Introducing the New Testament

OTHER TITLES BY THE AUTHOR

The Use and Abuse of the Bible
The Sunday Word

Introducing the New Testament

Henry Wansbrough

BLOOMSBURY

LONDON • NEW DELHI • NEW YORK • SYDNEY

Bloomsbury T&T Clark

An imprint of Bloomsbury Publishing Plc

Imprint previously known as T&T Clark

50 Bedford Square   1385 Broadway
London   New York
WC1B 3DP   NY 10018
UK   USA

www.bloomsbury.com

BLOOMSBURY, T&T CLARK and the Diana logo are trademarks of Bloomsbury Publishing Plc

First published 2015

© Henry Wansbrough, 2015

British Library Cataloguing-in-Publication Data

A catalogue record for this book is available from the British Library.

ISBN: HB: 978-0-56765-669-8
PB: 978-0-56765-668-1
ePDF: 978-0-56765-670-4
ePUB: 978-0-56765-711-4

Library of Congress Cataloging-in-Publication Data

A catalog record for this book is available from the Library of Congress

Typeset by Fakenham Prepress Solutions, Fakenham, Norfolk NR21 8NN
Printed and bound in India

Contents

Part IV The Catholic or Universal Epistles

Foreword

Once upon a time there was a young monk studying at the University of Fribourg. By the rules of the university he and all the other ardent young students were obliged to sit in a lecture-hall for three hours each week, listening while a Spanish friar read aloud from the textbook on Canon Law which he had written some years before. This was not easy, for the friar spoke in heavily accented Latin – it was well before the second Vatican Council abolished lectures in Latin – and the hushed silence was occasionally broken by a suppressed snore. However, this young monk had already been imbued with a love of scripture by an elderly monk of his monastery. In addition, he knew that an informed reading of scripture would bring fulfilment to his life by opening up a treasury of divine wisdom. So, instead of dozing like many of his classmates, he perseveringly worked his way, hour by hour, through an introduction to the Old and New Testaments. First he read the chapter on a Book of the Bible, then the Book itself, and then finally the introductory chapter again, to see what he had missed. You yourself, dear reader, might like to use this book in the same way on your own search. Furthermore, you will probably not need to scrape through the final examination in Canon Law – five minutes of rather stilted Latin question-and-answer – which a hurried reading of the textbook enabled the young monk to survive.

Part I

Preliminaries

1

Why Read the Old Testament?

1. The Revelation of God

There are questions about existence, life, destiny, purpose, ultimate reality which every human being must ask in moments of tranquillity, contentment or anguish. From our own resources we can penetrate only a certain distance below the surface. To some it may be plain that 'Ever since God created the world his everlasting power and deity have been there for the mind to see in the things he has made' (Rom. 1.20). On the Areopagus Paul speaks of the nations 'feeling their way towards' the Unknown God (Acts 17.27) tentatively, like people in the dark, with the implication of many a false step. By human efforts and philosophy alone little more can be known than the existence of the unknowable. Anselm of Canterbury's 'that greater than which nothing can be conceived' tells us little that is positive. It is the Christian faith that God revealed himself in the Bible through words and deeds in order to bring us into his friendship as a response to this gift of understanding. Christian faith rests on this understanding imparted by the Bible; the Christian believes that the whole Bible speaks of, leads to and focuses upon Jesus. This is not the only way of understanding the Bible, for the Jewish faith, which Christians accept as another valid way of understanding the Bible – valid but not Christian – does not lead to this conclusion (see preface to *The Jewish People and its Sacred Scriptures in the Christian Bible*, 2001).

2. The Old Testament

It would be absurd to attempt an introduction to the Old Testament in a couple of pages. Nevertheless, the revelation of God and of human meaning is so luminously depicted in certain moments of the Old Testament that the significance of these must at least be sketched. These moments introduce themes which will be developed and reach their plenitude in the fullness of revelation in the New Testament.

a. Dignity and Misery of the Human Condition

The human condition is clearly staked out in the earliest chapters of the Bible, in the myths of Genesis 1–11. To call a story a 'myth' does not in itself affirm or deny historicity. It simply attests that the story contains important truths, usually in some way religious truths, which are seen as a basis of customs, a way of life or existence itself. These are not historical stories but constitute an analysis of the human condition in the form of narrative. They assert in story form such truths as the dignity of the human race, created in the image of God, the mutual companionship of man and woman and human responsibility for preserving, developing and completing the divine purpose in creation. They hint at an ideal way of life, suffused with friendship, peace and harmony. However, they also attest the human awareness of repeated failure, of inability to maintain this ideal, even within the framework of the continuing, forgiving love of God. They proclaim also the conviction that, after an age of toil and trouble, good will eventually triumph over evil. The theme of the creation of human beings in the image of God is taken up and carried further in the New Testament by Paul, in the hymn of Christ as the first-born of creation and of the new creation (Phil. 2.6–11), in the incorporation of all those baptized into Christ into his risen life (Rom. 8.29) and their eventual share in the heavenly life of the Risen Christ (1 Cor. 15.49).

b. The Call of Abraham

This historical story (folk-history) of the Chosen People begins with the call of Abraham, and Abraham's own unshakable trust in God, the model of Christian faith (Rom. 4). The call is not exclusive to the physical descendants of Abraham, since the blessing on Abraham is to extend to the nations, for 'all the tribes of the earth shall bless themselves by you' (Gen. 12.2). As always, this text must be read in its canonical context: at the moment of the call of Abraham the patriarch may not have been aware of the breadth of his vocation and the extent of the promise. But by the time the account reaches the written form in which it stands in the Bible – the fifth or fourth century BC – the deeper understanding of this vocation had broadened to embrace Israel's vocation to bring salvation to the nations of the world (as in Isa. 60–6). This is the motif of the mission charge in Matthew 28.16–20, of Simeon's canticle in Luke 2.31–2, and of the whole of Paul's mission to the gentiles.

c. The People of God

The story of the escape from Egypt and the encounter with God on Sinai is the bedrock of the whole history of Israel. Whatever the basic facts of this meeting with God, described in awesome terms of thunder, lightning, storm and earthquake, it was the occasion on which Israel came to know that it had a special calling from God and a special vocation among the nations of the world. It is described in terms also of a marriage-covenant, and the time in the desert is conceived as a honeymoon period of fidelity. This covenant will be refreshed in the form of the New Covenant, promised in Jeremiah 31.3–34, and in Ezekiel 36.26 in the new heart and new Spirit. It will be completed by Jesus at the Last Supper (Mk 14.24), as the mediator of the New Alliance (Heb. 8.7–13). Two special aspects of this meeting with God were treasured: first, the name of the LORD, too holy to be pronounced, is here explained and paraphrased as 'a God of tenderness and compassion, rich in forgiveness and mercy' (Exod. 34.7); this is the basic definition of God, which echoes down passage after passage of the Bible. Jesus' mission to sinners is the embodiment of this forgiveness. Secondly, the Law was given, in the form of the ten commandments (Exod. 20.3–17) and the other precepts, which show how Israel must live in order to remain God's own treasured people; this will be perfected by Jesus, as Matthew shows in the Sermon on the Mount: 'you have heard it said… but I say to you…'. When

Jesus is challenged to pronounce on the first of the commandments (Mk 12.28), he replies in the words of the Law, given in Deuteronomy 6.4–5 and Leviticus 19.18.

d. King David

A new moment occurs in the history of Israel with the kingship of David. The LORD is the King of Israel, but David is his viceroy. David sanctifies Jerusalem, making it the city of the LORD by bringing up the ark to Jerusalem. Jerusalem will remain the symbol of God's dwelling among men, the symbol of the hopes of a new, restored age of perfection, the ultimate city of peace (Ezek. 48.35; Gal. 4.26; Rev. 21). Although David was not allowed to build the Temple himself, he was revered as the founder of the Temple worship, and the promises made to his descendants would endure for ever (2 Sam. 7.14; Ps. 2.7). The promise remained vivid throughout the dark days of the Babylonian Exile and beyond (Ezek. 35.24; in the Dead Sea Scrolls, e.g. 4Q252; 4Q399). So Jesus is hailed as the son of David (Mt. 1; Mk 10.47; 11.10), although his kingship is not of this world (John 18.36). The consummation of human history will be when he 'hands over the kingship to God the Father, having done away with every sovereignty, authority and power' (1 Cor. 15.24).

e. The Day of the LORD

In the writings of the early prophets a new conception begins to appear, the Day of the LORD (see p. 293). This will be a day which renews all justice on earth. In an era of exploitation of the poor by the rich it seems to have been awaited by the oppressive rich as a day of triumph, but Amos warns that for them it will be a 'day of darkness, not light, as when a man escapes a lion's mouth only to meet a bear' (Amos 5.18). As the threat of the great empires of Mesopotamia, first Assyria, then Babylon, increased, this Day of the LORD came to be seen as the visitation of God to correct and punish all Israel's infidelities and desertions, the superstitious flirting with other gods, the appeal for protection to other powers rather than to the LORD and shepherd of Israel. It was to be a day of disaster, represented in more and more cosmic terms and lurid imagery, a day of darkness at noon, the earth convulsed and stars falling from heaven. Once the disaster of the Babylonian Exile had occurred, and first Israel and then Judah had been driven from their lands, the application of these prophecies changed. It was now the enemies and oppressors of Israel who would be punished, the Day when Israel would be set free and restored in the LORD's favour.

Perhaps the most potent expressions of these confident hopes come in Ezekiel and Daniel. Ezekiel 40–8 gives a blueprint for the restoration of Jerusalem and its Temple to their former glory: the bones of the dead Israel will return to life (37.1–14), rivers of life-giving water will flow from the Temple (47.1–12), and the name of the city will be 'The LORD is there' (48.35). During the great persecution by the Syrian King Antiochus Epiphanes (167–164BC) the Book of Daniel sees Israel crushing the bestial empires which have oppressed it and emerging under the image of a Son of Man who will receive all power on earth from the One of Great Age (Dan. 7.8–14). The restricted community of returned Judean exiles centred on Jerusalem was buoyed up by these hopes, which became more vivid again under the domination by Rome in the century before Christ. They form the background to the proclamation first by John the Baptist, then by Jesus himself, that the Kingship of God had drawn near (Mt. 3.2; 4.17). The imagery of the Day of the LORD gives the meaning of darkness at noon and earthquake at the crucifixion and resurrection (Mk 15.33; Mt. 27.51; 28.2) and of the future coming of the Son of Man to gather his elect at the end of time (Mk 13.24–7; 1 Thess. 4.15–17).

In this sense the medieval pronouncement is valid, 'In the Old Testament the New Testament lies hidden; in the New Testament the Old Testament becomes plain'.

3. The Use of the Old Testament in the New

Luke reports on two journeys, each leading to a sacrament. On each occasion Jesus and his mission are explained by means of the Old Testament: the journey to Emmaus (Lk. 24.13–34) and Philip's meeting with the Ethiopian (Acts 8.26–40). On the day of Pentecost Peter explains what is happening by means of reference to the Old Testament: the coming of the Spirit is explained by reference to Joel 3.1–5, and the resurrection and exaltation of Jesus by reference to two psalms (Acts 2.17–35). The Old Testament is therefore the key to understanding the New. The principal ways in which the Old Testament is used, and 'becomes plain' in the New Testament are three, all closely related:

1. *Pesher*: this Hebrew word means 'interpretation'. This type of explanation of scripture is common in the Dead Sea Scrolls (1QpHab), in which phrases from the prophets are understood as predictions of events current in the writer's own time. The writer quotes a scriptural passage and then uses the formula, 'Interpreted, this means...', and refers to a current event. So Matthew has a whole series of fourteen occasions when Jesus is said to act 'in order to fulfil what is written in the prophet...'. Understanding the events of Jesus' ministry, Passion and Resurrection in this way was an important part of the earliest tradition. It occurs in the early traditional formula in Paul 'Christ died for our sins *in accordance with the scriptures*... he was raised to life *in accordance with the scriptures*' (1 Cor. 15.3–4). So many of the details of the Passion narratives fit this understanding of the scriptures that some think that they are inserted not because they were *known to have happened*, but because they *must have happened* that way, e.g. Mark 15.24, 34, fulfilling Psalm 21.

2. Typology: figures and events in the Old Testament are seen as preparatory types of which Jesus is the antitype. So, in the Infancy Narratives of Matthew, Jesus is seen as the son of David's line and the second Moses in Chapters 1 and 2 respectively; the story of the persecution by King Herod is told in such a way as to bring out its similarity with the persecution of Moses by the Egyptian Pharaoh. In the same way the gift of manna in the desert is seen as a type of Jesus' gift of the Bread of Life: 'it was not Moses who gave you bread from heaven, but my Father gives you the true bread from heaven' (Jn 6.32). The gospels understand the title 'son of man' to be a reference by Jesus to the Son of Man in Daniel 7.13, to whom all power on earth is given, a prerogative which Jesus is implicitly claiming for himself, for instance in Mark 2.10, 28; 14.62. Melchizedek, the priest-king of Jerusalem, is seen as a type of Christ, the high priest of the order of Melchizedek (Heb. 7).

3. Allusion: titles and qualities which in the Old Testament are ascribed to God are ascribed to Jesus, often without further explanation. God is the shepherd of Israel who feeds his flock (Ps. 23(22); Ezek. 34), but Jesus is this shepherd (Jn 10). God creates by his Wisdom (Prov. 8.22), but Jesus is the Power and the Wisdom of God (Jn 1.3; 1 Cor. 1.24). God will come in awesome splendour on the Day of the LORD, but it is the Lord Jesus who is to come (Mt. 25.31–46; 1 Thess. 4.15). The significance of so many symbols in the New Testament (living water, the cloud of divine presence) can be understood only by reference to the Old. In no Book is this so clear as in the Book of Revelation, which is full of symbols which make sense only against the background of the Old Testament; for example, the scene of the

heavenly throne-room (Rev. 4–5) draws its significance from Old Testament scenes of the heavenly court; the doom of Rome (Rev. 18) is modelled on the prophecies of the doom of Babylon in the prophetic writings.

4. Inspiration

From this briefest of surveys it becomes abundantly clear that the Bible is no 'flat' or 'cold' presentation of historical, geographical or scientific facts, but rather seeks to express the meaning of God's dealings with Israel and the nations as they are seen in the light of the Holy Spirit. The human authors express their understanding in the literary forms of their own culture, whether this be myth, folk-history, legal provisions, fiction, satire or poetry, according to the genius of each author. Many of the books of the Bible will have undergone an extended process of editing and revision. For instance, while the legal provisions of Exodus 20–2 envisage a primitive pastoral society, other provisions of the books of the Law reflect a later, settled monarchical and cultic background. Similarly, the Book of Isaiah was certainly not written by one person, but rather is a collection of prophecies on the same themes (from different points of view at different eras) stretching over a number of centuries. The tradition of the prophets developed: so Amos is basically pre-Exilic, with Amos 9.11–15 being added at a much later date. The Old Testament is an extended body of sacred writings which evolved over an extended period of time.

a. The Canon of Scripture

The question then needs to be posed: How did this body of sacred writings come to be gathered together? What makes them sacred? In the century or so after the destruction of Jerusalem by the Romans in 70AD the Jewish canon of scripture came to be formed. Among the much larger body of sacred literature some writings were felt 'to soil the hands', that is, the twenty-four Books were so holy that it was necessary to wash before and after handling them. Other, such as *1 Enoch*, were considered holy, but not to the same degree. Nor of course in the Hebrew Canon were any of the Books or parts of Books written only in Greek included. 'Canon' basically means 'yardstick' or 'norm'. The Old Testament Canon adopted by the Christian Church, where Greek rather than Hebrew was the dominant language, did include these Greek Books, such as Wisdom and Ecclesiasticus.

The Christian canon of the New Testament began to be formed at about the same time, though a good deal of variety existed for some time. Some Books, such as Hebrews and Revelation, were accepted in some areas and not in others. In the wake of the crushing of the Second Jewish Revolt (135AD) a rich ship-owner from Pontus, called Marcion, was so anti-Semitic that he unsuccessfully tried to bribe the Roman Church to discard the gospels of Matthew, Mark and John on the grounds that they were too Jewish. Other writings (e.g. the *Letter of Barnabas*) were included at one time or another among the 'books read in the Church'. The definitive list of twenty-seven Books, as we have it now, is usually considered to be the list given in the Festal Letter of St Athanasius of Alexandria in 367AD. In about 200AD Bishop Serapion of Antioch wrote to the Church of Rhossus (which was under his jurisdiction) forbidding them to read in Church the *Gospel of Peter*, on the grounds that its Christology was defective. This is important in that it shows that the name of one of the Twelve, indeed Peter himself, was not a sufficient guarantee that a book was authoritative. In the second century several other works bearing the name of an apostle circulated (for instance the *Gospel of Philip*, the *Gospel of Thomas*). It was only towards the end of the century that Irenaeus insisted successfully that there could be only four gospels, those which we have now. These were and are the norm for Christian belief. There is, therefore, the curiously circular situation that the sacred writings provide the norm of the Church, but the Church decides which writings constitute the norm: the Church both forms and is formed by the Canon of Scripture. The Bible is the book of the Church: in reciprocal ways the Church interprets the Scriptures and is judged by the Scriptures.

b. Dual Authorship

How does this revelation occur? Three preliminary factors must be borne in mind. First, revelation occurs in deeds as well as in words: it is the deeds of the Lord, recorded in scripture, which reveal the divine will and nature (the repeated forgiveness of God in the history of Israel, Jesus' miracles of healing) as much as the verbal expressions. Secondly, revelation is often a gradual process, in which a general idea is first expressed and then later filled out more precisely (conceptions of life after death). Thirdly, God's truth is revealed in the terms of a particular culture, which may need to be translated into the terms of another culture (so the relationship of creatures to creator is revealed in the terms of the world-picture of the time).

If the scriptures 'teach faithfully and without error everything that God wanted put into the sacred writings for the sake of our salvation', how is it that the human writers are true authors who 'made use of their powers and abilities in consigning to writing what God wanted' (Vatican II, *Dei Verbum*, #11)? How is it possible to reconcile the inspiration of the authors with their human free will? If God puts the thoughts into the minds of the authors, are they true authors? Did God dictate the words? Is inspiration merely a negative protection from error?

Theologians have struggled to find an analogy for this dual authorship. Many early icons show the Holy Spirit in the form of a dove sitting on the evangelist's shoulder as he writes, or God the Father shyly presenting the evangelist with the book from behind a curtain. These images suggest a form of divine dictation hardly compatible with the obvious personal characteristics of research and style proper to each author. Is the human author to be regarded as a trusted secretary, left to put the message in his or her own style and language, and occasionally making unimportant factual errors (Cardinal Newman was worried by the fact that Nebuchadnezzar is described in Judith 1.1 as King of Assyria, when in fact he was King of Babylon)? Origen likened the process to playing a musical instrument: God plays the human instrument, which is sometimes damaged or badly tuned.

It is more helpful to see inspiration as the enhancement of the author's faculties, by analogy with prophetic inspiration. The prophet is not so much one who foretells as one who sees as God sees, who sees the true meaning and character of events and situations. So when Jeremiah goes down to the potter (Jer. 18.1–12) he is enabled by divine inspiration and an enhancement of his faculties to see the analogy of the potter's operations to Israel's situation. On an earlier occasion he is enabled to see the significance for Israel of the name 'Watchful Tree' and of the angle of a cooking-pot (Jer. 1.11–14). So the inspired writer is enabled to perceive and express 'faithfully and without error everything that God wanted put into the sacred writings for the sake of our salvation'. This inspiration is not confined to the final author of a text, but is operative in the whole process of the formation and preservation of the text, observation, oral transmission (perhaps discussion), editing and final verbal expression. In the case of the gospels this would apply to the original observer of words or actions, to the story-teller who formed and handed on the story, to the community which preserved it, to any who may have edited it to clarify its significance, as well as to the final writer who fitted it into the pattern of his own gospel.

c. Methods of Interpretation

The approach of this book is that of the historico-critical method as the method of discovering the message of the Bible. This has not always been the most favoured method of interpretation in the Christian Church. Origen thought that the 'spiritual' sense of the Bible was far more important than the 'literal'. So, commenting on Genesis 18.1, he expostulates, 'What does it help me, who have come to hear what the Holy Spirit teaches the human race, to know that Abraham was standing under a tree?' He then proceeds to explain, by a rather tortuous etymology, that the Oak of Mambre stands for 'sharpness of sight' or 'insight'. Similarly, in the middle of an excellent discussion of the difference between John (2.13, at the beginning of Jesus' ministry) and the synoptic gospels (Mk 11.15, at the end of Jesus' ministry) over the timing of the Cleansing of the Temple, he explodes, 'Anyone who examines the gospels carefully to check disagreements over historicity will grow dizzy'; he asserts that the truth of the gospels does not lie in their material characteristics (*Commentary on John* 2.10).

Much of medieval Christian interpretation of the Bible consists of non-literal exegesis, which Origen would qualify as 'spiritual', principally of four kinds:

- Allegory – this has its place in the Bible itself, as in the interpretation of the parable of the Sower (Mk 4.14–20). Origen interprets the scarlet thread, by which the Prostitute of Jericho is identified, as a presage of the saving blood of Christ (on Josh. 6.4).
- Etymological – as in the passage of Origen above, reliant on the etymology (correct or incorrect) of the place-name 'Mambre'.
- Numerical – Bede explains the six water-jars at the marriage-feast of Cana (Jn 2.6) as the six previous ages of the world. For the 153 fish of John 21.11 Bede puts together all the numbers between 1 and 16 (=136), and adds the 10 commandments and the 7 days of creation.
- Typology – the full understanding of events in the New Testament is obtained by putting them into the mould provided by events in the Old Testament (see p. 334): Christ's sacrifice is to be understood as the fulfilment of the sacrifice of the Paschal Lamb (cf. Jn 19.36 following Exod. 12.46). The journey to a place of rest is understood in Hebrews 3.7–4.11 as the completion of the incomplete journey of the Hebrews to a place of rest in Canaan (see p. 324).

By contrast the successive stages of a historico-critical investigation may be characterized as:

1 The establishment of a correct critical text by such factors as comparison of manuscripts, versions and quotations in ancient authors (see p. 18). Two famous cases of necessary correction are the *Comma Johanneum* (1 Jn 5.7bc–8a), which occurs in no early Greek manuscript but crept into Erasmus' text via the Old Latin version; this is no longer considered part of the New Testament. Similarly, the last few verses of Revelation in Erasmus' first Greek edition are not an acceptable text: they were translated from Latin back into Greek by Erasmus himself because he was in a hurry and had no Greek manuscript for them to hand.

2 Linguistic analysis – establishment of the true linguistic meaning or correct translation according to contemporary usage. Did Jesus mean 'What I want is *mercy*' or '*love*' at Matthew 9.13; 12.7? Should Romans 9.5 be translated 'Christ who is above all, blessed God for ever' or 'Christ who is above all. Blessed be God for ever'? The issue is important for establishing Paul's teaching on the divinity of Christ.

3 The genre of the writing must be established. Is the Book of Jonah a historical account or is it a fictional satire on Jewish self-satisfaction? At the Baptism of Jesus is the splitting of the heavens a historical assertion or apocalyptic symbolism (Mk 1.10)?

4 There follow a host of critical and analytical questions, such as:
   - Source analysis. In the case of the gospels, is Matthew's version of the Lord's Prayer drawn from Luke, or vice versa, or are they independent, drawn from a further source? Which is to be trusted as the most authentic?
   - Editorial analysis (often called 'Redaction-criticism'). In the account of the Temptations, did Matthew put the temptation on the very high mountain as the climax in order to show the comparison with Moses, or did Luke put the pinnacle of the Temple as the climax to stress the centrality of Jerusalem?
   - Rhetorical analysis. A feature of Hellenistic rhetoric is *captatio benevolentiae* (flattery of the audience to win them). This appears in Paul's speech on the Areopagus (Acts 17.22–23) and to Agrippa (Acts 26.2–3), and in most of Paul's letters (e.g. Phlm. 4–6, and see p. 192). Another important rhetorical feature is the farewell-speech: such a speech is given of Jesus at the Last Supper (Jn 14.17), of Paul at Miletus (Acts 20.17–35), in 2 Peter (see p. 341).Features of Semitic rhetoric are balance and parallelism: Jesus riding simultaneously on a donkey and on a colt (Mt. 21.7), the bracketing of the Beatitudes at beginning and end (Mt. 5.3b, 10b).

- Canonical approach. A text must be considered not only for itself but in relationship to the development of this theme throughout revelation: the gradual development of belief in life after death as a background to 1 Corinthians 15. The Day of the LORD in the Old Testament becomes in the New Testament the Day of the Lord Jesus.
- The Jewish tradition of exegesis: the actualisation of scripture as at Qumran (see p. 8) or the Yelammadenu Sermon in John 6 (see p. 389).

The interpreter of the New Testament needs to be aware of all these currents and also other approaches. In recent times other agenda have also been important for the interpretation of the New Testament. These are the agenda for particular problems in the Christian life, in the search for guidance from the scriptures for a particular concern. These include liberation theology, which sees Jesus as the liberator from oppression, tyranny and injustice, and feminist theology, which concentrates especially on Jesus' message for the equal dignity of the sexes, stressing the important part played by women in the life of Jesus, in Paul's writing and in the life of the early Church.

2

How the New Testament Came to Us

1. Texts

a. The Transmission of Ancient Texts

The letters of Paul were intended to be read aloud and heard in the Christian assembly rather than read privately by individuals. The same will have been true of the gospels and all the other Books of scripture. In the modern world for certainty we like to have something 'on paper' (perhaps 'on screen'), whereas in the ancient world the oral tradition was preferred, and written records were considered less reliable. Before the invention of printing in the fifteenth century, texts had to be copied by hand. In classical antiquity this was normally done by professional scribes, either one scribe copying from a previous manuscript or a group of scribes writing at dictation – a primitive method of polycopying. This was not always done with absolute accuracy, for instance in written script the Greek abbreviation for 'God' could easily be confused with 'who' (1 Tim. 3.16); at dictation the Greek for 'ours' and 'yours' was pronounced almost identically and easily confused. Misreading was made all the more likely by *scriptio continua*, that is, there were no paragraphs, no punctuation, nor even gaps between words. In the Hebrew tradition the very letters of each Book of the Bible were counted in the hope of ensuring accuracy, but it was not unusual for a codicil to be added to a book, calling down a curse on anyone who copied the text inaccurately. Despite all efforts and all professionalism, several classical Greek and Roman authors joke about the possibility of miscopying of their own texts (e.g. Martial, *Epigrams* 1.115). This was obviously a frequent occurrence. The peppery St Jerome complains bitterly about mistakes made by profess-ional scribes in copying out his own works (Letter 71.5).

In the population at large, literacy levels were low, possibly only 10 to 15 per cent being able to read or write at all. In the second century a pagan writer called Celsus mocks the low level of education among Christians of his time. A century later the Christian scholar Origen, writing against Celsus, does not attempt to refute these charges, which we may take to be well founded. Origen himself found that there were so many variations in the text of the Greek Old Testament that he went to massive lengths in trying to re-establish the true text, setting out different versions in six parallel columns. The text ran to 6,000 pages; it was lost in the Moslem invasions of Palestine, and only fragments quoted by other writers survive. The first mention of profes-sional scribal work on the Christian Bible is when the Emperor Constantine, after his conversion to Christianity in the early fourth century, instructed Eusebius of Caesarea to have 50 copies of the Bible made and disseminated.

b. The Manuscripts

In the first Christian century two kinds of material were used for preserving written texts, papyrus and vellum. Papyrus (from which we get the word 'paper') was made from two layers of the papyrus plant, cut into strips, flattened and pressed together at right angles. Vellum or parchment (the name is derived from the town of Pergamum in Asia Minor) is made from animal skins, cleaned and dried. It is more durable but more expensive to make. The principal manuscripts of the Bible are of parchment, but in the last 150 years important caches of papyrus manuscripts have been discovered in the dry sands of Egypt, which add greatly to our knowledge.

Most literary works were in the form of scrolls, written on one side and rolled up. However, from the end of the first century Christians seem to have played an important part in development of the codex, or book, consisting of pages written on both sides and bound together on a spine. A codex uses less material and is easier to handle and transport, and in the long run is more durable. All the earliest Christian biblical papyri from the second century are in the form of a codex. The oldest, known as ℙ52, is a small seven–line fragment containing John 18.31–3 on one side and 18.37–8 on the other. It is dated by the style of handwriting to 100–125AD; the date is important, showing that John's gospel must have been written some years before that date; it is permanently on view in Manchester. The biblical scholarly world was briefly thrown into disarray in 1994 by the claim that the handwriting of ℙ64, a fragment of Matthew held at Magdalen College, Oxford, was mid-first century. This would have meant that Matthew was the earliest of all New Testament writings; however it is now firmly held that this fragment and two other fragments of the same are parts of the first book containing all four gospels, probably from the late second century.

The three principal sources for reconstruction of the Greek text of the New Testament are the Codex Vaticanus, Codex Sinaiticus and Codex Alexandrinus, all containing virtually the whole Bible.

- Codex Vaticanus was already in the Vatican library when the first catalogue was made in 1475. It was probably written at Alexandria in the mid-fourth century, and may be one of the 'codices containing the holy Scriptures' mentioned as sent to the Emperor Constans in 340AD.
- Codex Sinaiticus was discovered in the library of St Catherine's monastery on Mount Sinai in 1844 and 1859 by Constantin Tischendorff. He took the first clutch of 17 leaves to Leipzig in 1844. The main part was 'borrowed' in 1859 to show to the Czar of Russia, and was sold by Stalin to the British Library in 1933 for £100,000. A few leaves remain in St Catherine's. It is fully published online.
- Codex Alexandrinus was presented to King Charles I in 1628 by the Patriarch of Constantinople and is now in the British Library. It is the latest of the three, probably early fifth century, and is of a slightly different textual tradition.
- To these may be added the Codex Bezae, a bilingual (Greek/Latin) text, given to the Cambridge University Library by Theodore Beza in 1581, having been plundered from the monastery of St Irenaeus at Lyons in 1562. It was probably copied in the sixth century, but may be earlier. Some of the gospel readings are strikingly similar to quotations given in the works of St Irenaeus (c. 180AD).

Although these great manuscripts are the earliest witnesses to the full text, the papyri and other partial witnesses provide indispensable clues for the reconstruction of individual passages.

c. A Variety of Readings

Proof-reading is a special profession, demanding a high degree of training and accuracy, and even professional proof-readers make mistakes. The same is true of copying. Anyone who has copied a lengthy text will be aware of the dangers of carelessness, omission of lines, words or letters, jumping from one word to another of similar ending. In addition there are the dangers of incorrect 'corrections', when the scribe writes from incorrect memory, or thinks he knows what the text *should* be but is not (e.g. because this is what it says in another gospel), either on literary or theological grounds (e.g. because the text before him does not express the theology which the scribe thinks is correct). In 1707, John Mill of Queen's College, Oxford, after 30 years of study of the manuscripts, declared that they contained 30,000 variations of the text of the New Testament. It will be useful to give a range of examples from the gospels:

- Matthew 6.13 At the end of the Lord's Prayer some manuscripts of the Byzantine tradition add 'For thine is the kingdom and the power and the glory for ever. Amen.' This appears in Erasmus' Greek text, and so was translated into the King James Version, but it is not contained in Jerome's Vulgate Latin (which was based on a better and wider selection of manuscripts). It first appears in the *Didache*, added to the Lord's Prayer as a doxology.
- Mark 1.1 In some manuscripts the verse ends 'Jesus Christ, *son of God*'; in others simply 'Jesus Christ'. The longer ending adds clarity to the whole gospel, and gives a nice balance with the centurion's declaration (15.39) at the end of the gospel – but it could have been added later for just those reasons.
- Mark 1.41 In some manuscripts we read that Jesus was 'growing angry', in others 'moved with pity'. In their parallel passages Matthew and Luke both omit Jesus' anger, but they omit it also at their parallels to Mark 3.5 and 10.14. Does an angry Jesus not accord with their theology, or did a later scribe make the change at Mark 1.41? This is only one of many changes which can be argued to have been made on doctrinal grounds.
- Mark 16.8 In some manuscripts Mark's gospel ends here at the empty tomb. In others the meetings with the Risen Christ are included (Mk 16.9–20). After the later gospels, Matthew and Luke, had included such material, a scribe could have decided that it *ought to have been* in Mark too. But the style is quite different from the rest of Mark.

- Luke 2.14 ends either 'peace on earth, *good will to all people*' or 'peace on earth *to people of good will*', a difference of one letter in Greek, *eudokia* or *eudokias*.
- Luke 22.43–4 The angel comforting Jesus and his drops of sweat 'like blood' in the Garden are missing from some manuscripts. Without these details the pattern of the narrative is more balanced.
- Luke 23.34 'Father, forgive them for they do not know what they are doing' does not occur in some manuscripts. The theme of forgiveness is typical for Luke, and it provides a nice parallel with the martyrdom of Stephen in Acts 7.60 (written by the same author).
- Luke 24.12 The visit of Peter to the empty tomb is omitted by some manuscripts. It could have been inserted later, adopted from John 20.3–9.
- John 1.13 Most of the best manuscripts read the plural 'who *were* born' (referring to Jesus' followers), but many early Christian writers (Irenaeus, Tertullian, Origen) quote it in the singular, 'who *was* born', referring to Jesus.
- John 5.4 Mention of an angel disturbing the water of the pool is a later gloss, perhaps drawn from an old legend.
- John 7.53–8.11 The story of the woman taken in adultery is missing from all the oldest manuscripts. This story, complete in itself, is not in Johannine style and when it does occur in the manuscripts it occurs in different places (also in Luke 21, or at the very end of John). It could have been inserted here by a scribe to illustrate John 7.51 or 8.15.
- 1 John 5.7–8 in the Old Latin manuscripts used by Jerome for the Vulgate contained the only explicit biblical mention of the Trinity. It is not in any genuine Greek manuscript, and so was omitted by Erasmus in his Greek edition. This caused such fury that a spoof manuscript was forged, and Erasmus was persuaded to include the words in later editions.

In many of these cases different reputable scholars make different decisions. One of the most distinguished of all textual scholars, Bruce Metzger, the chairman of the panel which produced the latest United Bible Society Greek text, wrote a book explaining the decisions made for that publication by the panel of scholars (*A Textual Commentary on the Greek New Testament*, 1971). Occasionally the evidence is so evenly balanced that, with the utmost courtesy, he personally opts for a decision different from that of the panel of which he was chairman. So delicate are many of the questions.

2. Translations

a. The Latin Vulgate

The New Testament was written in Greek, and spread in that language to the West, for Greek was widely spoken in Rome among the educated classes as well as among slaves and immigrants. The first translations into Latin were made in Roman North Africa, a stronghold of the Roman Empire; these written texts were used by Tertullian and Cyprian in the third century. Other translations into Latin abounded, and by the time Jerome was commissioned by Pope Damasus in the 380s to revise the Latin of the New Testament he could claim that there were 'almost as many forms of the text as there are copies'. Although Jerome claims to have revised the whole New Testament, in fact he revised only the Gospels, and in his commentaries frequently criticises the Latin translations of the Acts, the Letters and the Book of Revelation. Translation of the remainder is commonly attributed to Rufinus the Syrian; together they constitute the 'Vulgate' or 'common' Bible. Jerome's own translation is a masterpiece of limpid and simple style, mirroring the simplicity of the original Greek. However, Jerome worked notoriously fast, and some of the later material is a little careless.

For some centuries the Latin Bible existed only in separate volumes, usually nine. The earliest mentioned all-in-one Bible (*pandect*) was produced in the mid-sixth century in the monastery of Cassiodorus, but the earliest extant exemplar is the Codex Amiatinus, produced c. 700 in St Bede's monastery in Northumbria. It was stolen from Abbot Ceolfrid's luggage as he was taking it to Rome; it is now in Florence. Two other copies were made, of which some leaves survive in the British Library; each copy of this great volume required 500 calfskins. The monastery was given a special grant of land to breed the animals.

The earliest claimed translation into English is also by St Bede, whose biographer claims that he translated the first six chapters of John; it has not survived. The earliest surviving translation into Old English is the magnificent West Saxon Gospels, made about 990 by Aelfric, Abbot of Eynsham. This is, however, not the oldest biblical translation into English, for a Latin psalter exists from 200 years earlier, with the Northumbrian Old English written above the Latin text.

The Norman Conquest put paid to any further attempts at translation into English, for French was the language of the literate classes until

1362 (the year in which the opening of Parliament was first conducted in English). Books were rare, and private Bibles too expensive even for the lower clergy to possess. In the matter of translation into the vernacular England lagged behind the rest of Europe, where translations into German, French and Italian were common by the thirteenth century. The first extensive translation into Middle English was made by (or at least under the guidance of) John Wycliffe in about 1380. But Wycliffe was denounced as a heretic and consequently all Bible translation was banned, except with special permission, by the Constitutions of Oxford in 1410. Those unable to read Latin had to remain content with devotional works, paraphrases and painted illustrations on the walls of churches.

b. The Renaissance and Reformation

A new impetus was given to the dissemination of Bibles by the invention of printing, but again England lagged behind. By the time Caxton produced the first book printed in England (1477) there were already Bibles printed in German, Italian, French and Dutch, to be closely followed by Catalan and Czech. Further impetus was given by the return to Greek sources, and especially by the desperate rush of Erasmus to produce the first printed Greek edition of the New Testament in 1516 before the publication of the magnificent Complutensian edition, which finally did not appear till 1520. As his Greek manuscripts did not contain the last page of Revelation, Erasmus himself translated the last five verses back into Greek from the Latin.

As the clamour of the Reformers to have direct access to the scriptural text grew louder, in 1520 William Tyndale, a young West Country scholar, offered himself to Cuthbert Tunstall, Bishop of London, as a translator. He was turned down. Unable to find a patron in London, he moved to the continent, and by 1525 was sending his translation of the gospels back to England, to be pilloried by Thomas More, the Lord Chancellor, and seized and destroyed by Bishop Tunstall. Tyndale was thought to have been infected by Luther, and some of the expressions he used diverged from the accepted ecclesiastical terms ('congregation' instead of 'church', 'presbyter' instead of 'priest', 'love' instead of 'charity'). By the time Tyndale was kidnapped and imprisoned, then garrotted and burnt at the stake in 1536, he had translated enough of the Bible to form the basis for the great tradition of the English Bible. After the break with Rome, King Henry VIII insisted that every parish church should have an open Bible, available to all (though he later added the proviso that it should not be read by women, apprentices and other such unreliable persons); this was known as the Great Bible.

In the course of the century other versions were circulated by various groups. Most important was the Geneva Bible (1560), sponsored by the English Puritans in Geneva, which rapidly became the most popular version. More for a niche-market was the Rheims-Douai version, translated by Gregory Martin for the exiled English Catholics (1582/1609), kept deliberately, and sometimes awkwardly, close to the Vulgate Latin text for purposes of controversy. Each of these had its own commentary and notes.

c. The King James Version (1611)

When James VI of Scotland became James I of England one of his first moves was to attempt to reconcile the Puritan tradition with the Elizabethan settlement of religion. At the Hampton Court conference in 1604 a new translation of the Bible without any notes was suggested. The King, eager to oust the Geneva Bible, and particularly its Puritan notes, took up this suggestion. An elaborate machinery of translators and revisers was set up, which engaged in the work the best scholars in the land, at a period of unprecedented scholarly, literary and poetical achievement, the age of Shakespeare, John Donne and Ben Jonson. It was to be authorized by the Privy Council and the King himself. In those Books which Tyndale translated some 80 per cent of his version is retained.

Every subsequent English version of the Bible has been heavily indebted to this translation, countless phrases of which have become part of the English heritage. It forms the explicit basis of the RSV, NRSV, ESV. To a lesser extent the JB/NJB and NEB/REB also benefit from it. Only the brilliantly idiosyncratic Knox version and the highly paraphrased GNB/Today's English Version break away from it. From a literary point of view the King James Version has never been surpassed, though more recent versions have profited from wider manuscript evidence and the continuing tradition of scholarship.

3

The Politico-Religious Situation

1. On the Fringe of the Roman Empire

a. The Hellenistic World, from Alexander to Pompey

Alexander the Great spread his empire as far as India. In the course of his conquests he passed through Palestine (a round tower at Samaria is dated to this period) on his way to Egypt, where a mysterious adoption by the god in the desert Temple of Siwa occurred. Nevertheless, in 323BC he died after a drinking bout, leaving no obvious heirs. Possibly his drink was spiked with poison. The empire was divided between his twelve senior generals, but within a few years most of these were eliminated, and the remains of the empire settled into three provinces, Macedonia, Syria and Egypt. A common culture, of which the language was Greek, seeped gradually over the whole area, combining with the indigenous local cultures. Palestine, the corridor between Syria and Egypt, was influenced and even dominated in turn by these two neighbours, according as each was more powerful. The small, threatened community of exiles returned from Babylon to Jerusalem, and, huddled round a partially restored Temple, struggled to retain their identity and fidelity to their way of life.

In 167BC the Syrian King Antiochus Epiphanes (175–164BC), as part of his attempt to overrun Egypt and unite all his subjects under his divine rule, attempted to stamp out this stubborn pocket of adherence to a monotheistic religion and its strange customs. The story of the ensuing Maccabean revolt and the protracted struggle between the Syrians and the Jews is told from the Jewish point of view in the Books of Maccabees, which does not disguise the fact that even some of the high-priestly families had been in favour of yielding to the Hellenistic influence and way of life, disguising their circumcision and building a gymnasium. Antiochus succeeded in plundering the Temple, setting up a statue to Zeus in place of the altar, and imposing a permanent Syrian garrison on the highest place in the city (now the Jaffa Gate), which lasted over 20 years. John Hyrcanus expelled the garrison and re-established Jewish independence, combining the offices of king and high priest in 135BC. He fathered a short-lived dynasty of Aristobulus and Alexander Jannaeus (note the Greek names, further evidence of the advance of Hellenistic influence!). The squabbling of the latter's sons invited the intervention of the Roman general, Pompey.

b. Rome Enters on the Scene

The entry of Rome into Asia was sparked by the bequest of the kingdom of Pergamum to Rome by its king, Attalus III, in 133BC. It was soon organized into the Province of Asia. Roman presence in the eastern Mediterranean increased over the next half-century until in 67/66BC the great general, Pompey, organized the whole eastern seaboard into a line of Roman provinces, backed by a line of client kings and rulers who owed their power and stability to their own Roman backing. Their function was to ensure the stability and peace of their territories and to spread the Roman influence, to civilize their peoples which Rome regarded as barbarian. Rome ruled these with a light touch, benefiting from their revenues, but governing indirectly by means of the local machinery, especially through 'free cities', which enjoyed certain tax exemptions. Among these client rulers was Antipater in Palestine. His son, Herod, was educated in Rome with Octavian, the future emperor Augustus, with whom he became good friends.

In 40BC Herod was granted the title 'King'. His relationship with the Jewish religious establishment was always tricky, firstly because he was only half a Jew, through his mother, secondly because he took seriously his task of spreading the Roman influence. His success in this may still be seen in the great buildings set up under his personal patronage and design, the castles of Massada, Herodium and Jericho, the great port which he named 'Caesarea' in honour of his patron, and above all in the magnificent Temple of Jerusalem. This made Jerusalem, according to Pliny, the Roman historian, 'far the most distinguished city of the East'. He was an autocratic tyrant, who would brook no rival, and did not hesitate to liquidate even members of his own close family on suspicion of their planning to supplant him. In his final years his megalomania seems to have got out of control. By attacking the neighbouring client king of Nabatea he lost his exemption from Roman taxes, and his kingdom was subjected to the Roman census reflected in Luke's Infancy Narrative. As he lay dying at Jericho in 4BC, in order to ensure due mourning throughout the kingdom, he gathered all the notables and ordered that they should be slain at his death.

At his death there were some vain and short-lived attempts to throw off the Roman yoke. The Jewish historian Josephus records uprisings led by various claimants to be a prophet or Messiah to head the promised rule of God. These were swiftly brushed off by the Romans and the kingdom was divided into four 'tetrarchies' ruled by his sons. The most successful was Herod Antipas, tetrarch of Galilee. He established his capital at Sepphoris, within sight of Nazareth (was the craftsman Joseph employed in building it?), and built also a new city on the shore of the Lake of Galilee, calling it 'Tiberias' in honour of the emperor. In the neighbouring tetrarchy his brother Philip named his city 'Caesarea Philippi'. The least successful was Archelaus, ruler of Judea and Jerusalem. His incompetence was such that not only was he refused the title of 'King' but after ten years he was deposed at the request of some leading men among the Jews, and the territory constituted a Roman prefecture.

Its constitution reverted to the situation before Herod the Great, in that the local ruler at Jerusalem was the High Priest and Ethnarch ('tribal ruler'), though now under the supervision of a Roman prefect established at Caesarea on the coast. This prefect had specific duties, such as the maintenance of peace and order, oversight of the all-important collection of Roman taxes, and judgment of legal cases involving Roman citizens or the death-sentence. The prefect had at his disposal a detachment of auxiliary soldiers, but in a serious military situation would be obliged to call on the legions stationed in the nearby province of Syria. In fact the Roman historian

Tacitus attests that all was quiet in Judea during the reign of Tiberius, 14–37AD (*Histories* 5.9.2).

There is no reason to believe that the land was swarming with Roman soldiers; even the 'centurion' at Capernaum (Lk. 7.2) could be a local officer of Herod Antipas, rather than a Roman officer. Pontius Pilate was the longest-serving of the prefects (26–36AD), and the fact that he remained in office so long suggests that his rule was successful and moderate. Josephus had the task of explaining to his Roman audience why the Jews rebelled against Rome (30 years later!), and attempts to fasten the blame on Pilate's misgovernment, but his evidence hardly supports this charge. Modern scholars are divided on the issue.

2. Galilee and Jerusalem

a. Galilee at the Time of Jesus

According to the synoptic gospels the ministry of Jesus occurred almost entirely in Galilee, though John shows him visiting Jerusalem four times. Josephus describes the countryside lyrically:

> The soil is universally rich and fruitful and full of plantations of trees of all sorts, so that by its fruitfulness it invites the most slothful to take pains in its cultivation. Accordingly it is all cultivated by its inhabitants, and no part of it lies idle. Its cities lie close together, and there are many villages, full of inhabitants because of the richness of the soil. (*War* 3.3.1)

The literary sources are either too late or too early to establish a pattern for life in Galilee at the time of Jesus, and guesswork filled the gaps. Serious archaeological surveys began only in 1967.

> Views of Galilee were dominated by the phrase 'Galilee of the gentiles', which was read as implying that Galilee was mainly gentile territory. In fact the phrase more probably refers specifically to the coastal region of Galilee, close to the Phoenician ports of Ptolemais, Tyre and Sidon – as opposed to the rest of Galilee (Joel 4.4; 1 Macc. 5.5). In Matthew 4.15 '*Galilee* of the gentiles' obviously is a mistranslation of Isaiah 8.23 '*district* of the gentiles'.

A feature which must have made a considerable mark in the Galilee of the time of Jesus is urbanization. The building of Herod Antipas' two great cities, Sepphoris and Tiberias, must have had a large impact on life in the country districts, including presumably a considerable drift of population from country to town. Yet there is no sign that Jesus had any contact with either of those cities. The location of his mission (at least according to the data from Q) seems to have been mainly the villages round the north shore of the Lake of Galilee, Capernaum, Bethsaida, Korozain. A certain amount of faithful Jewish culture is now attested for Galilee at the time of Jesus. At Sepphoris ritual baths, incense shovels and stone vessels predominate, together with absence of pig-bones. On the other hand the lower courses of the Hellenistic theatre at Sepphoris may date from the time of Herod Antipas, showing that Hellenistic dramas and shows were tolerated, which often involved some form of religious presentation. Furthermore, Antipas' city of Tiberias was built over a cemetery, which would make it unclean. Everywhere in Galilee the decoration on mosaics avoids animal and especially human representation. The road system, which would bring gentiles through Galilee for trade, was established only in the second century. Nevertheless, the balance is in favour of an observant culture. In Galilee, Jesus would have been moving and teaching mainly among observant Jews, without much opening onto the wider world. Although there is still considerable controversy on the matter, the dictum of E. P. Sanders still stands: 'On the whole, in Antipas's Galilee, which was Jesus's Galilee, the law was Jewish, the courts were Jewish, the education was Jewish' (*Jesus in Historical Context* [1993]).

Another guess was that the rich soil was farmed as great estates (*latifundia*) by oppressed peasants, working for absentee foreign landlords. The main evidence for this is the reconstruction of the gospel-source Q: the preoccupation of the Q-sayings with poverty, debt, peasant farmers, small transactions, homelessness might suggest such a situation in Galilee. However, other literary evidence is lacking for this estimate, and archaeological evidence necessarily cannot show evidence of rural poverty. There is certainly not enough evidence to establish that the crowds who followed Jesus were ground down by lack of resources and by over-taxation into desperate poverty. Even today a rural population can achieve a tolerable standard of living with very few resources. Of course there were poor, sick, widowed, maimed among them.

b. Jerusalem at the Time of Jesus

Jerusalem held a unique position in the heart and mind of every Jew. Geographically it was the crossing-point of the natural roads north-south and west-east. The Jebusite city had been one of the strongholds which the Hebrews could not capture and assimilate at their entry into Canaan. For David it was the joining-point between the northern kingdom of Saul and his own sphere of influence in the south of the country. He captured it, so making it his capital of the united kingdom. Astute politician that he was, he also made it God's capital by installing in it the Ark of the Covenant, the symbol of God's presence on earth. From this it acquired an aura which it has never lost. King Hezekiah further enhanced its centrality by insisting that the Passover, originally a family feast of nomads, must always be celebrated in Jerusalem. It became the city of pilgrimage, to which zealous Jews would journey for the great festivals three times a year. As the despoiling of the Temple in 597BC and the total Sack of Jerusalem in 586BC became the symbols of disaster, so the rebuilding of the Temple at the end of the century became the statement of renewed confidence. To Jerusalem and its Temple would flow the nations and their wealth as they came to 'draw water from the wells of salvation' (Isa. 12.3).

The Jerusalem of Jesus' day was a magnificent monument to Herod's wealth and building prowess; he is said to have been the richest man in the Mediterranean. His building programme was part of his remit to civilize, i.e. Hellenize, Judea, and at the same time to demonstrate that his (half-) Jewish heart was in the right place. The most sumptuous of the buildings was the Temple, settled on a platform enclosing three acres of ground, at the highest point 45 metres above the natural rock (which slopes away), reached from the South by a flight of 50 broad and monumental steps. It included a columned hall in the style of a Roman basilica. The largest stone is 45 feet long and 11 feet high, weighing some 600 tons. All the stones are faced in the characteristic Herodian style, smooth and with bevelled edges. Apart from this there was a massive fortress, the Antonia, overlooking the Temple, and a magnificent three-towered palace at the citadel, where later the prefect would reside when he came to Jerusalem. To provide water there were numerous large storage pools, some (e.g. the Pools of Siloam and Bethzatha) decorative and used also as ritual baths. As this provided insufficient water for the growing city, Pilate constructed an aqueduct of 27 kilometres from the so-called 'Pools of Solomon' south of Bethlehem, snaking along the contour-lines and tunnelling through one hill, with a fall of only 27 metres overall – a fine feat of engineering. On the higher and more salubrious western hill of Jerusalem, the grander residences, often built round a courtyard, have yielded elaborate frescoes and mosaics. It was a noble city, deserving of the wonder and admiration of the Galilean disciples (Mk 13.1–2).

For Jesus and his companions Jerusalem would have been a week's walk from Nazareth or Capernaum. There were two possible routes, either through the hill country and its fertile plains, risking the hostility of the Samaritans, or down the arid Jordan Valley to Jericho and then turning east up the canyon of the Wadi Qilt. The gospel of John recounts four visits of Jesus to Jerusalem, whereas Mark compresses them into one visit in the final week. According to John, also, when Jesus went up to Jerusalem he stayed with the family of Martha, Mary and Lazarus at Bethany, which is a half-hour's walk from Jerusalem on the way up from Jericho.

3. Judaisms of the Time of Jesus

a. The Parties Given by Josephus

Josephus tells us – or rather, tells his Roman audience – that there were three parties of the Jews, three groups or 'choices', Essenes, Sadducees and Pharisees, to whom he adds a 'fourth philosophy', the Zealots (*Antiquities of the Jews*, 18.1.5). His description is not entirely reliable because he is describing them to the Romans as 'philosophical sects', and trying to fit them into boxes which would be intelligible to the Romans. Of course not all Jews, even within Palestine, belonged to one of these parties. To begin with, there were also the 'Am Ha'arez (literally 'country people'), despised by the Temple hierarchy as ignorant of the Law (cf. Jn 9.34). These would have included the descendants of those who were never taken into Exile, and so never developed the strict and rigid way of life, centred on the three boundary-markers of Judaism (Sabbath, circumcision and clean food), evolved during the Exile. What proportion of the pre-Exilic population of the land was taken into Exile we do not know. Nor do we know what proportion of the reconstituted post-Exilic society they formed. The older inhabitants were certainly enough to make life difficult for those who returned from Babylon and settled back in Jerusalem as though they were the sole rightful owners.

1. **Pharisees** Josephus, who was himself a Pharisee, claims that they were the largest and most influential of the Jewish groups. Their chief concerns were three:

- Reverence for the oral Law, interpretations of the written Law which purported to be handed down from Moses. Many others rejected these interpretations.

- Purity, especially in matters of food and life-processes. This required frequent, or even daily, ritual baths for the sake of purification. In addition they were punctilious about washing their hands before eating, purifying dishes and not having contact with women in certain conditions. It must have been a major preoccupation.
- Exactitude of observance of the Law. Their legal experts who advised on correct observance, especially in cases of doubtful or conflicting obligations, were the 'scribes', who were literate and learned in the Law.

It is difficult to discern the degree of hostility between Jesus and the Pharisees. Obviously his interpretation of the Law often differed from theirs (Mt. 5.20–48), especially on the oral Law (Mk 7.1–23), but he engages in argument with them on their own terms and by their own methods (Mk 2.23–8; Mt. 15.4, 11). The disagreements often resemble 'in-house' arguments. Disagreement between Pharisees was notorious, for instance at the time of Jesus, between the two rabbinic schools of Hillel and Shammai, echoed in the discussion on divorce (Mt. 19.1–8). Jesus often interprets scripture according to the rules codified by Rabbi Hillel (e.g. Mk 12.31). It is notable that the Pharisees took no part in the processes which led to Jesus' death; they do not appear in Mark 14–15. Christian hostility to the Pharisees increased in the course of the writing of the New Testament because, after the Fall of Jerusalem in 70AD, the Pharisees were the chief opponents of Christianity within Judaism. This is particularly clear in Matthew (e.g. Mt. 23.1–36). The equation between 'Pharisee' and 'hypocrite' may well stem from this time rather than from Jesus' own lips; the rabbinic writings show that they were well aware of the dangers of 'pharisaism'. Pharisees belonged to no particular layer of society: high priests could be Pharisees, and so could manual workers such as Paul. Josephus says they were loyal to, and supportive of, one another.

2. **Sadducees** We know almost nothing about the Sadducees except from chance remarks of Josephus, contrasting them with the Pharisees. Even the origin and meaning of their name is disputed. They did not accept any belief in life after death: body and soul perished together (Acts 23.6–8). They differed from the Pharisees particularly on rules about purity and so were accused of rejecting the oral Law. They were aristocratic, and some but not all priests were drawn from their ranks. The vagueness about them in all the sources may stem from the fact that they were concentrated in Jerusalem and perished in the fall of that city in 70AD.

3. **Essenes** Essenes are described by Josephus but are never mentioned in the New Testament. Their importance for the New Testament stems from the mention by the Roman historian, Pliny, that there was a settlement of Essenes on the western shore of the Dead Sea, and hence the assumption that much of the material in the scrolls found in the area of Qumran depicts their ideas. These scrolls provide the only reliable witness independent of the New Testament for ideas current at the time of Jesus, and often contribute notably to our understanding of the New Testament. Particularly important is their apocalyptic attitude (see p. 33–4). They show a community waiting eagerly for the Messiah to bring in the eschatological Kingdom of God. They reject the Temple in its present condition, and believe that their community (rather than the Temple) is the true dwelling-place of God on earth. They too were founded by an outstanding figure, 'the Teacher of Righteousness', who is the one authority to whom they appeal. Their methods of scriptural exegesis are similar to those of the New Testament, particularly in their treatment of the fulfilment of scripture (see p. 8) A detail is that both communities use the text of Isaiah 40.3, 'the voice of one crying in the wilderness', of the herald of the Messiah. In these writings occur a number of New Testament expressions ('sons of light' and 'sons of darkness') and processes: the three-stage process for reconciling differences between brothers is the same in Matthew 18.15–17 and in the Rule of the Community. A text of six Beatitudes similar to those of Matthew 5.3–10 has been found at Qumran (4Q525).

The Qumran community was destroyed by the Romans in 68AD, after which little is heard of the Essenes.

4. **Zealots** For the sake of the Romans, Josephus calls the Zealots a 'fourth philosophy', but 'zeal' can have different meanings. Zeal for observance of the Law, after the model of Phinehas (Numb. 31.6), was highly praised. The cleansing of the Temple by Jesus is seen as an example of such zeal (Jn 2.17), and Paul claims the same zeal in his days as a Pharisee (Gal. 1.13; Phil. 3.6). The Zealots as such eventually emerge in 68AD as a group notable for their determination to expel the Romans and thus set Israel free, but political and religious motivations are often difficult to separate. A forerunner may be Judas the Galilean, who led a rebellion against the Roman census in 6BC, on the grounds that Israel belonged to God and that payment of taxes to Rome amounted to recognizing Caesar as Lord. However, during the life and ministry of Jesus there was no more than an underswell of discontent with the Romans; it was, after all, the leaders of the Jews who had invited the

Romans in for direct rule. Soon afterwards, Josephus tells us that Pontius Pilate was removed from office in 36AD because of his brutal suppression of a rebellion in Samaria. Religio-nationalistic fervour and widespread alarm was also provoked by the Emperor Nero's abortive plan in 41–4AD, to set up a statue of himself in the Temple. There is, however, no further trace of armed rebellion in Galilee and Judea until after that date, when a series of incidents rapidly escalated into full-scale warfare in 66AD. This culminated in the siege of Jerusalem and the sack of city and Temple by the Romans, led by Titus and Vespasian. The heroic last stand of the Zealots four years later at the desert stronghold of Massada is dramatically narrated by Josephus.

5. Herodians About the Herodians mentioned in Mark 3.6 and 12.13 we know almost nothing from the texts, except that they are vaguely paired with the Pharisees and try to catch Jesus out about payment of tribute. They may conceivably be supporters of Herod Antipas in Galilee, or in Judea they may be a party who want to see the family of King Herod the Great back on the throne.

b. Charismatic Galilean Rabbis

Apart from these parties enumerated by Josephus, two other tendencies significant for Judaism at the time of Jesus must be mentioned: the charismatic Galilean rabbis, and apocalyptic fervour. Several passages of the rabbinic writings mention charismatic Galilean rabbis who have a special, warm and personal relationship to God, and are claimed to have worked miracles. One of these, known in the rabbinic sources at Rabbi Honi the Rain-maker, or the Circle-Drawer, is briefly mentioned under the Hellenized name 'Onias' by Josephus, 'he was a righteous man and beloved of God. During a drought he prayed to God to put an end to the intense heat, and God heard his prayers and sent rain' (*Antiquities of the Jews*, 14.2.22). The same story is told with humour and at greater length in the Mishnah:

> Once they said to Honi the Circle-drawer, 'Pray that it may rain'. He prayed but it did not rain. What did he do then? He drew a circle, stood in it and said to God, 'Lord of the universe, your children have turned to me because I am like a son of the house before you. I swear by your great name that I will not move hence until you are merciful to your children.' It then began to drizzle. 'I have not asked for this,' he said, 'but for rain to fill cisterns, pits and rock cavities.' There came a cloud-burst. 'I asked not for this, but for a rain of grace, blessing and gift.' It then rained gently. (*mTaan* 3.8)

The story is told also, with slight variations, of his grandson. In a way which heralds Jesus' own use of the term, Hanan uses the intimate family name *Abba* for God (*bTaan* 23–4): School children come to 'Abba Hanan', asking him to give them rain. He prays, 'Lord of the universe. Do it for the sake of those who do not distinguish between the *Abba* who gives rain and the *Abba* who does not.' A comparable story of miraculous healing through prayer is told of another Galilean rabbi, Hanina in the generation after Jesus. He was a student of the great Rabbi Yohanan ben Zakkai. Yohanan asked Hanina to pray for his son, so he 'put his head between his knees and prayed and the son lived' (*bBer.* 34b). When Yohanan's wife reproached him for his inability to heal the illness, Yohanan replied that Hanina was like a son in the house of God, who must be humoured, whereas he himself was of higher standing. The fuller stories are too late to be good evidence for the time of Jesus, but the note in Josephus gives some assurance. Jesus may stand in the tradition of these charismatic rabbis.

c. Apocalyptic Fervour

The Jesus movement cannot be understood without reference to the apocalyptic writings of the time. The nature of apocalyptic writing is discussed with reference to the Book of Revelation, the final book of the New Testament (see p. 362). The expectation of a divine intervention to fashion a new world marks also the earliest writings of the New Testament (1 Thess. 4.13–5.11) and particularly 1 Corinthians 15.20–8. Much of Paul's moral teaching is dependent on expectation of an imminent divine intervention (e.g. 1 Cor. 7.26). It is voiced in the initial proclamation of both John the Baptist and Jesus (Mt. 3.2; 4.17). It forms the burden of Peter's speech on the morning of Pentecost (Acts 2.16–21).

Such an expectation was widespread in the Israel of the time. It is expressed in the earliest part of the *Book of Enoch* (*1 Enoch* 17–36) already at the beginning of the second century BC, and in the allegorical description of the history of Israel, leading to the triumphant vindication of Israel (Chapters 89–90). The same expectation is vivid in the Scrolls of Qumran (e.g. the 'Kingdom of Peace' in 1 QS 4.8), the preparations for a final eschatological war in the War Scroll (1 QM), and in various ways in many of the Qumran fragments. In wider spheres the promise of a renewed kingdom is rooted in the *Assumption of Moses,* 10 (dated to the first decade AD). The expectation of a 'Son of Man' after the model of the figure in the apocalyptic description of Daniel 7.13 is the clue to much of the use of that title in the gospels, and possibly also its use on Jesus' lips. This restoration eschatology gives a context to Jesus' miracles of healing and forgiveness and to his choice of the Twelve to represent a renewed twelve-tribe Israel. It also makes sense of his instructions that no time is to be lost, and of the crisis nature of the parables, particularly in Mark, and similarly of the Synoptic Apocalypse in Mark 13. Finally the apocalyptic signs at the death and resurrection of Jesus, the darkness at noon and especially the two earthquakes in Matthew, mark out that event as the fulfilment of the hopes of Israel.

Questions on Part One

1   What are the key concepts of the Old Testament which we need in order to understand the message of Jesus?
2   Can the evangelists be considered true authors or only secretaries? Is the analogy of a musical instrument played by God a useful one? If not, think of a better one!
3   If the text of the Bible is so uncertain, can it be our guide in life?
4   Do advances in knowledge of recent centuries render biblical teaching obsolete?
5   To what extent have I a right to decide what the Bible means to me?
6   Did God choose a good moment to send his Son?

Part II

The Gospels and Acts

4

The Origin of the Gospels

---

1. Before the Gospels

From the beginning of the Christian community witness to Jesus was important. The replacement for Judas among the Twelve was chosen from among those who had, according to Peter, 'been with us the whole time that the Lord Jesus was travelling round with us' (Acts 1.21), and so able to bear witness to the whole of Jesus' trajectory. Although the gospels were written in the cities of the Jewish Diaspora among gentiles, it is striking that many of the names in the stories are characteristic of Palestinian rather than Diaspora Judaism, e.g. Bar-Timaeus, Jairus (=Yair), Nathanael, Mary from Magdala. Paul, despite his fierce insistence that his authority to proclaim the gospel was a divine rather than a human mandate, went up to Jerusalem to check that his message was in accord with that of the apostles (Gal. 2.2). What and how much he learnt there we do not know, but presumably it included knowledge of Jesus' ministry; he twice quotes traditional formulae about the institution of the Eucharist and about the death and Resurrection of Jesus which he had clearly learnt by heart (1 Cor. 11.23–6; 15.3–6). He uses the official rabbinic terms for handing on tradition. It is significant for

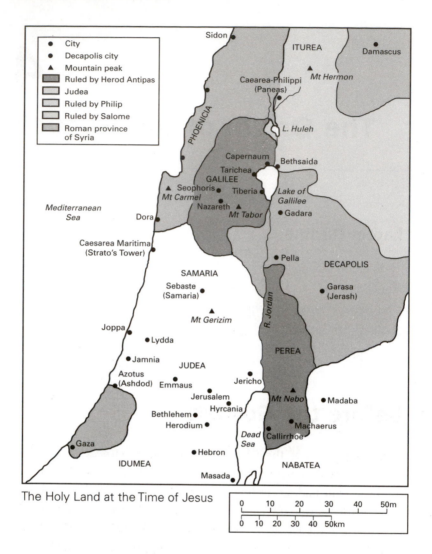

The Holy Land at the Time of Jesus

what would become the gospels that from the earliest times the memories of Jesus were always understood against the background of scripture. This is evident both in the first two accounts of evangelization (Lk. 24.27; Acts 8.35) and in Paul's memorized text (the text stresses that the events were 'according to the scriptures', 1 Cor. 15.3 and 4); it will be reflected in the gospels. Memorization was extremely important in education at that time, when books were rare and expensive, whole passages being memorized for use as examples of style. It has been suggested that, when the Twelve thought it would not be right for them 'to neglect the word of God so as to give out food' (Acts 6.2), they were unwilling to put aside their work of garnering and developing the traditions about Jesus. The teachers in the early Christian communities (Rom. 12.7; 1 Cor. 12.28–9, etc) will also no doubt have engaged in this process. Our earliest Christian writers tell of Papias, Bishop of Hierapolis at the end of the first century, eagerly listening to the traditions about Jesus from the elders or those who had known the Twelve, and – a few years later – of Polycarp of Smyrna passing on what he had learned from John 'concerning the Lord, his mighty works and his teaching' (Eusebius, *H.E.* 3.39.3; 5.20.4). At some stage it must have been thought appropriate that such traditions should be gathered together, and this is how the gospels came to be written.

2. The Gospels

The English word is derived from 'god-spel' or 'good word'. The corresponding Greek word is *euangelion*, or 'good message'. It enters Christian discourse through Paul, who frequently speaks of 'my *euangelion*' (Rom. 16.25; Gal. 1.11). He may have derived it from one or both of two backgrounds. In the religious cult of the emperors the term was used to qualify a piece of imperial good news of salvation, such as a victory or the birth of an heir, which was flashed round the empire to provoke a response of congratulatory gifts from provinces, city-states and other political units. The Good News of Christ is just such a joyful message. Paul may also be drawing on the use of the word in Isaiah 61.1, 'The Lord has anointed me to *bring good tidings* to the afflicted'. This usage may go back to the proclamation of Jesus himself; it certainly occurs on his lips in Matthew 11.5 and Luke 4.18. The first sentence of the gospel of Mark uses the term for the proclamation of the saving message. Matthew uses it twice for Jesus' own proclamation of the Kingdom (4.23; 9.35), and twice with the addition of '*this* gospel' (24.14; 26.13), in which case he may be intending to restrict the sense to the particular incident of the gospel message. Luke does not use the noun, but frequently uses the corresponding verb for the activity of spreading the good news.

None of the four canonical gospels originally included attribution to an author; all were anonymous. Papias' evidence about the authors is neither reliable nor easy to interpret, and most modern scholars form their opinion about the authors from the text of the gospels themselves, sometimes appealing subsequently to the external evidence for confirmation of their findings.

Until recently the type of writing called 'gospel' was considered to be without parallel in the ancient world. However, it pertains to the basic understanding of any text that the reader can situate it within some genre of literature (a biography is different from a political husting). It is now held that the gospels fall within the varied and well-attested Greco-Roman concept of biography, of which there are many subdivisions, including political propaganda and moral persuasion. In the first century there was a host of literary works of comparable length, on many subjects, history, medicine, astronomy, arms-manufacture, navigation, travelogues, novels as well as biographies. Luke explicitly ranges his gospel among them by his preface, which conforms to many of the conventions of this type of writing. Religious biographies in the broad sense were not unknown, and the respectful atmosphere, tinged with worship, occurs also in such works as Tacitus' *Agricola* and Philo's *De Vita Moysis*. Unique to the gospels, however, is the salvific claim of their message, expressed most clearly by John 20.31, 'these things are written so that you may believe, and that believing you may have life'. It is not, then, an unprecedented type of writing that is unique, so much as the conviction of the writers that their subject and message has the power to change the world for those who accept them that is unique. This does not exclude the gospels from the broad category of Greco-Roman biography.

3. The Basic Interrelationship of the Gospels

The three gospels of Matthew, Mark and Luke are clearly related very closely to one another, much more closely than John is related to any of them. They share the same basic outline, roughly the same order of events, the same way of telling stories and relating sayings, and even the basically same portrait of the good news of the kingdom and its preaching by Jesus.

This similarity among the first three gospels is best seen by contrast to John.

- The geographical outline is different: in the first three gospels Jesus goes to Jerusalem only once during his ministry, for the final week, whereas in John he pays several visits to Jerusalem.
- The order of events is different, for example the cleansing of the Temple comes early in John, introducing Jesus' ministry (Jn 2.13–22), whereas in the other three gospels it forms the climax (Mk 11.15–19).

- John relates many fewer miracles, but almost invariably these are developed by means of a subsequent long discourse of Jesus or by a controversy that brings out the sense and meaning of the event (for example the cure at the Pool of Bethesda continues into a discourse on the works of the Son, John 5; the multiplication of loaves flowers into the bread of life discourse (Jn 6.1–15, 22–66).
- While the Jesus of the first three gospels turns attention away from himself to the kingship of God, in John the kingship of God is mentioned only in 3.3–5; John concentrates rather on Jesus' gift of life.
- In the first three gospels, story-parables are an important vehicle of teaching, whereas the fourth gospel barely uses them, preferring instead extended images such as that of the Good Shepherd (Jn 10.1–18).

The similarity between the first three gospels may be roughly described in terms of the number of verses shared.

- Of Mark's 661 verses, some 80 per cent feature in Matthew and 60 per cent in Luke. Conversely, only three pericopes of Mark (the seed growing secretly, 4.26–9, the healing of the deaf-mute, 7.31–7, and the blind man of Bethsaida, 8.22–6) have no equivalent in either Matthew or Luke.
- Time and again long stretches of almost verbatim agreement between Matthew and Mark or Mark and Luke show that some literary relationship at the textual level must be postulated between them.
- Similarly, Matthew and Luke have some 220 verses in common, mostly of sayings-material, so that some literary relationship between these two is undeniable.

The possibility of viewing these three gospels together has led to the name 'Synoptic Gospels', and the difficulty of reaching an agreed solution to account for their relationship has been dubbed 'the synoptic problem'. Three proposed solutions to this problem will be outlined.

1. The Griesbach Hypothesis. Truly scientific study of this problem did not begin until in 1776 J. J. Griesbach produced a critical edition of a Synopsis of the Gospels, printing the gospels in parallel columns, and thus enabling the reader to see in detail the similarities and differences between them. His conclusion, published in 1789, was that Mark was nothing but a combination of Matthew and Luke. This thesis was revived by William R. Farmer in 1964. The theory is that the first gospel to be written was that of Matthew, written for Christians of Jewish extraction. Next, for the Christians of gentile origin,

but still before the destruction of Jerusalem, Luke was written. Finally Mark combined the two. The fundamental argument for this hypothesis lies in the order of pericopes. Wherever Mark departs from Matthew's order he supports Luke's. If there is a difference between the order of Matthew and Luke, Mark zigzags between the two, following first one, then the other. The same pattern is seen also for the material within pericopes. Mark has many double expressions, of which half occur in Matthew and half in Luke, e.g. Mark 1.32 has 'That evening, at sunset', where Matthew has in the corresponding passage, 'That evening' (8.16) and Luke 'when the sun was setting' (4.40). The theory is that Mark takes one phrase from each of the other gospels and combines them (so also Mk 1.42; 8.3; 10.29).

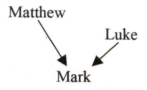

However, opponents of the theory claim that duality of this kind is a feature of Mark's own style, specifically a feature of his oral style, in which a certain repetitiveness aids the hearer. Mark serves as a quarry for his successors, with the result that sometimes Matthew takes one element and Luke the other. On many occasions Matthew keeps both Mark's elements, while Luke has only one, or Luke keeps both elements while Matthew has only one. Double expressions occur in Mark even where there is no parallel in Matthew or Luke; it should be considered a trait of Mark's own style rather than a combination of two sources.

The greatest difficulty for the Griesbach hypothesis is, however, to explain why Mark should have written a gospel (and why the Church should have accepted it) in which he deliberately omitted so much that is valuable: the infancy stories, the beatitudes, the Lord's prayer, the resurrection appearances and many other favourite passages which had already been included in Matthew and Luke.

The Two-Source Theory

Since it was proposed by C. Lachmann in 1835 this theory has won overwhelming acceptance at least as a working hypothesis. It still holds the dominant position in New Testament scholarship. The theory is that Mark is the first gospel, and was used independently by Matthew and Luke, neither of whom knew each other's texts. The large quantity of material shared by Matthew and Luke (but not in Mark), mostly sayings material, derives from a common source, known as Q (which stands for 'die Quelle', 'the Source' in German). The acceptance of this source has been greatly assisted by the mention by Papias of a collection of Sayings of the Lord in Aramaic made or used by Matthew.

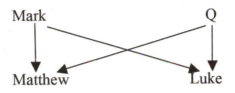

Considerable studies of this hypothetical document 'Q' have been undertaken to establish its shape and content. Its most striking feature is that it contains no account of the Passion and Resurrection of Jesus, and indeed shows no interest in these events, containing no hint that they were to occur. Kloppenborg suggests that Paul's stress on these events could be a deliberate corrective to their neglect in this very early document. The most important stress is on the threat of coming judgment; this frames the whole document (Lk. 3.7–9, 16–17 and 19.12–27; 22.28–30) as well as many of the sub-units isolated by Kloppenborg. Combined with these is criticism of the continual rejection of the prophets, and a promise of fulfilment through 'one who is to come'. Many of the sections isolated show a common structure, beginning with programmatic sayings, introducing a series of imperatives and concluding with affirmations of the importance of its message. Kloppenborg likens it to the 'widely attested genre in near Eastern literature', the instruction or sapiential discourse. Its principal function is social criticism and the destabilization of a corrupt society. Interests are in small transactions, debt, moths, treasure found, homelessness, renunciation. There is reference to the rule of God, but – by contrast to the canonical gospels – no interest in exegesis of the Torah, no disputes with Pharisees over legal observance of the Sabbath or food laws.

Some scholars would go so far as to postulate and elaborate at least two editions of the Q-document, and even postulate a Q-community. Would this have been classed as a Christian community, since it seems to have lacked any interest in the death and resurrection of Jesus? From its concern with the poor, peasant farmer and the threats against the lakeside villages, Capernaum, Bethsaida and Chorozaim (Lk. 10.13–15) and the silence about Judaea, it seems likely that Q should be placed in Galilee. Others, while accepting the existence of the Q-tradition, doubt whether it was ever a single document. Various answers have been given to the question why it disappeared: perhaps it had no reason for a continued independent existence, having already been fully copied into Matthew and Luke; perhaps it is still waiting to be found in the sands of Egypt.

The strongest arguments for this theory are the order of pericopes, the detailed editing and the mutual independence of Matthew and Luke:

- With Mark as starting-point it is possible to explain the order of pericopes in Matthew and Luke: Matthew follows Mark's order of pericopes strictly except when he is composing two series, the collection of miracles in Matthew 8–9 and the discourse on mission in Matthew 10. For these two collections he takes material that occurs later in Mark. Matthew is a careful and orderly teacher, who likes to assemble into complete collections all the material on one subject. Thus all the changes in Matthew's order are explained as anticipations in accordance with his teaching methods. Luke's changes of the Markan order are not to be explained so simply and schematically, for Luke is more creative in his writing and more independent of his sources than is Matthew. So he puts the rejection of Jesus at Nazareth (Mk 6.1–6) earlier and builds it up into the programmatic opening speech with which Jesus begins his ministry at Nazareth (Lk. 4.16–30). On the other hand Luke postpones until 5.1–11 the call of the first disciples and builds it into an important lesson in discipleship. Luke's most far-reaching change in order is the construction of the great journey to Jerusalem (9.51–18.14) by which he locates much of Jesus' teaching on the final journey to his death at Jerusalem.
- The argument from detailed editing can hardly be briefly summarized, though some impression of it may be given. Often Matthew and Luke improve the grammar and style of Mark's rough Greek; it seems perverse to argue in the opposite direction that Mark deliberately roughens a more cultured presentation. Matthew and Luke show a distinctly more explicit Christology than Mark. Mark is highly, even shockingly, critical of the disciples' lack of faith and understanding; Matthew and Luke both weaken this criticism, in a way that might be expected to have occurred at a time when reverence for the first leaders of Christianity was increasing.
- The mutual independence of Matthew and Luke is a crucial point, for if Luke knew Matthew (or vice versa) the links between Matthew

and Luke can be accounted for without the intervention of any Q. The large number of minor agreements between those two evangelists (some calculate that there are as many as 1,000) demands some explanation. It may be that Matthew and Luke used an earlier (or later) edition of Mark than our present text, which included (or omitted) a phrase. Clusters of agreement between Matthew and Luke do occur in a limited number of pericopes, and it is accepted that in these passages Matthew and Luke drew on both Mark and Q; they are known as 'Mark-Q overlaps', amounting in all to perhaps as many as 50 verses. The major examples are John's preaching, the Testing of Jesus in the desert, the parable of the mustard-seed, collusion with Satan, and the commissioning of the Twelve.

Mark as the Single Source

This theory of Michael Goulder (1974), building on Austin Farrer (1955), holds that the material in Matthew which is not drawn from Mark shows a consistency of method and approach which can only be the stamp of a single mind, so that it would be mistaken to postulate any other source for that part of it which is shared with Luke. Goulder 'finger-prints' Matthew to show a consistency of vocabulary, imagery and patterns of speech (pairs of parables, contrasts in parables, pairs of images). Luke can be 'finger-printed' in a similar way to show a characteristic method of story-telling and characterization, as well as a consistent care for the poor and underprivileged. A difficulty about this theory is that it postulates that Luke carefully cut down Matthew's long and structured discourses, estimating – it is claimed – that only a limited amount of teaching can be digested at one time. Another difficulty is that the theory attributes considerable freedom of inventiveness to both Mathew and Luke. A third difficulty is whether such a careful, modern scissors-and-paste method may be postulated of an ancient author. Doubt has also been cast on the central argument from vocabulary. The theory remains a minority opinion.

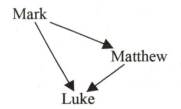

John and the Synoptic Gospels

It is difficult to establish any link between the gospel of John and the present text of the synoptics. It is not possible to prove that John intends either to supplement or to correct the synoptic tradition. Such links as there are seem to be more at the oral level, John and the synoptics using the same oral traditions. The relationships vary:

- Some stories are closely similar, though the authors have remodelled them to express their own theology, e.g. the Multiplication of Loaves and the Walking on the Waters (Jn 6.1–20), the Commission to Peter in Luke 5.1–11 and John 21.1–14.
- Some Johannine miracle-stories are of the same type as synoptic stories, e.g. Healing on the Sabbath in Mark 2.1–12 and John 5; the Raising of Jairus' Daughter, and of Lazarus in John 11.
- Some sayings in John may be different translations of the same Aramaic saying, e.g. John 1.26–7; 2.19 and Matthew 3.11; Mark 14.58; John 12.27–8 and Mark 14.36.
- There is a special link between John and Luke, especially in the passion and resurrection narratives. It has been argued both that John is dependent on Luke and vice versa.

4. Dating the Gospels

The images of destruction, and especially of the desecration of the Temple, are so prominent in Mark 13 that it is conventional to date the gospel of Mark at around the date of the Sack of the Temple in 70AD (cf. p. 31). It may have been written when the threat of destruction was becoming ever more pressing, or when the destruction was a dominant, fresh memory. Therefore the gospel is conventionally dated 65–75AD. It could be that Matthew and Luke, incorporating Q, were written within a dozen years after Mark. The theology of John is in many ways more explicit and developed, but this means only that the tradition matured differently, perhaps cut off from the synoptic tradition, not necessarily that John is later. The synoptic writers show only vague knowledge of the topography of Palestine (e.g. Jesus' strange route from Tyre to the Lake of Galilee via the Decapolis, Mk 7.31), whereas John has detailed knowledge of Jerusalem and its surroundings.

Further Reading

Burridge, Richard A., *What are the Gospels?* (Cambridge: Cambridge University Press, 1992): gospels compared to Greco-Roman biography

Eve, Eric, *Behind the Gospels* (London: SPCK, 2013): understanding the oral tradition

Goodacre, Mark, *The Synoptic Problem* (London: Sheffield Academic Press, 2001): a way through the maze

Rodriguez, Rafael, *Oral Tradition and the New Testament* (London: Bloomsbury, 2014): short, scholarly treatment in the *Guide for the Perplexed* Series

Senior, Donald, *Jesus* (Mahwah: Paulist Press, 1992): a gospel portrait

Stanton, Graham, *The Gospels and Jesus* ([2]New York: Oxford University Press, 2002): an introduction to gospel study, revised – methods and texts

Tuckett, Christopher, *Reading the New Testament* (London: SPCK, 1987): methods of interpretation

—*Q and the Early History of Christianity* (Edinburgh: T&T Clark, 1996): a different way through the maze

5

Matthew – A Gospel for the New Israel

1. Authorship and Date

If our conclusions in the section about the Synoptic Problem are correct, then Matthew was the second Gospel to be written. In this case, also, the author used the Gospel of Mark, which he edited and expanded in order, under the inspiration of the Holy Spirit, to express his view of the Good News of the Christ event. He used the elusive document Q, whether it was a written or simply a memorized document, and also some of his own material. As will become evident, the whole of the document clearly shows the style, mannerisms and interest of one mind. If Mark wrote – as is commonly held (but see p. 46) – within a few years either before or after the Sack of Jerusalem in 70AD, we should allow a decade or so for that first gospel to be disseminated, and for the Christian community to feel that there was another angle to the story than that presented by Mark. We might imagine that they came to Matthew and said, 'Mark has told us the story of Jesus, concentrating on the personality of Jesus and the necessity of suffering. But that is not the whole story; Mark does not give much of the teaching of Jesus. You are a fine and reliable teacher, with excellent ways of helping us to remember the lessons. Please incorporate Q and other important material into the Gospel.'

Who was this 'Matthew'? If the conventional date of the composition of the gospel is accepted, by the time the gospel was written, c. 85AD or later, any disciples of Jesus would have been very old, and hardly capable of the detailed work necessary for writing this gospel. Did Matthew 'rubber-stamp' it, and stand behind it as the authority? There is another alternative: the story of the call of Levi the tax-collector is told in Mark 2.13–14. In Matthew 9.9 the same story is told, but the disciple called is now named Matthew. In the list of disciples corresponding to Mark 3.18 'Matthew' is listed as 'Matthew the tax-collector' (Mt. 10.3). One could suppose that someone 'corrected' the story of the call of Levi, attaching it to Matthew instead of Levi. It is, however, surely unlikely that anyone would recount the story of his own call by Jesus in the words of someone else's call. Nor is it likely that the apostle Matthew, one of the Twelve, merely accepted without change so much of Mark's account. Hardly likely! There is a third possibility: is the gospel attached to Matthew simply because Matthew is twice mentioned, instead of merely being listed among the twelve disciples?

2. Shape

The Gospel according to Matthew is about twice as long as that of Mark. According to the generally accepted Two-Source Theory (see p. 42–3), Matthew has edited Mark, adding material from Q, and in addition some of his own material, much of which he may have received from the oral tradition. Much of this proper material shows similar popular characteristics, which suggest its origin in popular culture (angels, dreams, violence, heavenly phenomena); it is difficult to discern whether these features come from Matthew himself or from a source. With the addition of these insertions Matthew follows the outline of Mark, occasionally expanding it massively. There were many elements of the oral tradition which Mark had not included, particularly those of the teaching of Jesus.

As a careful and gifted teacher, Matthew gathers his teaching material into discourses, each on one particular topic (and for this reason it appears that Luke retains more closely the order of material in Q). Finally, Matthew puts before the Markan material his own narrative of Jesus' birth and babyhood, and after the Markan material Matthew adds two stories of the Risen Christ. The Gospel as a whole is given structure by the discourses on the Kingdom, which are arranged concentrically. The first and the last discourses are centred respectively on the entry and exit (so to speak) into the Kingdom, the second and penultimate respectively on the community in its outward work and in its home life.

a. Matthew 5–7 Sermon on the Mount – the basic qualities necessary for a disciple who makes a commitment to the Kingdom. It is placed in Mark's outline after Jesus' initial preaching, when he has drawn a huge audience (Mk 1.39).

b. Matthew 10 The Mission of the Community and the persecution this brings. In this Matthew gathers together material from Jesus' instructions in Mark about the initial mission of the disciples in Mark 6 and the warnings of persecution in Mark 13, adding other material from Q.

c. Matthew 13 Images of the Kingdom. In this central discourse Matthew uses and expands the parable chapter of Mark 4.1–33.

b' Matthew 18 Community Relationships. Matthew gathers together material from Mark, from Q and from his own tradition.

a' Matthew 24–5 Eschatological Discourse, the final coming. This discourse uses and expands Mark's eschatological Chapter 13.

The structure of Matthew overall may be viewed in five sections, preceded by the Infancy Stories and completed by the story of the Passion, Death and Resurrection of Jesus:

Preliminary 1–2 Infancy Stories
  Jesus the Second David
  Jesus the New Moses

1 3–4 First Meetings with the Disciples
    5–7 Opening Discourse: the Sermon on the Mount
2 8–9 A Collection of Ten Wonders
    10 The Mission of the Community

3 11–12 The Training of the Disciples
        13 Images of the Kingdom: Parables
4 14–17 The First-Fruits of the Kingdom
        18 Living in the Community
5 19–23 The Kingdom Approaches
        24–25 Eschatological Discourse

Climax 26–28 The Passion, Death and Resurrection

3. Structure and Style

1. Numerical structures and formulae are very important to Matthew; they would no doubt be important factors in the memory-work of a primarily oral society. So:

- There are 14 'formula quotations', biblical quotations introduced by roughly the same formula, 'this was done to fulfil what was said by the prophet X'
- The generations of Jesus' genealogy in Matthew are structured on the sacred number 7: 7 x 2 from Abraham to David, 7 x 2 from David to the Exile, 7 x 2 from the Exile to the birth of Jesus. The final Woes on the scribes and Pharisees also number 7.
- The Beatitudes at the beginning of the Sermon on the Mount are very carefully structured: the whole bracketed by 'the Kingdom of Heaven' (verses 3 and 10) – two halves, each of four blessings, each ending with 'justice' (verses 6 and 11) – the first half numbers 20 + 16 words, the second balancing with 16 + 20 words.
- Six corrections of the Law (5.21–36), each structured on the formula, 'You have heard it said…, but I say to you…'.
- The three good works of Judaism, each presented with the same formula cautioning against ostentation.
- There are also blocks of teaching in which Matthew first gives a principle, then follows it with applications or examples. In rabbinic teaching this was called *ab wetoledoth*, or 'father and descendants'. So at 5.20 he gives the principle 'I tell you, if your uprightness does not surpass that of the scribes and Pharisees you will never get into the Kingdom of Heaven', followed by six applications. Similarly the principle in 6.1, followed by the three applications in 6.2–18.

- The sevenfold indictment of the Jewish leaders is structured round, 'Alas for you, scribes and Pharisees, you hypocrites!' (23.13–29).

2. Matthew also has a liking for pairs, two elements either reinforcing or contrasting with each other: treasure in heaven, treasure on earth; light and dark; moth and woodworm; judgment given and received. The Sermon on the Mount ends with a volley of contrasts: narrow gate/broad road; sound tree producing good fruit/rotten tree producing bad fruit; sensible man building on rock/stupid man building on sand (7.13–27). These contrasts are often expressed by means of animals – always a memorable way of teaching – moth and woodworm, dogs and pigs, snake and fish, sheep and goats. Each of these animals stands for a particular quality, such as corruption, or cunning or simplicity. Particularly Matthew likes to pair parables: the mustard-seed and the leaven, the hidden treasure and the pearl of great price, the ten wedding-attendants and the talents. All Matthew's story-parables are based on starkly contrasting characters (unlike Luke's delicately painted likeable rogues): the two builders, the playing children, the wheat and the darnel, the good and bad fish, the two sons, the unmerciful servant and his victim, the wedding-feast and the guest without a wedding garment, the sheep and the goats.

3. The same rhythm is achieved in Matthew by the frequent four-point verbal balance (grapes from thorns/figs from thistles, 7.16; foxes have holes/birds have nests, 8.20), often including a four-point antithesis: 'the harvest is rich but the labourers are few', 'be cunning as snakes and innocent as doves', 'covered/revealed//hidden/made known' (10.26), 'confess before men/confess before my Father in heaven// deny before men/deny before my Father in heaven' (10.32–3). On some occasions Matthew's saying is based on a saying in Mark, but the parallelism and balance have been brightened up (compare Mt. 10.26, 33 with the corresponding passage in Mark).

4. Matthew also likes rhythms of three, for instance the same-shaped saying with three different objects: 'Lord, did we not prophesy in your name, drive out demons in your name, work miracles in your name' (7.2); similarly 'angry – raqa – fool' (5.22), 'ask, seek, knock' (5.22), kingdom – house – Satan (12.25–6). Three good works of Judaism (6.1–18), in the Lord's Prayer three petitions about God, followed by three petitions about ourselves (6.9–13).

The imagery used by Matthew is also richer than that of Mark. Mark uses four different animal images (camels, sheep, puppies, birds), whereas

Matthew uses 22 different animals. That he moves in a different world from Mark is shown by his use of economic and urban images: if Mark moves in the world of the corner-shop (sell, barter, pay, make and lose money) Matthew is almost ready for a supermarket (debt, banker, interest, merchant, unemployed). The same is true of money: Mark has only small coins, a denarius and *lepton*, a mere sliver of copper; Matthew parades also shekels, staters (four denarii) and the astronomical sum of ten thousand talents. Above all, the religious imagery is diversified (phylacteries, tithes, rabbis, proselytes). This shows where Matthew's true interests, positive and negative, lie; this shows the world from which Matthew came.

It is because of the brilliant teaching power of these memorable images and neat contrasts that Matthew has always been the most popular of the gospels, and until recently provided most of the readings in church. It may also be the reason why Matthew is put as the first of the four gospels. The attractive suggestion has been made that when Matthew says at the end of the parable-chapter, 'Every scribe who becomes a disciple of the Kingdom of Heaven is like a householder who brings out from his storeroom new things as well as old' (13.52), this is a self-portrait. By this he lays claim to the important prophetic role of wisdom in the community; he brings out from his storeroom the old traditions in a new way. The Greek word for 'scribe' really means 'writer'. Those who could read and write in the ancient world were few, so those who could read and check up on the Law would have a special position as lawyers, advising on how to observe the interlocking and often contradictory legal regulations. Matthew is eager to protect the reputation of the scribes, and so it is notable that he cuts out Mark's mentions of 'scribes' in the opposition to Jesus when there is no legal issue involved (in the passages corresponding to Mk 2.16; 3.22; 9.14). Similarly, they take no part in the plot to dispose of Jesus: Mark 14.1 ascribes this to 'the chief priests and scribes', while Matthew 26.3 attributes it to 'the chief priests and elders of the people'. He is perhaps defending his own position and his own friends.

4. Matthew the Jew

The paradox of Matthew is that it is on the one hand the most Jewish of all the gospels, obviously formed in Judaism, thinking in Jewish categories, using Jewish methods of argument, but at the same time the most starkly hostile to the Jews. Matthew's whole presentation of Jesus, his person, his work and his community, is largely in Jewish terms. The first incident after the baptism is the Temptations or Testing in the Desert. To the brief account in Mark, Matthew adds a series of three text-swapping confrontations with the Devil, where the two protagonists quote the scriptures at each other in a manner exactly reminiscent of rabbinic argument. The Matthean account is taken from Q, but the order in which these temptations come fits Matthew's Jewish scheme: for the final climax of temptation Jesus is taken onto a very high mountain, just as Moses was taken onto Mount Nebo before his death (Mt. 4.8; Deut. 32.48). So also the Sermon on the Mount opens with the Beatitudes, an opening blessing or congratulation frequent in the Old Testament and in contemporary writing, e.g. 'Blessed is anyone who has not sinned in speech' (Sira 14.1). The first two major sections are in the Jewish form *ab wetoledoth* (literally 'father and descendants', a heading followed by examples, one of the classic arguments codified by Rabbi Hillel, see pp. 192, 262), and the whole of the Sermon on the Mount is to teach a more perfect 'justice' or observance of the Law. Matthew continues to think in terms of observance of the Law, though he shows that Jesus conceives this in a way different to the teaching of his contemporary rabbis. In the infancy stories, Joseph is praised as 'just' (i.e. law-observant, 1.19), and 'just' is Matthew's highest form of commendation (16 times in the gospel, only twice in Mark). Similarly 'justice' occurs seven times in Matthew, never in Mark, once in Luke. At his baptism Jesus sets out to 'fulfil all justice' (3.13). In the Beatitudes the two sets of four Beatitudes are linked by Matthew's addition of 'justice' as a primary motive (5.6, 10).

In his treatment of the incident of plucking grain on the Sabbath, Matthew shows how concerned he is about legal observance; indeed, Matthew's handling of the Law suggests that it may well still have been observed in his community. He makes clear that the disciples' disregard of the Sabbath Law is justified by their hunger. To reinforce Mark's rather distant precedent of David, Matthew adds the precedent of priests breaking the Sabbath, with a neat rabbinical argument *a minori ad maius*. In a further contrast he omits Mark's sweeping dismissal of the Law, 'The Sabbath was made for man, not man for the Sabbath' (Mk 2.27), just as he will later omit Mark's sweeping dismissal, 'thus he pronounced all foods clean' (Mk 7.19). Instead, he adds as Jesus' far-reaching principle of interpretation the biblical principle, 'What I want is love not sacrifice' (Hosea 6.6, used in Mt. 12.7; 9.13; 23.23). When Mark depicts Jesus going into gentile territory, the region of Tyre, to meet the Syro-Phoenician woman, Matthew protects Jesus from the uncleanness of entering a gentile house by bringing the woman out to meet him (Mk 7.24; Mt. 15.22).

For Matthew the probative force of scripture is paramount. He presents events as taking place simply in order to fulfil scripture; 'All this happened in order that the word spoken by the Lord through the prophet should be fulfilled' is a formula recurring ten times (1.23; 2.15, 23; 4.14; 8.17; 12.17; 13.35; 21.5; 26.58; 27.9). Perhaps the most expressive passage is Matthew 11.4–5, when Jesus himself interprets his wonders in terms of Isaiah 35.5–6: John the Baptist had been expecting a Messiah of fire and judgment, so Jesus shows that his Messiahship is a matter of healing, and proclaiming good news according to the prophecies of Isaiah.

A further feature of Jewish writing at the time is the frequency of angels and apocalyptic phenomena. In Mark angels are rare; in Matthew they are mentioned some 20 times. Similarly the earthquake at the death of Jesus and the resurrection, not to mention the strange phenomenon of the sacred dead rising and walking into the Holy City (27.51–3). All of these are apocalyptic markers of the Day of the Lord, familiar from the Jewish apocalyptic literature of the time. An amusing feature of Matthew is exaggeration, a feature familiar also from rabbinic stories: he uses huge sums of money, the immense sum of ten thousand talents contrasted with a few weeks' wages (18.24), talents again in 25.14–28. The disciples are told not to take any gold in their pouches, whereas in Mark Jesus tells them not to take any coppers, a more likely currency for peasants (Mt. 10.9). An army is sent to burn down a city because a wedding-invitation was refused (Mt. 22.7); this may, of course, be an allusion to the destruction of Jerusalem by the Romans.

However, as well as being firmly anchored in Judaism, Matthew is perhaps the most critical among the evangelists of the contemporary practice of Judaism, and especially of the leadership of the Pharisees. This would fit a date towards the end of the century. After the Sack of Jerusalem in 70AD, many of the leadership-groups of the Jews (e.g. Sadducees and Essenes) were destroyed, and the Pharisees, who were a strictly religious group, were the only group that remained. Therefore the opposition to Jews who became Christians was overwhelmingly from them. Further, it has been surmised that the Gospel of Matthew was written at Antioch, where there was a large and prosperous Jewish colony, who were energetically persecuted and mocked by the non-Jewish population. The Christians, sprung from Judaism, would then have been in the unenviable situation of being the persecuted minority of a persecuted minority, which would give a particular point to Matthew's emphasis on persecution by the Jews. So Matthew carefully differentiates 'their' synagogues from Christian assemblies (4.23; 9.35; 10.17; 23.34), often with reference to persecution: 'you will be scourged in *their* synagogues'. There is biblical reason for this, 'they persecuted the prophets before you' (5.12): it is the fate of prophets to be persecuted. The Jews were of course not the only source of persecution, but 'you will be hated by all nations for my sake' (24.10–12), and Matthew brings persecution into special prominence as the finale of the Beatitudes, emphasized by his addition (5.10–12).

By countless little touches, Matthew alludes to the hostility of the Jews. To begin with, murderous hostility from the Jewish King Herod is contrasted with the homage from the oriental Magi ('Nations will come to your light, and kings to your dawning brightness… Everyone in Saba will come, bringing gold and incense', Isa. 60.3–6). In the story of the Centurion's Servant, Jesus stresses that 'In no one in Israel have I found such faith', and adds that the natural children of the kingdom will be thrown out in favour of 'many from east and west' (8.10–12). The synagogue-ruler, Jairus, in Mark 5.22 is changed into a mere 'ruler' to deny the beneficiary of the miracle any contact with official Judaism. The great sevenfold tirade of Matthew 23 is prepared by many little touches (3.7; 15.13–14; 11.16–24; 21.43–5). This tirade is in fact not extreme by the standards of the time; it seems mild when compared to the invective of Essene documents against the Temple Judaism which opposed them (e.g. Damascus Document 1.14–16, 20: 'they justified the wicked and condemned the just; they loathed all who walked in perfection'; 3.14). Such hostility from Judaism is finally confirmed at the trial before Pilate by the people, every one of them, shouting out 'Let his blood be upon us and on our children' (27.25). (This is no foundation for Christian anti-Semitism. Rather it looks towards the gruesome sufferings of the people of Jerusalem during the Roman siege in the next generation). Jewish responsibility for the condemnation of Jesus is further stressed by Pilate's biblical gesture of washing his hands (27.24–5). A final twist is given by the intensification of the mockery of the crucified Christ on the cross: the priests join in the mockery, and Matthew even puts into their priestly mouths the mockery of the just man by the godless in the biblical Book of Wisdom 2.13, 18: 'He calls himself a son of the Lord; if he is God's son, God will rescue him'.

5. Christology

The story of Mark is the story of the discovery of who Jesus is, an awesome figure who is yet intensely human, who is jostled by the crowds, who sleeps in a boat, 'his head on a cushion' (Mk 4.38), who puts up with the sarcasm of his own uncomprehending disciples. The disciples gradually discover a Messiah who must suffer and so enter into his glory. One important change Matthew makes in the way of telling the story is the beginning. Mark begins his story already at the baptism of Jesus, leaving open the possibility that this was the beginning of his significant career, or even the possibility that he was formally adopted as son of God at this moment. Matthew begins earlier, with two chapters on the birth and infancy of Jesus which already inform us who Jesus is.

a. Infancy Narratives

These two chapters of Matthew, the Jewish gospel, introduce Jesus as God's messenger to Israel, son of David, and a second Moses. Believing as he did that Jesus was born of the virgin Mary, Matthew had a first difficulty in showing that the Messiah Jesus was descended from the line of David.

There can be no doubt that Matthew believed that Jesus was born of a virgin, since it makes such a difficulty for his theme that Jesus was son of David. The virgin birth is one of the few facts that the Infancy Stories of Matthew and Luke share. It creates a difficulty, and the belief in the perpetual virginity of Mary increases the difficulty, since the 'brothers and sisters' of Jesus in Mark 3.32 and 6.3 then have to be explained as half-brothers and sisters (children of Joseph by another wife) or as cousins. Either of these explanations is perfectly possible. It has, however, been the belief of Christians since the earliest times.

The whole of Matthew 1 therefore leads up to the adoption of Jesus into the line of David. In Judaism, as in some other cultures, legal adoption constitutes quite as strong a claim on inheritance as physical parenthood, and Jesus is adopted into David's line by Joseph, scion of the House of David, naming Jesus, for only a father has the right to name a son. This is not Joseph's own choice, but is divinely ordained. When Joseph found that Mary was pregnant by the Spirit of God, he thought he should quietly withdraw from his engagement to marry her, presumably on grounds of his own unworthiness to mix in or rival the Spirit. It is at this stage the angel intervenes, and Joseph receives a divine message that he should continue. The emphasis is on the final climax, that is, the naming and so the adoption of the child.

The long and carefully crafted genealogy at the beginning of the gospel emphasizes the importance of this adoption. It is a sort of introductory drum-roll. Rather than detailing every one of the forebears, it rehearses the great figures of Israelite history, beginning with Abraham, the father of the race, to whom came God's original call and promises. As we have seen (p. 58), the genealogy is structured on a series of six 7s. The first stop on this tour, so to speak, is David, to whom the promises were made (in 2 Sam. 7) that his royal line and his special relationship with God would never cease: God would be a father to him and his heirs. The second stop is the Babylonian Exile, which is perhaps a hint that this new heir to Abraham and David would fully restore the nation of Israel and bring the promises to completion. In any case the recital of these great names of Israelite history would fill with pride and expectation any who valued the heritage of Israel.

So at the start of the gospel Jesus is depicted as the son of David, the heir of all the promises to Israel. Matthew returns to this several times. The blind men at Jericho hail Jesus, 'Have pity on us, son of David!' (20.30, 31), as do the other blind men cured by Jesus (9.27). Even the Canaanite woman shows her faith in the promises to Israel by giving him this title (15.22). Finally it reaches its climax in the cry at Jesus' messianic entry into Jerusalem, 'Hosanna to the son of David! Blessed is he who comes in the name of the Lord' (21.9).

In the second chapter of this introduction Jesus is depicted as the Second Moses. In accordance with the promise in Deuteronomy 18.15 that God would send another prophet like Moses, this figure has often featured in the expectations of Israel. It is picked up by Matthew. Just as the life of the baby Moses was threatened by the wicked king of Egypt, so the life of the baby Jesus is threatened by the wicked King Herod – both escaped. Just as Moses was driven into exile (after slaying the Egyptian overseer), so Jesus goes with his family into exile to escape death. There he stays until Joseph receives a message from the angel which almost exactly echoes the message to Moses, 'Go, for all those who wanted to kill you are dead' (Exod. 4.19; Mt. 2.20). This figure of Jesus as the Second Moses is particularly important in Matthew's presentation, showing that Jesus was the founder of a renewed People of God. So Jesus is taken up onto a high mountain from which he sees all the territories of the earth (Mt. 4.8, as Deut. 34.1–4), just as Moses was taken up onto Mount Nebo before his death, to see all the territories of Israel. Jesus teaches the new Law of the People of God seated on a high mountain, like Moses on Sinai (Mt. 5.1). At the Transfiguration, again, Jesus is a second Moses, his face shining radiant white, as did that of Moses at his descent from the mountain (Mt. 17.2, as Exod. 34.29). In this way Matthew shows the importance of Jesus as the giver of the new Law and the new founder of a People of God.

Other features of the Infancy Narrative further show the importance of Jesus in a Jewish way. The appearance of a star at birth is a standard feature of ancient legends of the East, reported at the birth of Nimrod, Alexander the Great, Mithridates and others. It shows that a new star has been born! Matthew makes use also of the reputation of Herod as a murderous tyrant – he was well known to have killed without pity any possible rebels or rivals, even three of his own sons – to set up a contrast between the Jewish king who tries to eliminate the new-born hope of Israel and the Wise Men from the east who pay homage to him. There will be the same contrast at the end of the gospel between the Jewish high priests who are determined to secure Jesus' death and the gentile Pilate who emphatically declares his innocence and – contrast with Herod! – names him 'King of the Jews' (27.37).

So, even before we come to Mark's starting-point of the baptism of Jesus, we already come to know the importance and significance of Jesus in Christian Jewish eyes.

b. Names and Titles

The names and titles which Matthew uses of Jesus also reveal his significance. Mark uses the title 'Son of God' as the bracket of his gospel at the beginning and end (1.1, 11; 15.39); in the course of the gospel the disciples are slowly discovering the awesome meaning of the expression. Matthew, by contrast, already shows Jesus as son of God by the name given by the angel, 'Emmanuel, God with us' (1.23). This is a more explicit bracket than Mark's; it is closed at the end of the gospel by the declaration of the Risen Christ, 'I am with you always, yes, to the end of time' (28.20), promising his divine presence and strength to his own people – now and always. In Mark, the centurion at the foot of the cross is the first person to recognize Jesus as Son of God, but in Matthew the divine nature of Jesus is so clear that Peter, even after his soaking in the water when he momentarily lost faith in Jesus, comes bursting out with the declaration, 'Truly, you are the Son of God' (14.33). This is all the more striking in that in Mark's corresponding passage the disciples are still puzzled and uncomprehending. Similarly, at Caesarea Philippi, Mark shows Peter finally arriving at the knowledge that Jesus is the Messiah; in Matthew, Peter gives a full confession, 'You are the Christ, the Son of the living God' (16.16). The divine nature of Jesus is so clear that it cannot be concealed; it is as though Jesus is already the Risen Christ in his awesome glory. Mark's careful structure of the gradual discovery of the personality of Jesus, hinged on Peter's recognition at Caesarea Philippi of Jesus as Messiah, is shattered: his full stature as Son of God cannot wait to be revealed by the centurion at the foot of the cross. It is significant that, while in Mark only the man possessed by evil spirits 'worships' Jesus (5.6), in Matthew the Wise Men from the East and several others offer Jesus this 'worship' (*proskynesis*), which is properly reserved for God alone (8.2; 9.18; 14.33; 15.25; 20.20). Most marked of all is the change of address to Jesus: in Mark he is called *kyrie* a couple of times (7.28; 12.51), but usually only 'Teacher' or 'Rabbi'. In Matthew he is regularly addressed by the disciples as *kyrie*. While this address can mean no more than 'Sir!', it is also the word used in the Greek Bible to translate the sacred name of the Lord; in biblical Greek it carries an awe of its own. It certainly, therefore, has a higher sense than 'Rabbi', and even hints at the divinity of Jesus.

c. Jesus and his Father

For his part, Jesus himself openly and frequently addresses God as his Father. He uses this appellation more than a score of times, giving the impression that the Father is the constant background of his thought, showing how close is the relationship between them. The chief contexts are two, the fulfilment of the Father's will and the confirmation of the Son's decisions by the Father. Thus anyone who will enter the Kingdom of Heaven must not merely call out 'Lord, Lord!', but must do the will of the Father, fulfilling the petition of the Lord's Prayer, 'Thy will be done' (6.10; 7.21). The fullness of this comes in Jesus' prayer in Gethsemane, when Jesus repeats his own prayer of acceptance of the Father's will (26.39–53).

How close are Jesus and his Father, and what is the relationship between them? A scene of extraordinary intimacy between Jesus and the Father is given in Matthew 11.26–7: 'I bless you, Father, Lord of heaven and earth, for hiding these things from the learned and clever and revealing them to little children. Yes, Father, for that is what it has pleased you to do. Everything has been entrusted to me by my Father, and no one knows the Son except the Father, just as no one knows the Father except the Son and those to whom the Son chooses to reveal him.' Here Father and Son are seen working in concert and in perfect love and harmony. This invitation of Jesus gives an exalted Christology, for it is strongly reminiscent of the invitation of divine

Wisdom in the Book of Wisdom 9.3–5. Here (as in Jn 1.39 and 6.44) Jesus' followers are warmly invited to share this intimacy between Father and Son. Elsewhere, too, the Son is the representative of the Father, standing in his place, so that in the context of persecution the same intimacy is promised, 'If anyone declares himself for me in the presence of human beings, I will declare myself for him in the presence of my Father in heaven' (10.32–3).

Indeed, Jesus is more than a mere representative of the Father, for, instead of Mark's promise of reward at the coming of God's kingdom in power, Matthew 16.28 has Jesus proclaim that his disciples will see the Son of Man coming in his own kingdom; this is tantamount to a divine claim. At the messianic entry into Jerusalem, Jesus is not merely coming in the name of the Lord but is himself hailed as the king (21.5 9). In the scene of the Last Judgment Jesus exercises the power and majesty on God's behalf; he is escorted by all the angels and seated on his throne of glory. But it is only God who is escorted by angels, and only God who sits on the throne of judgment. The glorious Jesus speaks on God's behalf, 'Come, you whom my Father has blessed' (25.34). In Mark we see God acting through and in Jesus on earth, so that the disciples in awe cry out, 'What sort of person is this?', whereas in Matthew we see God acting in and through Jesus in the divine judgment.

Consonant with this conception of Christ is the description of the wonders of Jesus. Matthew shows Jesus approaching in awesome solitude instead of the turbulent crowd-scenes of Mark. So, when Jesus goes to heal Simon's mother-in-law, the thronging disciples have disappeared; Jesus meets her on her own and she gets up to serve not 'them' (as in Mark) but only 'him' (8.15). In the same way, the Woman with a Haemorrhage seems to be alone with the awesome figure of Jesus, rather than, as in Mark 5.23–33, as part of a thronging crowd-scene. Jesus' dignity makes him stand out on his own. He is indeed human, but at the same time stands apart from humanity; he is not fully absorbed by human nature, and the divine glory is somehow felt to be shining through him already.

Nevertheless, things enter a new phase with Matthew's account of the Risen Christ. The significance of the resurrection is underlined by the apocalyptic earthquake, the explicit description of the interpreting angel, and the mixture of extreme fear and joy in the reaction of the women (28.8). The scene of Jesus greeting them has all the features of a divine appearance, Jesus' greeting of joy and his instruction not to be afraid. The reaction of the women is to worship him and, here, Matthew again describes their act of reverence by a word which is used only for the worship of God. The final scene on the holy mountain in Galilee (28.16–20) is couched in the terms of the vision of the glorious Son of Man in Daniel 7.13–14, who comes to the One of Great Age and receives all power on earth. This final scene may well be interpretative of the position of the Risen Christ and of his vital role in the mission of the Church, rather than a historical reminiscence of an actual occurrence. The position of the Risen Christ is even more powerful than the Son of Man in Daniel, for the Risen Christ has received all power in heaven as well as on earth. It is this which gives strength and confidence to the open-ended task of his followers.

6. Matthew's Theology: A Gospel for a New Israel

By his use of scripture Matthew shows that he is intensely aware that the history of Israel comes to its fulfilment in Jesus. Apart from the quotations and allusions of the Infancy Stories (see p. 58–60), this is frequently pointed by quotations from the prophets along the way. So 'Way of the sea beyond the Jordan, Galilee of the gentiles' (4.14) and 'he will present judgment to the nations' (12.17) attest to the fulfilment of the hope that salvation would spread from Israel to the nations. 'Listen and listen but never understand' (13.35) attests the renewed stubbornness of Israel. 'He himself bore our sicknesses' (8.17) focuses on Jesus the prophecies of the Servant of the Lord who would bring God's saving purposes to completion. 'Your king is approaching, humble and riding on a donkey' (21.5) expresses the chastened mood of humility and repentance in post-Exilic Judaism. Especially in the Passion Narrative the increased and explicit references to scripture show that this is the fulfilment of God's purposes. For example, Matthew changes Mark's offer of 'myrrhed wine' to Jesus on the way to crucifixion into 'wine mixed with gall' in order to fulfil a psalm (27.34).

This emphasis on the community of Israel touches not only the past but also the future. Woven into all Matthew's gospel is an ecclesiology of an organized community centred on Christ. Matthew's interest in the concept of community is shown by the fact that he is the only evangelist to use the word *ekklesia*, literally 'a gathering', called out to be together. It occurs frequently in the Greek Old Testament to denote the gathering of the People of Israel, the assembly of God. Paul and the Acts of the Apostles use the word frequently of Christian communities scattered round the eastern Mediterranean, and the later Pauline letters (Colossians and Ephesians) use it of the Church as such. Of the evangelists Matthew alone uses it, first at 16.18 where Jesus promises to build 'his *ekklesia*' on the Rock; it is Jesus' assembly, corresponding to the Old Testament 'assembly of God'. Secondly it is used in the teaching on relationships within the Church (18.17). For Matthew, therefore, the *ekklesia* of Jesus has come to represent the assembly of God. As the heart of God's choice of Israel as God's people was his presence among them, first in the Tent of Meeting, and then in the Temple, so the heart of Jesus' choice of the *ekklesia* is his presence among them. This is the theme-tune of the gospel, from the Emmanuel-prophecy in 1.23 to the final promise of the Risen Christ in power to be with them for all time (28.20), which bracket the gospel. It recurs also in the chapter on the community as the heart of their relationships among themselves (18.19), 'where two or three are gathered together, there am I, among them'.

This presence of Jesus in the midst of his community receives its iconic expression in Matthew's version of the calming of the storm: the boat is the ship of the Church, confident in the presence of Jesus. So instead of the sarcastic reproach of the disciples to Jesus, 'Teacher, don't you care that we are lost?' (Mk 4.38), Matthew has the confident plea to Jesus, 'Lord, save us! We are lost' (8.25). Instead of the reproach of Jesus and the puzzlement of the disciples (Mk 4.40–41), Matthew gives simply the awe of the disciples at Jesus' power (8.27). This is allied to the increased confidence and understanding on the part of the disciples. Time after time, where Mark shows the disciples failing to understand and earning a rebuke from Jesus, Matthew shows them being complimented by Jesus for their comprehension, or at any rate the rebuke softened (Mk 4.13; 8.17). Instead of Jesus' often quite insistent rebukes for their lack of understanding or hardness of heart in Mark (e.g. Mk 6.52; 8.17), in Matthew they are simply reproached for their 'little faith' (Mt. 6.30; 8.26; 14.31; 16.8). Instead of confusion and astonishment at Jesus walking on the water, Matthew shows Peter daring to join Jesus on the water, and the disciples confessing Jesus as son of God (which in Mark does not occur till the centurion makes this confession after Jesus' death). It is as though Matthew does not want the future leaders of the Church to be seen failing. For the same reason, the insensitivity of the sons of Zebedee in asking for the best seats in the Kingdom immediately after the second prophecy of the Passion is avoided by putting the request in the mouth of their mother (compare Mk 19.35 with Mt 20.20).

Peter, of course, is far from perfect, and – for all his enthusiasm – his faith fails when he attempts to join Jesus on the water (14.28–31 – this passage is characteristically Matthean, containing some 17 words and phrases typical of Matthew among its 66 Greek words; it must have been composed by Matthew); Peter is still a man of little faith. The story of the Coin in the Fish's Mouth shows that he has a special bond of affection with Jesus. Nevertheless, not only is he frequently the leader and spokesman of the disciples in passages unique to Matthew (14.28–31; 16.17–19; 17.24–27 – in 17.4 he leads with 'Let *me* build...' instead of Mark's 'let *us* build...') in passages concentrating on the training and preparation of the disciples, but Matthew delicately spares him reproach: Jesus' reproach in Gethsemane is now directed to all the disciples, not to Peter alone, 'Could you (plural) not watch with me one hour', 26.40, instead of Mark's singular 'you'). Nevertheless, the last we hear of Peter is when he is 'weeping bitterly' (26.75 – the 'bitterly' is added by Matthew); there is no special mention of Peter at the empty tomb, as in Mark 16. Peter is the model of the enthusiastic but weak disciple who always starts well, but has not the strength to withstand persecution without the help of Jesus.

It is difficult to recover the source of Jesus' promise to Peter, which occurs in this form only in Matthew 16.18–19, but several features of the language suggest that it goes back to an Aramaic origin. Matthew may have had an alternative source, since the same sort of promise occurs in Luke at the Last Supper, and in John at the breakfast-party with the Risen Christ, and Matthew may have simply inserted it here as the most suitable place in his gospel. In any case the promise indicates some form of leadership in an organisation, just as does the promise to the Twelve of sitting on twelve thrones in the Kingdom (Mt. 19.28). Whereas in Mark the chief task of the disciples is to 'be with Jesus' and to proclaim the arrival of the Kingdom (Mk 3.14), in Matthew they receive detailed instructions for their mission for the whole of Matthew 10. Similarly the arrangements for seeking out the lost sheep (18.12–13) and for settling disputes in the community presuppose an enduring community. This three-stage arrangement is similar to that of the community at Qumran: first a private chat, then with witnesses, finally in public before the community (compare Mt 18.15–17 with 1 QS 5.25–6.2). Not only Peter, but the community as such is given the power of forgiveness which will be honoured in heaven (16.19 and 18.18).

The emphasis of the parables is also an indication that Matthew is setting up arrangements for a considerable period of time (see p. 135). Mark's parables have been called 'crisis parables' (*Krisisgleichnisse* in German), stressing that the crisis of the Day of the Lord is now imminent upon the hearers – 'the Kingdom of God has drawn near' – as the time of harvest, marriage, judgment has now arrived with the coming of Jesus. The accent in Matthew is different, for a period is envisaged before the imminent end, during which the hearers must prepare themselves. Thus the wedding-guest must provide himself with a wedding-garment (a standard rabbinic figure of good works, 22.11–14), the wedding attendants have to wait until midnight and be alert, with oil for their lamps (25.1–13), servants must use their talents until the owner returns (25.14–30), the nations will be judged on their exercise of love (25.31–46). These parables have all the more prominence and weight because they are added by Matthew to the eschatological discourse, giving a pronounced accent to the emphasis on the delay of the final judgment. Earlier, Matthew stresses that there are wheat and weeds (13.24–30), or good and bad fish (13.47–50) within the Kingdom, which will not be sorted out until the end-time.

> A feature of all Matthew's parables is the sharp black-and-white contrast between two chief characters: the two builders (7.24–27), the playing children (11.16–17), the two servants (18.21–35), the two sons (21.28–32), the talents (25.14–29), the ten wedding-attendants (25.1–12), the sheep and goats (25.31–46).

These parables, and the arrangements made for life in community presuppose an interval before the end, just as the Qumran *Rule of the Community* presupposes a settled community awaiting the coming of the Messiah for some time, which the community must live faithfully. The follower of Jesus must forgive seventy times seven times, which also implies a time-lapse.

The ultimate confirmation of the endurance of the Kingdom upon earth is given by the final charge by the Risen Christ on the holy mountain in Galilee. For all his emphasis on the completion of the community of Israel, Matthew gives to the gentile mission considerably more prominence than does Mark. The task which the disciples are given, to 'Go and make disciples of all the nations' (28.19), can scarcely be finished in a short time; thus the delay of the Second Coming and the space left for the gentile mission are closely linked. Whereas in Mark the only explicit contact of Jesus with gentiles during his ministry concerns the Syro-Phoenician woman, in Matthew such contacts play a much larger part. In Matthew's corresponding story of the Canaanite Woman her full faith is expressed: three times she calls Jesus 'Lord' as well as 'son of David', and she is explicitly praised for her faith (15.21–8). The centurion of Capernaum must be a gentile, since he is the model of 'many will come from east and west to take their places in the Kingdom' while the children of the Kingdom are cast out (7.11–12). Matthew adds to the parable of the Wicked Tenants not only allegorical features which stress the failure of Israel to respond either to the early or to the later prophets (Mt 21.35, 36), but also the threatening codicil, promising the Kingdom to 'a people who will produce its fruit' (21.43). This is immediately followed up by the highly allegorical parable of the Great Wedding-Feast, in which the gentiles are symbolised by the guests press-ganged to the feast after the refusal of those originally invited (22.5–10).

Further Reading

Boxall, Ian, *Discovering Matthew* (London: SPCK, 2014): lucid, wide-ranging, intelligible

France, R. T., *Matthew, Evangelist & Teacher* (Exeter: Paternoster Press, 1992): comprehensive and far-sighted

Goulder, M. D., *Midrash and Lection in Matthew* (London: SPCK, 1974): Matthew's imagery and poetry

Luz, Ulrich, *Studies in Matthew* (Grand Rapids: Eerdmans, 2005): collected essays on particular topics

Senior, Donald, *Matthew*[Abingdon NT Commentaries] (Nashville: Abingdon, 1998): complete, thoughtful, succinct

Sim, David C., *The Gospel of Matthew & Christian Judaism* (London:T&T Clark,1998): Matthew's attitude to Judaism

Mark, the First Evangelist

1. Authorship and Date

The Gospels have often been compared to a four-sided prism, presenting four different aspects of the gospel-message. Each of the gospel-writers was a theologian, offering his own particular angle of the message, with his own emphasis. Hence the Greek titles of the gospels, 'the gospel *according to* Matthew/Mark/Luke/John'. It is the Gospel which is important, not the personal identity of the writer. Not until the second century were names associated with these four gospels to distinguish them one from another, 'the Gospel *according to* X'. Who was this Mark?

Marcus is one of the most common names in the Greco-Roman world. It was one of the seven classic *praenomina*, like *Marcus* Tullius Cicero or *Gaius* Julius Caesar. In the New Testament three men named Mark are mentioned:

1 John Mark, a young man of Jerusalem (Acts 12.12; 15.38 etc), whom Paul later dismissed from his team, but who is mentioned as a companion by the author of Colossians 4.10;

2 Mark who was a fellow-worker of Paul during his imprisonment (Phlm. 24);

3   Mark who is with the author of 1 Peter 5.13 in 'Babylon', a code-name
    for Rome.

The association of Mark with the author of 1 Peter may have been responsible
for the traditional link of the gospel of Mark with Peter, and even for the
theory that Mark was Peter's secretary, taking down the gospel at his dictation.
The difficulty about this is that 1 Peter is now normally accepted as pseudonymous (see p. 336), that is, not really written by Peter, but merely attributed to
him by a convention of the time. However, in favour of the tradition it must
be said that Eusebius quotes the saying of Papias, Bishop of Hierapolis at the
beginning of the second century, that Mark was the ερμηνευτης (interpreter)
of Peter, and soon afterwards Justin quotes a sentence of Mark as coming from
'Peter's Memoirs'. These are good evidence for the early tradition.

The theory was further fostered by the anxiety somehow to attribute the
gospel to an apostle, which both current scholarship and current Church
authority see to be unnecessary. The author must, of course, have been
associated with the apostolic circle. Current theories of inspiration (see p.
11) see the important factor to be that the gospel material was cherished
within the apostolic community at every stage of its transmission, oral and
written, not merely that it was written down by an apostle (or in the case of
the Petrine theory of Mark, by an apostle's secretary).

When was this first Gospel written down? This was an era when
the spoken word was considered superior to the written word. Written
materials were expensive and literacy was rare, at least in the non-elite
circles where Christianity began. The stories would have been told and told
again, the message being passed around by word of mouth. Paul, writing his
letters in the 50s, shows no knowledge of any written record. He appeals to
the traditions about the institution of the Eucharist and about the death and
resurrection of Jesus, which he received and passed on by word of mouth
(1 Cor. 11.23 and 15.3–5). He introduces his quotation with the technical
terms used for handing on the rabbinic oral tradition. It seems most likely
that the writing-down of the message occurred when the first generation of
Christians were getting old.

In any attempt to establish a date for Mark the most useful passage is
Mark 13, where the central threat is 'the abomination of desolation' or 'the
disastrous abomination' (Mk 13.14): 'When you see the disastrous abomination set up where it ought not to be…'. This quotation of Daniel 9.27,
originally referring to the statue of Antiochus Epiphanes briefly set up in the
Temple in 164BC, may be an allusion to the Emperor Gaius' proposal to set

up a statue of himself in the Temple in 40–44AD. This would situate Mark 13 (or at least its outline) in the early 40s. On the other hand, the author may be using both allusions in a symbolic and prophetic way to refer to the destruction of the Temple in 70AD, when the Temple was burnt to the ground, and no such statue set up (Josephus, *Jewish War*, 6.4.250–84). A decision on such an important matter, which could shift the composition of Mark some 30 years earlier, eludes us.

No other clear information is available about the author. It seems unlikely that Mark knew the Holy Land. His knowledge of Jerusalem is distant and sketchy (contrast John, who mentions the Sheep Gate, the Pool of Bethzatha, the Pool of Siloam and other known places in Jerusalem. John also mentions Bethphage and Bethany, villages just outside Jerusalem). Mark leads Jesus by a very roundabout route from Sidon to the Lake of Galilee *via* the Decapolis (7.31), which suggests that he was unaware of the topography. He also seems unaware that he gives the unfortunate Gerasene swine a run of 30km from Gerasa (now known as Jerash) 'down the cliff' to drown themselves in the Lake (5.13). This may be the reason why some texts (and Mt. 8.28) read 'Gadara', for Gadara is only a dozen kilometres from the lake. The great second-century scholar Origen solved this problem by locating the event at the place now known as El Kursi, a hill above the eastern shore of the lake itself.

It is often thought that Mark was writing for gentiles, and the association with Peter in Rome is often used as an extra argument for this. In fact, of course, the vast city of Rome itself included a large Jewish population. Though Mark is not so coloured by Jewish lore as Matthew is, it will already be clear that a basic understanding of Mark presupposes a wide knowledge of the Old Testament, and, for the profound meaning and allusions of many passages, demand a detailed knowledge of the scriptures. If Mark was directed to a gentile audience, these gentiles were well versed in the Hebrew scriptures.

2. Structure and Style

a. Features of Mark's Writing

In considering the Gospels it is valuable to study the special message and angle of each evangelist, a method known as Redaction History, since it involves studying the way in which each evangelist edited ('redacted') the tradition. For Matthew and Luke it is easier to do this than in the case of Mark, for it is possible to note the changes made by each of these to the text of Mark, and so discern their particular emphases. Thus, in the sentence after the Baptism of Jesus Matthew makes several small but significant changes to Mark's text:

Mark 1.12	Matthew 4.1
And at once the Spirit drives him out into the desert.	Then Jesus was taken up into the desert by the Spirit.

1 Mark begins very many verses with 'And', and in Ch. 1 alone has 'and at once' nine times; Matthew avoids this, and substitutes a favourite word of his own, 'then'.
2 Mark repeatedly uses the historic present tense ('drives'); Matthew avoids this and uses the more sophisticated past ('was').
3 Matthew frequently inserts the name 'Jesus' into Mark's text, presumably out of devotion.
4 Matthew's 'taken *up*' is preparing for the theme of Jesus as the New Moses, taken up onto the high mountain.

On the whole Mark writes in a primitive, unsophisticated Greek. It has been described as 'kitchen Greek', the sort of Greek which slaves around the Mediterranean would have spoken, and which is found scrawled as graffiti on the walls of ancient buildings at Pompeii and elsewhere.

However, it is less easy to discern Mark's techniques than it is to discern those of Matthew and Luke, since we have no predecessor against whom we could compare Mark. Nevertheless Mark is sufficiently consistent in his verbal and compositional techniques for us to discern a number of clear characteristics. These show that Mark was primarily an oral teacher and a story-teller of genius. One can imagine that the community came to Mark and said, 'Mark, you are such a good story-teller that we choose you to write it all down'. Here is a list of the more prominent features of Mark's writing. They need to be understood and remembered, since they will be widely used in what follows.

1 The 'and' and 'and at once' or 'again' (26 times) with the historic present gives a breathless speed to the narrative which emphasizes the urgency of Jesus' message. In Mark 1 alone 'and at once' occurs nine times. Mark seldom uses subordinate clauses (e.g. clauses introduced by 'because' or 'although') but prefers parataxis (straightforward main clauses joined together).

2 Mark repeatedly uses two phrases of similar meaning for emphasis, e.g. 1.32 'at evening//when the sun had set', or 1.42 'the leprosy left him//and he was cleansed', or 2.20 'then//on that day'. Particularly frequent are double questions: 4.30 'What can we say that the kingdom of heaven is like?//What parable can we find for it?' (or 3.13; 4.40; 6.2). This repetition is a technique of oral teaching.

3 Mark zooms in, to focus on one memorable material object: 4.38 Jesus was asleep in the stern, *his head on the cushion*', or 5.27 'she *touched his cloak* from behind', or 6.28 'he brought the *head on a dish*'.

4 A delayed explanation with 'for...', rationing the information till a question might arise in the mind of a reader, when it could have been logical to explain earlier: 1.16; 2.15; 5.8; 16.4, 8.

5 The sandwich-technique, by which Mark inserts a piece between two halves of another piece in such a way that the outer halves and the central piece illustrate and clarify one another. Thus

> 2.1–4 Story about physical healing
>> 2.5–11 Story about healing of sin
> 2.12 Story about physical healing

Here the physical healing constitutes a proof that Jesus can effect the healing of sin, which is unseen.

> 3.20–1 Jesus' family fail to understand him
>> 3.22–30 The scribes misunderstand him
> 3.31–5 Jesus' family fail to understand him

Opposition both from the scribes and from Jesus' own family stresses the general failure to understand what Jesus is about. This leads straight on to the parable of the Sower, Jesus' own reflection on the meagre response to his teaching.

> 4.1–9 Parable of the Sower
>> 4.10–12 Jesus' use of parables
> 4.13–20 Parable of the Sower explained

The scriptural quotation in v. 12 is a crucial clue to the understanding in the early community of why the Jews did not respond to Jesus' message: it was foretold in scripture that they would not do so. This verse of Isaiah is used also in John 12.40 (at the end of Jesus' ministry) and Acts 28.26–7 (at the end of Paul's ministry). Here it is a turning point in Jesus' ministry.

11.12–14 The fruitless fig-tree cursed

11.15–19 The Temple rubbished

11.20–5 The fig-tree found to be withered

The enclosure of the rubbishing of the Temple within the story of the fig-tree shows that Jesus' action in the Temple certifies the barrenness of the rituals there performed.

6 The controversy-technique. This occurs in the controversies about divorce, about Jesus' authority in the Temple, about paying tax to Caesar and about the yeast of the Pharisees.

	Divorce	Authority	Tax	Yeast
(1) The opponents put a question to Jesus	10.2	11.27	12.14	8.16
(2) Jesus replies with a counter-question	10.3	11.30	12.15	8.17
(3) The opponents give inadequate answer	10.4	11.33a	12.16	8.19
(4) Jesus clinches the matter	10.5	11.33b	12.17	8.21

In each case Jesus' answer goes more profoundly into the matter than his opponents expected (or wanted!) to hear.

7 Triple repetition for emphasis. This is a common feature of folk-literature (e.g. Little Red Riding-Hood, the Wolf and the Three Pigs, the Three Bears, Dick Whittington and the three peals of bells).

The prophecies of the Passion:	8.31	9.31	10.32
'Stay awake'	13.33	13.35	13.38
The failure of the disciples in the Garden	14.37	14.40	14.41
Witness against Jesus	14.56	14.57	14.63
Peter's denials	14.68	14.70	14.71
Pilate's questions to the crowds	15.9	15.12	15.14

b. The Overall Pattern of Mark

These seven instances of pattern show that Mark is a real author, receiving his material in an oral and flexible form, and shaping this material consistently according to his own patterns of thought in such a way as to bring out the lessons and emphases which he wishes to underline. For the understanding of Mark as a whole, however, it is important to be aware of the architectonic lines of the whole story:

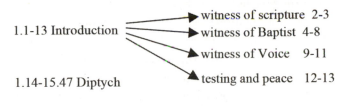

The diptych: this consists of two panels, opposite and parallel to each other, in which the disciples are slowly discovering who Jesus is. In each panel the disciples three times fail to understand and are rebuked by Jesus. In each panel they finally achieve understanding after a blind man is given his sight (at Bethsaida and Jericho respectively); this is placed symbolically to signify the disciples receiving their insight. In the former instance it is also significant that the cure takes place in two stages, first a dim sight and then the full vision.

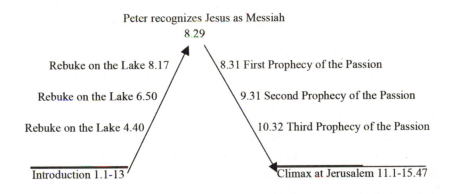

The gospel begins with an Introduction, in which the reader/listener is told – still somewhat mysteriously – who Jesus is, namely, that he is 'son of God', whatever that may mean (see p. 84). First comes the witness of scripture, then the witness of John the Baptist, then the overwhelming witness of the Voice from heaven. This witness is all the more overpowering because it uses the conventions of apocalyptic (see p. 362), and alludes especially to Isa 42.1 ('my beloved son, in whom I am well pleased' is a possible alternative translation to 'my chosen one in whom my soul delights'). Finally the Testing in the Desert shows Jesus in the messianic peace with the wild animals (as Isa. 11.6–9) and ministered to by angels (Ps. 91[90].11), a return to the peace of the Garden of Eden.

Next begins the first half of the diptych, two panels, hinged in the middle (8.29), one matching the other. After the introduction, the curtain comes down, so to speak, and the actors on stage (the first disciples) have no idea who Jesus is – only we, the privileged readers, know that. The actors discover slowly and painfully who Jesus is from a crescendo of incidents in which they are repeatedly bowled over by Jesus' charismatic authority.

> It is already striking that the first four disciples simply respond to the call of this charismatic stranger without any psychological preparation or knowledge of him. There follows a crescendo of amazement. First (1.27), all are amazed that he teaches on his own authority, unlike the Jewish religious teachers, whose instruction would be based on the opinions of previous revered teachers. Then the crowds are amazed at Jesus' cures of physical ailments. Next Jesus claims to forgive sins, which is understood as an implicit claim to divine powers (2.7), confirmed by the physical healing which Jesus puts in parallel to it. Then Jesus acts in ways which flout the sacred Laws, first those of uncleanness by eating with sinners and tax-collectors (2.16), and then the Sabbath, likening himself to the precedent of David, and even claiming to be master of the Sabbath (2.25–28). A new height is reached when Jesus calms the storm on the Lake (4.35–41). This receives its significance from Psalm 106.23–30, for there the despairing, storm-tossed sailors 'cried to the LORD in their need', in response to which the LORD 'stilled the storm to a whisper'; now Jesus stands in the place of the LORD. The disciples are filled with awe, but – with a Markan double question – they are still rebuked for their lack of understanding.

Three times they are rebuked, each time on the Lake of Galilee, for their lack of understanding (4.40; 6.50–1; 8.17). This leads up eventually to Peter's declaration at Caesarea Philippi, which, however, is immediately preceded by the symbolically placed gift of sight to the blind man of Bethsaida. At Caesarea Philippi Peter's eyes are at last opened, and he declares (8.29), 'You are the Christ'. This is the turning point of the gospel.

Peter has reached the truth that Jesus is the Messiah, but he immediately shows his failure to understand what this implies, what sort of Messiah Jesus is. So in the second half of the diptych there follow the three great formal prophecies of the Passion. Each of these is misunderstood, the first by Peter's rebuke to Jesus (8.32), the second by the squabble about precedence (9.33), the third by the sons of Zebedee asking for the best places (10.35–40). After each of these failures Jesus reiterates that his followers must share his Cross.

Finally comes the climax at Jerusalem. At they leave Jericho and enter the Wadi Qilt for the final three-hour walk up to Jerusalem (look at a map!), the cure of the other blind man, Bartimaeus, signals that the disciples, too, are at last about to receive their full sight. The full revelation of who Jesus is occurs in two scenes, first the scene before the High Priest, where Jesus for the first time accepts the three great titles, 'son of God', 'Christ' and 'son of man'. The second scene of the final revelation is the acknowledgement by the centurion, the first human being to give Jesus the title, 'son of God' (15.39). Whatever the centurion meant by that formula, Mark hears it with Christian ears. So the declaration of the Voice at the baptism, 'You are my beloved Son', has returned again with the declaration of the centurion. This title therefore functions as a bracket which binds together the whole gospel, showing that the whole gospel is precisely about the revelation of the personality of Jesus as son of God.

There are other balances between the two halves of the diptych, for example the group of controversies with the Jewish leaders in Galilee at the beginning of Jesus' ministry (2.1–3.6) and at the end in Jerusalem (12.1–37). Mark has gathered these two groups of controversies together, just as he gathers together the parables in 4.1–34.

Mark's practice of gathering incidents together at least raises the question whether Mark's presentation of the ministry at Jerusalem in a few days is not itself a gathering together of incidents which in fact occurred over a wider time-span. So Mark creates a succinct sequence of the confrontation between Jesus and the Temple authorities, centred on his demonstration in the Temple, which will lead to his death. The overall arrangement of John differs widely from that of the synoptic gospels, which of course ultimately stems from Mark. In the Christian celebration of Holy Week preference is given to the synoptic arrangement, in which Jesus makes only one visit to Jerusalem, at the end of his ministry. On the other hand, John presents four visits to Jerusalem over the course of Jesus' ministry, beginning with the Cleansing of the Temple. Each time Jesus goes up to Jerusalem in John the authorities attempt to get rid of Jesus, but they succeed only when Judas gives them the opportunity on the eve of Passover. This offers at least as plausible a scenario as the single short visit to Jerusalem given by Mark. Just as at the beginning of Jesus' ministry Mark offers a sample day of his activity (1.21–38), so his careful time-indications serve to knit together the Jerusalem incidents into a tight time-frame: 'next day' (11.12), 'next morning' (11.20), 'two days before the Passover' (14.1), 'on the first day of Unleavened Bread' (14.12).

The messianic entry into Jerusalem is hailed as the coming of the Kingdom, and is followed immediately by the rejection of the system operated in the Temple, characterizing it as being a 'robbers' den' rather than a 'house of prayer for all the peoples' (11.17) – another hint that Jesus' mission was not confined to Judaism but was open to all peoples.

Finally the question must be asked about the originality of Mark's written gospel, how closely it is related to Mark's sources, and whether previous collections of written material should be posited. Scholars have suggested that Mark was using previous collections of material, especially for the Passion Narrative. There is no proof of any such collections, nor is it necessary so to limit Mark's inspired originality. The material is taken from the oral tradition, but just as his own repeated stylistic features are continually to be seen, so also his skill in arrangement. After the beginning of Jesus' mission with the call of the disciples, the story opens with a sample day of Jesus' activity in Capernaum (1.21–45), continues with a collection of progressively hostile confrontations with Jewish authorities (2.1–3.6), which leads into a summary of Jesus' rejection (3.20–35), before Jesus reflects on this rejection as the beginning of a collection of parables (4.1–34). The sequence, entirely different from that of John, is Mark's own, just as his placing of the cure of the blind men of Bethsaida and Jericho is symbolic of the opening of the eyes of the disciples which is about to occur.

Mark's Criticism of the Pharisees

Throughout the Gospel there runs a continual undercurrent of criticism not of Judaism as such (it is not anti-Semitism) but of the current Pharisaic practice (see p. 29). Jesus is criticized by the scribes, that is, the lawyers, experts in the Law of Moses and its application, first when Jesus claims to forgive sin (2.6), then at his keeping company with sinners and tax-collectors (2.16). It is the Pharisees who complain at his lack of fasting (2.18) and his breaking the Sabbath (2.24). The lawyers from Jerusalem next accuse Jesus of being in league with Beelzebul (3.22). An extended controversy over Pharisaic practice follows in 7.1–23: the Pharisees accuse Jesus of neglecting the oral traditions of the elders about ritual cleanliness – a specifically Pharisaic concern – to which Jesus replies that the oral traditions are used to subvert the Ten Commandments themselves. Mark interprets Jesus' teaching here as completely sweeping away the laws about clean and unclean food (7.19). It is notable that, in the passage (7.6–7) where Jesus quotes from Isaiah, he is represented as using the Greek version of the Bible rather than the Hebrew; this betrays the hand of Mark rather than Jesus' own speech. Again in 8.11 the Pharisees try to test Jesus by asking from him a sign – a request which he denies – and in 8.15 Jesus warns the disciples against 'the yeast of the Pharisees and the yeast of Herod'. When the Pharisees question him about divorce he attributes the legislation permitting divorce to their 'hardness of heart' (10.5). This repeated and stringent criticism of the Pharisees has given them a bad name in Christian circles. It is worth noting, however, that by the standards of contemporary writing (compare the Qumran criticism of the Temple Judaism from which the sect had split off) the criticism is not harsh. Matthew is also using the Pharisees as negative role-models for Christians, examples of the legalism and even pomposity which he wishes to discourage. The controversies gathered in Mark 12 represent the opposition to Jesus as coming from several Jewish groups, Pharisees, Herodians and (for the first time) the Sadducees.

Mark's Portrait of the Jewish Authorities

However, in the great prophecies of the Passion it is the elders, the chief priests and the lawyers (8.31; 10.33) who 'will condemn him to death and hand him over to the gentiles', for the Pharisees took no part in the Passion of Jesus. At Jesus' disturbance in the Temple the chief priests and the lawyers, who after all are the authorities in the Temple, confirm their determination to do away with Jesus (11.18). Correspondingly, in the narrative of the Passion it is overwhelmingly the chief priests, the lawyers and the elders who drive the action forward (14.43, 53; 15.1, 3, 11, 31). The legal responsibility for the decision to crucify Jesus remains firmly with Pilate, but he three times declares Jesus' innocence, while Mark makes it quite clear that it is the chief priests who incited the crowd which Pilate wanted to placate by this decision (15.11–15). This corresponds to the report of the Jewish historian Josephus (*Antiquities of the Jews*, 18.3) that Pilate condemned him 'at the instigation of the principal men among us'.

In his negative portrait of the Jewish authorities, therefore, Mark makes a sharp distinction between the opposition of the Pharisees to Jesus' attitude to, and teaching on, legal observance and the lethal hostility of the chief priests and elders which brings him to his death. Less clearly defined is the position of the Herodians. In 3.6 the Pharisees are said to join them in plotting to get rid of Jesus, and Jesus warns against the yeast of Herod (8.3); it was, after all, Herod Antipas who had executed John the Baptist, an event which Mark clearly represents as a prelude to the Passion of Jesus.

Mark and the Gentiles
A significant contrast is also presented between Jews and gentiles, for immediately after Jesus' rejection of the Pharisaic interpretation of the oral law in 7.1–23 occurs the only confrontation in Mark between Jesus and a gentile. Jesus challenges the Syro-Phoenician woman in brusque terms, applying to her the injurious term 'dog' used by Jews about gentiles. Her courageous and witty riposte wins for her the cure of her daughter, an exact parallel to the cure of the daughter of the Jewish synagogue official, Jairus (5.21–43): Jesus' ministry is also to the gentiles. At the end, immediately after the tearing of the veil of the Temple reveals the emptiness of the Jewish worship, the gentile soldier becomes the first to profess Jesus as Son of God.

3. Mark's Portrait of Jesus

The heart of the gospel is the gradual revelation of the person of Jesus. To the reader it is enigmatically revealed by three witnesses in the introduction to the gospel.

First the scripture bears witness to Jesus, in a mixed quotation from Exodus 23.20 and Malachi 3.1, followed by another quotation from Isaiah 40.3. This is enigmatic because it is unclear both whether the 'messenger' is the Baptist or Jesus and who is the 'you' in verse 2. In Malachi the quotation given as 'who will prepare the road before *you*' ends 'before *the* LORD'. In the quotation from Isaiah the 'road' is the 'road of the LORD'. Is Jesus the messenger before the final coming of God, or is John the messenger before the coming of Jesus the LORD? The quotations themselves, therefore, are full of presage; there is already almost the suggestion that Jesus is the LORD. This is the same ambiguity as is present in Ezekiel 34, where it is unclear whether the promised shepherd is God himself or his representative.

Another weighty presage is the eschatological overtone of 'the desert' in verse 2 and the constant mention of 'the Spirit' in verses 8, 10 and 12. In the Jewish historian Josephus, there is mention of several figures who claim to be Messiah, and they all appear from the desert. Similarly, the community of Qumran (the origin of many of the Dead Sea Scrolls, see p. 31) went out into the desert specifically to wait for the Messiah, who is so important in these texts. The Baptist proclaims that the coming figure will baptize in the Spirit; the Spirit comes down upon Jesus at his baptism, and then drives Jesus out into the desert. But, as Peter's speech at Pentecost will make clear by the use of the prophet Joel 3.1–5 (in Acts 2.17–23), the coming of the Spirit is one of the chief eschatological signs. The Spirit is a constant feature of the promises of the Messiah, such as Isaiah 11.

The second witness is John the Baptist, whose clothing shows him to be a prophet like Elijah, the prophet whom Malachi 3.23–24 says will return to herald the final coming of God. His message is that a turning point has come, for the meaning of 'to repent' is primarily to change one's ways and one's whole scale of values. He is preparing a purified community for the Messiah, and this witness is said to be accepted by 'the whole of Judaea and Jerusalem'.

The third and overwhelming witness is the apocalyptic Voice from heaven. A Voice from heaven is, in the rabbinic writings, an authoritative indication of God's will. It is here strengthened by heaven being 'split open' (the Greek uses the same word as the English 'scissors'), as in the awesome vision of the divine throne in Ezekiel 1.1. The Voice addresses Jesus as the Son of God in terms of Isaiah 42.1, for 'my son' is an alternative translation of 'my servant'. This introduces the idea that Jesus is the Servant of the Lord prophesied by the four Servant-songs in Isaiah, in which (especially in the last Song, Isaiah 52.13–53.12) the idea of suffering is prevalent. It must be noted that in Mark the Voice is addressed to Jesus himself, and is to be heard as a revelation to him, not to the bystanders, as in the more familiar version of Matthew. It is therefore one of the principal clues to the understanding of his mission.

After this Jesus goes out into the desert to a messianic renewal of idyllic peace with the animals and attended by angels. This must be understood as a preliminary eschatological reversal of the disorder and evil wrought by the Fall. The forty days is a conventional number for a long period of preparation, as the forty years of Israel preparing to enter the Promised Land, or Elijah's forty days in the desert in preparation for his mission (1 Kings 19.8), or the forty days of preparation of the disciples for their mission between the Resurrection and the Ascension.

After this begins the diptych, in the first leg of which the disciples begin slowly to discover who it is that has called them to follow him, as they witness how he teaches new dimensions of love, heals the sick, welcomes sinners, liberates from bonds and from contempt and alienation, provides food (as did the prophet) for his followers and – like God – dominates the sea and the storm.

From his first proclamation onwards Jesus concentrates on the Kingdom of God rather than his own personality: 'The time has come and the Kingdom of God is close at hand' (1.15). In this formula 'the time has come' might be clumsily translated 'the significant moment has been fulfilled', for it implies reference to the long-awaited fulfilment of the prophecies; it designates a joyful opportunity rather than being a simple time-marker. The significance of Jesus' cures is that they bring these prophetic promises of healing, from Isaiah onwards, to fulfilment. Jesus does not make claims for himself, but sees himself simply as a sower, concentrating on the outcome of his sowing. This is further illustrated by the simple images of his parables, a wedding-feast, new wine in new wineskins (2.19–22), a lamp to be put on a lamp-stand, a seed developing unaided, the mustard-seed growing to many times its size (4.21–32). Jesus himself concentrates on his Father's will: he goes out to pray in secret (1.35; 6.46), and in particular to his Father, whom he addresses by the Aramaic term *Abba* (14.36), a relationship so treasured by Christians that it is retained even in the Greek text of the New Testament. He does not engage with the spirits who acknowledge him as 'Holy One of God' (1.26) or 'son of the Most High God (5.7). His concern is only with others, 'I come to call not the virtuous but sinners' (1.17); 'the son of man came not to be served but to serve' (10.45). There is a strong awareness of his role as messianic shepherd – a role constantly attributed in the Old Testament to God himself. He takes pity on them 'because they were like sheep without a shepherd' (6.34).

In the account of the Feeding of the Five Thousand Mark represents Jesus as the divine shepherd of Psalm 22, feeding the people on 'green grass' beside the 'flowing waters' of the Lake (6.34–42). The account also carries overtones of the future Christian community in the Eucharistic overtones of 'he raised his eyes to heaven and said the blessing' and in the twelve baskets of scraps, alluding to the twelve tribes of the new Israel. There are further biblical overtones from the similarity to the account of the prophet Elisha feeding his followers in 2 Kings 4.42–44: there is the same process of disbelief and dialogue between the prophet and his followers. Only Jesus' power is many times greater.

With supernatural acumen the evil spirits recognize Jesus as son of God, but no human being recognizes him as such until after his death. The report of general opinions given by the disciples, that he was John the Baptist, Elijah, or one of the prophets, is no doubt correct (8.28). It is not until the eyes of the blind man of Bethsaida are opened that Peter at last acknowledges Jesus as Messiah, the fulfilment of the promises. Even Peter then fails abysmally to appreciate what this means. In the second leg of the diptych the disciples learn unwillingly and painfully that Jesus can attain his goal only through suffering and death. They learn also that disciples must be prepared to share this suffering, for after each of the prophecies of his own Passion he makes uncompromising demands of his disciples: they must take up their own cross (8.35); they must be prepared to cut off a hand which causes sin (9.43); they must be the servant of all (10.44). But again, it is not until the eyes of the blind man of Jericho have been opened that we reach the climax at Jerusalem. There, before the High Priest, Jesus finally accepts the titles of Messiah and Son of God (14.62). There he also adds his own preferred title, 'son of man'.

There is some evidence that on Jesus' lips this expression is no more than an Aramaic reticent self-designation, used in the gospel only by Jesus himself, to avoid boasting or shocking. Thus, 'The son of man is master even of the Sabbath' (Mk 2.28) could mean either 'I am master even of the Sabbath' or be merely another version of the pervious verse, 'The Sabbath was made for man, not man for the Sabbath'. However there are three occasions in Mark (8.38; 13.26; 14.62) where the context shows that Mark sees the expression 'son of man' as an allusion to the glorious figure of the Son of Man in Daniel 7.13. In Daniel's vision the Son of Man comes to the

Most High to receive all power on earth. In these three cases, therefore, the title would be a claim to divine authority. This accounts for the High Priest's outraged cry of 'Blasphemy!' at the trial scene (Mk 14.64).

The first human being, however, to recognize Jesus as 'son of God' is the centurion at the foot of the Cross (15.39) What did the centurion mean by this, and what does Mark mean? The Roman world was so peopled by demi-gods and heroes that the gentile centurion may have meant no more than we might express by 'a fantastic person'. In Judaism the expression was variously used: the angels are sons of God (Job 1.6), Israel itself is son of God (Hosea 11.1), later the just man is son of God (Wis. 2.18). The phrase expresses a special choice, mission and blessing from God, but the true meaning of it in this case has been being illustrated in the course of the whole gospel, from the Voice at the Baptism onwards. Thus in Mark, taken on its own, it is not clear that Jesus is divine, or at least not clear in what sense he is divine. He brings the Kingship of God to fulfilment, and the line of messianic biblical promises that God would visit his people. Jesus speaks with the authority of God. God is at work in the ministry of Jesus, not least in the final work of giving his life in the complete union of loving obedience to the Father, which provokes the centurion's acclamation.

The story does not finish there: the completion is the empty tomb. Most probably Mark's own gospel ends at Mark 16.8, the remaining verses being added later, after Matthew's and Luke's resurrection stories had provoked the view that a gospel should end with stories about the Risen Christ. These verses have a different style and vocabulary; they can easily be read as summaries of other New Testament materials. If Mark finishes at 16.8, he is hinting that Jesus has been vindicated by God and a new life has begun with the divine acceptance of Jesus' total, loving obedience on the cross. The awed reaction of the women leaves open unlimited possibilities of the divine action in the world, and there is no need to limit this to particular stories. The encounter at the empty tomb is not so much a proof that the tomb is empty as an explanation of what has happened. The angel interprets the event, and, four times, the awe and fear of the women is expressed. In raising Jesus from the dead, God has acted decisively in the world, ushering in a new era. The future of Christianity is open-ended.

4. Why did Mark Write his Gospel?

Every writer has an overall plan or purpose in writing. We will here make three suggestions, not mutually exclusive, about Mark's purpose.

a. Passion Narrative with Extended Introduction

Mark's Gospel has been described by Martin Kähler (1835–1912) as 'a Passion Narrative with extended introduction'. Kähler maintained that all we can really know about Jesus is that he was crucified and rose again. Certainly the Passion is strongly emphasised, not only in that it is described in two whole chapters but also in that there is strong emphasis on the Passion from the beginning. The hostility of the Jewish authorities is evident from the early controversies in Galilee. First, we are given a sample day in Jesus' Galilean ministry of healing (1.21–45), which leaves an impression of the wonder and admiration created by Jesus. But immediately afterwards hostility begins: the scribes object to Jesus' claims to forgive sins (2.6–11) and to his eating with sinners (2.16). The Pharisees complain that Jesus does not fast (2.18) and that he breaks the Sabbath (2.24). It is at the end of this sequence that the Pharisees began to plot to kill Jesus (3.6). This is surely an over-reaction at this stage, for the clash has surely not yet become death-dealing. It may be Mark's hint to the reader of the eventual outcome. Another significant Markan hint is the sandwiching (cf. p. 73) of the martyrdom of John the Baptist by the expedition and return of the disciples on their missionary journey, suggesting that there is no Christian mission without martyrdom (6.7–30).

Once Peter has acknowledged Jesus as the Messiah, the dark atmosphere thickens. Each of the three great prophecies of the Passion (8.31; 9.31; 10.32–4) is shaped to stress that Jesus' triumph can be won only by suffering – an example of Mark's triple repetition for emphasis. Peter bridles at this, and receives the heaviest rebuke in the Gospel: Jesus calls him a Satan, a tempter (8.33). Each time, this prophecy is misunderstood: the disciples shy away from the message of suffering, and Jesus has to repeat to them that anyone who wishes to follow him must deny himself, take up his own cross and so follow him (8.34; 10.38). This may also be the reason why Jesus so frequently tells the disciples to refrain from proclaiming the message: after the Transfiguration they are instructed not to tell anyone what they have seen until the Son of Man has risen from the dead (9.9). They are puzzled because they do not understand what 'to rise from the dead' can mean. Thus the threat of the coming Passion and Death of Jesus is present throughout the gospel.

> Since 1902, Jesus' commands to silence about his healings and other works of power have been characterized as 'The Messianic Secret', following a book of that title by William Wrede (*Das Messiasgeheimnis in den Evangelien*). Wrede suggested that these commands are unhistorical and are simply a clumsy attempt to explain why Jesus was not recognized as the Messiah: he did not allow the disciples or those whom he healed to reveal it. This would also explain why so often, after some public teaching, Jesus gives further teaching to his disciples in private (e.g. 7.17–23). However, this secret has been described as 'the worst kept secret in history', for the unclean spirits whom Jesus expels proclaim loudly for all to hear that Jesus is 'the Holy One of God'. A double explanation of 'the secret' is more satisfactory:
>
> 1 The commands of silence to the disciples are part of Mark's theology of suffering. The disciples are forbidden to spread the message until they have fully understood that Jesus' triumph can come only after his Passion. The resurrection makes sense only as God's vindication of Jesus after his suffering. The disciples are slow to understand this, just as they are slow to understand that they too must bravely suffer persecution. Hence the contrast with the unclean spirits who perceive and broadcast the true significance of Jesus.
> 2 The real mystery is why Jesus was not recognized as Messiah by the people who had been prepared for this over long ages. This is explained in 4.10–13, an explanation sandwiched (in the Markan style, see p. 73) between the parable of the Sower and its allegorical meaning: it was foretold in scripture that this would be so. The quotation from Isaiah 6.9 is used three times in the New Testament for this purpose, once here in Mark, once at the conclusion of Jesus' ministry in John, and once by Paul in Rome, at the final climax of the Acts 28.

The Failure of the Disciples

A related theme is the failure of the disciples to understand Jesus. They start well enough. The first four disciples respond with immediate alacrity to Jesus' call (1.16–20). The disciples are the privileged recipients of the mystery of the Kingship of God (4.11). They fulfil their mission and are congratulated and encouraged to rest by Jesus (6.30–1). However, their weakness is seen (4.13) in their failure to understand the parable of the Sower. They fail to rely calmly on Jesus in the storm on the Lake, though the fact that they turn to him at all shows a certain amount of trust; nevertheless there is a sharp exchange, the disciples treating Jesus to sarcasm, and Jesus replying with an accusation of cowardice (4.38–40). In the story of the Woman with a Haemorrhage they are again sarcastic (5.31). At the first Multiplication of Loaves they douse him with sarcasm, 'Are we supposed [deliberative subjunctive] to go off and buy…?' (6.37), and Mark himself adds the critical finale of 6.52. On two further occasions on the Lake they are rebuked with the characteristically Markan double question (7.18; 8.17), and on each occasion of the prophecies of the Passion they misunderstand and show that they have failed altogether to grasp the message of suffering. When it really comes to the crunch, at the time of the Passion, three times (Markan repetition for emphasis!) the disciples callously fall asleep in the garden of Gethsemane, just as Jesus is struggling in prayer to his Father. Then they all run away, and Peter denies Jesus three times. This consistent pattern is thrown into even sharper relief by the adjustments made by Matthew and Luke, who both tone down the constant rebukes by Jesus (e.g. Mt. 14.33; 16.9), as though to spare the Twelve, the leaders of the apostolic community.

Several attempts have been made to explain this criticism of the disciples. T. J. Weedon has suggested (1968) that there was abroad in the Christian community an understanding of Jesus as a θειος ανηρ (Divine Man), a notion that Jesus was simply a miracle-worker like Apollonius of Tyana (late first century). In this theory, Jesus' check on the disciples and his frequent prohibition of spreading the news of his healings is the 'Messianic Secret' engineered by Mark to correct such a naive and one-sided view of Jesus. S. G. F. Brandon suggested (1958, taken up again by Aslan Reza in 2012) that Jesus was in fact a political revolutionary. It was only after his failure, and the failure of the Jewish Revolt in 70AD, that his followers changed their tune to make him a religious figure; the 'Messianic Secret' would thus be a lame attempt to pretend that even during his lifetime he was secretly understood as a religious rather than a revolutionary figure. Neither of these explanations accounts for all the evidence, and a more straightforward solution is required: Mark stresses so strongly the need to take up the cross because the community for which he wrote towards the end of the century was undergoing persecution and was finding it difficult to accept. Even some of the leaders of the community may have failed, like the Twelve, and even, like Peter, denied their Master. Jesus is, as Francis Moloney puts it, 'a never-failing presence to the ever-failing disciples'.

b. The Good News

In the last analysis Mark must be understood through its title, 'The beginning of the Good News of Jesus Christ' (1.1). The expression 'Good News' (ευαγγελιον) was taken over by Mark from Paul. Originally it was a pagan term, used in the worship of the Roman Emperor. When the Emperor won a significant victory, or had some special news to spread, such as the birth of a son and heir, it would be quickly posted round the Roman world so that appropriate congratulations might flow in to the Emperor. The noun is adopted and used more than 50 times in the Pauline writings to express the triumphant sacred news which Paul had to bring. The corresponding verb, 'to announce good news' is used by Isaiah (e.g. 61.1, quoted by Lk. 4.18) of the eschatological bringing of good news to the poor. This provides the eschatological context for Mark's proclamation.

One important aspect of Mark's eschatological proclamation is the breathless urgency which characterizes it. In common with other Christians of the first generation, Mark saw the coming of Christ as ushering in the final age of the world. The use in Greek texts of the Aramaic expression *Maranatha* ('Come, Lord' or 'Our Lord is coming') is strong evidence of the urgency for Christians of the final coming of Christ. Paul teaches that Christians should live in the vivid expectation of the coming of the Lord: 'The time is growing short' (1 Cor. 7.29; 1 Thess. 5.1–3). In Mark this is evident from the beginning, the first proclamation of Jesus, 'The time has come, and the Kingdom of God is close at hand. Repent and believe the Good News' (1.15) and the urgency of Jesus' instructions to his disciples when he sends them out on their first mission (6.8–11). In Mark the Old Testament images of harvest and the final eschatological wedding of God to his people apply to the present coming of Christ (2.19; 4.3–5; 12.1–10), whereas in Matthew there is a tension between the present coming and waiting for a future coming, which leaves room for a record of good works on which people will be judged (Mt. 22.12; 25.31–46).

Nowhere is this urgency more dominant than in the eschatological discourse of Mark 13.5–32. Unlike all the other brief and incidental units of the gospel, consisting of only a few verses of story or succinct and pithy sayings of Jesus, this speech of Jesus before his departure is one single, long discourse, warning his followers of the threatening final disasters. It begins and ends with a series of pressing warnings: 'Be on your guard' (13.2, 5,

9, 23, 33); 'Keep awake' (13.34, 35, 37). Each section is built on a warning from the prophecy of Daniel which is plucked from its original context and applied to the final days. The first, about the 'desolating abomination' (13.14, quoting Daniel 9.27, where it referred to the destruction of the Temple in the time of the Maccabean persecution) predicts the eschatological upheavals and persecutions which will beset Christians as the end-time approaches. The second (13.26, quoting Dan. 7.13–14) predicts the coming of the Son of Man to rescue his chosen ones amid these cosmic disasters. The imagery suggests that the sack of Jerusalem by the Romans in 70AD was seen as the symbol of the imminent coming of Christ, though others have attached the imagery to events of 30 years earlier (see pp. 70–1). The urgency of this message has served to date the final composition of the gospel at a time very near to that historical event. The final section of the discourse (13.32–6) attests in parabolic language that no date can be given for the threatening moment. The message is apocalyptic: persecution of the community will be inevitable, but the Lord will rescue his own.

Further Reading

Camery-Hoggatt, Jerry *Irony in Mark's Gospel* (Cambridge: Cambridge University Press, 1992): an enlightening particular study

Hooker, Morna, *The Message of Mark* (London: Epworth, 1983): broader themes of the gospel

—*The Gospel according to Mark* [Black's NT Commentaries] (London: A&C Black, 1991): steady, authoritative commentary, useful 'additional notes'

Moloney, Francis J., *The Gospel of Mark* (Peabody, MA: Hendrickson, 2002): a detailed, thorough commentary, preliminary to the next book:

—*Mark, Storyteller, Interpreter, Evangelist* (Peabody, MA: Hendrickson, 2004): an inspiring small volume

Räisänen, Heikki, *The 'Messianic Secret' in Mark's Gospel* (Edinburgh: T&TClark, 1990): study of a particular problem

7

Luke the Historian

1. Authorship and Date

a. Authorship

The two works, the gospel of Luke and the Acts of the Apostles stem clearly from the same author: their vocabulary, style, themes and approach leave no doubt about the matter. From the name 'Luke' we can tell little; 'Loukas' is a Greek form of 'Lucius', which was one of the commonest names in the Roman world. The name occurs three times in the New Testament, each time as a companion of Paul (Phlm. 24; Col. 4.14; 2 Tim. 4.11). However of these only the first is definitely by Paul; the others may well be pseudepi-graphical, and so merely feed off the first. The Colossians passage describes Luke as 'the beloved physician', yet there is nothing particularly medical about the writing ascribed to Luke. Some passages scattered over the Acts (16.10–17; 20.5–8; 21.1–18; 27.1–28.16) are written in the first person plural – they are known as 'the we-passages' – thereby associating the author with Paul on some stretches of his sea-voyages. It is, however, best not to set too much store by this association, for there are definite differences of approach between Paul and this author. One puzzle would be that the Acts shows no knowledge of the letters which Paul would have been writing in the course of these journeys.

As will become clear from the discussion of structure and style, the author (whom we call 'Luke') was a more educated writer than Mark, composing in a Hellenistic idiom for a mainly gentile audience.

b. Date

Reliant on Mark and Q, but writing from his own inspired angle and adding material of his own, it is difficult to tell when Luke wrote. It could hardly be less than a dozen years after Mark wrote, perhaps in the mid-1970s, perhaps earlier (see p. 70). Luke's handling of the synoptic apocalypse (Mk 13) leaves no doubt that he was aware of the Sack of Jerusalem in 70AD. Instead of the prophetic and symbolic language of Mark, Luke speaks of 'Jerusalem surrounded by armies' and the 'devastation' of the city; he says concretely, 'they will be carried off to all nations as prisoners of war, and Jerusalem will be trampled by the nations' (21.20, 24).

2. Structure and Style

Plan of the Gospel

Birth and Childhood of John the Baptist and of Jesus	1–2
Prelude to the Public Ministry of Jesus	3.1–4.13
The Galilean Ministry	4.14–9.50
The Journey to Jerusalem: the Challenge of the Apostolate	9.51–19.27
Teaching in Jerusalem	19.28–21.38
The Passion and Death of Jesus	22–3
After the Resurrection	24

---

a. The Historian

Several features of Luke's gospel mark him out as a historian. First, he presents his account as a history. Booklets of a length comparable to his gospel (the longest of the synoptic gospels) were common at the time. Some were histories, others booklets on navigation, medicine, arms-manufacture, astronomy. Luke likens his work to these by giving it a preface (1.1–4) which contains all their usual features: a dedication, a claim to have researched the topic and consulted the experts (in this case the eyewitnesses – he never claims to have been an eyewitness himself), and a claim to do something which had not been done before. In Luke's case this is 'to write an ordered account'.

b. An Ordered History

This claim to write an ordered history does not necessarily suggest that the other gospels are *dis*orderly; but Luke gives it a new sort of order, new in several respects.

a Events re-ordered

Luke normally follows the order of events given in Mark, but he rearranges some events to make a more logical sequence.

- So he puts the scene of Jesus' expulsion from Nazareth (Mk 6.1–6) earlier (Luke 4.16–30) in order to make it the scene of a sort of manifesto by Jesus at the beginning of his ministry. Here Jesus declares that he fulfils the role of a prophet, full of the Spirit and quoting Isaiah, 'The spirit of the Lord has been given to me'.

- Mark 1.16–20 has the call of the disciples right at the beginning when they have no experience of Jesus and are simply spell-bound by this charismatic personality. Luke delays the call of the disciples (5.1–11), until after Peter and the others have some natural motivation for following Jesus because they have seen some of Jesus' miracles (the Cure of Peter's Mother-in-law) and heard some of his teaching.

- Mark 3.31–5 puts a confrontation between Jesus and his family who have rejected him as the last straw *before* Jesus' sad reflection on the Sower and his unsuccessful sowing, contrasting Jesus' own family with his faithful listeners. Luke (8.19–21) puts this meeting *after* the chapter of parables. Instead of being separated by a barrier of other people sitting around Jesus (Mk 3.34), his family have direct access to him. Luke carefully removes the criticism of Jesus' family in Mark 3.21, 33–4. By this means he presents Jesus' mother as the ideal role-model who hears the Word of God and keeps it – as one would expect, after the Annunciation.

- It is plain from the Acts of the Apostles that Luke is a traveller, and journeys are for him the locus of revelation. So the Journey to Emmaus (Lk. 24.13–35) and Philip's meeting with the Ethiopian (Acts 8.26–40) bring important revelations. In the same way, Luke 9.51–19.27 gathers together teachings on the difficulties of following Jesus into the great journey up to Jerusalem, where Jesus is to give the full example of commitment and perseverance by his Passion and death. This journey is signalled already at the Transfiguration, when they are speaking about his 'parting' which he was to accomplish in Jerusalem (9.31): the journey is about to begin. We are reminded that this is the purpose of Jesus' journey by the laments over Jerusalem at 13.34–5; 19.41–44 and finally 23.28–31.

If Luke is a traveller, Jerusalem is the still point, the hub round which the story revolves – just as Rome will be the end-point of the story of Acts, the journey from Jerusalem to Rome. It is arguable that Luke changes the order of the Temptations in the desert to bring the end-point to Jerusalem, setting the third temptation on the pinnacle of the Temple (4.9). The second half of the gospel is constituted by the great Journey up to Jerusalem. The Resurrection appearances take place in and around Jerusalem. Accordingly, Luke adjusts Jesus' words. In Mk 14.28 Jesus proclaims that they will see him in Galilee. In Lk 24.6 he proclaimed in Galilee that they would see him. It is from Jerusalem that the gospel is proclaimed 'to the ends of the earth' (Acts 1.8).

b Parallels

Another way in which Luke orders his narrative is by laying it out in parallels. In the Infancy Narratives he sets the stories of John the Baptist and Jesus in parallel, first showing how great the Baptist is, and then showing that Jesus is even greater:

At the Annunciations

Zachariah & Elizabeth childless	Mary is childless
Zachariah is 'righteous'	Mary is 'full of grace'
John will be great in God's sight	Jesus will be great
John will be filled with the Spirit	Jesus to be Son of the Most High
John will bring Israel back to God	Jesus will reign on David's throne
Zachariah questions the angel	Mary questions the angel
and is struck dumb	and is blessed

Zachariah sings a canticle	Mary sings a canticle
(*Benedictus*)	(*Magnificat*)

At the birth and circumcision of the two children

John is named 'God's favour'	Jesus is named 'Saviour'
Family and friends rejoice	Angels in heaven rejoice
John grew up his spirit matured	Jesus increased in wisdom, in favour with God and men

As we shall see (pp. 166–7) Luke uses this technique widely in the Acts of the Apostles, to show that the life and work of the early Church carries on the work of Jesus himself. So Luke builds a parallel between the miracles of Jesus and those of his followers, between the pastoral work of Peter and that of Paul, between the judicial procedures against Jesus and against Paul.

c Pairing of women with men
Another element in Luke's history writing which may be considered a matter of order is the pairing of women with men. Writing for the Hellenistic world, where women had a more important role (there are many inscriptions describing women as presidents of synagogues in the Diaspora), Luke is careful to show that the message of the gospel applies to women no less than to men. Hence the parallel annunciations to Zachariah and to Mary, the parallel appearance in the Temple of Simeon and Anna, the raising to life of Jairus' daughter and of the Widow of Naim's son, the recovery of the man's lost sheep and the woman's coin (15.4–10). Possibly also the repentance of the Woman at Simon's House (7.36–50) and of Zacchaeus at Jericho (19.1–10). Correspondingly, in Acts 5.1–11 Sapphira is just as guilty as her husband Ananias.

In the same vein of giving women their due, Luke presents Mary as the perfect disciple. In the Infancy Story it is Mary's consent which allows the Incarnation to occur. This is twice stressed, both by the Blessing on Jesus' mother cried out by a woman, to which Jesus replies that it is those who hear the word of God and keep it (Lk. 11.28) and in Luke's rearrangement of the scene of rejection of Jesus' family in Mark 3.32–5: by slight changes, Luke 8.19–21 makes Mary the paradigm of those who hear the word of God and keep it. She is also explicitly mentioned as present for the prayer of the earliest community (Acts 1.14).

C. A World History

Although Luke uses Mark, his style and imagery show that he is writing for a more sophisticated and more Hellenistic audience than Mark.

- He regularly improves Mark's primitive Greek, and he uses a far more sophisticated style and vocabulary. His vocabulary runs to over 2,000 words, by contrast to Mark's 1,350 words and John's 1,000 words. He frequently uses compound words and is familiar with the niceties of Hellenistic Greek.
- Luke's world is no longer the world of the countryside: Mark has only eight images of economic life (buy, barter, pay, measure, etc), to which Luke adds 32 more, such as creditor, debtor, do business, profit, bill, steward, swindle, bank. His world is the life of the town, with builders, robbers, midnight visitors, travellers, the wealthy and their guests. His warnings about the dangers of wealth suggest a richer audience than that of Mark.
- He omits strange-sounding Semitic names like Boanerges, Gethsemane and Golgotha, and all of the Hebrew words which occur occasionally in Mark (*talitha kum*, etc).
- He dates the events of Jesus' birth and baptism by the ruling Roman, local and religious authorities (1.5; 3.1–3). In the same way, in the accounts of the Acts he will be carefully accurate in his recordings of the diverse titles and functions of magistrates, known to us from secular historians and inscriptions, in the various cities of the eastern Mediterranean: *strategoi* at Philippi (Acts 16), proconsul at Corinth (18.12), Asiarchs and *grammateus* at Ephesus (19.31, 35), *hegemon* at Caesarea (Acts 23). About events in the popular memory of the past he is less accurate. For instance, the 'census of the whole world', 'the first', under Augustus (Lk. 2.1–2) is a confused memory of the unpopular first registration and census of Judaea, shortly before King Herod died in 4BC, a decade before Quirinius was governor of Syria. He also reverses the historical order of Theudas and Judas in Acts 5.36–37.

d. A Creative Historian

On the whole Luke is following Mark's order of events, though he makes considerable changes, omitting two large sections, Mark 6.45–8.26 and Mark

9.41–10.12. He also prefaces Mark's material by the Infancy Narratives. He is editing Mark's account to stress the lessons which he finds important, and he does so by means of his own techniques. The parallelism of the infancy of John the Baptist and Jesus has already been mentioned, and also the parallel between men and women. A further pair of parallel stories is the Disciples on the Road to Emmaus (24.13–35) and the Ethiopian Official (Acts 8.26–40), for these share the same pattern (a journey → puzzlement → meeting → instruction based on the Bible → enlightenment → sacrament → continuation of the journey).

Luke's parables also have a special pattern (see p. 137). Instead of Mark's parables of the Kingdom and Matthew's parables of final reward and punishment, Luke's parables are often examples of behaviour (the Rich Fool, the Pharisee and the Tax-Collector at prayer). Instead of Mark's agricultural parables, and Matthew's parables of contrasting good and bad characters, Luke's are principally about mixed characters, amiable or clever rogues who are neither wholly good nor wholly bad, the Friend at Midnight and the Unjust Judge, who both turn out well in the end, the Crafty Steward, the Rich Man who repents too late. Luke builds up Matthew's story of the Two Sons (Mt. 21.28–32) to give an example of repentance through two mixed characters (the prodigal Son, Luke 15.11–32). A repeated characteristic of his parables is the anti-hero's self-doubting monologue, 'What shall I do now?' (12.17; 16.3; 20.13). On several occasions a parable seems to be based on a saying in the Old Testament: the Rich Fool (12.13–21) on Sira 11.18–20, the Unjust Judge (18.1–8) on Sira 35.14–15, the Places at Table (14.7–10) on Proverbs 25.6. On another occasion Luke turns the incident of Jesus cursing the fig-tree into a parable (13.6–9) to teach his lesson of repentance. Some of Luke's long parables (the Great Feast, the Pounds) are drawn from Q, but here, too, we meet Luke's characteristic preference for direct speech (14.17–19, as in the Healing of the Centurion's Boy, 7.4–5).

Certainly much of Luke's sayings material is taken from Q, but it is questionable how much other sources should be postulated. The conventions of historical writing differ from one age to another. The meaning of a life or an incident is often put as a speech in the mouth of an important character; does this account for Jesus' programmatic speech at Nazareth, in which he announces his mission (4.16–30)? Further, a biographical convention was to gather together sayings of a great leader to his followers at a final supper. So Luke gathers together sayings of Jesus about the future of the community and places them at the Last Supper

(22.21–8); the sayings about Peter's leadership occur in different contexts in Matthew 16.18–20 and John 21.15–18. Is the story of the cleansing of the ten lepers (17.11–19) built up from the Markan story of the cleansing of a single leper to stress the lesson about Samaritans (Mark 1.40–5//Luke 5.12–16)?

Luke obviously has a brilliant talent for teaching a theological point by means of a gripping story, such as the Journey to Emmaus as the story of the Christian apostolate, or the Conversion/Vocation of Paul (Acts 9.1–19). Stories of a great man's childhood are often more illustrative than factual; are the Infancy Narratives built up by Luke from the essential data which he shares with Matthew, that Jesus was born at Bethlehem of the virgin Mary, betrothed to Joseph, and brought up at Nazareth? Is the scene of repentance and conversion at the Crucifixion based on a source unavailable to or passed over by Mark, or is it a Lukan expression of the saving power of the death of Jesus?

3. The Lukan Portrait of Jesus

a. The Prophet

The concentration in the Infancy Narrative on the Temple and its servants shows that for Luke Jesus is heir to the promises to Israel. In what way? In the programmatic speech at Nazareth Jesus presents himself as the prophet anointed with the Spirit; this is the sense which the anointed *Christos* will bear throughout the gospel, ready to be reflected by the presence of the Spirit in the apostles throughout the story of the Acts. At Nazareth he declares himself a prophet. At the raising of the Widow's Son at Naim they acclaim, 'A great prophet has risen among us' (7.16). It is as a prophet that Jesus must die at Jerusalem (13.33–4), and as a prophet that he weeps over the fate of Jerusalem. Only in Luke's account is he explicitly mocked as a blindfolded prophet (22.64) – ironically, even as his prophecy about Peter's triple denial is being fulfilled. The disciple on the road to Emmaus characterises Jesus as 'a prophet powerful in action and speech before God and the whole people' (24.19). At the end, the Ascension is a deliberate allusion to the ascension of Elijah in a fiery chariot (2 Kgs 2.11): as Elisha succeeds Elijah, so the apostles will carry on the task of Jesus. The theme of prophecy fulfilled is everywhere, not only in the Passion prophecies of Luke 9.22, 44; 18.32–3, or the lament over Jerusalem which frames Jesus' ministry in Jerusalem (19.41–44 and 23.28–31, a warning of the Sack of Jerusalem in 70AD), but also in the promises for the apostolic mission: they will receive power from on high (24.49, fulfilled at Pentecost, Acts 2.1–13), they will tread down serpents (10.19, fulfilled in Acts 28.5), they will be judges over Israel (22.30, fulfilled Acts 5.1–11). The work of a prophet, however, is not simply to foretell the future but to be God's spokesman, who sees the significance of events and situations, as Jesus does by his constant teaching.

b. The Lord

Jesus is more than a prophet, for he is also called 'the Lord', which Luke and his hearers well know is the Greek translation of the Hebrew divine Name. In Mark, Jesus is addressed (in the vocative case) as 'Lord!', but this can mean little more than 'Sir!', but it is never used clearly of Jesus with the article, '*the* Lord'. It is, however, so used in Luke's own editorial additions (7.13, 19; 10.1, 39, 41; 11.39; 13.15; 17.5, 6; 18.6; 19.8; 22.61). This must at least have overtones of the divinity, suggesting that Jesus is seen as God himself. In the Acts it is often difficult to discern whether 'the Lord' means God or the Risen Christ. In the vocation-experience of Paul on the road to Damascus (Acts 9.1–15) the awesome appearance of 'the Lord' is certainly represented as a theophany because of its similarity to divine vocations in the Old Testament; equally clearly it is Christ that appears, and this is the same Christ who moves through the pages of the gospel as 'the Lord'. Peter's speech at Pentecost shows that, at the Resurrection, Jesus was in some way 'exalted to the right hand of God' in accordance with Psalm 110 (109) as Lord, and yet it is already the same Lord who is to be seen in the gospel.

This explains the easy sense of command which Luke associates with Jesus. Not for Luke is the tortured prayer in the Garden. For him Jesus is preparing for the contest, the *agon* (22.44, a word used elsewhere of athletic contests): Jesus does not fall prostrate, but kneels in the attitude of earnest prayer, prays once and rises to his feet at the end of his prayer. Luke is showing not the desperation of Jesus but his example to his disciples to pray in time of testing and persecution; the incident is framed by the instruction to 'pray that you enter not into temptation' (22.40, 46).

Of all the evangelists, Luke especially stresses the need for prayer, both in Jesus and in his disciples. At key moments of his life Jesus is seen to be praying: at his baptism (3.21), before the crucial scene of Peter's profession of faith (9.18), before the Transfiguration (9.28). Jesus habitually goes off on his own to pray (5.16; 6.12); prayer is obviously the 'default mode' of his own life. The disciples come and find him praying when he teaches them to pray (11.1). He teaches them to 'pray continually' and with the tax-collector's humility rather than the Pharisee's complacency (18.1–11). Perhaps the most moving of all such occasions is the prayer in the garden before the Passion; in Luke, Jesus' prayer at his supreme time of testing – which is to be the model for that of the disciples in their time of testing – is centred wholly on his Father's will, without any regard for himself (22.40–6). The same utter yielding to the Father is the centre of his final prayer on the cross, 'Into your hands I commend my spirit'. Luke also gives us, from Q, the exultant prayer of Jesus thanking the Father for the intimacy which he enjoys with the Father and which he passes on to his disciples. Luke himself enriches it with the fullness of the Trinitarian cry of joy in the Spirit with which he introduces it (10.21). Such warmth in prayer glows from the beginning of the gospel in the canticles which respond to the saving events voiced by Mary, Zachariah, Simeon and the angels themselves.

Luke's form of the Lord's Prayer differs slightly from Matthew's. The address, simply 'Father' instead of Matthew's 'Our Father in heaven' is simpler, which imparts a noble simplicity and intimacy. It does not include the petition about the Father's will, perhaps leaving the prayer more centred upon the Father's own kingship rather than the human response. Both these differences may be Matthaean additions (compare p. 63), for Matthew is especially aware of the community dimension (whence 'Our'), and often brings to the fore the importance of 'doing the will of God'. In the second part of the prayer, which centres more on human need, two little features (a change of tense to the insistent aorist of 'give', and 'each day') stress our utter dependence on God.

Throughout the Passion, Jesus is in control: he knows that Judas is about to betray him with a kiss (22.48); he commands the disciples not to impede the arrest, as he heals the high priest's servant, and calmly faces the hour of darkness. The mockery by the soldiers is omitted (perhaps to spare Jesus the affront, perhaps to avoid the impression of hostility between Jesus and the Romans). On the way of the cross he is sufficiently in control to speak to the women of Jerusalem, and even, later, to continue his mission of pardoning and saving, forgiving those who nail him to the cross and welcoming the penitent to heaven. Instead of the seeming cry of abandonment as his last word, Jesus himself lays his life in his Father's hands: 'Father, into your hands I commend my spirit.'

c. The Saviour

Another favourite conception of Jesus in Luke's mind is as 'Saviour'. In the Old Testament this is a special title for God, the Saviour of Israel, both in the context of saving Israel from Egypt or from other aggressive enemies, and in especially in eschatological contexts, where God will come to save his people from all the evils that threaten (Isa. 49.25; 63.9). This concept is not at all used in Mark and Matthew, but suddenly springs into prominence in Luke in the message of the angels to the shepherds, 'Today is born to you in the city of David a Saviour who is Christ the Lord' (2.11). Luke may be seizing on the prominence of saviour-cults in Roman religion. The divine emperor is frequently hailed as 'saviour' on inscriptions, and saviour-cults abounded. It was possible to be initiated into a host of such cults, by secret religious rites, often several of them, which guaranteed salvation from the multiple uncertainties of life. Luke is claiming that only Christ, and not these other figures, is the true Saviour. This claim becomes more important in the later letters of the New Testament, as Christianity spreads round the Greco-Roman empire, especially the Pauline Pastoral Letters (see p. 307).

It has sometimes been claimed that Luke has no teaching on soteriology, that is, on *how* this salvation occurs. This is chiefly because he has no equivalent to Mark's declaration of Jesus, 'The son of man did not come to be served but to serve *and to give his life as a ransom for many*' (Mk 10.45). True, Luke does not use the image of ransom from slavery, an image which goes back to the freeing of Israel from slavery in Egypt. Nor does he use the image of vicarious sacrifice, the idea so popular in some circles, that Jesus on the cross took upon himself the suffering deserved by human sin, satisfying a demanding (not to say vengeful) God. On the other hand, Luke is the only evangelist who gives the words of Jesus at the Last Supper as, 'This is my body, *given for you*'. Salvation is indeed won by the death of Jesus. It is, however, highly significant that in the equivalent of Mark 10.45 he has – and this is placed at the Last Supper – 'Who is greater, the one who reclines at table or the one who serves? Surely the one who reclines at table? But I am among you as one who serves' (22.25). In Luke's thought Jesus is the model for his followers, and is conceived as timelessly among them, even now, as their model of service. As Jesus serves, even to the extent of giving himself for his followers, so must they in their witness to him. This is shown in the Acts of the Apostles (see p. 166), where their witness is patterned on his, their trials and martyrdoms modelled on his.

In the death of Stephen, the first of the disciples to die for Christ, there is a deliberate link with the death of Jesus. At the 'trial' by the Council before his martyrdom, Stephen sees the glory of God and Jesus as the Son of Man standing at God's right hand (Acts 7.55–6), just as Jesus before the Council had said, 'from now on you will see the Son of Man enthroned at the right hand of the power of God' (Lk. 22.69). Both Jesus and Stephen pray for the forgiveness of their executioners. Similarly, when Paul is being tried by the governor, the governor brings the case before the Jewish monarch, just as Pilate sent Jesus to Herod Antipas. Luke is, therefore, careful to show that the trials and death of the followers of Jesus mirror his own.

d. The Risen Christ

Mark ended his gospel at 16.8 (the remaining verses being added later), leaving it open-ended, reverberating with the fear and amazement of the women. Luke makes several additions which both intensify this terrified disbelief and show it to be unjustified. At the same time he is preparing for the future mission of the disciples.

1 The visit of the women leaves them stunned. They were 'at a loss' (v. 4) and 'scared stiff' (v. 5 – two intense and rare words). The Eleven to whom they report think them 'delirious' (v. 11 – the Greek word used, *liros*, comes from the same root). Even Peter, who takes a quick check in v. 12, is left simply 'amazed'. After the stalwart disbelief and despair of the two disciples on the Road to Emmaus (see below), the same reaction is repeated when the Risen Christ appears in the Upper Room: three strong words in vv. 37, 38 ('stunned with fear', 'scared stiff', 'thrown into confusion').

2 They should have known better. Firstly, Jesus had warned them in Galilee that the Resurrection could occur only after suffering and death; it was 'necessary' (v. 7, the word Luke uses 18 times for the

necessary fulfilment of scripture). Secondly, in the Upper Room the risen Christ explains to them from the whole of scripture just how it had to be fulfilled (v. 44). Writing for the Hellenistic world, it was important that Luke should insist on the physicality of the Risen Christ. In Hebrew anthropology, life after death consists in the continuity of the whole person, but in the Hellenistic world, influenced by Platonism, life after death might be conceived as the continuance of the soul after the death and dissolution of the body. By the invitation to touch him, and by actually eating fish, Christ shows that he is no mere 'spirit'.

3   The narrative is full of the promise of the Good News. The women begin it by announcing all these things to the Eleven (v. 9). Then in the Upper Room the disciples are given full instructions about proclaiming repentance for the forgiveness of sins and about witnessing to Jesus – two expressions which will become keywords in the Acts. They are given further reassurance by Christ's high-priestly blessing (modelled on the blessing of Simon the High Priest in Sira 50.20), and his Ascension as a prophet like Elijah. This brings them to three reactions which are to be characteristic of the Christian community: thanksgiving, joy and worship of Christ in the way that only God may be worshipped. This word for worship has been used in Luke only at the Testing of Jesus in the desert (4.7–8), where Jesus himself pronounced that only God may be 'worshipped'.

Between these two incidents Luke has inserted the exemplary story of the Christian apostolate on the Road to Emmaus. The two disciples set out on a journey (always Luke's ideal of revelation), ignorant but open and well-intentioned. Christ meets them in the scriptures. At the sacrament (of the Eucharist) they recognize Christ. Then they return and themselves continue the apostolate. In Luke's best manner the story is superbly crafted on a chiasmus, that is, a series of wrappings in which beginning corresponds to end, with the climax in the centre:

  a. Going from Jerusalem
    b. talking together
      c. Jesus came up
        d. their eyes were held
          e. hope frustrated
            f. they went to the tomb
              g. Jesus alive

f.' they went to the tomb

e.' hope fulfilled

d' their eyes were opened

c' Jesus left them

b' talking together

a' going to Jerusalem.

This is the model of any Christian apostolate, which we will see fulfilled in the Acts of the Apostles. Raymond Brown speaks of two bridges, one at the beginning of the gospel, joining the Old Testament to the New, and the other, at the end of the gospel, joining the era of Jesus to that of the Church: 'In Luke 1–2 OT characters representing Israel come across the bridge to meet Gospel characters; in Acts 1 the Jesus of the Gospel comes across the bridge to instruct the Twelve and prepare them for the coming Spirit.' This bridge is constituted also by the readiness of the group of apostles to proclaim the Good News and bear witness to Christ.

4. Theological Themes of Luke

a. The Gospel of the Spirit

In Mark the Holy Spirit play a relatively small part. The Spirit comes down on Jesus at his baptism, but after the introduction the Spirit is mentioned only twice more, in the distant past, as the inspiration of the Psalms (Mk 12.36), and in the future as the guidance and strength of the missioners (Mk 13.11). In Luke the situation is wholly different, especially where Luke is writing independently, without Mark as a background. But already Luke has carefully re-fashioned the scene of the baptism of Jesus: it is no longer simply the baptism, but rather it is the descent of the Spirit on the occasion of Jesus' baptism; the baptism is only the time-marker for the descent of the Spirit – 'as Jesus was being baptized...' – the main clause is 'the Spirit descended' (3.21). From the beginning the Spirit of God has burst upon the scene to guide the action: already in the Infancy Stories the Spirit has taken over: John the Baptist, Mary, Zachariah, Elizabeth and Simeon are all filled and moved by the Spirit (1.15, 17, 35, 41, 47, 67, 80; 2.25–7). Immediately after the baptism Jesus is 'full of the Spirit' as he leaves the Jordan, and is led by the Spirit into the desert (twice in one sentence!). At the end of his testing he comes back again into Galilee 'in the Spirit' (4.14).

This emphatic presence and action of the Spirit will be continued, especially where Luke is composing his own scene, as in Jesus' programmatic speech in the synagogue at Nazareth, which is a special celebration of the Spirit (4.18). Although the Spirit is not explicitly mentioned in many passages, this stress on the Spirit which gives direction to the mission endures throughout the gospel, and will of course return much more explicitly in the Acts. Especially, the Spirit is present in the presentation of Jesus as the Spirit-filled prophet, whose prophecies are fulfilled (see p. 98). A particularly significant passage comes at the return of the disciples from their first mission, and Jesus, 'filled with the Holy Spirit', rejoices in his closeness to the Father and in the revelation given to infants, that wonderful prayer of Trinitarian intimacy, as though confirming and rejoicing in the work of the Spirit during their mission. The Spirit is the life of the Church (10.21–4). Finally, with his last words, Jesus commits his Spirit to the Father (23.46), closing his own earthly mission and opening the door to the further mission of his disciples.

b. Luke and the Gentiles

At the programmatic proclamation in the synagogue of Nazareth which Luke brings to the beginning of Jesus' mission (Lk. 4.16–30) Jesus declares that he fulfils the role of a prophet, full of the Spirit, quoting Isaiah: 'The spirit of the Lord has been given to me.' Jesus here declares that he brings salvation to the gentiles, as did the prophets Elijah and Elisha. All flesh will see the salvation of God (3.6) as in the full prophecy of Isaiah. This is a major feature in all Luke's writing. His second volume describes the mission to the gentiles and the spread of the faith to the centre of the Roman Empire, but already in the gospel he highlights Jesus' concern for the gentiles. Already in the Temple Simeon promises that Jesus will be 'a light of revelation to the gentiles', even before mentioning 'the glory of your people Israel' (2.32). Accordingly, Luke's genealogy of Jesus goes back, not as in Matthew to Abraham, but to Adam, the founder of all the human race (3.38). The faith of the presumably gentile centurion at Capernaum is praised as greater than any in Israel (7.1–10). Into the parable of the Great Supper (14.21–3), Luke inserts a little allegory: the messengers first bring in to the banquet the crippled and beggars from the city (often representing the Chosen People) and then go out beyond the city to gather in the gentiles from the highways and byways. Especially stressed is the response of the Samaritans, the nearest neighbours and so the most hated rivals of the

Jews. So the parable of the Good Samaritan contrasts the generosity of a Samaritan with the narrowness of the observant Jewish officials (10.29–37). The story of the Ten Lepers (17.11 19, possibly a Lukan creation, built on the basis of the healing of a single leper, 5.12–16) climaxes with the praise of the one Samaritan leper, contrasting with the ingratitude of the other presumably Jewish lepers. In the final charge to the apostles, making the transition to the second volume, the Risen Christ instructs them to preach repentance not merely to Israel but to all nations (24.46).

Luke's omissions are further indication that this gospel is written with gentiles in mind. He shows little interest in the controversies over Jewish legal observance, which would be less relevant to a gentile readership, except in so far as they illustrate Jesus' personality. For example he omits Mark 2.27 and the whole discussion about observance of the oral tradition in Mark 7.1–23. He omits the discussion of the prescriptions about divorce in Deuteronomy (Mk 10.1–12), retaining only Jesus' ruling against divorce (Lk. 16.18); he omits also the discussion of the important commandments of the Law (Mk 12.32–3). All this suggests that he avoided discussions which would be opaque or irrelevant to gentiles. His warnings about the dangers of wealth suggest a richer audience than that of Mark and Matthew (see p. 54). His world is the life of the town, with builders, robbers, midnight visitors, travellers, the wealthy and their guests. He uses larger sums of money than Mark: in Mark 6.8 Jesus tells the disciples to take no coppers in their belts, whereas in Luke 9.3 he tells them to take no silver in their belts. The sums of money used are a sure indicator of the financial condition of the hearers! In Matthew the sums of money are huge (no gold in their belts, Matthew 10.9, a debt of ten thousand talents, Matthew 18.24), but this is typical of rabbinic exaggeration

c. Outreach to the Poor

Moving as he does in a rich world, it is all the more striking that the poor and the needy are a special concern to Luke. Above all, he is concerned to warn the rich of the dangers of wealth and the importance of using their wealth generously and well. Again this is a sign of the audience: there is less point in addressing the poor about their poverty than in addressing the rich about their peril and their obligations.

From the start the overriding misfortune of Zachariah and Elizabeth was that they were childless; this is a dreadful deprivation and humiliation (1.25) in such a society, if only because it meant they could not be parents of the Messiah. Mary, for her part, is obviously subject to the humiliation of being thought a betrothed adulteress. Furthermore, there is no room for her to put the new-born child, born far from home. He is greeted by no one more dignified than impoverished shepherds (contrast the wealthy oriental Magi of Matthew's account), and his parents have to make the Temple-offering of the very poor.

This is only the preface to Luke's consistent attention to the poor. To bring good news to the poor is an element in Jesus' programmatic manifesto in the synagogue at Nazareth (4.18). His followers, too, must be poor, for only in Luke is it stressed at the call of disciples that they left *all* to follow him (5.11, 28). Again and again such a demand accompanies the call to follow Jesus: the ruler (Matthew's rich young man) who wants to follow Jesus, must 'sell all he has' (18.22). Most absolute of all, Jesus proclaims, 'None of you can be my disciple without giving up all that he owns' (14.33), a passage unparalleled in the other gospels. Elsewhere, too, he insists, 'Sell your possessions and give to those in need' (12.33). Curiously, this demand for total poverty does not always seem to be observed: Zacchaeus gives only half his property to the poor (19.8). In the Acts, too, the demand has waned, for the crime of Ananias and Sapphira was not to keep money back for themselves, but to lie that they had handed it all in (Acts 5.4).

The two repeated elements are care for the poor and the dangers of wealth. Both of these are stressed in Luke's version of the Beatitudes. By contrast to Matthew's eight Beatitudes, which dwell on Christian attitudes (poor in spirit, etc), Luke's are more stark and material; they are blessings pointedly and directly addressed to those who are actually poor, hungry, weeping and hated. They are clinched by the four 'Woes' on those who are free of such disadvantages. In the sequel to the Beatitudes Matthew gives instruction on observance of the Law, ending up with the command to be perfect (perhaps 'whole' or 'complete', Mt. 5.17–46); by contrast Luke follows his Beatitudes with instruction on generosity and alertness to the needs of others, ending up with, 'Have pity, just as your Father has pity' (Lk. 6.27–36).

We are constantly reminded that the situation of the rich is a dangerous one. The Pharisees are criticized because they loved money (16.14) rather than for any dishonesty. In another passage even they are offered a clean bill of health – by generosity rather than by legal observance, 'Give alms from what you have, and look, everything will be clean for you' (11.41). Perhaps the fiercest little vignette in the whole gospel is addressed to the rich man who planned to extend his barns to accommodate his increasing wealth:

'Fool, this very night I shall demand your life from you, and then whose will be the store you were preparing?.(12.20)'. The dangerous situation can be redeemed only by generosity, as in the case of the Good Samaritan, or as the Rich Man fails to do to Lazarus. The force of Luke's teaching may be seen in the adjustments made in this story: the background may be a Palestinian story about a poor scholar and a rich tax-gatherer whose situations are reversed in heaven (j. Sanh. 6.23e). But when Luke adapts the story he not only refrains from saying anything about the merits of Lazarus and the faults of the rich man. He positively removes the built-in good qualities of the poor man (a scholar of the Law) and the bad qualities of the rich man (an unclean tax-collector). It is the position itself of being rich or poor which determines the place in the next world.

Frequent slight touches show the importance of this lesson for Luke: at 6.30 he changes the tense so that the instruction reads, 'Give *habitually* to everyone who asks you, and never ask the one who takes your possessions for their return'. In the story of the Cure of the Centurion's Boy, Luke inserts the Jewish elders; their function is to tell Jesus about the centurion's generous gift towards building the synagogue (7.3–5); there is none of this in Matthew's version.

d. Repentance and Forgiveness

A principal theme of Luke, which runs throughout his writing, both in the gospel and in the Acts, is the need for repentance and the welcome which God affords. Dante described Luke as *scriba mansuetudinis Christi*, the scribe of the gentleness of Christ. Jesus is the healer; he even heals the high priest's servant at the time of his own arrest (22.51). Luke does not show human emotion on Jesus' part, neither disturbance nor anger. He cuts out Jesus' anger from his version of Mark 1.41 and 43, his annoyance at Mark 3.5 and 10.14, and the fierce reproach to Peter in Mark 9.33. He spares the disciples, too, by removing Mark's sarcasm of the disciples to Jesus (Mk 4.38) and changing Mark's 'Why are you so cowardly? Have you no faith' into simply 'Where is your faith?' (Lk. 8.25). The disciples are not made to admit their failure as at Mark 9.28. At the Passion the disciples are not shown running away (Mk 14.50), and indeed all Jesus' friends are explicitly mentioned as present at the crucifixion (Lk. 23.49). A moving touch is Jesus' glance at Peter after his third denial, which brings Peter to repentance (22.61).

In this especially Jesus is seen to be the icon of God, expressing God's own forgiveness of human failing. Perhaps the most prominent aspect of the revelation of God in the Old Testament is the divine forgiveness. This is the meaning of the unpronounceable Name of God, given to Moses, when God passes before him, crying out, 'The LORD, the LORD, God of tenderness and compassion, slow to anger, rich in faithful love and constancy, maintaining his faithful love to thousands, forgiving fault, crime and sin' (Exod. 34.6–7). This is the concept of God which echoes down the scriptures, appearing again and again: Deuteronomy 5.9–10; Psalm 86.15; Jeremiah 32.18; Jonah 4.2, etc.

Correspondingly, in both volumes of Luke, conversion and acceptance of repentance are almost a necessary pre-condition of the call. Each of the speeches of Peter and Paul in Acts ends with a call to repentance and conversion. Peter must admit that he is a sinner before he becomes fit to be called (5.1–11). Luke shares with Mark and Matthew the saying of Jesus, 'It is not the healthy who need the doctor but the sick. I came to call not the upright but sinners' (5.31–2). Prominent among his additions are the calls of the two sinners, the woman who had a bad name in the town (7.36–50) and Zacchaeus, the fraudulent tax-collector (19.1–10) – again a pair of woman and man. In the former case the sinner is contrasted with the discourteous Pharisaic host; in the latter the contrast is underlined by the bitterness of the citizens. In the parables a similar pair of man and woman who find the lost sheep and lost coin occasion joy in heaven (15.4–10). While Matthew 21.28–32 provides a typical black-and-white contrast between two sons, Luke's parable of the Prodigal Son (15.11–32) brings the story to life not only by his delicate characterisation of the repentant rogue and the insanely welcoming father, but also by the contrast with the dutiful elder son who forfeits all sympathy by his spiteful self-righteousness. Jesus continues to the end his mission of welcoming sinners, for Calvary is a scene of repentance: the road to Calvary is dominated by the mourning and repentance of 'large numbers of the People' and 'the daughters of Jerusalem' (23.27–8). Jesus forgives his executioners, as will do also Stephen at his martyrdom (Acts 7.60), and the death of Jesus is greeted by a general movement of repentance from the watching crowd (23.48). Perhaps the most forceful of all is Luke's presentation of the Good Thief (23.40–3): having doubly acknowledged his guilt, he wins acceptance simply by turning to Jesus.

A comparison of vocabularies is instructive. 'Forgiveness of sins' occurs in Mark only as part of the Baptist's message (1.4) and in Matthew only at Jesus' words over the cup at the Last Supper (26.28), whereas in Luke it occurs five times and again five times in Acts. 'Repentance' occurs once in Mark, twice in

Matthew (both in the context of the ministry of the Baptist), but in Luke-Acts eleven times. Similarly the verb 'to repent' twice in Mark, five times in Matthew, but fourteen times in Luke-Acts. Neither word occurs at all in John.

In the last analysis, therefore, it is the healing mission of Jesus which endures to the end. To this answers the human response of repentance. This is the only objective of the apostolic preaching, as we see both in the final charge to the disciples ('that in his name repentance should be preached to all nations for the forgiveness of sins', 24.47) and in the constant conclusion of the apostolic exhortations of Peter and Paul in Acts.

e. The Salvation of Israel

Luke's message of salvation for the gentiles brings him considerable problems. One of the central themes of the Acts is that the Jews for a second time rejected the message of Jesus, the Good News for which the nation had been being prepared since the time of Abraham. In the gospel the Jews rejected Jesus. In the Acts first Jerusalem again rejects the Good News, as is certified by the martyrdom of Stephen, then three times Paul is driven by the Jews to turn away from them and to the gentiles. On each occasion, of course, some of the Jews are incorporated into the Christian community, but the nation as a whole rejects the Good News. Does this mean that the promises of God have failed? The answer to this worry is in the Infancy Narratives. It was important to show from the start that God had not deserted his people, and that the Saviour had come to fulfil their hopes. This is the message of the first two chapters.

The style of Luke 1–2 is deliberately reminiscent of the language of the Greek Old Testament. Such expressions as 'in the days of', 'it happened that', 'and behold', 'the time came for her to have her child' are all strongly biblical. The whole theme of an angelic announcement of a special birth is biblical. The childless Zachariah and Elizabeth are reminiscent of Abraham and Sarah, the prohibition of strong drink is reminiscent of the announcement of Samson's birth, belonging to God 'from his mother's womb' is reminiscent of the prophet Jeremiah. Mary's canticle is closely modelled on that of Anna, mother of the prophet Samuel. The little note about the growth of the child at the end of both stories echoes the note at the end of the stories of the young Samson and the young Samuel (Judg. 13.24; 1 Sam. 2.21). The actual poverty, the simplicity and the faultless spirituality of the characters carries the taste of the spirituality of the Poor of the LORD, so characteristic of the post-Exilic later prophets: they are perfectly observant of the Law, waiting devotedly for the coming of the Messiah, expectant but patient, making no claim of their own, but waiting for the LORD. This is the spirituality of Zephaniah 2.3: 'Seek the LORD, all you humble of the earth, who obey his commands.'

Among the most precious of these Old Testament reminiscences are the Canticles of Mary, Zachariah and Simeon. Once the Lord is born, everyone starts to sing. The canticles of rejoicing are piled one upon another, and all are primarily an expression of joy at the fulfilment of the promises to Israel.

> It is not necessary to hold that Mary's song was taken down *verbatim* by Luke, though no doubt she may be assumed to have been present when Zachariah and Simeon sang their canticles of joy. The *Magnificat* is built on allusions to Anna's song of joy at the birth of Samuel, and the *Benedictus* runs in the same vein of biblical poetry. They do fit well into the contemporary spirituality of those awaiting the Messiah, such as the *Hodayoth* of Qumran (1 QH) and the Pharisaic *Psalms of Solomon* 17–18, both stemming from around this time. Nevertheless, Luke's genius being what it is, the *Magnificat* is the perfect expression of the gratitude of the joyful young girl, nourished on the Bible. With the prospect of marriage and family-life before her, she has been stopped in her tracks by the divine invitation. To the angel she can reply in no more appropriate way than in the words of the promises to David (2 Sam. 7.11–16) of an eternal dynasty. Conscious of her own unworthiness, she pours out to her elderly cousin, in balancing biblical couplets, her joy at the reversal of situation for which Israel had so long been waiting. The elderly priest, for his part, appropriately sums up the history and hopes of Israel, founded on the promises to Abraham and to David. It has been proposed that the slightly aggressive touches in the *Benedictus* (2.71, 74) suggest that these canticles are best understood as hymns from the time of the Maccabean resistance movement of the early second century BC. However, Luke shows such variety and adaptability of style that we have no right to rule out the possibility that he composed them himself.

Quite apart from the careful parallelism of the John Baptist and the Saviour Jesus, the episodes are composed in Luke's best manner, each with an entry, a dialogue and an exit. The first appearance of Jesus in Mark is compatible with a theory that he became Son of God at his baptism. One of the purposes of the Lukan Infancy Stories is to show that, besides being the fulfilment of the promises, he was Son of God from the first moment of his existence. Only the final episode, which neither has a parallel nor (like the Visitation) draws the two chief actors together, stands out as being more like the non-canonical infancy stories. Its purpose is to show that the 12–year-old Jesus is already Son of God, already living in an intimacy with his Father which transcends all human relationships.

Further Reading

Drury, John, *Tradition and Design in Luke's Gospel* (London: Darton, Longman & Todd, 1976): enlightening, despite its age

Fitzmyer, Joseph A., *Luke the Theologian, aspects of his teaching* (London: Geoffrey Chapman, 1989)

Harrington, Wilfred, *Luke, Gracious Theologian* (Blackrock: Columba Press, 1999)

Shillington, V. George, *Introduction to the Study of Luke-Acts* (London: T&T Clark, 2007): thorough, scholarly, for students

8

The Gospel of John

---

1. Authorship and Date

a. Authorship

Traditionally this gospel has always, since the third century, been associated with John the Apostle, as have also the three Letters and the Book of Revelation. There are, however, marked differences between these writings, as well as obvious similarities, which have in more recent times resulted in their being attributed not to a single individual but to a school of writers. The situation is further complicated by uncertainty about the composition of the gospel. During much of the twentieth century the field was dominated by the theory of Rudolf Bultmann, who held that the gospel was finally edited by an Ecclesiastical Redactor, relying upon two sources, a Signs Source and a Passion narrative; in this case who would count as the author? Other important theories have been those of Raymond E. Brown, who posited five separate stages of composition, and most recently Urban von Wahlde, who has analysed the work into three major editions with some later additions.

The association with John is based on a reference in the (added) final chapter to a disciple 'who vouches for these things and has written them down, and *we* know that this testimony is true' (21.24). This statement may refer only to the final chapter, but it also echoes 19.35, which speaks of 'the evidence of one who saw it, trustworthy evidence, and he knows he speaks the truth'. Both these references are to the source of the testimony rather than to literary authorship. The unnamed disciple of 21.24 is the beloved disciple who leaned on Jesus' breast at the last supper. At the end of the second century Irenaeus voiced the tradition that the Beloved disciple was John, son of Zebedee (both sons of Zebedee were present in 21.2). Others have suggested that it was Lazarus, whom Jesus loved so tenderly (Jn 11.33–5). This Beloved Disciple appears altogether four times in the gospel, at the Last Supper, at the foot of the Cross, at the Empty Tomb and at the lakeside in John 21. It has been suggested that this is the picture of the ideal disciple, who is close to Jesus at the Eucharist, who participates in the Passion, who believes in the Resurrection and who is the source of witness and tradition, that is, the disciple whom Jesus loves. Rather than an imaginary figure, it may be based on a particular disciple whose name is deliberately withheld in order to permit such generalisation. In any case, it tells us little about the literary authorship of the gospel. If the analysis, or even the approach, of Raymond Brown or Urban von Wahlde is correct, it would be a mistake to seek a single author of the whole gospel. Rather, the material will have been re-handled at several different stages, each contributing its own features and emphases.

b. Date

The earliest papyrus fragment of the gospel ($\mathfrak{P}$52), consisting of John 18.31–3 and 37–8, is dated by its style of handwriting to the first half, probably the first quarter, of the second century. This shows that the gospel had reached Egypt by that date. There is no agreement whether John intends to correct or supplement the synoptic gospels, or is merely partially dependent on the same sources. In many ways the theology of the gospel is more developed than that of the synoptic gospels, but this does not necessarily imply that it was written later. Different communities and different authors may develop differently.

Certain features may suggest that developments have occurred for which time is required. The stress on realized eschatology, that the Spirit is present among the disciples now, rather than a future eschatology, looking forward to an imminent Second Coming, may suggest that the fervent expectation of a Second Coming seen in Paul (1 Cor. 7.29–31; cf. 2 Thess. 2.2) has waned. Similarly the fierce hostility from 'the Jews', and in particular the fear of being 'put out of the synagogue' (Jn 9.22; 12.42; 16.2), may reflect conditions towards the end of the first century, as in Matthew. But these are no more than possibilities.

2. Structure and Style

Different Patterns

The gospels of Matthew and Luke follow the pattern of Mark, so that the three gospels are called 'synoptic', that is, they may be looked at together, e.g. in parallel columns. On the whole they are composed from independent units of tradition, stories and sayings of a few verses, placed together by the evangelist. John has not only a different overall shape but also a different pattern. The most notable difference in the overall shape is that, while the synoptic gospels (apart from the Lukan Infancy Narratives), show Jesus making one visit to Jerusalem as the climax of his ministry, John shows Jesus going to Jerusalem four times. Linked to this difference is another: in the synoptic gospels Jesus 'cleanses' the Temple as the final climax of his ministry which leads directly to his arrest and death, whereas in John this cleansing comes at the beginning, as the introductory statement of his purposes, after which the authorities become increasingly hostile but succeed in arresting him only on the fourth visit to Jerusalem. It is difficult to decide which chronology is correct, for there are good theological reasons for either arrangement. For the last century or two it used to be scholarly orthodoxy to hold that John had little historical foundation. In recent decades, however, the tide has turned, and it is granted that at least in some cases John has strong historical foundations. Particularly about Jerusalem the knowledge of the synoptic gospels is sketchy and distant, whereas John shows detailed knowledge, confirmed by archaeology, of such places as the Pools of Bethzatha and Siloam, the Sheep Gate, and the locality of Bethany and Bethphage.

Instead of a multitude of short miracle stories, featuring healings and exorcisms, parables and individual sayings of Jesus in the synoptic gospels, John has no exorcisms, few miracles (almost all of which are developed at length and followed by a reflective commentary or dialogue) and no parable-stories. Instead John uses great archetypal symbols like light and water. Instead of quoting passages of the Old Testament which are fulfilled by Jesus, John prefers allusion to such passages, leaving the reader to draw a personal conclusion.

A seemingly small distinction expresses major difference: Mark has a brief historical introduction (Mk 1.1–14) explaining who Jesus is by the Baptism. Matthew and Luke preface this by their Infancy Narratives to show that Jesus was Son of God from the beginning of his life, not just from the baptism. John gives a poetic and theological preface to show that the eternal Word of God became man in Jesus. In the synoptic gospels Jesus proclaims the Kingdom or Kingship of God, his Father, whereas in John there is barely a mention of the Kingdom of God (3.3, 5); the gospel is centred much more obviously on the person of Jesus. Jesus proclaims himself as the Son of the Father, the light of the world, the good shepherd, the way, truth and life. He uses the divine name of himself (8.28, 58) and speaks quite openly of his own pre-existence (10.30–8; 14.9; 17.5)

John contains also unmistakable literary features which seldom appear in the synoptic gospels. Three examples:

1 Irony is often important in Mark (when Jesus is mockingly hailed by the soldiers as 'King of the Jews', Mk 15.18), but in John it may be the foundation of whole extended scenes, such as the Healing of the Man Born Blind: the blind man sees and 'the Jews' are blind. The High Priest says that it is better that Jesus should die for the people, not knowing what he says (11.50). 'The Jews' condemn an innocent man, but do not enter the Praetorium, to avoid ritual defilement (18.28). They think they are condemning Jesus when in fact they are condemning themselves.

2 John often works on more than one level. Jesus sometimes seems deliberately to mislead his audience, as when he speaks to the Samaritan woman about 'living water': he means the water which is a symbol of the Spirit, but she naturally thinks he means flowing water of the well (4.10). Speaking to Nicodemus, he talks of being born 'again' or 'from above' (3.3), which Nicodemus takes of a repeated natural birth. The living bread from heaven is not material food like manna, but sometimes is divine revelation, sometimes the Eucharist (6.26–58).

3 Repeatedly Jesus' teaching edges forward by misunderstandings and puzzled questions. There always seems to be a second level of

understanding which some accept and some reject. An air of awe and mystery makes itself felt in the poetic and elevated diction of the gospel.

3. The Composition of the Gospel

A certain amount of confusion and repetition suggests that the gospel was not composed in one draft.

a. Three Special Cases

a The Woman Taken in Adultery (7.53–8.11)

Several of the most important ancient manuscripts of the gospel do not contain this story. Others include it in different places. It does not have any particular Johannine features, and both style and vocabulary are more like Luke's writing. The theme of welcome for a repentant sinner is also typical of Luke. It is generally considered an ancient story, part of the authentic tradition of Jesus, but originally independent and incorporated only subsequently into the gospel. It may have been inserted in this position to illustrate the previous passage, 'Surely our Law does not allow us to pass judgment on anyone without first giving that person a hearing' (7.51) or the following passage, 'I judge no one, but if I judge my judgment will be true' (8.15).

b Breakfast with the Risen Christ (Jn 21.1–23)

This comes after what seems to be a conclusion of the gospel (20.30–1) and itself has a similar conventional conclusion (21.24–5). The passage combines some linguistic features which are quite typical of John (the use of the double name 'Simon Peter') with others which are quite untypical (the mention of the sons of Zebedee). A defensible opinion is that it was written by someone other than, but familiar with, the writer of the first 20 chapters. There is also the major difficulty that it seems to be a second version of the call of Peter and disciples after a miraculous catch of fish, given also much earlier in the story of Jesus in Luke 5.1–11. Has John used the same tradition in a different time-frame? The passage includes the gift of authority to Peter which comes elsewhere in other gospels (21.15–18, compare Matthew 16.17–19 and Luke 22.31–34), but also makes a fitting conclusion, looking towards the future of the community.

Who is this Beloved Disciple, and who is the author of the gospel? The disciple is here presented not as the author of the gospel but as the authority who stands behind this chapter, 'who vouches for these things and has written them down, and *we* know that this testimony is true' (21.24, compare 19.35), different from the author(s) of this chapter. Some have suggested that the Beloved Disciple is merely an idealized figure, a figure of the Church, the ideal of a beloved disciple, since he was close to Jesus at the Eucharist (13.23); he shared the Passion with Jesus and was closely linked by Jesus to his mother (19.26); he understood and believed at the empty tomb (20.2–8); now he is presented as the witness to the Jesus tradition. These four elements constitute the lasting witness of the Church. On each occasion he partners Peter, who is to be martyred. Others suggest that the Beloved Disciple was an unnamed minor figure in the apostolic tradition, possibly the disciple also mentioned, but not named, in 1.35–40; the name is suppressed so that the portrait may function as a model or ideal.

c   The Prologue (1.1–18)

Mark begins his gospel at the baptism of Jesus, the declaration of the voice from heaven and the descent of the Spirit. This could leave the impression that Jesus became Son of God at the Baptism. Matthew and Luke rule this out, since each adds a prologue which shows the quality of Jesus from the first moment of his existence. John, however, goes back even further, to show that the Word which became flesh in Jesus existed before time began. He begins his gospel with the first words of the Bible, 'In the beginning', already therefore alluding to the Word in creation, and he continues with a sort of Wisdom hymn, drawing on the concept of God's Word, the self-expression of God and so God's own creative image.

- This is paradoxical because as an overture to the gospel it revolves round many of the chief themes of the gospel, light and darkness, acceptance and rejection, the Son and the Father, witness, life, the glory of God. It adumbrates the story of the gospel, about the acceptance or rejection of Jesus.

- Yet the chief idea, the Word, occurs nowhere else in the gospel; it is drawn from the Wisdom literature of the Old Testament. In Hellenistic thought, and especially Jewish Hellenistic thought (Philo), the Logos or Word is what brings order and good sense and shape to the world. So the Logos is what makes sense of the world. God created by his Word and by his Wisdom, and God's Word and Wisdom form the template of creation. So God's Word represents God acting in the world. This is best seen in the great poems of creation, Proverbs 8.22–31 and Wisdom 7.21–8.1. Hence the presentation of Jesus as the Word become flesh is already tantamount to a claim that Jesus is God acting in the world.

- It is poetic and rhythmical in form, more a meditation than a story. It is, however, linked to the story by the two historical mentions of John the Baptist. These were perhaps the original opening of the gospel, onto which the prologue has been grafted.
- It is in the shape of a parabola, beginning with God, ending with God, yet in the middle coming to earth and 'the children of men' who accept or reject the Word. Acceptance or rejection will be issues throughout the gospel.

The Word with God   The Word with God

Creation   Re-Creation

John the Baptist   John the Baptist

Light   Glory

Rejection   Acceptance

Children of God

- Theologically this is the high point of the gospel, beginning and ending with the living and vibrant relationship of the Word 'towards' God (v. 1) and the Son 'into the bosom of the Father' (v. 18), the fulfilment of the Law of Moses, but transcending the gift of the Law in grace and truth.

b. Disjunctions and Dislocations

There are certain passages in the gospel which seem to have been misplaced: John 4 ends in Galilee, John 6 is again in Galilee, but John 5 suddenly finds itself in Jerusalem, and John 7.1 shows Jesus going up again to Jerusalem. If John 5 is put after John 6 this frenetic journeying is avoided, but was John interested in chronological or geographical continuity? Continuity of narrative is no interest of John.

There seem to be several versions of the discourse of Jesus after the Last Supper: at 14.30 Jesus says, 'Come now, let us go', but three more chapters follow (Chapters 14, 15–16, 17). John 17 has its own peculiar form, a prayer of Jesus as priest consecrating himself to the Father, possibly a meditation on the Lord's Prayer. John 13 is teaching about faith; John 14 and 15 partly overlap in teaching about love in a persecuted community; they contain four significant sayings about the Paraclete, who is mentioned nowhere else.

The Lazarus incident (Jn 11–12) seems almost a block on its own, especially after a seemingly final summing-up of Jesus' ministry in 10.40–2. It starts abruptly and independently: 'There was a man named Lazarus' (11.1). Yet it is the climax of the signs given in John 1–12, the gift of life which will lead to Jesus' own death. It shows Jesus at his most human, weeping for his friend, and his most divine, granting him the gift of life.

There are passages which seem to duplicate material, such as the inter-rogation of John the Baptist (1.22–35), or a series of sayings about the relationship of Jesus to the Father (5.19–31), as though there were two versions of the same incident, both of which are incorporated.

c. A Solution

Starting from the conflicting uses of 'the Jews' in John, Urban von Wahlde has elaborated a convincing solution: there are three different stages or editions of the gospel, marked by different literary and theological features. Each edition develops and carries further the position with regard to Jesus.

- In the first 'the Jews' means 'the inhabitants of Judaea', and their leaders are the Pharisees, the chief priests and the rulers. They are hostile to Jesus, and their hostility increases, but they behave like real people, in that there is division among them and discussion is still possible. In the second and third editions 'the Jews' is used indiscriminately of the enemies of Jesus who refuse to accept his message. All discussion is excluded. At the time of the second edition the community is still within Judaism, but is threatened by 'the Jews'; by the third edition the community has left Judaism behind.
- A second feature of difference is the treatment of the wonders of Jesus. The first edition is centred on the 'signs' or 'works' done by Jesus, often called 'the works of the Father'; these are the cause of faith and lead to faith. They are narrated at length, two in Capernaum and three in Judaea, and there is an important focus on the convincing character of these signs. So in the first edition Jesus is condemned by the chief priests and Pharisees for his signs and 'the evil he has done', whereas in the later editions, where his claims are more exalted, he is condemned

for his 'blasphemy'. This first edition provides the chronological and geographical framework of the gospel; its approach was most similar to the synoptic gospels.

- A third feature is seen in the Christology: in the first edition Jesus is described as the Messiah, or Elijah, or 'the Prophet' like Moses; he makes no divine claims and says nothing about a special relationship of the Son to the Father. In the second edition the Christology is much 'higher', centred on the relationship of the Son to the Father, expressed in long dialogues and debates rather than in narrative. The Son is the plenipotentiary agent of the Father, and the equality of the Son to the Father is stressed. Jesus is the Wisdom of the Father and gives the Spirit which will impart a saving knowledge of who Jesus is. Thus the chief impetus of the second edition is to fill out the reverence due to Christ.

- The second edition is distinguishable also by other literary features: the technique of advance by misunderstanding, for Jesus seems almost deliberately to puzzle his hearers. So, for example, Jesus says 'Destroy this Temple and in three days I will rebuild it', meaning the Temple of his body; his hearers naturally understand it of the physical Temple (2.19–21). Or Jesus' use of 'living water' when speaking to the Samaritan (4.10). In the background is also 'the Hour' of Jesus, a mysterious and threatening entity, finally an element in Jesus' triumph, the climax of the story. Instead of emphasis on the 'works' of Jesus, the stress is on 'witness', especially the witness of the community to Jesus. There are sophisticated Jewish arguments, such as John 5 (how God works on the Sabbath) and John 6 (a formal discourse on Moses and the Bread of Life).

- The third edition has several features which bring it close to the First Letter of John. Clearly a crisis had occurred over the attitude to Jesus. He is now called 'Lord' in a divine sense, as God is called 'Lord' in the Old Testament (20.28). He is the Son of Man, in a powerful sense, as a heavenly saviour. He is not only 'Son' but 'only-begotten Son' and pre-existent ('before Abraham was I AM', see 3.13; 6.62; 8.28, 58; 13.19). The eschatological and apocalyptic sense becomes far stronger: the drama is played out against a dualism of spirits, the Evil One contrasting with the Spirit of Truth, who is also the Spirit of Jesus, the Paraclete who is the presence of Jesus in the community. The criterion for salvation is no longer faith, but is the love shown for the 'brothers' in the community.

A clear example of the development is presented in the story of the Man Born Blind. The first edition (9.1–17 + 24b–34) gives a straightforward story with good topographical detail (recent excavations show that the Pool of Siloam was a purification-bath, built in the second century BC and destroyed by the Romans in 70AD; this would serve to cleanse the man from the uncleanness incurred by blindness) Jesus' opponents here are Pharisees, who have a real and typical argument about legal observance. Then (vv. 18–24a) 'the Jews' of the second edition take over, and here it is a question of the later disputes about expulsion from the synagogue for acknowledging Christ. Such disputes will have occurred at the end of the century, rather than in the time of Jesus himself. It is evident from the letters of Paul that Paul was still himself proud of being Jewish, a Jewish believer in Christ, and that the first generation or two of believers in Jesus as the Christ remained within the synagogue community. There is no question yet of expulsion from the synagogue. After the renewed altercation (vv. 24b-34) with the Pharisees, who claim to be followers of Moses, comes a final passage from the third edition (vv. 35–9), where Jesus is given the full titles of 'Lord' and 'Son of Man' and is 'worshipped'.

The dialogue with the Samaritan Woman has a similar pattern. The first edition includes only vv. 4–9, 16–18, 25–30, 39. Here the woman is amazed that Jesus will associate with a Samaritan and use her 'unclean' cup; she recognizes him as a prophet. The second edition adds a typical advance by misunderstanding, in which the two spar with each other with a sort of playful audacity (as in the Nicodemus incident). By these means the understanding of Jesus as more than a prophet advances.

In the story of the raising of Lazarus (11.1–46) the first edition is full of circumstantial detail about the personalities and Jerusalem and Bethany, quite similar to the stories of the synoptic gospels. The third edition adds – or perhaps interprets – the story in the light of a much more developed Christology: Jesus is called 'Lord' and 'Son of God' and himself claims to be 'the Resurrection and Life' (vv. 23–7). There is also the characteristic dichotomy between light and darkness (vv. 9–10).

4. The Christology of John

St Augustine in his eulogy of John does not explicitly distinguish the different stages of development in the gospel: 'John, though scorning to tread upon earth, rose by his very first words not only above the earth, above the atmosphere, above the heavens, but even above the whole army of angels and all the array of invisible powers'. Other more recent authors have said John's Jesus is 'a stranger to this world', 'a pre-existent divine being whose real home is in heaven'. It is therefore all the more valuable to distinguish the stages of deepening understanding shown by the Christology of the different editions.

The first edition has a predominantly Jewish Christology: Jesus is seen as a prophet like Moses. The prologue already introduces Moses as a forerunner of Jesus, whose work Jesus brought to perfection. In the first meetings with the disciples in John 1.35–49 he is greeted with Jewish titles: 'Rabbi', 'Messiah', 'Son of God' (a title which does not of itself mean 'the Word Incarnate' but in Judaism can have a much looser sense, denoting unity of love and purpose). Again, in the first version of the arguments with the Pharisees in the Temple (7.31–2, 40–52) the discussion is about whether Jesus can be the Messiah, a title within Judaism. After the healing of the Man Born Blind, the first discussion with the Pharisees is about whether Jesus is the expected Prophet like Moses and the Messiah (9.24–35).

This assimilation of Jesus to Moses is a constant feature of the gospel. Jesus declares that the son of man must be lifted up as a saving sign, just as Moses lifted up the serpent in the desert (3.14). He provides living water, as Moses provided water in the desert (4.13–14; 7.37–9). The manna at the time of Moses in the desert is only a sign of the true bread of heaven: 'it was not Moses who *gave* you bread from heaven, it is my Father who *gives* you bread from heaven' (6.32). As Jesus fulfils these figures of Moses, so also the basic narrative structure of the gospel stresses that Jesus is the fulfilment of the institutions of Judaism: Moses provided the water of the Law, but at Cana Jesus turns this water into the wine of the messianic banquet. The six water-jars for purification surely symbolize the incompleteness of the Law (one short of the perfect number 7, so a symbol of radical incompleteness), transformed into the lavish fullness of the messianic banquet (160 gallons of wine). The first public sign Jesus gives by the cleansing of the Temple shows that the Temple finds its true meaning in Jesus (2.13–22), making the Passover his own. The Jewish festival in 5.1 is given meaning by Jesus' act of healing. At the Jewish feast of Shelters Jesus calls believers to come for living water not to the Spring of Gihon but to him (7.2, 37). Finally Jesus is the Passover Lamb, killed at the same time as the Passover lambs were sacrificed in the Temple (19.14, 31).

The second stage in the development of the Christology of the gospels is centred on the relationship of the Son to the Father. This is most clearly expressed in the discussion in the Temple (5.19–30) after the cure of the sick man at the Pool of Bethesda. The expression 'the Son' without qualification is used only three times in the synoptic gospels, expressing the intimate relationship between son and father, where Jesus addresses God as 'Father' (Mk 14.36). This reaches a new dimension in John: in the discussion in the Temple on the Sabbath Jesus claims the privilege of working on the Sabbath as God works on the Sabbath. God must give life and judge on the Sabbath, since babies are born, and people die and must be judged on that day. In working on the Sabbath Jesus makes himself equal to the Father (5.18). This is expanded in the passage which follows: the Son does the work of his Father: the gifts of life and judgment have been entrusted to the Son, so that the Son judges and gives life, to the honour of the Father; those who listen to the Son listen to the Father, and the dead respond to the voice of the Son as to the voice of the Father. It is not two gods doing the same work, but the one work done by the Father and the Son indistinguishably; this is, so to speak, a dynamic definition of the equality and the close relationship of the Son to the Father. The dynamic definition, in terms of action rather than being, reflects a Hebrew way of thinking rather than the static definition of classic Trinitarian theology.

Discernible in this is the relationship of the agent or *Shaliah* (one sent), familiar from Jewish writing of the time: the agent is like the one who sent him, ranking in honour as the principal himself, carrying out the mission of the principal with full responsibility and reporting back to the principal. In John the expression of this is that Jesus is the agent in all these ways; he is honoured as the Father (5.23), does the will of the Father (6.38); his teaching is not his own (7.16–17) and he seeks the glory of his Father (7.18; 8.54); he returns to the Father (13.3). Furthermore, the agent can appoint his own agents in his turn, as Jesus appoints his apostles (20.21). In the second edition it still remains open that the Son could be considered subordinate to the Father. Particularly this is the case because the Son is repeatedly said to be 'sent' by the Father, just as the disciples are 'sent' by Jesus as his agents.

In the third edition, however, any subordination is ruled out. Jesus is freely spoken of as 'the Lord'. There must be, in the use of this title, some opposition to the imperial Roman cult. The Roman emperor claimed a divine status as 'Lord', and was acclaimed all over the eastern Mediterranean area as Lord (see p. 361). There were altars to the Lord Emperor in every town, temples in big cities and, in the greatest centres, festivals of Rome and the Lord Emperor. This was a regular and important feature of life, an essential element in the cohesion of the empire. To this, John's usage stands in stark contrast. For Pliny, the governor of Bithynia in the early second century, the test case for Christianity was whether a suspect would proclaim

'The Emperor is Lord', or insist on confessing 'Christ is Lord'. This is the background to Paul's saying, 'No one can say "Christ is Lord" unless he is under the influence of the Holy Spirit' (1 Cor. 12.3). In the Greek version of the Bible 'the LORD' is used to render the unpronounceable divine name revealed to Moses, and it is in this strong sense that it is used of Jesus by John (4.1; 6.23; 20.2; 21.7), and above all in Thomas' confession, 'My Lord and my God' (20.28), which brackets the gospel at the end, as the Prologue bracketed it at the beginning. Most explicitly, there are three occasions when Jesus uses the divine title 'I AM', or 'I am He', the divine Name revealed to Moses. On two occasions this is recognized by 'the Jews' as a divine claim and rejected as blasphemy (8.28, 58); on the third, at the arrest of Jesus, the soldiers fall back and involuntarily do homage to Jesus (18.5–8).

In this Christology Jesus speaks of his own pre-existence (6.62; 17.5, 24) 'before ever the world was' or 'before the foundation of the world'. It is allied to the apocalyptic expression, 'Son of Man', prominent in the late-first-century apocalyptic writings of Judaism, *1 Enoch* and *4 Ezra*, where 'the Son of Man' is an eschatological figure based on the Son of Man in Daniel 7.13–14, a pre-existent and messianic figure, more than human, who will reveal all things at the end of time (1.51; 3.13–14; 6.62; 8.38). By the Man Born Blind Jesus is worshipped precisely as Son of Man in 9.35–8.

Allied to this expression of Jesus as the eschatological revealer-figure of the Son of Man is the presentation of Jesus as the Wisdom of the Father come down from heaven, inviting all to share the divine gifts. In the Old Testament the Wisdom of God is a divine figure, the means by which God creates the world and gives life (Prov. 8.30–5), the only-begotten of God (Wis. 7.22), the fountain of living water (Ben Sira 4.10–15), who invites all people to the banquet of Wisdom. In the same way, in John 6, Jesus fulfils the will of the Father and invites his hearers to share his banquet, promising life to those who believe in him and eat the true bread of life. In the same way Jesus claims for himself a number of titles or qualities which in the Old Testament belong to God: 'I am the Good Shepherd' (10.11, but God is the Shepherd of Israel), 'I am the light of the world' (8.12, but the Lord God is our light), 'I am the way, the truth and life' (11.25; 14.6). The highest quality of all, a sort of external expression of the divinity that cannot be fully experienced, is the 'glory' of God. In Jesus the disciples saw the ineffable glory of God, the glory as of an only-begotten Son (1.14), seen at Cana in the miracle of the wine (2.11). The final act of Jesus' life is his glorification (17.1–5), with the glory which he had before the world existed, and which was experienced by Isaiah in the Temple (Isa. 6, cf. Jn 12.41).

There is, therefore, a progressive deepening of the understanding of Jesus through the successive editions of the gospel, using different images drawn from the Old Testament tradition, to express Jesus as the Jewish Messiah, the emissary of the Father, and eventually the Son of Man who communicates the Wisdom and the glory of the Father.

5. Theological Themes in John

a. Judgment

Running through the gospel from beginning to end is the theme of judgment, in the human reaction to the revelation of Jesus. The sole criterion of this judgment is belief in Jesus, 'so that believing you may have life' (20.31). This is announced in the prologue by the strong dichotomy between those who accept and those who reject Jesus (1.11–12). It is strengthened by the constant use of legal terminology: true, false, judge, judgment, and, especially, witness. Jesus came to witness to the truth (18.37), and the final stress is on the witness of the Beloved Disciple (21.24).

There is a constant process of division: Jesus judges no one. Those who meet Jesus judge themselves by their reaction to Jesus, either acceptance or rejection, so that belief leads to life, refusal to believe leads to judgment. In the first meetings, the disciples tentatively accept Jesus, and then at Cana they believe in him and see his glory, while 'the Jews' refuse belief at the scene in the Temple (2.13–22), after which the evangelist again meditates on the mission of the Son and the judgment it evokes (3.11–21). The Samaritan Woman, after misunderstanding, gradually comes to accept Jesus, while Nicodemus remains undecided. Then there are scenes where we see the division continuing: over the healing at the Pool of Bethzatha, over the acceptance or refusal of the Bread of Life, the declarations of Jesus in the Temple, over the Man Born Blind, and the Raising of Lazarus. This is summed up in the conclusion of the ministry of Jesus. And so it continues in the Passion Narrative, until the final climax is reached at the rejection of Jesus by the Jewish authorities before Pilate.

The scene of the Samaritan Woman is enriched by the typical Johannine technique of misunderstanding and gradual advance. It is almost as though Jesus is deliberately misleading and provoking her; they are enjoying their sparring-match together! On one level he breaks the barrier between Jews and Samaritans, and shows her that he is a prophet by his penetrating knowledge of her marital circumstances. At another he introduces the ideas of living water, of worship in the Spirit, of feeding on the will of the Father, each deepening the religious revelation. As a third step he takes the dialogue to the level of the harvest of everlasting life (4.36–8).

Similarly the healing at the Pool of Bethzatha begins with a synoptic-type story of Jesus healing the sick, continues with blanket opposition and rejection from 'the Jews', and issues in reflection on judgment and the relationship between Father and Son (5.20–3, 27–9).

The Bread of Life discourse begins after two synoptic-type miracles which show Jesus as the true Moses, providing bread in the desert for his followers and crossing the sea (5.1–21). It continues with a discourse in the style of contemporary preaching, based on two texts, one from the Law and one from the Prophets (6.31 and 45), as Jesus teaches on two levels that the Son of Man is the Bread of Heaven as the Wisdom of the Father (6.32–49), and then that he is the Eucharistic bread of life (6.51–8). Again it finally issues in judgment, as some accept and some reject his words (6.60–70).

The scene of the Man Born Blind is again full of oppositions, the two levels of physical and spiritual sight or blindness, the irony of the understanding of the unlettered blind man and the incomprehension of the sophisticated 'Jews', the acceptance by the cured man or the rejection of the Son of Man, and judgment on those who claim to be followers of Moses (9.39).

Then the teaching ministry of Jesus is summed up by the parable of the Good Shepherd and his sheep, contrasting with the judgment on those who reject the witness of the works of the Father and of the scripture (10.25–30).

Finally the Raising of Lazarus gives a typical Johannine paradox: Jesus' gift of life to Lazarus brings him to his own death: the Judeans believe in Jesus and witness to him, while the Pharisees condemn themselves by judging that he should die (11.43–53).

The climax of the rejection of Jesus comes in the scene of the judgment before Pilate. It is arranged in a chiastic structure, a series of envelopes around the central, focal member:

a. 18.28 Jews demand Jesus' death   outside the Praetorium
 b. 18.33 Pilate questions Jesus   inside the Praetorium
  c. 18.38 Pilate declares Jesus innocent outside
   d. 19.4 Jesus crowned King   inside
  c' 19.4 Pilate declares Jesus innocent outside
 b' 19.8 Pilate questions Jesus   inside
a' 19.12 Jews obtain death   outside

In a carefully balanced scene, focused (in the centre) on Jesus being crowned king, Pilate three times declares Jesus innocent of the charges brought against him. They will not enter the Praetorium lest they be ritually defiled, but are happy to condemn an innocent man. Jesus is crowned as king and seated on the judgment seat. By proclaiming that they have no king but Caesar they deny the basic tenet of Judaism, that God is king; so condemning, they are condemned.

Even afterwards the judgment will continue through the witness of the apostles and the Holy Spirit. The discourses after the Last Supper are so placed according to the Hellenistic conventions of a great man making a final speech at a meal, to prepare his disciples for their future task of carrying on his work (cf. p. 97). The witnesses will be the disciples and the Spirit, who will witness about Jesus (13.21; 15.26–7), a witness who will bring the disciples into persecution just as Jesus was opposed and persecuted. The legal terminology is intensified in the four sayings about the Paraclete (14.16–17, 26; 15.26; 16.7–15), an 'advocate' who will carry on the work of Jesus by leading the disciples into full understanding of the message of Jesus, and will bring the hostile world to judgment (16.8, 11). As Jesus bore witness to the truth before Pilate (18.37), so the Paraclete will bear witness to the world (15.26).

b. The Spirit

The presence of the Spirit in the Johannine community comes to prominence in the final discourses, but it is hinted from the beginning. The witness of the Baptist (1.32–3, again the legal terminology) is that he saw the Spirit come down upon Jesus and 'remain' upon him, the verb which will be used so prominently of the mutual indwelling of Jesus, the Father and the disciples (Jn 14–15).

A special dimension of the Spirit comes to light in 2.22: the disciples will understand the significance of Jesus' saying only after the Resurrection. In the same way they will understand about living water only when the Spirit is given (7.39), so these sayings concern the Post-Pentecostal period of the Church. In the conversation with Nicodemus we are told about those who are born of the Spirit (3.5–8), and in the Bread of Life discourse that 'the Spirit gives life' (6.63). This brings into action the Old Testament sayings about the life-giving spirit of God, which brings the nation back to life (the vision of the Valley of the Dry Bones in Ezek. 37.1–14) and makes the desert bloom (Ezek. 47.1–12), or the promise of Joel 3.1–3, quoted by Peter at Pentecost (Joel 3.1–5) about the Spirit poured out on all mankind. In the Dead Sea Scrolls of Qumran this Spirit is seen as a purifying Spirit, a spirit of holiness and a Spirit of truth who will guide the community into deeper understanding (1QS 3.5–8; 4.21–2). This spirit will be given to the disciples at the 'Johannine Pentecost' in the upper room after the Resurrection (20.22), giving them a mission of forgiveness and authority.

In the third edition of the gospel the Spirit is 'another Paraclete' (14.16), bearing witness to Jesus, so a personal Spirit who takes the place of Jesus, like Jesus himself, sent by the Father in Jesus' name, and leading the community into all truth. These passages are therefore vital for the self-understanding of the community: the Spirit takes the place of Jesus as leader and helper. It is a major theme of the Final Discourses (especially John 15) that Jesus 'remains' among his followers. The trial, which was such a prominent feature of Jesus' mission, continues in the life of the Church. The whole of the Christian life is summed up in the gift of the Spirit (7.37–9 'Anyone who is thirsty should come to me and drink'), but especially in true worship in the Spirit (4.21–2) and in Baptism (1.33; 3.34) and the Eucharist (6.63).

c. The Hour of Jesus

The Johannine Passion Narrative is very different from those of the synoptics, both in its story and in its theology. There is no Agony in the Garden, no trial before the high priest and his council, no crowd-scene at Pilate's residence, and the scene at the crucifixion itself is very different. More important, the events narrated express a different image of Jesus. Some of these differences may be the result of different factual knowledge, but the vital difference is theological. Jesus is not so much the Suffering Servant as the triumphant Lord.

The synoptic gospels depict Jesus before the Jewish council as they decide on a charge to bring against him before Pilate. In John the decision to eliminate Jesus was already taken as a response to the acclaim which he received for raising Lazarus from the dead. It is couched in a rich irony, for the high priest, saying more than he knows, announces that it is better that one man should die for many. It is notable that in John the arresting party includes a detachment of soldiery, and the word *speira* normally describes a Roman unit of auxiliaries. Does this mean that Pilate had already been brought into the case and had supplied soldiers? The high priest's palace was adjacent to the governor's residence, and it would be only normal for the governor, on arrival from Caesarea, to discuss with the city authorities any possible trouble-spot.

Typically of the Johannine Christology, there is no scene of the Agony. John omits as much as possible of the humiliation of Jesus. There is none of the terror at his approaching torture, no mockery by the high priest's servants, no cry of anguish from the Cross. The agonized prayer of Jesus in the Garden is replaced by a reflection in 12.27–8, where Jesus, granting that his soul is sorrowful even to death, refuses to opt out, since his Hour of glorification has come, the Hour for which he came into the world, that moment for which the reader has been waiting since it was first mentioned at Cana. This is the Hour at which (Johannine ambiguity) he will be lifted up/exalted (3.14; 8.28; 12.32) to draw all people to himself. Consistently with this outlook, at the arrest of Jesus when they approach Jesus he declares his divinity by 'I am He' and the soldiers fall to the ground involuntarily in worship, and they cannot arrest him until he has given permission.

In the scene before Annas, which replaces the interrogation presided by Caiaphas, it is Jesus who calls the shots and dominates the scene, continuing his teaching in the Temple. In the same way, standing before Pilate Jesus again dominates the scene, and Pilate loses all authority by his weak and foolish remark, 'What is truth?', especially in a gospel in which witness to the truth has been of primary importance. Then the kingship of Jesus is confirmed by the final chiasmus of the trial (see p. 127), and again by Pilate's refusal to withdraw his proclamation of 'King of the Jews', having been told that it is a kingship not of this world. Jesus carries his own Cross as a standard of triumph; there is no mention of Simon of Cyrene.

At the crucifixion itself there are no mocking bystanders, no cry of dereliction, no agonising thirst. Jesus cries, 'I am thirsty' only to fulfil the scriptures. He is in perfect control as he commends his mother and the Beloved Disciple to each other, thus at his death forming the first Christian community. It is only when he is ready and has willed it that he gives up his spirit, or rather 'gives over' his Spirit, to the newly-formed Christian community.

An integral part of the Hour of Jesus is his exaltation at the Resurrection. In John's account we may divide this into three scenes:

1 Visits to the Empty Tomb. These are somewhat confusing in John, for the evangelist combines two oral traditions, the first about Mary Magdalen (20.1, 12–16), probably from the earliest edition of the gospel. This is interrupted by the visit of Peter and the Beloved Disciple, as always working in partnership (20.2–11). Peter has the authority of being the first witness to the grave-clothes, but the Beloved Disciple shows the sensitivity and love to appreciate their meaning.

2 Final dispositions for the disciples. These bring to completion the promises of the final discourses at the Last Supper, in four elements, corresponding to those promised by Jesus: the blessing of peace (as 14.27–8), the disciples' joy at seeing the Lord (fulfilling 16.21), the gift of the Spirit (as 15.26). The Spirit breathed upon the disciples must recall the creative gift of life breathed into Adam (Gen. 2.7) and Ezekiel's vision of the Valley of Dry Bones (Ezek. 37.1–14), which signifies the renewal of life for Israel. Finally, the authority with which Jesus sends them out as his own agents to complete his mission (Jn 17.18). The scene is repeated for the sake of Thomas, with a double new emphasis: first, his confession of faith provides a final bracket of the gospel, 'My Lord and my God', the fullest confession of the divinity of Jesus, linking back to the prologue; secondly the blessing on future believers, opening out the perspective to that of the whole Church and world.

3 The Meeting with Jesus at the Lakeside (see p. 117). Here Peter, tested and forgiven for his triple failure, stands for authority and perseverance till the death of martyrdom, while the Beloved Disciple stands for the enduring witness of the message of Jesus, giving the message to the author of the gospel, but going beyond it, to 'remain' until the Lord comes.

Further Reading

Brown, Raymond, E., *The Gospel according to John* (Geoffrey Chapman, 1971); still unsurpassed

Edwards, Ruth, *Discovering John* (London: SPCK, [2]2014): succinct and enlightening

Harrington, Wilfred, *John, Spiritual Theologian, the Jesus of John* (Dublin: Columba Press, 1999)

O'Grady, John F., *According to John* (Mahwah: Paulist Press, 1999): a brief
treatment of individual passages

Van der Watt, J., *Introduction to the Johannine Gospel and Letters* (London:
T&T Clark, 2007): model scholarly short textbook

Von Wahlde, U., *The Gospel and Letters of John* (Eerdmans, 2011): 3 volumes

9

The Parables of Jesus

To begin with, it is important to clear away two confusions:

1 A parable is not necessarily a story. The Hebrew term *mashal* (plural *meshalim*) denotes, more widely, any imaged saying, usually slightly riddling, demanding reflection to disclose its full meaning. Two important story-parables in the Old Testament are those of Jotham (Judg. 9.7–15) and Nathan (2 Sam. 12.1–4). Such imaged sayings are much used by country people everywhere. In Hebrew the Old Testament Book known as 'Proverbs' is entitled *meshalim*, e.g. 'The words of a tale-bearer are tasty morsels that go right down into the belly' (18.8). 'A stitch in time saves nine' is definitely a *mashal*. So is 'No one sews a piece of unshrunken cloth on an old cloak'. (Mk 2.21)

2 The saying in Mark 4.11–12, 'To those outside everything comes in parables, so that they may look and look again but not perceive', has often been interpreted to mean that Jesus used parables positively to prevent all but his chosen disciples from understanding his message. This frustrating interpretation is wrong. Mark is quoting Isaiah 6.9 as an explanation of the baffling fact that on the whole Israel failed to recognize the Messiah for whom the people had so long been

prepared. It is so used at the end of Jesus' public ministry in John for the same purpose (Jn 12.39–41), and again as the climax of refusal by the Jewish elders at the end of Paul's mission in Acts 28.26–7. By Mark it is sandwiched (see p. 73) between the parable of the Sower and its allegorical interpretation. Just as many of the events of Jesus' life were explained as being 'in accordance with the scriptures' (e.g. 1 Cor. 15.3–5), it was obviously generally seen as the reason why Israel had not responded: it was foretold in the scriptures that they would not do so. In addition, the expression 'outsiders' (literally, 'those outside') in Mark 4.11 occurs nowhere else in the gospels, but five times in Paul; it presupposes an already-formed community, such as existed in the early Church. Furthermore, the word 'mystery' occurs nowhere else in the gospels, but is a central Pauline term for the final revelation at the end of time, culled by Paul from Hellenism. The saying expresses more the missionary experience of the apostles than the situation of Jesus himself.

1. The Parables in Mark

Each of the synoptic gospels has a unique treatment for the parables. John has little use of parables; he gives only the image of the Good Shepherd in 10.1–18 (and perhaps the image of the Gateway in 10.9 should be regarded as a separate image) and the Vine and the Branches in 15.1–6. Characteristically, both of these are centred on the relationship of his followers to Jesus himself. All Mark's parables are describing the Kingdom/Kingship of God, for the centre of Jesus' message in Mark, from his first proclamation (1.15) onwards, is the pressing arrival of the Kingship of God. For this he has any number of images, the Seed Growing Secretly (4.26–9), the Mustard-Seed (4.30–2), the Watchful Servants (13.34), all about the arrival of the Kingship of God. In addition Mark gives us plenty of little *meshalim*, for instance in Mark 2 alone: 'it is not the healthy who need the doctor but the sick', images of the bridegroom, the unshrunken cloth, the wineskins, 'the Sabbath was made for man, not man for the Sabbath'; all of these teach about the coming of the Kingdom and the human reaction to it.

Mark has only two big story-parables, each of which is placed at a turning point of Jesus' message of the Kingdom, the Sower and the Wicked Tenants (4.1–9 and 12.1–9). The Sower comes (with other parables, forming Mark's parable-chapter) at the turning point when Jesus turns from instructing the crowds to instructing the disciples. Not only have the scribes accused him of being in league with Beelzebul, but even his own family have failed to understand him (3.20–35). Nevertheless, the parable finally displays the same optimism as the seed-parables (4.20–32) about the growth of the Kingdom: note the increasing yield, 30→60→100-fold, as opposed to Matthew's warning reversal of the figures to 100→60→30-fold!

The Sower is the only parable in Mark which is fully allegorised, an allegory which is probably not from Jesus himself (4.13–20). The 'lure of riches' has no place in the world of Galilean peasantry, and persecution was a feature of the early Christian community rather than of Jesus' own ministry. The meaning given to the principal image, the seed, as the Word is more familiar from the apostolic preaching than from Jesus' own ministry. In this case the parable, rather than being a warning against the obstacles to perseverance as a Christian, may well be Jesus' own reflection on his failure of his mission to the many and his turning to a few disciples who will produce much fruit.

The parable of the Wicked Tenants, in its turn, comes centrally in the Jerusalem ministry of Jesus, flanked by the crucial cleansing of the temple and rejection of Jesus' authority, and the group of four controversies which sums up the Jerusalem opposition to Jesus. It constitutes, therefore, an image or illustration of the bankruptcy of the leadership of Israel.

2. The Parables in Matthew

From a literary point of view the most striking difference between Matthew's and Mark's parables lies in Matthew's use of contrasts. In Mark the only two parables where contrast enters in, and then not strongly, are the Sower and the Mustard seed. Matthew substitutes the Tares for Mark's Seed Growing Secretly for the sake of the contrast between the good and the bad growth. Similarly, to the Q parable of the Great Feast (Lk. 14.8–11) he adds the Man without a Wedding Garment for the sake of the contrast. He adds to the end of Mark's Wicked Tenants the contrast of the nation which does yield fruit. Of all Matthew's 21 parables only three do not have any contrast (the Leaven, the Hidden Treasure and the Pearl). This is in line with Matthew's general stress on contrasting personalities; for him, contrast is a major vehicle of teaching: from the Infancy stories onwards Herod is set against the Magi, and Pilate against Caiaphas. Such contrasts are also a common feature of rabbinic example-stories.

Another rabbinic feature of Matthew's parables is their dramatic exaggeration. His sums of money are astronomical: the Unmerciful Servant's debt of ten thousand talents (18.24) would make Bill Gates flinch. To bury even one talent (perhaps a million pounds) in the ground (25.24) would make any Jewish flesh creep; it could hardly be counted 'a small thing'. The king surely overreacts when he sends his private army to burn the city of the reluctant guests (22.7), and again by his punishment of the Man without a Wedding Garment (22.13). Some might think the exclusion of the Foolish Virgins unChristianly severe (25.12), and the scene of the Last Judgment has an apocalyptic splendour (25.31–46).

A third notable feature is Matthew's expansion into allegory. Thus the meaning of the Wicked Tenants is made clearer by the detail that the son is thrown out of the vineyard before being killed (21.33), instead of his body merely being jettisoned after death (Mk 12.8): Jesus died outside the city. The burning of the city of the reluctant wedding-guests (22.7) may also be an allusion to the burning of Jerusalem when it was sacked by the Romans.

Theologically, too, there is considerable difference between Matthew and Mark. In Mark the crisis of decision is now, at the coming of the Messiah, although there is still some room for growth and some alert waiting to be done (13.32–7). In Matthew the waiting period is much longer: instead of Mark's 'late or midnight or cockcrow or early in the morning' (Mk 13.35), for him 'you do not know which *day* your Lord will come' (24.42). The importance of this period is, however, stressed by the expansion of Mark's concluding figure (Mk 13.33–6) into four separate parables, the Burglar, the Servant in Authority, the Ten Virgins and the Talents, before being summed up in the parable of the Sheep and the Goats. For Matthew this expansion makes it evident that there is still important opportunity for good works, and that it is on behaviour in the interval that disciples will be judged. A wedding garment (22.11) is a standard rabbinic figure for good works. More specifically, in accordance with Matthew's stress on the community, judgment will be given on forgiveness (18.23–35) and on care for the brothers and especially the 'little ones' (25.40, 45). The lesson of forgiveness is stressed also in Matthew's addition to the Lord's Prayer (6.14–15). Both aspects are underlined by the message of positively going to look for the lost sheep (18.12).

Perhaps the greatest stress of all in Matthew is on the coming judgment. Thus the Tares (13.24–30) replaces Mark's Seed Growing Secretly because it leads on to the harvest-time of judgment. It is confirmed by the Drag-net (13.47–8), forming a neat bracket for the two pairs of parables, the

Mustard-Seed and the Leaven, followed by the Hidden Treasure and the Pearl – obviously Matthew likes pairs of parables! The same lesson of final reward or disaster is painted by the Two Builders (7.24–7) and the repeated refrain of weeping and gnashing of teeth (8.12; 13.42, 50; 22.13; 24.51; 25.30).

3. The Parables in Luke

Luke's use of parables is considerably different from that of Mark and Matthew. Luke takes over all the story-parables of Mark (the two key-parables, the Sower and the Wicked Tenants, and also the Mustard Seed and the Watchful Servants). Others are shared with Matthew, so presumably from Q. Luke's own parables, however, are of a quite different stamp, not describing the Kingship of God nor pointing to its consummation in the final judgment. They are more concerned with recommending individual virtues; so they have been characterized as imperative rather than indicative.

Unlike Matthew's characters, which are black-and-white, rather wooden figures, either wholly good or wholly bad, Luke's characters are interesting in themselves, partly good and partly bad, people who do the right thing for the wrong reason, rascals who turn out well and sacred figures who turn out badly, often amiable rogues with whom the reader sympathizes. Thus, while Matthew has a parable of the Two Sons (21.28–30), who both change sides with no explanation, Luke has the story of the Prodigal Son (15.11–33), bursting with character in all three major actors: the Prodigal begins by insulting his father and turns out right in the end, rather to his own surprise; the Father sacrifices his own dignity out of affection for his son; the dutiful Elder Son ends up surly, inventing stories about his brother's loose women and refusing to join the celebrations. Luke seems to have taken Matthew's story and humanized it, enriching it with his own concern for repentance and forgiveness. Luke's stories also reflect a socially and economically more sophisticated world of distant travel, banks and investments. He also frequently employs the literary device of the anti-hero's (there are no heroes in Luke parables!) deliberative monologue, 'What shall I do now?' This occurs also in the Rich Fool (12.17), the Unjust Steward (16.3), the Unjust Judge (18.4), the Pharisee and the Tax-Collector (18.11, 13 – not deliberative but monologues). The same sort of dilemma occurs in the Good Samaritan (10.31–2), where the priest and the Levite face the dilemma of defiling themselves by touching the luckless and lifeless victim.

Another attractive feature of Luke's story-telling is his use of direct speech (14.17–19); everyone is chatting at every opportunity – and not only in the parables (compare the version of the Centurion's Boy in Matthew 8.5–13 and Luke 7.1–10).

Others of Luke's parables recommend the virtues which Luke sees to be essential: repentance (the Two Debtors, 7.36–50; the Barren Fig-Tree, 13.6–8), generosity to those in need (the Friend at Midnight, 11.5–10), the dangers of wealth (the Rich Fool, 12.12–21; the Rich Man and Lazarus, 16.19–31), humility (the Wedding Guests, 14.7–11; the Pharisee and the Tax-Collector, 18.9–14), persistence in prayer (the Friend at Midnight; the Unjust Judge, 18.1–8), the need to reckon the cost of discipleship (the Defendant, 12.58–9; the Tower-Builder, 14.25–30; the Warring King, 14.31–33).

We have seen that Luke is a master at building up a story (see p. 98). He turns the Markan incident of the Barren Fig-Tree into a parable. For other parables he seems to draw on hints in the Wisdom Literature, e.g. the Rich Fool from Ben Sira 11.18–20, the Unjust Judge from Ben Sira 35.14, the Wedding Guests from Proverbs 25.6–7. Even the Good Samaritan may lean on the story in 2 Chronicles 28.15.

4. The Origin of the Parables

Confronted with such a range of differences between the parables in each of the synoptic gospels, one is bound to ask to what extent all the parables come from Jesus. Was there a large pool of stories from which each evangelist selected a particular group, for the parables more than any other feature have their own particular characteristics in each of the three authors? Mark's parables are almost all built on simple agricultural images, stressing the pressing immediacy of the Kingship of God. Matthew takes over these parables, but adds others which stress the need to make use of the time before the final coming of Christ to serve the community, and which threaten punishment at the Last Judgment; he does this by the use of sharply contrasting pairs of people. Luke takes up many of the same parables from Q (and in Matthew and Luke the Mustard Seed is a Mark-Q overlap, see p. 45). He also adds other parables giving examples of virtuous or dastardly conduct, enlivened by brilliantly sketched character-representations.

In some cases (e.g. Matthew's Two Sons and Luke's Prodigal Son) it is possible to see how the evangelist may have developed a story to express his own special emphases in the gospel message. Each evangelist underlines different aspects of the teaching of Jesus. It is, however, difficult to see how all three sets of story-patterns which illustrate this teaching can stem from one mind.

Further Reading

Dodd, C. H., *The Parables of the Kingdom* (London: James Nisbet, 1935): magisterial

Drury, John, *The Parables in the Gospels* (London: SPCK, 1985): full of fresh insights

Hendrickx, Herman, *The Parables of Jesus* (London: Geoffrey Chapman, 1985): detailed examination of all the parables

Jeremias, Joachim, *The Parables of Jesus* (London: SCM, 1970): classic

10

The Historical Jesus

How much can we know about the historical Jesus? It has long been obvious that there are marked factual differences between the gospels, especially between the synoptic gospels and John. The early Christian writers, e.g. Augustine, accounted for this by comparing the gospels to a four-sided prism: the gospel-writers each have their own particular angle in telling the story, just as any good story-teller will have. Another difficulty is that it is immediately clear that the gospels are not written as a modern biography would be. Are they, indeed, biographies at all (see p. 40)? The word 'gospel' means 'Good News', and a record of the good news of Jesus Christ is not necessarily a factually accurate account according to the canons of modern historical writing. Each of the evangelists has his particular stress or accent, and underlines particular aspects of the message. Furthermore, the chronological framework of Jesus' life is quite uncertain. We do not even know how long his ministry lasted; the accepted duration is three years, but this rests simply on three mentions of the Passover festival; the duration of his ministry could have been considerably more or less. Mark narrates the confrontation in the Temple as the climax at the end of Jesus' ministry, whereas John puts it as an introductory statement of position. Matthew gathers the principal teachings of Jesus into five large blocks, beginning with the Sermon on the Mount (see p. 51); Luke gives many of the same teachings in a wholly different arrangement. Can we know anything for certain about the story of Jesus?

1. Oral History

The basic difficulty in seeking the historical Jesus is to separate event and interpretation. Every historian or narrator views events within a certain framework which must itself be interpretative; there is no such thing as an uninterpreted narration. The stories about any character, certainly any ancient character, are already interpreted history. The story of Jesus is viewed by the evangelists as Good News of salvation, and as the culmination of the history of Israel; it is presented within this category. The basic difficulty for the modern critic is to separate event from interpretation, for these are often presented side-by-side: for example, the death of Jesus on the Cross is fact, whereas the earthquake, the rending of the Temple veil and the sacred dead entering the Holy City (Mt. 27.50–3) are interpretation.

The information behind the stories is sound enough. Richard Bauckham has recently shown that the eyewitnesses to the events and stories have Palestinian Hebrew names (Bar Timaeus, Yair/Jairus, Mary of Magdala, Lazarus/Eliezar, Joseph of Arimathaea/Ramathaim) as opposed to the Hellenized names known for Jews of the Diaspora, where the stories developed into the gospels. This is a first indication of the fidelity of the stories to their source. Especially John knows Jerusalem in a detail increasingly confirmed by modern archaeology (the Sheep Gate, the Pools of Bethzatha and Siloam, the approach to Bethany). However, in oral cultures stories are handed down with their significance already built into the story. This is inherent in the nature of story-telling, even in modern times. The stories of Jesus are told in such a way that their significance will be clear against a biblical background. Four examples serve to illustrate this aspect of the story-telling.

1   In the Feeding of the Five Thousand (Mk 6.30–44) Jesus is depicted as the shepherd of Psalm 23 [22], feeding his sheep on pastures green, near restful waters. He is the prophet like Elisha feeding his followers in a desert place (2 Kgs 2.42–4). He is also the Messiah restoring

Israel, for the formation of hundreds and fifties is no random number but corresponds to the messianic army of the Dead Sea Scrolls, and the 12 baskets to the 12 tribes of the New Israel. Jesus is proleptically celebrating the Eucharist surrounded by his followers. This is not to say that no such event ever occurred, but simply that its significance is built into the description. Is it the same event as the Feeding of the 4,000 or not? In the same way, there are two stories of the miraculous catch of fish, one early in Jesus' ministry (Lk. 5.1–11), the other after the Resurrection (Jn 21.1–13): are they the same incident or different? Which is the correct position? It is impossible to strip these stories down to the 'bare facts' of the case.

2 The Calming of the Storm (Mk 4.35–41) and the Walking on the Water (Jn 6.16–21) are narrated in a way deliberately to recall Psalms 77[76].20; 107[106].23–30, making clear that Jesus is the divine power whose way led through the sea, saves them from the perils of the sea and leads them to the haven they desired. Luke omits the story of the Walking on the Water, perhaps because he considers it a duplicate of the Calming of the Storm. In Mark, the disciples are amazed and uncomprehending, whereas, in Matthew, Peter shows his faith by attempting to join Jesus on the water, and acknowledges Jesus as Son of God.

3 The Passion Story itself is as much a commentary as a narrative (see pp. 153–61). Both the Markan and the Johannine accounts, different as they are, accord with the statement of the Jewish historian, Josephus (*AJ* 18.3.64), that Jesus was sentenced to crucifixion by Pilate at the instigation of the Jewish authorities. How much did his followers, who all fled, know to have happened and how much did they reconstruct from what *must have* happened for the scriptures to be fulfilled? Both Markan and Johannine accounts correspond to the linguistic and stylistic traits of these authors and bring their very different theological emphases to a climax. At the same time, detail after detail is shown to correspond to scriptural expectation, even if Matthew 27.34 needs to change Mark's 'vinegar' to 'gall' (Ps. 68[67].22). Some of the details indicate that this is the Day of the Lord (the naked young man in Mk 14.52 from Amos 2.16; the darkness at noon in Mk 15.33 from Amos 5.20), other details present Jesus as fulfilling the prophecies of the Suffering Servant in Isaiah 53, or Psalm 22[21].

4 The extreme case is perhaps the Infancy Narratives, where Matthew and Luke share the basic facts (an endangered birth at Bethlehem

to a betrothed virgin from Nazareth) but develop the story in very different ways. Matthew gives a scriptural *midrash* or meditation to illustrate that Jesus is the Second David and the New Moses, receiving the homage of the Wisdom of the East, while Luke shows Jesus, prophesied champion of the oppressed, receiving the homage of the heavenly host and of indigent, hireling shepherds. Stories of the infancy of a great man are of a genre all their own, and may be expected to be coloured by hindsight from a later date.

2. The Early Debate

Critical questions about the gospels began to be raised from the time of the so-called Enlightenment. The early debate is conveniently summed up in *Von Reimarus zu Wrede*, the German title of Albert Schweitzer's great book published in English in 1910 as *The Quest for the Historical Jesus*. Reimarus claimed that the gospel picture of Jesus is a fraud, invented by his followers after his death, and that the genuine Jesus was an unsuccessful political revolutionary; this claim was so shocking that it was published only after Reimarus' death in 1768. Some decades later, in 1835, D. F. Strauss published his *Life of Jesus*, holding not that the disciples were attempting to deceive but that they were expressing by means of myths their belief that Jesus was the Jewish Messiah; this established a distinction between the historical Jesus and the mythical Christ of Christian belief. A further alternative was introduced by William Wrede in 1906 (see p. 83), the idea of the messianic secret: Jesus did not consider himself to be the Messiah, but was so considered by his disciples after his death; they invented Jesus' commands to silence and their own misunderstanding to pretend that Jesus had deliberately kept his claim to be Messiah secret, not allowing it to become publicly known. The same sort of claim was made by S. G. F. Brandon in 1967. He interpreted Jesus in terms of the political violence of his day, seeing Jesus as a Zealot, determined to throw off the Roman yoke. After he had failed and been executed his followers scrubbed out this violent aspect and reinterpreted him in a spiritual way.

Schweitzer himself, however, in summing up the debate, saw Jesus as an eschatological visionary. He was first expecting the eschaton, the end of the time, to arrive when he sent out his first missionaries. When they returned, he was forced to re-think his perspective; he then saw that he himself must go up to Jerusalem to move the wheel of history forwards. His vision was wrong, for the world did not come to an end: 'The wheel rolls onward, and the mangled body of the one immeasurably great man, who was strong enough to think of himself as the spiritual ruler of mankind, is hanging upon it still' (*The Quest for the Historical Jesus*, p. 365).

3. Bultmann and the History of Forms

A score of years later, in 1921, Rudolf Bultmann, perhaps the most significant figure in the whole debate, moved discussion forward with his *History of the Synoptic Tradition*. In this work he concentrated on the oral forms in which the tradition would have been handed on before it was committed to writing, attempting to distinguish the core of units of the gospel from the later accretions of myth. It is now generally agreed that he was too ready to ascribe both sayings and actions attributed to Jesus to the inventive genius of the early Church. The early Christians felt themselves to be under the inspiration of the Spirit of Jesus, and attributed their own expansions to Jesus himself. Even the parables of Jesus have been liberally enlarged in their gospel versions by allegorical meanings. Consequently in his 1926 book *Jesus* Bultmann declared that we can know almost nothing about the actual life of Jesus. Such was the authority of Bultmann, especially in Germany, that, with rare exceptions such as C. H. Dodd (*Parables of the Kingdom*, 1935; *The Apostolic Preaching and its Developments*, 1936), little attempt was made in the following decades to research into the historical Jesus. For Paul's theology, for instance, Bultmann maintained that it was necessary to know only *that* Christ was crucified, not why this occurred, nor any details of Jesus' life.

4. The New Quest for the Historical Jesus

After the Second World War, by a paper, *The Problem of the Historical Jesus*, published in 1954, Ernst Käsemann, himself a former pupil of Bultmann, re-opened discussion of the historical Jesus, asserting that knowledge of the historical Jesus was indeed possible, and could be controlled by certain criteria. Günther Bornkamm, similarly a pupil of Bultmann, followed closely with a great classic life *Jesus of Nazareth* (1956), whose significant second chapter is entitled 'The Man who fits no Formula', for Jesus transformed all the expectations of the Jews. Jesus accepted none of the standard titles of the Messiah and none of the standard expectations of such a figure. The subsequent period was devoted to developing these 'criteria', or, as they are more aptly known (R. H. Fuller), 'indices' – for they must be used with flexibility.

Among the suggested indices are:

- Double dissimilarity: a teaching to which nothing similar has been found in Judaism or in early Christianity, which shows that the saying has not simply been transferred from either of these, and should be attributed to Jesus. In itself this is far too demanding, for it would make Jesus 'a monster', not consonant with anything that went before, and without effect among his followers. Only a few sayings pass this very strict criterion, e.g. 'Leave the dead to bury their dead' (Mt. 8.22), a saying thoroughly shocking in Judaism, and of which there is no trace in subsequent Christian history. We would be able to know very little about Jesus.
- Multiple Attestation: a teaching which is attributed to Jesus in several different sources, e.g. Paul as well as the gospels (the words of Institution of the Eucharist, Jesus' prohibition of divorce), may be considered authentic.
- Coherence: if a saying has been established (e.g. 'my blood poured out for many' by Multiple Attestation) other sayings which cohere with it may be accepted. So, in this case, the saying shows that Jesus saw his death as serving many others, and so other sayings on service may be accepted: 'came not to be served but to serve'.
- Embarrassment: sayings which fail to express due reverence for Christ ('The Son of man does not know the day or the hour'), the submission of Jesus to John the Baptist, the death of Jesus as a despised criminal, would not have been invented by the early Church.
- Friend and Foe: items accepted by Jesus' enemies as well as his friends, e.g. exorcisms (since Jesus' opponents admitted them but attributed them to dependence on Beelzebul), are marked as true history.

Other weaker indices have been suggested and may be useful:

- Agricultural imagery: the imagery of Jesus' teaching, and especially the parables, in Mark is uniformly agricultural, but contrasts to that of the parables in Matthew and Luke.

- Aramaic background: sayings which betray translation from Aramaic may be from Jesus, e.g. 'his soul' is a clumsy translation of 'himself' in Aramaic ('whoever wants to save his soul…', Mk 8.35) – but other people than Jesus spoke Aramaic!

The difficulty of this approach was that there was no uniformity of application or of objective yield. It was used both to support and to combat the same positions, for instance on Jesus' approach to apocalyptic, to legal observance, to political revolt, to the Temple. The most destructive use of the method is associated with the Jesus Seminar, a group of university teachers who, from 1985 onwards, in a blaze of carefully engineered publicity, set about estimating the historical value of each of the sayings of Jesus in the four gospels and in the *Gospel of Thomas*, which was assessed as having at least as good historical value as the canonical gospels. Some 18 per cent of the sayings were estimated to originate with Jesus. After this the method could be used only with extreme caution. Even though the findings of the Jesus Seminar were fiercely sidelined by mainstream scholarship, they did at least show the dangers of excessive reliance on these criteria.

5. The Third Quest

In 1967 Geza Vermes, a Hungarian Jewish scholar who for a time embraced Catholic Christianity, initiated a new movement to re-evaluate the Jewishness of Jesus against the background of Jewish culture of the time. This was much assisted by the discovery of the Dead Sea Scrolls in the previous decade (of which Vermes has always presided over the standard English translation). Jesus began to be seen more specifically against the background of contemporary Jewish culture:

1. The charismatic Galilean rabbis attested by Jewish writings from the second century onwards. These *hasidim*, intensely pious rabbis who prayed frequently, had a warm and loving relationship to God as their *Abba* or Father, and through their prayers worked miracles of healing and rain-production not unlike the healings and nature-miracles of Jesus (Jesus, however, worked signs and wonders not by prayer but on his own authority).

2. The Dead Sea Scrolls show a society in eager expectation of an imminent eschatological Messiah. They reject the Temple and see the community as the true dwelling-place of God. They have many

spiritual traits which appear also in the teaching of Jesus (the processes of reconciling differences in Mt. 18.15–17), and many terms which reappear in the gospels: there will be a final battle between the sons of light and the sons of darkness. They see the coming of the Messiah similarly in terms of the actualisation and fulfilment of scriptural prophecy.

3   A third finding of Vermes was the understanding of the term 'son of man'. This expression occurs some 14 times in the gospels, being used always and only by Jesus of himself; it is his favourite self-designation. As Bornkamm showed, this is the only title that Jesus accepted; he never accepts the title of Messiah or any other. In the gospels the term must be viewed on two levels: it sometimes carries allusion to the Son of Man in Daniel 7.13 (e.g. Mk 8.38; 13.26; 14.62). Vermes, however, maintains that none of those passages stems from Jesus, and that this titular use is foreign to Jesus. Jesus himself uses the expression in the same way as certain second-century rabbis, as a delicate self-reference to avoid shocking or boasting. The *sense* of the Aramaic expression is 'a member of the human race', though in this case the *reference* is to the speaker. Thus Jesus would be making a delicate but insistent claim that the power of God was at work in himself (e.g. in Mk 2.10, 28) so that he can forgive sin or even change the Law, both divine prerogatives.

These aspects of Galilean culture form an attractive background to Jesus' ministry. He can be seen as a travelling holy man, bringing the presence of God to a reality by his charismatic ministry of exorcism, healing and teaching, embodying in his own self the rule of God or God's Kingship. The power of God is working through him to dispel suspicion, sin and sickness, to rescue from fear and alienation, to bring freedom from evil social and cultural constraints. He is never self-regarding and aims only to do the will of his Father. Not until the further developments of John does he make claims for himself, 'I am the light of the world', 'the Father and I are one.'

The Jewish background is prominent also in the work of E. P. Sanders, primarily a scholar of Judaism at the turn of the eras. He initiated the Third Quest for the Historical Jesus, basing his reconstruction not on sayings but on events, and especially the 'demonstration' by Jesus in the Temple, the culmination of Jesus' activity, demonstrating the barrenness of the cult and worship centred there. Sanders put forward a list of 'virtually unassailable' facts about Jesus:

1 He was baptized by John.
2 He was a Galilean, who preached and healed (not merely exorcized).
3 He called disciples, known as 'the Twelve' (their names are less certain).
4 He confined activity to Israel geographically.
5 He had a controversy over the Temple.
6 He was crucified by the Romans outside Jerusalem.
7 His followers continued his mission after an experience of Jesus after his death.

These are brute facts, and have been generally accepted. The crux is how they are to be read and interpreted:

1 John Dominic Crossan, a member of the Jesus Seminar, sees Jesus in the light of the Cynic philosophers. The Cynics were a group of philosophers, typified by Diogenes, who lauded and advocated poverty and dispossession. Many of the sayings of Jesus fit this attitude, and it is said that it would have appealed to the hard-pressed Galilean peasantry – if indeed they were hard-pressed in that agriculturally rich and fertile area. It would be a mistake to ally Jesus too closely to the philosophical movement, for the Cynics were overwhelmingly an urban phenomenon, whereas Jesus avoided cities and exercised his ministry in the countryside. However, many of the values seen in his teaching, and especially in Q (see p. 43), are advocating a simple, radical life, free from artificial social constraints.

   In much the same way, Marcus Borg sees Jesus as advocating a 'brokerless Kingdom', sweeping away the restricting ritual and machinery of the Temple and legal observance, advocating a straightforward, unmediated approach to God as a loving Father.

2 E. P. Sanders and N. T. Wright, each in his own way, see Jesus as positively restoring Israel, returning to the true meaning and purpose of the Law, and setting up the Twelve as leaders of a restored twelve tribes. The Temple was the symbol of the old Israel and its values, of which Jesus predicts that no stone will be left upon another. Jesus was indeed an eschatological prophet, seeing that the moment of God's renewal, the fulfilment of the prophecies, was pressing upon them and that he was the instrument of this. But he had not necessarily worked out all the modalities and implications of this situation, still less its future progress. He brought the judgment, the healing, the forgiveness and the blessing of God to reality. This has been expressed that

Jesus was the symbol of God (Roger Haight) or – in more technical language – the sacrament of God (Karl Rahner).

6. A Focus Example

To focus these rather general statements some examples may be given in Jesus' use of scripture, the basic commandment and revelation of God, which Jesus uses in a new way.

1 A basic pattern may be seen in Jesus' language. It is the balanced, gnomic language of a sage. What is remarkable is that there is always a four-member saying which includes an appeal to the basic meaning of scripture:

What God has joined let no man separate (Mk 10.9).
Man is not made for the Sabbath but the Sabbath for man (Mk 2.27).
Abandoning the command of God you exalt the tradition of men (Mk 7.13).
Give to Caesar what is Caesar's and to God what is God's (Mk 12.17).

2 In the discussion, Jesus also goes beyond the sense in which scripture had been taken, and in each case a further ruling of God's Law is implied; the unexpected sting being in the tail. The second member transcends the first meaning accepted by the interlocutor.
3 In each case a basic law is enunciated. The first ruling appeals to the biblical Creation account where man and woman are joined together, putting forward a teaching more demanding than the accepted practice. The second, similarly, where man is more important than the Sabbath (the reference to Genesis is clear in the Greek εγενετο= 'was made'). The third, in its Markan context, looks back to the important fourth commandment of the Decalogue, and the fourth saying looks back to the basic Law of Israel, 'you shall love the LORD your God above all things' (Deut. 6.5).

We have, therefore, in these instances consistent examples of the rhythmical, gnomic speech of Jesus the sage, using scripture to return to the basic teachings of Israel, renewing the Israel of God by clearing away the dead practices of contemporary interpretation.

Further Reading

Bauckham, Richard, *Jesus and the Eye-Witnesses* (Grand Rapids: Eerdmans, 2006)

Bond, Helen K., *The Historical Jesus* (London: T&T Clark, 2012): thorough, scholarly, in the *Guide for the Perplexed* series

Dodd, C. H., *The Founder of Christianity* (London: Collins, 1971): a classic work

Evans, Craig, *Life of Jesus Research* (Leiden: Brill, ²1996): an annotated bibliography

Johnson, Luke T., *The Real Jesus* (San Francisco: HarperSanFrancisco, 1996): well-informed, combative

O'Collins, G., *Jesus, a Portrait* (Maryknoll, NY: Orbis Books, 2008)

Stanton, Graham, *Gospel Truth?* (London: Fount, 1997): sparked by a new manuscript claim

Sanders, E. P., *The Historical Figure of Jesus* (London: Penguin, 1995): an authoritative resumé of the data

Vermes, Geza, *Jesus the Jew* (London: SCM, 1994): classic but tendentious

11

The Passion of Jesus

In the course of the presentation of the four gospels a number of comments have been made which contribute to an understanding of the passion narratives. However, so central is this story to the Christian message, and so diverse are the gospel accounts, that a special account of these central events is required. This will reflect a basic difference between the presentation by Mark and that of John, for the former (the basis also for that of Matthew and Luke) concentrates on the suffering and humiliation of Jesus which prepares its reversal in the vindication at the Resurrection, while the latter regards the event as a single moment, the Hour of Christ's triumph.

1. Preparation

Martin Kähler's characterization of Mark as 'a Passion Narrative with extended introduction' has been sufficiently explained (p. 85); the Passion is a threatening presence from the beginning of the narrative until its realisation. Similarly in John the 'Hour' of Jesus, a concept introduced already at the Marriage Feast at Cana, is a mysterious beacon which shines

Jerusalem at the Time of Jesus

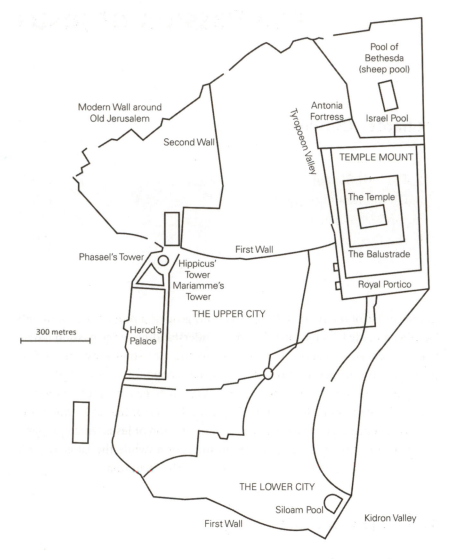

Pool of
Bethesda
(sheep pool)

Modern Wall around
Old Jerusalem

Antonia
Fortress

Israel Pool

Second Wall

Tyropoeon Valley

TEMPLE MOUNT

The Temple

First Wall

The Balustrade

Phasael's Tower

Hippicus'
Tower

Mariamme's
Tower

Royal Portico

THE UPPER CITY

300 metres

Herod's
Palace

THE LOWER CITY

Siloam Pool

Kidron Valley

First Wall

intermittently throughout the gospel of John (p. 129). Thus it is with widely different expectations that the reader of Mark and of John approaches the events themselves.

2. The Last Supper

We do not possess a full account of the Last Supper. Mark tells us only of two separate incidents, the identification of the Traitor and the institution of the Eucharist as a memorial of Jesus' gift of himself. John does not relate the institution of the Eucharist (perhaps because he wishes to postpone the institution of sacraments until after the death of Jesus), but does narrate Jesus' symbolic act of service in washing the feet of the disciples. He also includes the extended final speeches of Jesus outlining the meaning of his actions and the future of the community. Luke, the Hellenistic historian, also adds a much shorter farewell speech about the future of the community (cf. p. 98). These will fit easily into the cadre of a Passover meal, but do not demand it. There is a difficulty about the date: in Mark's account Jesus is crucified the day after celebrating the Passover; in John's account Jesus dies at the same time as the Passover lambs are being sacrificed (Jn 18.28; 19.36, cf. Exod. 12.46). At the beginning of John's presentation of Jesus, John the Baptist has introduced Jesus as 'the Lamb of God' (Jn 1.29); now we see the full sense of that title.

If John's timing is correct, the Last Supper occurred on the day before the Passover (it must be remembered that in Judaism the day *begins* in the evening, that is, the solemn meal occurs *the evening before* the day of rest). In this case Jesus used a non-passover solemn meal to make his own Passover. The Jewish Passover celebrated God's covenant with Israel on Sinai; now Jesus makes his own Passover to institute the new covenant prophesied by Ezekiel and Jeremiah. This will fit – not without difficulty – with the preparations for the meal (Mk 14.12). On the other hand, it solves a difficulty, that otherwise both Jewish and Roman authorities treated the sacred day as an ordinary day for meetings, a trial and an execution.

3. On the Mount of Olives

The synoptic gospels tell the story of the Agony in the Garden ('Gethsemane' means 'garden of olives'; Luke avoids the name, as he avoids other Semitic names which might puzzle his Hellenistic audience). Mark gives a picture of Jesus distraught by fear but loyally accepting the will of his Father. The scene is made more intense by the triple repetition of Jesus' prayer and of his rebuke to the disciples. The failure of the disciples (cf. p. 76) perhaps reaches its high point in the flight of the young man, naked, which also indicates the fulfilment of Amos' prophecy of the Day of the Lord (Amos 2.16: 'On that Day even the bravest of warriors will run away naked'). Matthew slightly tones down the horror of Jesus' expectation. Luke further diminishes this horror, depicting a scene where Jesus is firmly in control, praying a single time only, kneeling in the attitude of Christian prayer and providing an example to the disciples of earnest prayer in a time of trial (Lk. 22. 40, 46). John has no account of such a prayer in the Garden, but puts a Johannine version of the prayer in the mouth of Jesus well before the Last Supper (12.27–8). The Letter to the Hebrews (5.7) invokes also this intense prayer before the Passion, 'aloud and in silent tears', which suggests that there were several versions of the prayer Jesus must have made before his Passion.

In the synoptic gospels the account of the arrest concentrates again on the blood-chilling duplicity of the traitor (Mk 14.45, cf. v. 20). It is significant that in Matthew 26.49 Judas calls Jesus 'Rabbi', though elsewhere the disciples invariably address Jesus as 'Lord'; Judas is no longer a disciple. Luke, the *scriba mansuetudinis Christi* (p. 108), is careful to state that Jesus heals the servant's severed ear. In John, however, the scene has an entirely different atmosphere. Jesus, undimmed by any apprehensive prayer, controls the situation. He interrogates his captors, and when he responds to them with the divine name, 'I am' (18.5, repeated thrice for emphasis), they involuntarily fall back and fall to the ground in worship. It is only when he has signified his consent that they can arrest him. An important historical detail from John is the presence of a Roman military detachment, which indicates that the Roman authorities were already involved; had the high priest already alerted the governor?

An important element of interpretation is provided by Matthew, fulfilment of scripture (26.31, 54). Throughout the account of the Passion occur details which accord with the scripture, especially with Isaiah 53 and Psalm 22. At least some of these are artificial: so Matthew 27.34 changes Mark's narcotic with myrrh (Mk 15.23) to a poison of gall in order to fulfil Psalm 68.22. How much of the details did the disciples – who all fled – know, and how much did they supply from what *must have* happened in order to fulfil the scriptures? In other words, how much is a historical record of what happened, and how much an interpretation of the events, pointing out that the crucifixion accorded with God's will revealed in the scriptures? Is the spitting on Jesus a record of what happened or an allusion to Isaiah 50.6? Do the two others crucified with Jesus merely fulfil 'he was numbered among evil-doers' (Isa. 53.12), the division of his clothes merely fulfil 'they divide my clothing among them, cast lots for my robe' (Ps. 22[21].19), the last words of Jesus fulfil Psalm 22[21].2 in Mark and Matthew, or Psalm 31.6, in Luke?

4. The Trial of Jesus

a. The Legal Context

In the client-states on the edges of the Roman Empire normal government was left in the hands of the local rulers, in this case the High Priest. There is no external evidence that a formal Sanhedrin existed at this time, though of course a High Priest might gather advisers around him ('sanhedrin' means 'gathering'; it is used of 'gatherings' also in the plural, e.g. Mk 13.9). There was no question of a formal sentence of death by any Jewish court, for capital punishment was reserved to the governor (Jn 18.31, backed up by inscriptional evidence). Even the governor need hold no formal trial, for only Roman citizens had formal rights; on provincials the governor could merely use his own discretion. Josephus gives us the framework, that Jesus 'was condemned to the cross by Pontius Pilate at the instigation of the leading men among us' (*Antiquities of the Jews*, 18.3.64). Legally, the responsibility lay with the governor.

Opinion is divided on whether Pilate was a good or a bad governor. Josephus and Philo attempt to pin on his maladministration the blame for the rebellion of the Jews against the Romans in 66AD, thirty years after Pilate was withdrawn from Judea. They attempt to blacken his character by telling stories about him which could have other explanations; any occupying foreign governor is a potential target for abuse from his subjects. An argument in his favour is that Rome left him in charge for ten years instead of the usual two years. During all that time Caiaphas was High Priest, again an exceptionally long tenure of office, which argues stability and contentment. Pilate came up to Jerusalem only during moments of potential tension, and, while there, his residence was next to that of Caiaphas. They must have worked together! Hence the significance of the Roman detachment at the arrest of Jesus (Jn 18.3).

b. The Jewish Hearing

We know almost nothing about Jewish procedures at this time. Evidence from Jewish writings at least a century later is worthless, for everything was changed by the Sack of Jerusalem in 70AD, in which the Sadducees, who had been in charge of the Temple, were wiped out. The hearing before Caiaphas is largely Mark's composition.

- It has a similar pattern to the hearing before Pilate; the two fit together.
- It is a classic Markan 'sandwich' (see p. 73): Peter – Jesus – Peter, contrasting the steadfastness of Jesus with the timidity of Peter.
- Like many of the incidents in Mark's Passion narrative, it is build on a 'triple', in this case the three accusations (vv. 56, 58, 60).

The point of Mark's narrative is Jesus' self-identification in v. 62 as Son of God, Messiah, and most of all Son of Man, with allusion to the glorious Son of Man in Daniel 7.13. At last, in his position of prisoner, Jesus makes known his true status by his claim to share God's mobile throne, alluding to the vision of God's awesome throne in Ezekiel 1. To this claim the High Priest cannot but react with a horrified cry of 'Blasphemy!'

Matthew's presentation of the scene follows Mark's closely; perhaps his most significant change is to note that after his denial Peter wept 'bitterly'. Luke rearranges the timing, filling the night-hours with Peter's denial at the fireside and the mockery of Jesus by his guards, though the taunting of Jesus as a prophet fits better after his claims to be the Messiah than before. Luke dispenses with Caiaphas and with the false witnesses, presenting more a kangaroo court where they ask Jesus directly the two questions: whether he is the Messiah and whether he is the son of God. This suffices for a decision to take him off to Pilate.

John's version of the Jewish hearing is radically different. No decision is needed, for it has already been taken long ago (11.53). It is replaced by a confrontation with the powerful Annas, father-in-law of Caiaphas, at which Jesus stands his ground and leads the interview, merely continuing his teaching – to the discomfiture of Annas. That this scene with Annas is the replacement of the Caiaphas scene is shown by Peter's denial, which now sandwiches this scene.

c. The Trial before Pilate

The hearing before Pilate, as recounted by Mark, is hardly an account of a trial: Jesus' accusers seem (v. 12) to have called Jesus 'king of the Jews'. Pilate puts one question to Jesus, to which he receives no answer. He is convinced of Jesus' innocence and briefly turns all his attention to an attempt to release him. Apart from the silence of Jesus, fulfilling Isaiah 53.7 (as Mk 14.60, both with the characteristic Markan double negative), the purpose of the scene is to show the determination of the crowd, egged on by the chief priests, to have Jesus crucified. After the single question, all attention is concentrated on the contrast with Barabbas. There is no evidence elsewhere in the Roman world for such an amnesty; one can only say that it might be a gesture towards celebrating the festival of the liberation of the Hebrews from slavery in Egypt.

To the Markan account Matthew adds details which increase the guilt of the Jewish crowd:

- Jesus is twice called 'Christ' or 'Messiah', thus relating him to the promises to Israel (Mt. 27.17, 22).
- Pilate's wife's dream stresses the enormity of the deed, for a dream is a favoured Matthean indication of the divine will (2.19, 22).
- By washing his hands Pilate attempts to slough off the guilt by a biblical gesture prescribed by Deuteronomy 21.6–8.
- The crowd, on the verge of a riot, is described as 'the people' (v. 25), a term which indicates the sacred People of God. However, against the anti-Semitic conclusion that this crowd took on national blood-guilt for all time, it must be said that this acceptance was amply fulfilled 'on us and on our children' by the horrors of the siege of Jerusalem in 70AD.

As Matthew stresses details from a Jewish viewpoint, so Luke includes several details from his Hellenistic viewpoint:

- He introduces (in vv. 2 and 5) a charge of sedition, which really would interest a Roman governor, though this charge is swiftly buried under the issue of kingship.
- He insists repeatedly that Pilate can find no grounds against Jesus (vv. 4, 14, 22), finally underlining that 'their voices prevailed' and that Pilate 'gives him over to their wishes'. Luke is always eager to show that there is no hostility between Christianity and Rome (see p. 165). This is perhaps the reason why he omits the mockery of Jesus by the Roman soldiers given in Mark 15.16–20. Pilate's half-heartedness is shown by his order that Jesus should merely be 'whipped', a corrective punishment (v. 16), much milder than the brutal flogging which preceded crucifixion.
- Through the mention of 'Galilee' (v. 5) he neatly inserts the incident with Herod Antipas, ruler of Galilee. Here again (see pp. 94, 164)

Luke is using parallels to show that Paul continues the life and mission of Jesus, for Paul is examined first by a Roman governor, then by a ruler of the Herod family (Acts 25–6). Typically, also, the link created through Jesus effects peace and reconciliation between enemies.

As elsewhere in the Passion Narrative, however, John wholly re-structures the trial before Pilate (see p. 127), making it at the same time a climax of Jesus' triumph and a dreadful climax of self-destruction by the Jewish leaders. Before Jesus, crowned as king and enthroned on the judgment-seat, the Jewish leaders, thinking they are condemning Jesus, in fact condemn themselves: 'we have no king but Caesar'. If God is not king, the Jewish faith has no purpose.

5. The Crucifixion

The Roman torture of crucifixion was too familiar and too gruesome to bear description; the material details are not given to us, for the evange-lists concentrate on the interpretation of this final event. Hence, despite traditional representations, we do not know the shape of the cross nor how Jesus was fixed to it. We do not know whether the Romans yielded to Jewish susceptibilities by allowing him a scrap of clothing. We know only that during the siege of Jerusalem the Roman soldiers fixed the escapers to the gibbets in different ways to amuse themselves and as a dread warning to onlookers (Josephus, *Jewish War*, 5.11. 451).

This interpretation focuses on various aspects:

1 It is the Day of the Lord (see pp. 56, 292). This is shown by the darkness at noon – a theological rather than a meteorological observation (Mark 15.33) – the rending of the veil of the Temple, the earthquake and the entry of the sacred dead into the Holy City (Mt. 27.51–3).
2 In Mark's and Matthew's accounts Jesus' last words form the intonation of Psalm 22, which leads from the distress and humiliation of God's servant to the exultant worship of God and the vindication of the sufferer. Other allusions to this psalm show its importance: the mockery (v. 8–9, quoted in Mt 27.39 and 43), the thirst (v. 16, in Jn 19.28), the division of the clothes (v. 19, in Mk 15.24).
3 The ironical acclamation by the centurion (Mk 15.39), the first recog-nition of Jesus as 'son of God', signifies that the opening to the gentiles begins at Jesus' death.

4 For Luke the whole scene is an occasion of conversion and repentance (cf. p. 108–9): first, the mourning of the women of Jerusalem in biblical terms (Lk. 23.27–31), then Jesus' forgiveness of his executioners (v. 34, an uncertain text), then the conversion and welcome of the 'Good Thief' (v. 39–43), and finally the general repentance (v. 48).

5 For John this is the triumph of Christ. Jesus carries his own cross, unassisted by Simon of Cyrene (Jn 19.17). He is officially declared King by Pilate in the three world-languages, despite the protests of the Jewish leaders (v. 19–22). He completes his work by forming the first Christian community in entrusting his mother and the beloved disciple to each other. Only then, when he has declared, 'It is complete', does he voluntarily give over them his Spirit (v.30).

Further Reading

Senior, Donald, *The Passion of Jesus in the Gospel of Mark* (Wilmington: Michael Glazier, 1984), *Matthew* (1985), *Luke* (1989), *John* (1991): a detailed treatment of the facts and theology of each account

Wansbrough, Henry, *The Passion and Death of Jesus* (London: Darton, Longman & Todd, 2003): a briefer account

12

Acts of the Apostles

The title of this second volume of Luke's writing is controversial. It is not 'the Acts of the Apostles', for it is neither all the acts nor acts of all the apostles. There is no record of the wide apostolate of most of the Twelve, nor any record of how Christianity was brought to such important centres as Antioch and Rome, let alone Alexandria or India. One convenient chapter-division is:

1–7   The early, ideal community at Jerusalem.
8–15   The early missions and the opening to the gentiles.
16–28 Paul carries the gospel to 'the ends of the earth'.

The plan is given in Acts 1.8, 'You will be my witnesses not only in Jerusalem but throughout Judaea and Samaria, and indeed to the ends of the earth', for Rome, the capital of empire, is known in Jewish documents (e.g. the *Psalms of Solomon* 8.15) as 'the ends of the earth'.

Luke prefaces this second volume with an introduction similar to but shorter than the preface of his first volume (see p. 93). Like other such pairs of volumes in the ancient world, there is a slight overlap or interlock – Raymond Brown calls it a bridge (see p. 104) – for both volumes describe the Ascension and the return of the disciples to Jerusalem (Lk. 24.50–53;

Acts 1.6–12). The two scripts were separated only in the second century, when the first scroll was hived off to join the other gospels. There is, however, a major difference between the two works, Luke and Acts, in that the gospel is dependent for its outline and much of its content on Mark's gospel and, to a lesser extent, on Q. Where Luke is independent of Mark, for example in the Infancy Narratives, the Resurrection Appearances and a large number of Parables, he spreads his wings remarkably and shows his own style, versatility and theology. For Acts it is quite unclear whether he is dependent on any written source.

1. The Purpose and Genre of Acts

a. A Hellenistic History?

Is it factually reliable? Acts shows an impressive knowledge of the highly varied constitutions and magistrates of cities (see p. 96) and details of travel between them. But how much did he know about Paul? There are also passages where the author narrates in the first person, 'we', implying that he was travelling with Paul. The author who stands behind this 'we' claims to have travelled with Paul on the part of his second missionary journey from Troas to Philippi (16.10–17), and to have joined Paul again when he sails from Philippi to Palestine some years later (20.5). The intervening gap was the period of perhaps seven years, when most of Paul's important letters were written, a gap which might explain why Acts never mentions the letters. Such a partial companion might well have had a different viewpoint on many matters, and thought that Paul's worries about observance of Jewish Law were now less important than the relationship between Christians and Rome. Attempts to show that the use of 'we' was a literary convention for a travel account have now been abandoned, and the simplest explanation is that the author was at least using an eyewitness account. But there are also elaborate and dramatic set-pieces which contain considerable improbabilities: why in 16.21–39 does Paul not disclose his Roman citizenship earlier and so spare himself the flogging? How does it happen that the earthquake merely shakes free the bonds of the prisoners without harming them? Why does the gaoler think he will be held responsible? Why are the magistrates unaware of the earthquake? In 14.19–20 Paul is left for dead and then strolls back unconcernedly into the city and sets off on his travels. Such dramatic scenes are, however, fully in accord with the conventions of the time. Quintilian, the Roman arbiter of style, encourages an author to include without specific evidence events which always occur in particular circumstances, such as burnings, rape and slaughter at the storming of a city.

Another important difference from modern history-writing is that in historical writing of the time, by convention, a speech in the mouth of a chief character might be used to express the author's view of the issues rather than what was actually said at the time. The author's commentary is put in the form of this speech; the speech records what *should have been* said, or *might have been* said, rather than what actually was said. Thus the speech of Stephen before his martyrdom (7.2–53) sums up the history of Israel as an interpretation of the second failure of Jerusalem to accept the salvation promised to Israel. On the other hand, students were trained to write in imitation of the style of particular persons. Luke's account of Paul's speech at Athens (Acts 17.24–31) has many similarities to Paul's own natural theology in Romans 1, and his conventional farewell speech at Miletus (20.18–35) chimes in well with his letters.

b. An Apologia?

A recurrent element in Acts is the attempt to show the compatibility between Christianity and the Roman Empire. Everything stresses the friendly relationship between Rome and the new movement, and the approval of Roman authorities for Christianity. This is in sharp contrast to the Book of Revelation, in which Rome, and particularly the worship of the Roman Emperor, is the great enemy. In Acts the first gentile convert is a Roman centurion (10.1–48). The proconsul of Cyprus, 'an extremely intelligent man', became a believer (13.7, 12). The magistrates at Philippi are embarrassed and frightened at having flogged and imprisoned Paul and Silas, both Roman citizens (16.37). The proconsul of Achaia will have nothing to do with accusations against Paul, asserting that Roman law has nothing to say on the matter (18.12–17). The Asiarchs, priests of the cult of Roma at Ephesus, are friends of Paul and send him helpful private messages (19. 30–1). Finally, Paul is plucked from persecution at the hands of hostile Jews by a fair-minded and well-disposed Roman tribune, who labours tirelessly and vigorously to ensure that Paul escapes their malicious and underhand plots and ambushes. Paul, repeatedly declared innocent by two Roman governors, nevertheless appeals to the emperor himself, and has no charges brought against him at Rome. Since Acts was clearly written for a

Christian audience, it is more likely that it seeks to persuade Christians that they have nothing to fear from Rome than to persuade Rome that it has nothing to fear from Christianity.

An important issue raised by this question is whether Luke created Paul's Roman citizenship in order to explain his journey to Rome. Paul himself nowhere mentions his citizenship in his letters, even when trying to win the confidence of the Romans (Romans 1.1–15; 15.14–16.20). On the contrary, he was flogged three times by Roman lictors (2 Cor. 11.25), which would have been utterly illegal if he were a Roman citizen. A handful of Jews are known who were also Roman citizens, but none of these were observant Pharisees, as Paul was. Further legal difficulties are his appeal to Rome despite his acquittal, and his seeming freedom while a prisoner in Rome – *custodia libera*, a condition known only of Herod Agrippa (Josephus, *Antiquities*, 18.161–238), a Head of State, so an entirely different situation. The legal situation presupposed by the narrative is impossibly contorted.

c. A Succession Narrative?

C. H. Talbert in 1974 has used the parallels between the two volumes to suggest that, in a period of controversy between different interpretations of Christianity, Luke intended to show that Pauline Christianity is the true successor of Jesus, just as Moses passed on his leadership to Joshua (Numb. 27.15–23; Josh. 1.1–5) and Elijah passed his cloak and spirit to Elisha (2 Kgs 2). In this scheme there are two successive eras: by the presence of the Spirit in the disciples, the era of the apostles corresponds to the era of Jesus. This can be plotted in detail:

Luke	Acts
1.1–4 Preface dedicating to Theophilus	1.1–5 Preface dedicating to Theophilus
3.21 Jesus praying at his baptism	1.14 Disciples praying in Upper Room
3.22 Spirit descends in visible form	2.1–13 Spirit descends in visible form
4.16–30 Jesus' opening sermon: Prophecy fulfilled, Jesus rejected	2.14–40 Peter's opening address: Prophecy fulfilled, Jesus rejected
5.17–26 Lame man healed by Jesus	3.1–10 Lame man healed in Jesus' name
5.29–6.11 Conflict with religious leaders	4.1–8.3 Conflict with religious leaders

7.1–10 Centurion invites Jesus, finds faith	10 Centurion invites Peter, finds faith
7.11–17 Dead raised to life, sits up	9.36–43 Dead raised to life, sits up
9.7–9 Death of John, witness to Jesus	8.60 Stephen's death, witness to Jesus
10.1–12 Mission of 70 to gentiles	13–20 Missions of Paul to gentiles
9.51–19.28 Jesus journeys to death in Jerusalem	19.21–21.17 Paul journeys to death in Jerusalem
13.33 His awareness of impending death	21.23 His awareness of impending death
22.21–36 Jesus' farewell discourse	20.18–35 Paul's farewell discourse
22–3 Jesus' trials (Sanhedrin, Roman, Herod)	23–26 Paul's trials (Sanhedrin, Roman, Herod)
Jesus slapped by High Priest's servant	Paul slapped at high priest's command
Roman thrice declares innocent	Romans thrice declare innocent
Jews cry 'Take him away'	Jews cry 'Take him away'.

The parallels are unmistakable; this parallel pattern is confirmed by Luke's use of parallels in the Infancy Narratives (see p. 94), and the parallel between Peter and Paul (see below), but the purpose is wider than contemporary controversy. The major importance of this theme is that the life of Jesus is continued in the life of the Church. The Good News of Jesus is not merely proclaimed by the apostles, but may be seen being continued in the life of the apostolic community, inspired and led by the Spirit of Jesus.

d. Historical Novel?

In 1987 Richard I. Pervo suggested that Luke uses the literary techniques of contemporary novels to make his serious instruction also entertaining, fulfilling Horace's adage, 'He who joins utility with charm, entertaining at the same time as edifying the reader, carries off the prize'. Pervo lists 33 episodes of exciting and miraculous escapes (e.g. 5.19; 12.4–19; 16.25–6), imprisonment, martyrdom, mob-scenes, trials and shipwreck. Plentiful use is made also of irony, mockery and burlesque (e.g. 14.8–18). All of these are standard features of novels of the period. Although this thesis has been heavily criticized, it must be remembered that contemporary historians (e.g. Polybius) allowed a certain amount of embellishment for 'dramatic history'. Luke may have used the same techniques.

2. The Speeches of Acts

A large proportion of Acts consists of speeches, principally by Peter and Paul, but on one important occasion by Stephen. In accordance with the conventions of Greek historiography, it is through the speeches that we hear the author's comment and understand how he sees events; the speeches are therefore an essential expression of Luke's theology and view of events.

a. Peter's address to the crowd at Pentecost (2.14–39)

This speech sets the whole tone for the book, concentrating principally on two themes:

- Fulfilment of scripture. The speaking in tongues is explained as the fulfilment of Joel 3.1–5, further stressed by the addition of 'In the last days'; this is the sign ofthe arrival of the eschatological outpouring ofthe Spirit. Then the resurrection is presented as the fulfilment of Psalm 15 (14).8–11, and the exaltation of Christ as the fulfilment of Psalm 110 (109).1. Luke is here using the contemporary *pesher* method, familiar to us from the scripture commentaries of the Dead Sea Scrolls, in which current events are explained as the fulfilment of the prophets (see p. 8).
- Universality of salvation: all who call on the Name of the Lord will be saved, even those who are far away (2.21, 39). The theology ofthe Name ofthe LORD, denoting the full power of God, is important in the Old Testament, especially Ezekiel 36.20–23. Now an important referential shift has taken place: God 'has made this Jesus both Lord and Christ' (2.36). The name of the LORD is now overwhelmingly 'the name of the Lord Jesus' (1.21; 7.59; 8.16; 11.17, 20; 15.11; 16.31, etc). The Name, patronage and power of the Lord Jesus stand in the place of the Name, patronage and power of the LORD God. Christians are those over whom the Name of Jesus or of Christ has been called.

This first of these themes prepares for one of the major focus points of the Acts. The early chapters narrate the second chance given to Jerusalem to embrace the fulfilment of the promises, a chance that is again rejected. It comes to an end with the martyrdom of Stephen (8.3). Then begins the expansion of the community according to the plan laid down already in 1.8 (Jerusalem → Judaea and Samaria → the ends of the earth). It is initiated by two highly significant moves.

- First the apostle to the nations is brought into the community by a divine intervention, the call on the Road to Damascus. The importance of this incident is underlined by its triple repetition (the story, its repetition to the Jews in the Temple, its repetition to the gentiles at Caesarea).

There are minor differences between the three accounts given by Acts. These are compatible with the historian's ideal of *variatio*. There should be slight variations in each telling of a story, accommodating it to the audience. Hence to the Jews in the Temple Paul stresses his Jewish upbringing and Ananias' orthodoxy (21.3-5, 12). In the Hellenistic court-scene at Caesarea he inserts a classical proverb (26.14). Other variations in 'who sees what' are different ways of expressing that Paul's companions were aware of but did not fully share in the experience. The basic story is full of allusion to the conversion of Heliodorus in 2 Maccabees 3.24-36, the conversion of the persecutor of God's people who is struck down and healed, to become a devoted adherent and messenger of the faith. Another open question is the relationship of this incident to that described by Paul himself in 2 Corinthians 12.2-4.

- Next the first gentile, Cornelius, is admitted to the community. Again the importance of the event is underlined by its triple repetition (the story, its repetition to the community by Peter, its summary by Peter at the Council of Jerusalem) and by its heavenly endorsement (the Spirit comes down on Cornelius and his household before Peter has finished speaking to them).

The scene of the Council of Jerusalem is difficult to interpret. We have two partial accounts, one from Luke (in Acts 15) and one from Paul (in his letter to the Galatians 2). At the very least the two accounts stress different aspects. According to Acts the dispute about accepting gentiles arose at Antioch and Paul went up to Jerusalem to settle the matter. There, after speeches by Peter and James, the participation of the gentiles was accepted, and four conditions were imposed on them, four measures to avoid upsetting the Jewish Christians. These conditions are given in a letter addressed not to the whole Church but to a particular comer of the Church; it does not fit well here, and Luke may have added it. In Paul's own account Paul went up to Jerusalem, seemingly on his own initiative, pointedly taking with him Titus, an uncircumcised gentile, just to check that he was doing right. There he spoke with the leaders of the Church, and a division of spheres of activity was decided, Paul to the gentiles, Peter to the Jews. There is no account of a full meeting of the Church. A dispute with Peter at Antioch about sharing between Jews and gentiles is *narrated* after this. If in fact the event occurred *before* the meeting at Jerusalem the two accounts fit together much better. (In English translation the verbs of Galatians 2.11 and 14 are usually put in the aorist, but the Greek could equally well be translated by the English pluperfect, 'When Cephas *had come down* to Antioch, I *had opposed* him' and 'I *had said* to Cephas in front of everyone...')

How accurate is Luke's account? It is possible that Paul is narrating the events merely from his own viewpoint, to secure his position. It is also possible that Acts builds up the meeting (Peter's last appearance in the Acts) to increase the solemnity of the decision to include gentiles. The unity of the Church is one of Luke's major concerns, and it is possible that he omits to mention the row between Paul and Cephas/Peter to tone down the ferocity of the disagreement.

b. Stephen's speech

This speech sums up the history of Israel as Luke sees it, ending with the second chance given to Jerusalem (7.2–53). Jerusalem was given one chance by the ministry of Jesus; when that has been rejected, a second chance is given by the ministry of the apostles in Jerusalem. It is a masterly speech, a selective reading of history, marking the end of the Jerusalem phase of the Church, and preparing the opening to the gentiles, truly a turning point. It echoes the situation of Moses, who also was twice rejected by his people, who had said (as Peter already remarked at the end of his speech to the people in 3.22); and Moses had said (Deut. 18.18) that God would raise up another prophet like himself. The speech falls into three sections.

- It begins with God's promises to Abraham, drawing in the listeners with 'my brothers, my fathers' and the promise to *'our* ancestors' (three times). This selective version of the history already contains two warnings: Abraham was given no land of his own (and nor will the material Temple be God's final choice), and it was only on a second visit that Joseph was recognized by his brothers (just as Jerusalem has been given a second chance to recognize Jesus), vv. 2–16.
- The centre of the speech is about Moses, vv. 17–43. He was rejected by his people, twice, just as Jesus would be. In a series of rhetorical anaphoras ('this is the one who…', vv. 35, 36, 37, 38, 39) the hearers are told how Moses prepared the way for Jesus, sent as leader and redeemer, working miracles and signs as a prophet, entrusted with words of life, and rejected even a second time. The people merely turned to idolatrous worship in the desert – just as Stephen's hearers would be content with an idolatrous worship.
- The capstone of the failure of Israel was the building of a Temple 'made with human hands'. Here Stephen uses a poisonous word, rendered odious by its allusion to the constant rejection by Isaiah of idols 'made with human hands'. Worship cannot be tied to the Temple by their 'pagan hearts and pagan ears', when 'heaven is my throne and earth my footstool' (vv. 49–51). We are ready to turn to the gentiles, and it is no wonder that the hearers reacted with fury.

c. Peter's speech to Cornelius

The corollary of Stephen's record of the Jewish rejection is Peter's proclamation of God's acceptance of all people. His speech to Cornelius (10.34–43) is the first telling of the story of the Good News of Jesus, to which the apostles have been appointed witnesses. It begins – as does Luke's gospel – with the anointing with the Spirit, and is full of the universality of salvation: 'all nations', 'Lord of all', 'all those in the power of the devil', 'all who believe' (10.35, 36, 42, 43).

d. Paul's speeches to Jews and gentiles

We have heard Peter's speeches to Jews and gentiles; now comes the pair of Paul's speeches to Jews and gentiles (13.17–41; 17.22–31). The former is naturally full of scripture, carefully used: Peter's speech to the Jews had centred on the patriarchs (3.12–26), Stephen's speech had centred on Moses (7.17–43), now Paul's on the promises to David. It is warm and welcoming, 'our nation, our ancestors, my brothers' (13.17, 26, 32); the leaders of the people are partially excused, for in crucifying Jesus they unwittingly fulfilled the prophecies. The speech at Athens is a special masterpiece, taking on the philosophers on their own ground. Paul actually draws support from two pagan philosophers, and at the same time gently pokes fun at the Athenians. He seems to compliment them, but in fact mocks them ironically, calling them 'god-fearing', a word which could mean either 'reverent' or 'superstitious'; they also eagerly grab the wrong end of the stick about Resurrection. However, both these speeches have special Pauline features: the title 'Son of God' (13.33) is important in Paul's letters, and the natural theology of the speech to the Athenians is echoed in Romans 1.

e. Paul's Farewell at Miletus

Another classic speech by Paul is his farewell speech at Miletus (20.18–35), his only speech to Christians, and a mirror-image of Jesus' final discourse. It both justifies Paul's past conduct, with many phrases and sentiments typical of his letters, and warns of future disturbances in the Church (cf. p. 13).

f. Paul's Defence-Speeches

The series of four defence-speeches of Paul (before the Jews in the Temple, before the Sanhedrin, before Felix and before Festus and King Agrippa) owes much to the delight in court-scenes evinced in contemporary novels. The speeches seek to emphasize again and again that Christian belief in the Resurrection is the heritage of Judaism, that Paul, the faithful disciple of the strictest stream in Judaism, is doing no more than crowning Jewish belief. Furthermore, there is no cause for alarm or dissension in the relations of Christianity and Rome. Luke's literary skill is seen at its best in the final speech by Paul's elaborate flattery of the king (26.2–3), his use of a classical Greek proverb (v. 14), the play on light in Paul's vision and light to the gentiles (vv. 13, 17), and the way Paul picks up and sanitizes the king's sarcastic quip (vv. 24–9).

g. Paul to the Jews of Rome

Paul's final speech to the Jewish leaders at Rome (28. 25–8) provides a fitting conclusion to the book. Arrived at 'the ends of the earth' he for the third time registers how he is being forced to turn from the Jews to the gentiles, as at Antioch In Asia Minor and Corinth in Greece. On each occasion it had been stressed that Paul was forced into this position by the obduracy of the Jews. On each occasion it was sealed by a biblical gesture (16.46; 18.6; 28.25–28). Here Paul explains his action by the prophecy of Isaiah, a passage obviously used in current apologetic, since it is quoted both in the parable-chapter of Mark (4.12) and in the final summing-up of Jesus' ministry in John 12.40. This confirms the whole thrust of Luke's double work.

3. The Ecclesiology of Acts

a. The Spirit in the Acts

The two most important elements in the overlap between the ending of the gospel of Luke and the opening of Acts are that the Eleven are to be witnesses to the Risen Christ, and they are to wait in the city until they are clothed with power from on high (Luke 24.48–9; Acts 1.8). After the Ascension they return into the city, where their first action is to complete the number of twelve. Not till the number is complete can the New Israel begin to function, but it is noticeable in this election that no mention of the Spirit is made. The birth of the Church occurs at Pentecost, on the Feast of Weeks, 50 days after Passover. Already, since at least the second century BC, this feast had been the commemoration of the giving of the Law on Sinai, and so the formation of the Old Testament community, in which both wind and fire are symbols of the presence of the LORD. According to the tradition, on this occasion there was a mighty wind, and the Spirit came down on the heads of the elders in the form of fire in the desert, in the same way as at Pentecost. The presence at this event of the large numbers of pilgrims from all over the world – for that is what the list of heterogeneous peoples implies – points to the distribution of the Church all over the world.

Thereafter we are continually told of the members of the community being filled with the Spirit, just as judges, prophets and other rulers of God's people in the Old Testament were filled with a divine spirit of courage or counsel. As Peter explains, from the prophecy of Joel, this is the messianic and eschato-logical people of God (Isa. 11.2), the fulfilment of Jesus' promise in Luke 11.13. Peter is so filled with the Spirit at his speech before the Council (4.8), and the whole community as they begin to proclaim the gospel (4.31). Stephen and all the chosen Seven are filled with the Spirit (6.3, 5). The Samaritan believers receive the Spirit at the hands of Peter and John (8.17), and Paul at the hands of Ananias (9.17). The Spirit directs Philip to go to meet the Ethiopian, and again to continue on his journey afterwards (8.29, 29). The Spirit jogs Peter to go to meet the messengers of Cornelius (10.19). At the reception of the first gentile into the community there is a sort of mini-Pentecost (10.44–7), with the same consequence of speaking in tongues. The community at Antioch in Pisidia is filled with joy and the Spirit at Paul's departure (13.52).

More particularly, the Spirit guides the community, both positively and negatively. It guides the community at Antioch to select Barnabas and Saul for their mission (13.2). It guides the decision of the community gathered in council (15.28). It checks Paul on his journey, and then, in the form of a vision, encourages him to cross into Europe (16.6–7). Similarly it guides him on other journeys. All this is a way of expressing the detailed guidance of the Church by the divine will. It indicates a constant and pressing guidance of the messianic community by the Spirit to which there is no parallel in the Old Testament.

> In the Acts there is regular competition between the Spirit of God and other spirits which are at work. It is almost as though each new advance in the spread of the Good News is opposed by a manifestation of an opposing spirit, perhaps representing the opposition of evil. This suggests that in the Roman world for which Luke was writing there were thought to be influential, generally magical, spirits. Simon in Samaria 'practised magic arts' (9.9) and tried to buy the Spirit. Another Jewish magician is found in attendance on the proconsul of Cyprus (13.6), a sooth-telling slave-girl at Philippi (16.16–18) and some Jewish exorcists at Ephesus (19.13–16). These serve as foils to demonstrate the power of the Spirit of God in Paul, which triumphs over them all.

b. The Ideal Community

The early chapters of Acts give a picture of the Christian community which seems to be a blueprint of the ideal community. The outline is repeated in several summaries: 2.42–6; 4.32–5; 5.12–14. The chief element, repeated in each of the summaries, is sharing, a sharing of life and possessions. This *koinonia* was a key element in the early communities, stressed in almost all Paul's own letters (Romans, both Corinthian letters, Galatians, Philippians and Philemon). The most important element of all is that they were 'united, heart and soul'. Again, this is a keynote of all the action in Acts; it is stressed ten times by the author that they did everything *homothumadon*.

- Community of goods was practised also in the community of Qumran, which suggests that it was felt to be an important element in an eschatological community, in which each received according to individual needs. The summaries stress that all goods in the Jerusalem community were held in common and that the members sold what they owned. However, this is partly contradicted by the story of Ananias and Sapphira (5.1–11), whose sin was not that they failed to give in all their money, but that they lied that they had done so. Moreover, the feeling that some of the community were being neglected, and the need to select officials for the distribution who would be more sympathetic to the 'Hellenists', show that the system did not always run smoothly (6.1). Paul's collection for the poor at Jerusalem, which features so largely in his letters (Rom. 15.25–8; 1 Cor. 16.1–4; 2 Cor. 8–9; Gal. 2.10), shows the extent to which this 'communion' obtained also between geographically separate communities: other communities were concerned for the Jerusalem community, though Acts 21.18–25 suggests that the gift was coolly received. These texts show that in the Pauline communities complete community of goods was not practised, but only generosity. Perhaps Acts is presenting an ideal rather than the actual fact.

There are two historical difficulties here.

1 The account of the selection of the Seven (6.1–6) gives a strange result: there are obviously two sub-communities involved. If there was unevenness in the distribution of food between the needy among the Hebrew-speaking widows and the 'Hellenists', one would expect that those who would take over the distribution would be drawn from both communities. In fact they all have Greek names. This would suggest that the whole function of distributing alms was transferred from the Hebrew-speakers to the Hellenists, which would not solve the problem, but simply transfer it! It has been suggested that Luke was eager to underline the unity of the community, and that the disagreement was more profound than the text admits, and that the Seven are a parallel hierarchy to the Twelve, with authority over the Hellenists in the community. The powers of the Seven are not confined to presiding over the distribution of food, for Stephen works signs and wonders among the people (6.8) as well as making the significant speech before his martyrdom. Philip also has a significant role in teaching and baptizing the Ethiopian and proclaiming the Good News in the coastal regions (8.26–40).

2 It is clear from Paul's letters that he was nervous about the reception of the collection which he delivers to them in Acts 21. He regarded it as a recognition of the Jerusalem community by the communities which he had formed, a sort of tribute from the daughters to the mother-city. There had clearly been difficulties with the Jerusalem community about observance or non-observance of the Law by gentile Christians, and the collection may have been intended as a gesture of reconciliation. The oddly fragmentary account in Acts 21.19–26 suggests that it was somewhat grudgingly accepted. Paul may even have been forced to 'launder' the money by using it to pay for the performance of a vow in the Temple.

Perhaps Luke is presenting an ideal of peace and love to which the historical reality does not fully correspond.

- Prayer-life was in common also, for they went as a body to the Temple every day (2.46). The continued participation in the worship of the Temple may be the reason why Luke shows Jesus as 'cleansing', or purging, the Temple, rather than symbolically rubbishing it (compare Lk. 19.45–6 to Mk 11.12–21). We do not, of course, know how long the followers of Jesus continued to worship in the Temple. After the first persecution by the Sanhedrin the community is represented as praying together in a house (4.23–31).
- The Eucharist was celebrated in their houses (2.46). The Greek really means 'at home', suggesting that the original Eucharist was a family celebration rather than a public act. We do not know what public rooms were available to the earliest community, though 120 persons were present for the election of Matthias (1.15). A communal celebration in the Temple would hardly have been possible!
- Apart from worship the most important activity was to proclaim the Good News, and so to bear witness to the Resurrection, even under persecution, as their persistence despite the warnings of the authorities and the martyrdom of Stephen shows. It is difficult to know how widespread the persecution was, or how literally to take the statement that Paul 'asked for letters addressed to the synagogues in Damascus that would authorise him to arrest and take to Jerusalem any followers of the Way' (9.2), for there is no other evidence that the high priest had authority over communities outside Judaea. Within Judaea King Herod Agrippa I had James executed and was planning the execution of other members of the community, including Peter (12.1).

- An important example of the decision-making process within the community is given on the occasion of the reception of gentiles into the community. First Peter is required to justify himself (11.1–18). Then the success of Paul's apostolate raises the question of the degree of their observance of Jewish Law. For this, the community meets, the difficulty is explained, the opinion of the leaders is given, a decision is made by 'the apostles and elders' and accepted by the whole community, and then communicated as the decision of 'the Holy Spirit and ourselves'. It is received with delight at the encouragement it gives (15.6–31).

> There are historical difficulties about this scene cf. p. 170. First, the quotation of Amos 9.12 in James' speech uses, and needs to rely on, the Greek version of the Bible (reading 'Adam' rather than the 'Edom' of the Hebrew text). Since we cannot suppose that the Greek Bible was used at a meeting in Jerusalem, the speech must have been composed by Luke. Secondly, the apostolic letter is addressed (v. 23) to one particular small area rather than to the Church as a whole. Thirdly, Paul's own writings and rulings show no knowledge of this decision. Perhaps the author combines elements from different occasions, leaving the reader with the decision which eventually prevailed.

4. The Christology of Acts

There are three peculiarities of the Christology of Acts, all of which add to our understanding of how Christ is seen.

a. The Initiative Rests with God

In all the speeches of Acts it is God who takes the initiative in directing the course of Israel's history. The life and the wonders of Jesus are referred back to God, thus 'Jesus the Nazarene was a man commended to you by God through the miracles and portents and signs that God worked through him' (2.22). They are considered not the works of Jesus but the works of God, worked through Jesus. This is consonant with the whole of Luke's treatment of the events of saving history. In Stephen's long summary of Israel's history it is God who initiates each stage, the call of Abraham, the fulfilment of the promise to Abraham, the Exodus, the call of Moses, the settlement in Canaan and permission to build the Temple. Paul, too, in his address to the Jews of Pisidian Antioch, concentrating this time on David, attributes all the impetus to God. Consonantly with this, the resurrection is always described as the action of God. In the three great prophecies of the resurrection in Mark (Mk 8.31; 9.31; 10.34) Jesus will *rise* (*anistemi*) from the dead. In Acts, on the other hand, the intransitive 'rise' is used only once (Acts 17.3), whereas six times God *raises* Jesus from the dead (2.24, 32; 3.26; 13.32, 34; 17.31). Similarly, using the verb *egeiro*, Paul often uses the passive 'he was raised' (Rom. 4.25; 6.4; 1 Cor. 15. 4, 12, 13, etc), whereas Acts always has explicitly 'God raised him' (Acts 3.15; 4.10; 5.30; 10.40; 13.30, 37); for the author of Acts this is the supreme act of God. In the account of the Ascension it is again stressed that all the initiative rests with God: the disciples are to await the fulfilment of the promise of the Father (Acts 1.4), 'the Father decides the times by his own authority' (1.7), and Jesus is the passive recipient of the divine action: he 'was lifted up' (1.9, 11) and the divine cloud 'took' him from their sight (1.9).

In the same way Luke stresses constantly that God has brought to fulfilment the promises made to his people, to Abraham, Moses and David. It is consistent with this that he calls Jesus '*the* Christ', that is, '*the* Messiah'. For Paul, 'Christ' had become part of Jesus' name, no longer consciously a messianic title, but in Acts 'the Christ' is used with the article. This keeps the conception closer to the Old Testament usage, and to the prophecies of the Messiah. It is specifically a Greek translation of the Hebrew 'Messiah' (2.31, 36; 3.18; 4.26; 5.42; 8.5; 9.22; 17.3; 18.5, 28; 26.23). Jesus is therefore depicted as 'the Christ', the long-awaited anointed one sent by God in fulfilment of the promises.

b. The Servant of the Lord

In Deutero-Isaiah there are four poems about a Servant of the LORD, who will bring the vocation of Israel to fulfilment through suffering. Whether these songs in their original context refer to the prophet himself or to Israel as a nation is not clear, but particularly the fourth song, Isaiah 53, the Song of the Suffering Servant, has been seen as a prophecy of the suffering and death of Jesus.

In the Passion Narrative and elsewhere there are a number of quiet references to the Songs of the Suffering Servant of the LORD in Isaiah 53, for example the stress on Jesus' silence before his judges (Mk 14.60–61; 15.4–5 and parallels) has been interpreted as an allusion to Isaiah 53.7, 'He never opened his mouth, like a lamb that is led to the slaughter-house, like a sheep that is dumb before its shearers'.

In the Hebrew of Isaiah the 'servant' is designated by the Hebrew word *'ebed,* which can be translated either 'servant' or 'son'. In the Greek version, however, it is translated by the Greek *pais,* which can only mean 'child' or 'son'. The use of this expression in the earliest community, in Peter's speech at Pentecost (Acts 3.13, 26, 'God raised up/glorified his *pais* Jesus' – 'God carried out what he had foretold when he said through all his prophets that his Christ would suffer', 3.18) and in the prayer of the apostles under persecution (4.27, 'they made alliance against your holy *pais* Jesus whom you anointed') therefore suggests that the earliest community saw Jesus specifically as this servant of the LORD who would accomplish the purposes of God by his suffering, and would be vindicated by God. This title therefore introduces the whole rich Christology of seeing Christ as the Suffering Servant/Child of the Lord in Isaiah. It may also be echoed in the 'hymn' of Philippians, where Jesus is described as 'taking on the form of a servant' (Phil. 2.7), though the word here used is not *pais* but *doulos*). This may provide a link to the sayings of Jesus where he describes himself and his followers as servants and serving: 'The Son of Man has come not to be served but to serve and to give his life as a ransom for many (Mk 10.46).

c. Jesus Lord and Saviour

The word *kyrios* has a wide range of meaning. It can be used in the vocative as a polite and honorific address, simply meaning 'Sir!'. It is, however, also the Greek rendering of the Hebrew sacred name for God which is too holy to be pronounced. In Mark, Jesus is frequently addressed as *kyrie*; but the word is never used of Jesus with the definite article, *'the* Lord'. Luke is less careful, already influenced by the later usage, allowing post-resurrection language to slip in. Thus Elizabeth, in her greeting Mary, asks why 'the mother of my Lord' should come to her (Lk. 1.43) and the angels at Jesus' birth sing 'today is born to you a saviour who is Christ the Lord' (Lk. 2.11).

In the Acts, however, *kyrios* is used freely of Jesus, and this with specific reference to biblical texts where it originally referred to the LORD God. The 'great Day of the LORD', mentioned by Joel 3.4, is now referred to the day of the Resurrection of Jesus (Acts 2.20). More especially, 'all who call on the name of the LORD' (Joel 3.5) is used regularly of the followers of Jesus, and 'those who call on the name of the Lord' becomes a technical term for Christians (Acts 9.14, 21; 22.16, etc). There is, therefore, a referential shift: the sacred word or name which referred to God is now referred to the Risen Christ; the Risen Christ is put in the position of God and is so addressed. This is particularly clear in the account of the martyrdom of Stephen. Jesus had asked forgiveness from God for his killers and had died with 'Into your hands, LORD, I commend my spirit' (Lk. 23.46) on his lips; Stephen dies saying, 'Lord Jesus, receive my spirit' (Acts 7.59) and asks forgiveness for his killers, 'Lord, do not hold this sin against them'.

In the same way, in the Old Testament 'Saviour' is a divine title, especially in the context of saving from the Babylonian Exile (Isa. 41.14; 43.14; Jer. 50.34). In the New Testament also the title is normally reserved for God: 'My spirit rejoices in God my saviour' (Lk. 1.47); 'God's power for the salvation of everyone who has faith' (Romans 1.16); 'by the command of God our saviour' (1 Tim. 1.1); 'to God our saviour alone be glory' (Jude 25). In the gospels both John and Luke once refer to Jesus as saviour (Lk. 2.11, 'today is born to us a saviour'; John 4.42, 'truly this is the saviour of the world'). It is not until Acts that the same referential shift occurs: this divine attribute is freely applied to Jesus: 4.12 'in none other is there salvation'; 5.31. 'God has raised him up to be leader and saviour' – God himself has given to Jesus the divine prerogative of being Saviour; 13.23, God has raised up for Israel one of David's descendants, Jesus, as saviour'. The prerogative of God as Saviour is now shared with the Risen Jesus (cf. p. 00).

By the use of these two titles the divine quality of the Risen Christ is clearly proclaimed in the Acts of the Apostles.

Further Reading

Clark Kee, Howard, *Good News to the Ends of the Earth* (London: SCM Press, 1990): the theology of Acts

Pervo, Richard I., *Profit with Delight* (Philadelphia: Fortress Press, 1987): on the literary genre of Acts

Shillington, V. George, *Introduction to the Study of Luke-Acts* (London: T&T Clark, 2007): thorough, scholarly, for students

Questions on Part Two

1   Which is your favourite gospel and why?
2   Is it enough to say that Jesus is the symbol of God?
3   Who was really responsible for the death of Jesus?
4   Does it contribute to our understanding of Jesus to know that his life fulfilled the Old Testament?
5   How do the conventions of modern history writing differ from those of the New Testament?
6   If you were giving instructions to a gospel-writer, what would they be?

Part III

Paul's Life and Letters

Part III

Regulation and Law

13

Judaism in the Roman Empire

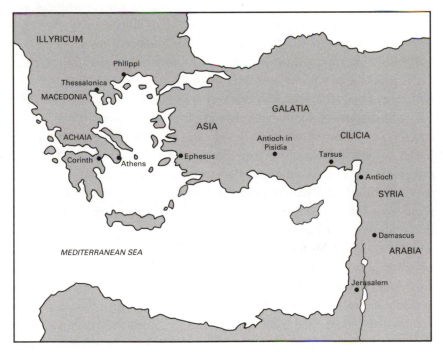

Significant places in the activity and travels of Paul

1. The Roman Empire

At this moment of history the eastern Mediterranean was more united than it has ever been, before or since. This is part of what some have called the *Praeparatio Evangelica* (preparation for the gospel) or, on another level, the *Pax Romana* (Roman peace). The whole of the Mediterranean basis – and in some directions for hundreds of miles inland – was subject to Rome. Rome was ruled notionally by the Senate, but by the last half-century before Christ the power of the Senate had waned, and the government had fallen into the hands of the powerful dynasty of the Caesars, Julius Caesar and his successors, notably for our purposes Octavian/Augustus (31BC–14AD) and Tiberius (14–37AD). The Romans themselves liked to claim that the empire had fallen into their hands by chance and through defensive action rather than through imperial aggression, and this is reflected in the Roman system of government. The Romans left things as much as possible as they had been. There were, of course, armies and governors stationed around the empire, whose functions were to keep peace and to maintain the flow of taxes and other revenues to Rome. But as far as possible day-to-day government was left in the hands of local territories, chiefly semi-independent city-states who had their own constitutions and their own systems of government. This ensured the maximum flow of money into Rome at the expenditure of the minimum of effort. Rome was, after all, only one city-state among many, though its population and aristocracy were becoming increasingly international. The streets of Rome were much like those of London or Manchester, where all races mixed together, though the government remained in the hands of a small clique of Etonians. To the unsympathetic, Rome could be represented as the Whore of Babylon seated on the Seven Hills of Rome, while the wealth of all nations flowed to her (Rev. 17–18). But the fact is that there were few large-scale movements of discontent or rebellion. Rome's interest in the East had first been aroused by King Attalus of Pergamum's willing bequest of his territory to Rome in 133BC, and in 6AD the leaders of Judea positively invited Rome to replace the corrupt and ineffective Archelaus (son of King Herod the Great) by direct rule. The unified empire and culture made travel and mutual understanding between the component nations more fluid then even before or since. Even the language was a unitive factor: when Julias Caesar lay stabbed and dying, he spoke to Brutus in Greek rather than Latin (not '*Et tu, Brute*' but '*Kai su, teknon*' [You too, my son?])

2. Jews in the Roman Empire

It was an important part of the *Praeparatio Evangelica* that the Jews had spread widely all over the Mediterranean territory. Since the beginning of the Hellenistic era many new cities had been founded (prominent among them the many cities named 'Alexandria' after Alexander the Great, and especially the great Egyptian city of Alexandria), and a great commercial expansion taken place. Especially prominent were the Jewish colonies in coastal trading cities, such as Antioch, Corinth, Thessalonika, Salamis (Cyprus), Berenice (Cyrene). Their trading and banking aptitudes were helped by their family and ethnic ties of trust and loyalty. The *Sibylline Oracle* 3.271 in the first century BC says *pasa gaia sethen pleres kai pasa thalassa* (every land is full of them and every sea) – echoed in Josephus (*Antiquities* 14.7.2). The Roman consul in 142BC sent round a circular letter to protect them (1 Macc. 15.16–23). They had special exemption from military service because of the Sabbath, the right of assembly and permission to observe their religious customs, even to the extent of exporting the Temple tax to Jerusalem (*Antiquities* 14.10, 20–4). Philo reports 'on the Sabbath days thousands of houses of learning were opened in all the cities' (*De Spec. Leg.* 2.15.62). The wide spread and the solidity of these communities would have ensured Paul of an initial welcome on his missionary journeys.

Inscriptions (some in Hebrew, some in Greek) show that Jewish communities in the various cities had various names, such as citizen-body (*politeuma*), synod, synagogue, directed by a council of elders or leaders and a president elected for a certain period or for life. This body was a legal person, so that payments could be made to it. In Acts 14.23 Paul is said to have set up just such a constitution in his earliest Christian communities, though human organisational structure in the Corinthian community seems to have been notably lacking. Paul's early persecution of Christians suggests that the religious courts had also civil jurisdiction (Gal. 1.14; Phil. 3.6); this would account for his own flogging later (2 Cor. 11.24).

14

Paul's Life and Letters

1. Sources

In secular terms Paul was a nobody, an itinerant Jewish craftsman who inspired groups of people in several cities to follow a new Jewish cult. We cannot expect his story to be reflected in any secular historian. A secondary source is the Acts of the Apostles, but the primary source must be Paul's own letters, what he says about himself. Each of these has its difficulty.

The Acts of the Apostles is of course written according to the canons of ancient historical writing, among which slavish attention to factual accuracy was not included see p. 164–7). The main purpose of that second volume of Luke is not biographical, but is to show the development of the early community of the followers of Jesus as it spread 'to the ends of the earth'. Luke has his own theological concerns and emphases. Two of these are to show that Paul was very thoroughly grounded in Judaism, and that there is no cause for hostility between Christianity and Rome. Thus when Paul is represented as claiming in the Temple that he studied under Gamaliel, one of the most respected rabbis in Jerusalem at that time, the reader is drawn to ask, 'When and how much?' Did Paul come to Jerusalem at an early age and receive his basic education, or the whole of his education, at the feet of Gamaliel? Was his formation chiefly in Judaism or in the Hellenistic wisdom of the city of his birth, Tarsus, a Hellenistic university centre? Is Paul's Roman citizenship an invention of Luke to underline the friendship between Christianity and Rome?

There are several difficulties about Paul's Roman citizenship:

1 As the tribune remarks (Acts 22.28) Roman citizenship was highly prized. How did Paul acquire it? It is suggested that his family may have gained it by serving in the Roman army.
2 Paul never mentions his Roman citizenship in his letters. One would expect that, certainly when he is intent on securing the favour of the Roman congregation at the beginning and end of the letter to the Romans, he would mention his citizenship.
3 There are cases of Jews who were Roman citizens, but it is difficult to believe that a zealous Pharisee like Paul could give the necessary degree of loyalty to the emperor.
4 Paul himself says that he was three times beaten by the Roman lictors' rods (2 Cor. 11.25). It was illegal so to beat a Roman citizen.
5 Paul's appeal to Caesar when he has already been acquitted is legally puzzling.
6 Paul's so-called *custodia libera* in Rome (Acts 28.16) is unprecedented. The only partial parallel is the tetrarch Herod Agrippa, who was so held for a short time (Josephus, *Antiquities*, 18.161–238). As a head of state he was in a very different situation.

It would not be beyond the conventions of contemporary historical writing for Luke to use Paul's Roman citizenship as a means of carrying his story as far as Rome. The theological question is whether such a highly imaginative historical construction, which dominates the final third of Acts, can be a vehicle of inspiration.

Nor are Paul's own letters a straightforward source for his life. First, Paul gives biographical information only accidentally, in the service of particular pieces of persuasion; they may not be the full story. Secondly, only seven of the letters are almost universally agreed to be genuinely by Paul. The Letter to Philemon is universally accepted, and shows Paul as an old man and a prisoner. Since the letter presupposes fairly easy travel between Paul's prison and Colossae, this imprisonment may have been at Ephesus, the capital of Asia Minor. An imprisonment, perhaps the same, is mentioned also in Ephesians 3.1 and Colossians 1.24–9, and at any rate Colossians is widely accepted as authentically Pauline. When was/were this/these imprisonment(s)? The theology of Colossians and Ephesians, considerably developed over that of the seven 'authentic' letters, suggests that, if they are genuine, the imprisonment was late in Paul's life. A good deal more biographical information – sometimes called 'Paul's second career' – is offered by the Pastoral Letters, but of these only 2 Timothy is considered possibly genuine by some scholars; the information cannot be safely used to reconstruct Paul's life (see pp. 196, 304–5).

There is, however, enough information given in Paul's own letters to underpin the claim that the outline given in Acts is not far wide of the mark. It may be used, somewhat hypothetically, to supplement the information of Paul's own letters. With these reservations, we may outline Paul's life in four sections.

2. Upbringing and Formation

Acts 22.3 tells us that Paul was born at Tarsus in Cilicia and trained by Gamaliel at Jerusalem. We do not know how old he was when he went to Jerusalem, nor how long he stayed there, both important factors in assessing the effect of this education on Paul's thinking. After his visit to Jerusalem after his call to Christianity, he returned to Tarsus, again for how long we do not know (Acts 9.30). What is clear, however, from Paul's writing is that he is thoroughly conversant with both Jewish tradition and Hellenistic thinking. He was born into the former, and remained staunchly proud of his Jewish credentials:

> 2 Corinthians 12.21–22: I can be as brazen as any of them [claimants to be apostles of Christ], and about the same things. Hebrews are they? So am I. Israelites? So am I. Descendants of Abraham? So am I.

> Philippians 3.5–6: I was born of the race of Israel and of the tribe of Benjamin, a Hebrew born of Hebrew parents, and I was circumcised when I was eight days old. As for the Law, I was a Pharisee; as for working for

religion, I was a persecutor of the Church; as far as the Law can make you perfect, I was faultless.

The Hellenistic culture could have been acquired at either Jerusalem or Tarsus. This city of his birth was a prosperous, fun-loving (Philostratus, *Vita Apollonii* 1, 7) trading city, an intellectual and philosophical centre, whose administration was re-structured by Augustus' former tutor, Athenodorus. Jerusalem also, however, had been being progressively subjected to Hellenistic influence for a couple of centuries, and most recently by Herod the Great (see pp. 23–6).

At any rate, Paul is thoroughly conversant with both traditions, His knowledge of and affection for the Hebrew tradition needs no proof, for it is the backbone of his whole thinking. The detail of this may, however, be here illustrated by two examples. He is capable of word-play on the Hebrew root of the word *Amen* (2 Cor. 1.17–20), which means stability or firmness, as well as confirmation of someone else's statement or prayer. Paul plays on this double sense when writing that Christ is the *Amen* of the Father's promises. He also makes frequent use of the strict rules for exegesis of scripture which were codified about this time (traditionally by Rabbi Hillel). One of the most frequent is the argument *qahal wehomer*, arguing from one case to another, 'even more so' (Rom. 5.9, 10, 15). Another, more obscure, is *gezerah shawah*, interpreting one text by another which shares the same word, though in a different sense, Deuteronomy 27.26 and 21.23 in Galatians 3.10–14; they share the same words, 'cursed be everyone who'. This is a highly technical matter, and evidence of careful formation in the rabbinic tradition.

On the other hand, Paul uses *captatio benevolentiae* (see p. 13), *sorites* ('pile-up') in Romans 10.14–15, and the whole of Galatians has been analysed according to the canons of a classic lawyer's speech for the defence (p. 257). He frequently uses images from the Games, which were a feature of contemporary popular culture similar to the modern craze for football (Gal. 5.7; 1 Cor. 9.24–7; 2 Cor. 4.9; Eph. 6.14–17). More importantly, he normally quotes the scripture in the Septuagint version, showing that this was his familiar Bible. Paul's presentation of Christ as the Wisdom of God relies on the Wisdom literature of the Greek Bible, which was not normally accepted by the rabbinic tradition (1 Cor. 1.17, 24; Col. 1.15). If we accept the evidence of the speeches of Acts we see Paul giving a highly polished speech in the Greek style of rhetoric before King Agrippa at Caesarea (Acts 26.2–18).

Paul's education was, then, cosmopolitan, fitting him for the apostolate in both the Hebrew and the Hellenistic worlds.

3. The Road to and from Damascus

Apart from Paul's presence at and connivance in the martyrdom of Stephen (Acts 8.58), the next we hear of Paul is what he describes as his 'call' on the road to Damascus, repeated thrice for emphasis (see pp. 168 or 169). Luke's message here is that the persecutor of the Church has become its defender. Acts does not tell us that Paul actually 'saw' Jesus as Paul himself claims (1 Cor. 9.1). It may be that Luke does not wish to put Paul on the same level of apostle as the Twelve and the others who saw the Risen Jesus (15.5–6). Although the speeches of Acts are compositions of Luke rather than verbatim reports, this is a prime case of suitability of words to the speaker. The words 'Saul, Saul, why are you persecuting me?' touch the heart of Paul's theology, for which incorporation of the Christian into Christ is a central focus. It is tempting to think that the scene described in Acts may be the external appearance of the experience described by Paul himself in apocalyptic language in 2 Corinthians 12.2–4:

> I know a man in Christ who, fourteen years ago, was caught up – whether still in the body or out of the body, I do not know, God knows – right into the third heaven. I do know, however, that this same person – whether in the body or out of the body, I do not know, God knows – was caught up into paradise and heard things which must not and cannot be put into human language.

After a few days, according to Acts, Paul began his mission of preaching, but in consequence of a Jewish plot had to flee the city. This gives us our first date for Paul, for he himself says that he was let down over the wall of Damascus to escape an official of King Aretas of Nabataea (2 Cor. 11.32), and Aretas was made governor of Damascus by the emperor Caligula, who reigned 37–41AD; Paul's escape must therefore be after 37AD. Paul says that he went from Damascus into Arabia, which probably indicates Nabataea, the Arabian kingdom of Aretas, centred on Petra, a rich staging-post for caravans coming from the East. According to Acts, Paul's first missionary activity was in the Roman Province of Cilicia (southern Turkey). Paul would have returned to the important Jewish-Christian community at Antioch in Syria, and was commissioned by them as a companion to Barnabas; they set up communities and appointed elders to lead them, the normal constitution of the Jewish communities of the Diaspora (Acts 13.1–14.28). It was the report to the Church of Antioch after this mission that raised the hot topic of the inclusion of gentiles in Christian communities which Paul and Barnabas laid before the Church at Jerusalem (15.1–6).

4. Paul's Missions

After the verdict given at this meeting began the main body of Paul's travelling missions. Whether the major disagreement between Peter and Paul occurred before or after the Jerusalem meeting is unclear. At any rate, it was now that Paul split off from his previous Jewish team of Barnabas and John Mark and made his own way, gathering his own lieutenants, Silas and Timothy. It is widely held that the journeying reported in Acts 15.40–21.15 is streamlined by the author into two journeys. One awkwardness of this schema is that the 'we'-passages, where the author of Acts is depicted as accompanying Paul, are abrupt, and spread over the whole period (16.10–17; 20.5–15; 21.1–18; 27.1–28.16); it would be more coherent if they occurred consecutively. According to Acts, Paul seems to have had two main centres for his missionary activity, Ephesus in Asia Minor and Corinth in Greece. In Ephesus he stayed at least two years (Acts 19.10) and in Corinth at least 18 months (18.11). The period in Corinth may give us a firm date, for Paul was brought before the tribunal of Gallio, and we know from other sources that Gallio was pro-consul, resident in Corinth in 50–51AD. At Ephesus there was some incident which Paul describes, perhaps in images, as fighting with wild beasts (1 Cor. 15.32). This may be the imprisonment alluded to in Philippians 1.7, 13–17, for Ephesus would have had a Praetorian residence. Luke may have omitted to mention this out of a desire to save Paul from the humiliation of imprisonment. It must have been during this period of travelling pastoral work that Paul wrote most of his letters.

Paul himself paints a vivid picture of his activity during this period, the discomforts and dangers of solitary travel in those days, the conflict with authorities both Roman and Jewish, and his own anxieties, in 2 Corinthians 12.23–8. He compares himself with others who flaunt themselves as servants of Christ:

> I have worked harder, I have been sent to prison more often and whipped so many times more, often almost to death. Five times I had the thirty-nine lashes from the Jews, three times I have been beaten with rods, once I was stoned, three times I have been shipwrecked and once adrift in the open sea for a night and a day. Constantly travelling, I have been in danger from rivers

and in danger from brigands, in danger from my own people and in danger from pagans, in danger in the towns, in danger in the open country, danger at sea and danger from so-called brothers. I have worked and laboured, often without sleep; I have been hungry and thirsty and often starving; I have been in the cold without clothes. And, to leave out much more, there is my daily preoccupation, my anxiety for all the Churches.

Paul was travelling in a world where brigandage was rife and lone travellers were liable to be swept up and sold into slavery, where frail barques and primitive navigation made sea-voyages perilous, where life was cheap and strangers were suspect, where Jews might take offence at his claim that Jesus was Messiah, and Romans might take offence that Jesus, rather than the Emperor, was Lord. Major routes had magnificent roads (though the lone foot-traveller would often find himself pushed aside by official or military traffic), contrasting sharply with unmapped and tortuous lesser paths. The road system in Asia Minor was already good, and was being improved throughout the first century AD. At its best the system made travel a real possibility: the future emperor Tiberius travelled 200 miles in 24 hours from Ticino to reach his dying brother Drusus in Germany. A merchant from Hierapolis in Turkey claims on his tombstone to have travelled 72 times to Rome.

For Paul it would have been less easy. The roads were infested with brigands, ready not only to despoil but to kidnap and sell into slavery any serviceable person. In some areas 'the district was overrun by packs of enormous wolves, grown so bold that they even turned highwaymen and pulled down travellers on the roads or stormed farm-buildings' (Apuleius, *Metamorphoses*, 8.15). The major roads had inns at more or less regular intervals, but for the lone traveller these would provide little security and no privacy. They were, however, an improvement on huddling down in a cloak at the roadside, an open prey to robbers or other predators. This itinerant craftsman, with his minimal bag of tools, working night and day to support himself while he spread his message, would have cut no striking figure amid the monuments, marbled porticoes and colonnaded streets of Greek cities of his apostolate. He was attempting to guide unruly communities into a new way of life and new loyalties, with high ideals and plenty of human faults, spread over a vast area with limited communications.

5. Paul's 'Second Career'

From the earliest times many have been tempted to go beyond the firm evidence of Paul's own letters. Romans 1.10 and 15.24 show that Paul was planning a visit to Rome on his way to Spain. We do not know for certain whether these plans ever materialized. At the end of the first century 1 Clement 5.7 reports that they did, but this may be sheer speculation. In the personal, chatty notes at the end of letters, the Pastoral Letters mention travels to Ephesus, Macedonia and Nicopolis in Greece, and 2 Timothy 1.8, 17 detail a search for Paul as a prisoner in Rome. These would suggest a continued pastoral activity, but the question of the evidential value of these letters remains unresolved (see pp. 189, 304–5).

There is a rich legendary tradition about Paul's martyrdom by beheading outside the walls of Rome. If Peter was martyred at Rome, it is highly fitting that Paul should also bear similar witness.

6. Letter-Writing in the Roman World

Many letters have survived from the Roman world. Some are mere scraps, often found preserved in the dry sands of Egypt, such touching fragments as letters from schoolboys to their parents (much the same as their modern equivalents, asking for more pocket-money!). One voluminous correspondent was the lawyer and politician Cicero, about a century before Paul, whose letters to his family and friends have been collected into eight books. Another was the statesman Pliny, the tenth book of whose letters comprises 121 letters exchanged between himself as governor of the Roman province of Bithynia (northern Turkey) and the Emperor in Rome, sent by the regular imperial post, some 60 years after Paul's letters. He would write with such trivial questions as the age at which municipal firemen should be appointed, and what equipment should be provided for them. He also writes to ask how the Emperor wishes Christians to be treated. His description of their activities gives us invaluable information about Christian life and liturgy at the time. Both of these clearly wrote with an eye on subsequent publication.

Paul did not write for literary publication, but sometimes directs, as in 1 Thessalonians 5.27, that the letter is to be 'read out to all the brothers'. Colossians 4.16 directs 'after this letter has been read among you, send it on to be read in the church of the Laodiceans, and get the letter from Laodicea for you to read yourselves'. At any rate some of Paul's letters were treasured and preserved, though of course we have no guarantee that all his letters have survived to be collected into the body of letters which we now have.

7. The Shape of a Letter

As with modern letters, there was a stock formula of beginning and ending, which needs to be appreciated. It would be a mistake for future historians to deduce from twentieth-century English letters that 'Dear…' implied any affection. The email-greeting 'Hi!' is similarly meaningless. One needs to know the customs, such as the convention that 'Yours very sincerely' is not warmer, but rather more formal and distant than 'Yours sincerely'. Letters written in French have a different set of conventions, such as the formal and courtly ending. Paul's letters have a definite set of conventions.

- *Praescriptio*

Paul normally begins 'Paul to so-and-so' or 'to the church in such-and-such a place', sometimes joining to his own other names, perhaps subordinate co-authors or secretaries. It is difficult to be certain of the part in the composition of the letters played by the various secretaries mentioned, (A computer study conducted by Anthony Kenny reveals only the Letter to Titus as standing out linguistically. This suggests that Sosthenes, Timothy and the others were merely taking dictation rather than composing or improvising). This formula is similar to the curt Roman formula '*Maximus S.D. Minimo*' ('Maximus wishes health/safety to Minimus'). But Paul follows it with a blessing, 'Grace and peace'. The latter half of this corresponds to the set Jewish formula '*Shalom*' ('Peace'). From Paul's pen, however, this may have a fuller sense, for 'peace' has become a special Christian greeting. The Christian message as a whole is called 'the good news of peace' (Acts 10.27). One of the faults of unbelievers is that they did not recognize the way of peace (Rom. 3.17), for 'God has called us in peace' (1 Cor. 7.15), and Jesus Christ 'is our peace' (Eph. 2.14).

With this, Paul has coupled the greeting usually translated 'Grace'. This, too, is a special Christian word. The basic idea behind this concept is favour freely bestowed without any merit. Just as a king or potentate spontaneously and unpredictably chooses a favourite on whom he lavishes his favours, so does God. The favours bestowed are only the sign of a living and vibrant relationship. So the 'grace' which Paul wishes in his letters is the relationship of God's gracious favour.

- *Thanksgiving*

Paul follows the initial greeting with a thanksgiving. This occurs quite frequently in other letters of a religious character. Paul thanks God in prayer for the qualities and Christian life of his correspondents. This thanksgiving is normally rather rotund and formal, even rhetorical. It compliments the recipients of the letter on their faith and fidelity. This makes the deliberate absence of such a thanksgiving in Galatians all the more stunning: Paul has no praise to give them, but simply pitches straight in, 'I am astonished that you are turning away so promptly from the one who called you'. The thanksgiving normally also stresses the main theme of the letter. So in 1 Thessalonians one of the main themes is the future coming of Christ. This is reflected in the conclusion of the thanksgiving: 'You are now waiting for Jesus, his Son, to come from heaven. It is he who will save us from the Retribution which is coming' (1.10). In 1 Corinthians, where the gifts of the Spirit form a major theme, Paul thanks God that 'you have been richly endowed in every kind of utterance and knowledge... and so you are not lacking in any gift' (1.5–7).

- *Conclusion*

It was common enough to conclude a letter, even dictated, with a short passage which is especially personal; this was often in the chief author's own hand (as in Gal. 6.20). It would include good wishes. In secular letters the usual form for this is '*erroso*' ('be strong' or perhaps 'take care'). In Paul, however, this also has the form of a blessing, very often 'The grace of our Lord Jesus Christ be with you'.

8. The Authenticity and Order of Paul's Letters

a. Opinions on the authenticity of Paul's letters are still thoroughly divided. The situation espoused by this book is that there are three groups:

1 Eight authentic letters:
   Romans, 1 Corinthians, 2 Corinthians, Galatians, Philippians, 1 Thessalonians, 2 Thessalonians (this is less certain than the others), Philemon.
2 Deutero-Paulines:
   Ephesians, Colossians (the latter could just possibly be authentic).

3   The Pastoral Letters
    1 Timothy, 2 Timothy (held by some to be authentic), Titus.

b. The order in which these letters are printed has nothing to do with chronology. They are printed in two groups, each in decreasing order of length. The first group consists of letters addressed to Churches, the second of letters addressed to individuals. The chronological order of writing is very difficult to establish, especially if some letters (notably 2 Cor. and Phil.) each consist of several letters put together (mostly in decreasing order of length). However, something can be said:

- 1 Thessalonians is most probably the earliest of the letters.
- 2 Thessalonians (if authentic) was probably written soon afterwards.
- Galatians must have been written before Romans, since it presupposes an earlier situation.
- 1 Corinthians must have been written before any part of 2 Corinthians, but whether it precedes Romans or not remains unclear.
- Philippians (at least in part) and Philemon were written from prison, probably late in Paul's career. In both letters he mentions his bonds, and in Philemon he calls himself an old man.
- Colossians must precede Ephesians, for Ephesians re-uses phrases from Colossians.
- If 2 Timothy is authentic, it precedes 1 Timothy and Titus.

9. Paul's Moral Teaching

a. Gospel Teaching

Neither in Paul nor in the rest of the New Testament does the scripture provide a 'ready-reckoner' or 'dial-an-answer' solution to moral problems. The synoptic gospels provide teaching on a variety of moral issues, especially in Matthew's Sermon on the Mount (Chapters 5–7). In the last analysis, however, in Matthew the judgment will depend uniquely on how we have treated 'the little ones' – understood by some to mean the needy, by others to mean missioners (as Mt. 10.42). Luke's Sermon on the Plain (6.20–49) and his parables are also fertile sources of moral instruction; indeed, the whole of the Great Journey up to Jerusalem, with its teaching on the hardships of the apostolic calling (9.51–19.27), could be regarded as moral teaching.

    In John, on the other hand, only two things are necessary, belief in Jesus and love. The whole gospel is built on the division which occurs between those who believe and those who refuse belief. All the actors in the drama judge themselves by whether they accept or refuse belief in Jesus (see p. 126). At the same time love is paramount: the new commandment which Jesus finally gives at the Last Supper (Jn 13.34) is the commandment of love, which is stressed throughout the following final discourses (Chapters 14–16). In this, John rejoins Mark's account of the dialogue of Jesus with the lawyer about the greatest commandment (Mk 12.31), and Matthew, whose great corrections to the Law of Moses are bracketed by the commandment to love (Mt. 5.21–48). Few details, however, are given about how this commandment should be applied, at least not details which are specific to Christian teaching. Matthew lays great stress on forgiveness (e.g. 18.12–35) and Christian attitudes or habits of mind (his Beatitudes), and Luke on the danger of wealth and the need to use it generously.

b. Paul's Dilemma

In the matter of moral teaching Paul is firmly skewered on the horns of a dilemma. On the one hand his conviction that salvation has been won by Christ leads him to reject any suggestion that salvation can be earned by deeds, such as by obedience to the Law of Moses. On the other hand he is convinced that some actions are incompatible with Christianity. In this he is in harmony with other attitudes to the Jewish Law, for in Judaism it was always taught that the Law is a precious gift of God, teaching Israel how to behave as God's people: 'Be holy as I am holy' (e.g. Lev. 11.44). The question therefore is different: Salvation is not won by obedience to God's Law in the Law of Moses. But to what extent is it necessary to obey the Law of Moses in order to be God's people? Salvation is not won by such obedience: is it then necessary, and to what extent? One basic difference must be the starting-point: incorporation into God's people is won no longer by observance of the boundary-markers, circumcision, Sabbath and clean food, but by faith in Christ, expressed in baptism. By this the Christian is incorporated into Christ, becomes one being with Christ, is shaped and lives by Christ's Spirit (see p. 216).

This should be an end of the matter: the Christian lives with Christ's Spirit and is led by Christ's spirit. The works of the Spirit are obvious enough, listed in Galatians 5.22–24, and opposed to the works of the flesh (that is, unredeemed humanity) listed in 5.19–21. The trouble is that Paul is well aware that he does not always act according to the Spirit (Romans

7.14–24). There is, therefore, still room for external guidance in moral matters. Hence Paul can give guidance on behaviour which is fully in accord with the Law of Moses (Rom. 12.1–13.13). Only the motive is different: 'let your armour be the Lord Jesus Christ; forget about satisfying your bodies with all their cravings' (Rom. 13.14)

c. The Community

Since Christians form the Body of Christ they should act like Christ, in unity and fraternity. In First Corinthians this is brought home particularly in two matters, the Eucharist and the gifts of the Spirit. The way that the Eucharist was celebrated at Corinth, with privileges for the rich and contempt for the poor, was no way of expressing the Body of Christ. Paul chides them that, if they behave like this, they are guilty of the death of Christ for failing to recognize the Body of Christ. He chides them also that they glory in the gifts of the Spirit, without realizing that the true purpose and splendour of the gifts of the Spirit is that they build up the Body of Christ; they are for the good of the whole – each member contributing some special gift – rather than for the splendour of the individual. Whatever your gift, whether it be healing, leadership, understanding, interpretation of tongues or of prophecy, all are for the building up of the community. The gift is primarily for the community rather than for the individual.

d. Conscience

Paul may lay down rules for what he considers action according to the Spirit. This he does in 1 Corinthians 10.14–30 about food which has been offered to idols, and attractive because it is sold off cheap in the market. Is it tainted by this offering? Paul thinks not, since the gods to which it was offered do not exist. Others, however, cannot see this reasoning, and are scandalized by Christians who eat such meat. To Paul the scandal is more important than the convenience, and Christians who are led by the Spirit in a certain direction should be allowed to follow the prompting of the Spirit to themselves. Similarly in the case of marriage: to Paul it seems that the imminence of the final coming of Christ and the disastrous tension which will precede it are so pressing that it is not worth marrying and exposing newborn children to the horrors to come. If, however, a young couple are so wildly in love that they can no longer bear to be apart, let them marry (1 Cor. 7.36–40). The pressing nature of the eschaton is such that 'our time is growing short'. 'the world as we know it is passing away', so that 'those who have wives should live as though they had none, and those who mourn should live as though they had nothing to grieve over', but the administration of these principles is left to the conscience of each individual (1 Cor. 7.29–31).

Further Reading

Barrett, C.K., *Paul, an Introduction to his Thought* (London: Continuum, 2001): magisterial

Dunn, James D.G., *Cambridge Companion to St Paul* (Cambridge: Cambridge University Press, 2003): brief outline of his theology

Fitzmyer, Joseph A., *Paul and his Theology, a Brief Sketch* (Englewood Cliffs: Prentice-Hall, 1988): magisterial

Gombis, Timothy, *Paul, A Guide for the Perplexed* (London: T&T Clark, 2010): short handbook of his theology

Hooker, Morna, *Paul, a Short Introduction* (Oxford: One World, 2003): magisterial

Horrell, David G., *An Introduction to the Study of Paul* (London: T&T Clark, 2006): textbook

Murphy O'Connor, Jerome, *Paul, a Critical Life* (Oxford: Oxford University Press, 1996): biographical, using close knowledge of the terrain

15

The Letter to the Romans

1. The Christians of Rome

It would be an egregious mistake to picture the Rome of the period as being inhabited by Italians. The population of Rome has been estimated by ancient historians as being by this time only 12 per cent of Italian origin. A constant complaint is voiced by Juvenal, that the Orontes (a river in Syria) now flows into the Tiber, indicating the immense numbers of orientals then resident there; there had been steady immigration, mostly as slaves, for 250 years. Greek was as commonly spoken in Rome as Latin, and many of the professional classes and skilled workers were of Greek origin. A Roman, by now and certainly later, came to be judged not by his blood but by his way of life. Just as a native of Chichester or Caesarea had as much right to expect advancement in the Roman Empire as a native of

Ostia, so an inhabitant of the city of Rome was as likely to be black as the descendant of local stock.

Rome was the capital of the world, and proud to be mistress of the world. Financially, Rome was practically the owner of the world too, for much of the land in the provinces of the Roman Empire was owned by the upper classes of Rome, having defaulted to them as a result of loans made at wholly unsustainable rates of interest. Taxes flowed into Rome from the provinces, though they could be remitted in times of crisis from earthquakes, famine or other natural disasters. Some idea of the central position of Rome in all trade may be gained by the list of imports to Rome (including slaves) given in the satire on the impending fall of Rome in Revelation 18.12–13. Already, a century before Paul writes, Cicero claims that not a penny changed hands in Gaul without being entered on Roman ledgers. Administratively, too, to an extraordinary extent Rome controlled what went on in the provinces, from the appointment of local rulers to minute details: a provincial governor can be found writing to the Emperor in Rome about the composition and equipment of a local fire brigade (Pliny, *Letters* 10.33). Rome was linked to all the provinces not only by a system of magistrates governing the provinces but also by a swift, efficient and frequent imperial postal system. More subtly, local rulers were encouraged to send their sons to Rome for education and Romanisation; Herod the Great a firm friend of the Emperor Augustus, sent his sons there for education. Herod's grandson, Aristobulus, moved to Rome to spend his last years there in the 40s; it is an attractive guess that Jewish members of his household (mentioned in Rom. 16.10) may have been the first Christians in Rome. In any case, by the year 64AD Christians were well enough known in Rome for Nero to blame them for the great fire.

Josephus (*Antiquities of the Jews,* 17.6) claims, no doubt with his customary exaggeration, that at the death of Herod the Great in 4BC there were 8,000 Jews in Rome. A host of synagogues is known from inscriptions, with an organisation of *gerousia* (Council of Elders) and *gerousiarch, archisynagogos* (President), etc, the sort of organisation common in the synagogues of the Diaspora, though without any central organisation such as is known at Alexandria, with its Jewish ethnarch. Jews and their habits were well known and thoroughly mocked in Rome as early as Horace: *credat Judaeus Apelles,* 'let the Jew Apelles believe *that*', he says (*Sermo* 1.5.100), as though everyone knew that Jews would believe anything. The sententious Seneca criticises them for wasting one-seventh of life by their observance of the Sabbath (quoted by Augustine, *De Civitate Dei,* 6.11). It is significant that Paul does not use the term *ekklesia* of the Christian community at Rome: they were not a single community. He does use it of an individual grouping round Aquila and Prisca (Rom. 16.5). The list of greetings in Romans 16 suggests that Paul is greeting members of at least four independent synagogues.

The most significant factor is the expulsion of Jews (how many? certainly not all of them) from Rome under Claudius in 49AD, by an edict which probably lapsed at his death in 54AD. The Roman historian Tacitus (*Annals* 15.44) links this expulsion to a disturbance sparked off by 'Chrestus', a common slave-name. The name is pronounced the same as 'Christus', which suggests that it may have been a disagreement between Christian and non-Christian Jews. The presence of so many Jews back in Rome when the letter was written, many of whom Paul had no doubt met in the east, shows at least that the edict was no longer effective. It is not unreasonable to suppose that an important factor in the Roman congregations was this return of the Jews after the gentile Roman Christians had lived, believed and worshipped on their own for some years; a fair amount of tension would not be surprising, and could well have been significant for the composition of the letter.

2. The Purpose of the Letter

The Letter to the Romans is the longest, most intense and most important of all Paul's letters. Yet there is considerable question why it ever came to be written. Several factors may have played a part.

G. Bornkamm put forward the theory that Romans should be regarded as Paul's Last Will and Testament. He argues that there is no mention of information received from Rome, to which Paul might be responding. On the contrary, the letter forms a sort of summing up of previous controversies, interests and debates. Any impression of controversy is misleading and comes from the diatribe style of exposition. The Reformation scholar Melanchthon called Romans a *Christianae religionis compendium*, 'a compendium of the Christian religion'. However, there needs to be some reason why Paul should have written thus to the Romans; it cannot be simply a motiveless letter out of the blue, an unprovoked meditation on the truths of Christianity.

Peter Stuhlmacher holds that Paul is considering his impending visit to Jerusalem to hand over the money he has collected (see on 2 Corinthians 8–9), knowing that he will have to justify his position with regard to the relationships of Jews and gentiles in the Christian Church. 'It is very likely that Paul intends to defend himself before the Christians in Jerusalem with arguments similar to those presented in Romans. But Jerusalem is not the letter's principal destination. The Apostle's main intention was to achieve a consensus with/ between the Christians in the metropolis' (Stuhlmacher, p. 236).

With such a motif must, however, be at least integrated another, Paul's concern about his proposed journey to the West, to Spain (Rom. 15.23). There he would be on totally unfamiliar ground, even linguistically. Did Paul speak Latin? Even if he did, he would find in Spain a medley of dialects with little relation to conventional Latin. There would be no maps to guide him, no Diaspora Jewish communities to welcome him. On the other hand, Rome had ruled Spain for two and a half centuries, sending thither governors, troops and merchants. There would be plenty of people at Rome, no doubt even among its Christians, who knew Spain well. But if Paul's reputation among the Christians of Rome was that of a dedicated opponent of the Law, then he could hardly expect whole-hearted support. After the row with Peter at Antioch, after his uncompromising attack on the Judaisers in Galatia, his bitter and sarcastic mockery of Judaisers at Philippi and Corinth, it would require only slight over-simplification by his wounded opponents to secure him just that reputation. If he was to win the support of the Roman congregations, he must first set out his real stance towards the Law.

Finally, in a community composed of Jewish and gentile Christians there may well have been tensions about the value of Judaism and its Law, intensified after the enforced temporary absence of some of the Jewish Christians, which Paul sets out to explain to them.

In any decision on the matter, the style of the letter must certainly be considered, particularly two factors:

1 Paul is treading carefully and gently. When he is fighting against opponents he does not spare them: the Galatians are called 'fools' or 'senseless' (Galatians 3.1); he wishes the troublemakers there would

'let the knife slip' (5.12). He lashes the Corinthians with sarcasm (1 Cor. 1.26; 3.2; 2 Cor. 10.12). He even pressurizes Philemon unmercifully (Philemon 14, 19–21). Nothing of this to the Romans! Quite apart from the usual initial compliments about their faith, he handles them with kid gloves: 'Brothers, I have often planned to visit you – though until now I have always been prevented – in the hope that I might work among you as fruitfully as I have done among the gentiles elsewhere' (Rom. 1.13), hardly daring even to offer them advice (15.14–15). He writes with respectful awe, as though to a superior community.

2   The seemingly aggressive style, technically called 'diatribe', is used in ancient literature for dialogue within a school of thought, not against enemies. This technique of setting up an artificial opponent, and interrogating that opponent, is of its nature suitable when there is no direct opponent in view whose opinions are known. It is used amply in Romans, so that one can see Paul sorting out his ideas, e.g. 2.1–5, 17–25; 3.27–4.21; 9.19–21; 11.17–24. Features of the style are:

- Little rushes, changes of direction, sharp questions and emphatic answers.
- Interpellation in the second person: 'You preach that there is to be no stealing, but do you steal? You say that adultery is forbidden, but do you commit adultery?' (Rom. 2.22).
- Imaginary dialogue with short, sharp question and emphatic answer, often a volley of these: 'Is there any advantage in being circumcised? A great deal in every way' (3.1) or an answer suggested and then disputed.
- Paul's favourite answer is literally 'let it not happen', used by him as one might say 'heaven forbid!', or 'out of the question!'; this occurs ten times in Romans alone.

3. The Plan of Romans

As is normal in Paul's letters, the main division is into two parts, the first about belief (Chapters 1–11), the second about action (Chapters 12–15). Between the two parts, Chapters 9–11 on the situation of Israel are regarded by some as an appendix to Chapters 1–8, by others as the climax to which Chapters 1–8 lead up.

4. The Justice of God and the Wrath of God

a. The Justice of God

The first section of Romans (1.17–5.21) is dominated by the twin concepts of the wrath and the justice of God. In the first two sections of the letter Paul sets out to show that all humanity is sunk in iniquity, first the gentiles (1.18–32), then he turns on the Jews themselves and points out that they are no better (2.1–3.8), finally summing it all up with proof from a catena of scripture-quotations (3.9–20).

Since the Reformation the letter has often been viewed through the Augustinian spectacles of Luther: the basic problem is the wrath of God: human beings are worthless and hideously sinful – how can they escape God's wrath? Human beings have sinned, so God's justice must punish them. This is in fact a fundamental misunderstanding of the concept of God's justice.

The word-group based on *dikaiosune* ('justice of God') occurs overwhelmingly in two letters only: 60 times in Romans and 13 times in Galatians. Otherwise it occurs only 15 times in all the other Pauline letters. The term is clearly a forensic and relational term. To the modern mind justice is related to keeping a set of rules or a law. A judgment is just if it adheres to the law. An arrangement can be called 'just' if it puts into practice the principles which stand behind the law. To the Jewish mind, however, the concept is entirely different. Hence the *dikaiosune* of God is often translated by the archaic word 'righteousness', which has no currency in secular modern English, and can be used as a sort of wild-card. What does this word mean?

In the Bible the relationship of *dikaiosune* is not to the Law but to God's promises. It is God's fidelity to his covenant promises, his reliability. It is not connected with fairness, or human deserts, or assessment of merits. The clearest way of finding the meaning of a word in the Bible is often to see the parallel terms which are used. Hebrew poetry works primarily by parallelism, stating the same truth twice in parallel ways or expressions. Especially in the Psalms and in Deutero-Isaiah God's justice is put parallel to God's saving power, or his judgment in favour of Israel, quite divorced from any merits on Israel's part.

> So Psalm 7.11: 'God is an upright judge // slow to anger'.
> Isaiah 46.13: 'I am bringing my justice nearer // my salvation will not delay'.
> Isaiah 51.6: 'My justice is suddenly approaching // my salvation appears'.
> Isaiah 51.8: 'My justice will last for ever // and my salvation for all generations'.

Similarly in Jewish literature of the first century, roughly contemporary with Paul, as shown in the texts of Qumran:

> 1 QH 11.17 I have known that righteousness is yours // and that salvation is in your favours.
> 1 QH 11.31 Cleanse me by your righteousness, even as I have hoped in your goodness.

Occasionally this justice positively violates or runs contrary to human notions of justice, which demand the punishment of offences:

Daniel 9.16   In your justice turn away your anger // for we have sinned.
1QS 11.9–12   He will wipe out my transgressions through his right-
                eousness …
                From the source of his righteousness is my justification.

So close is the righteousness of God to being God's power to save and help
Israel that in the LXX it can translate the Hebrew *hesed*, 'mercy' (Gen. 19.19;
20.13; Exod. 15.13) as well as the more obvious *zedek*, 'justice'. This whole
view of God as a saving God whose very nature is to pardon is rooted in the
explanation of the name and nature of God given in Exodus 33–4. After the
disaster of the golden calf, the first of Israel's many desertions of the Covenant,
Moses prays to see God's glory. God descended in a cloud and pronounced
the sacred Name, immediately giving an exegesis or explanation of that
Name, 'God of tenderness and compassion, slow to anger, rich in faithful love
and constancy, maintaining his faithful love to thousands, forgiving fault,
crime and sin' (Exod. 34.6–7). Only after this strong assertion of forgiveness
does God briefly mention 'letting nothing go unchecked, punishing the
parent's fault in the children'. How deeply rooted in the consciousness of
Israel is this conception of God as forgiving may be seen by the number of
times this passage is recalled, either by direct quotation or by allusion. The
'justice' of God, therefore, is God's trueness to himself and to his promises as
expressed, and ever and again renewed, in the Covenant with Israel.

b. The Wrath of God

The puzzle is not so much God's justice as his anger. The Greek *orge* is
normally translated 'anger', but God's anger is different, and this is why it is
best translated by a strange word, 'wrath'. To begin with, this excludes the
petulance and irrationality which is often associated with human anger.
But how can God's anger find place beside divine 'justice'? God's Covenant
with Israel is not one-sided; it demands absolute loyalty from Israel, and
excludes loyalty to other gods and other standards. That is why it is often
expressed as God's 'jealousy'. Even to David's line, God does not promise
not to punish, only not to punish with that annihilating absoluteness which
might be expected of a divinity: 'if he does wrong I shall punish him with a
rod such as men use, with blows such as mankind gives. But my faithful love
will never be withdrawn from him' (2 Sam. 7.14–15). God's punishment will
always be corrective rather than vindictive.

When, after multiple infidelities and disloyalties, Israel is eventually
punished by exile, the seeming end of Israel's special status, Ezekiel presents

his audience with a God who was forced willy-nilly into this catastrophic position by Israel's failure to recognize him for what he is. God's inability to protect and rescue Israel according to his Covenant with them is described by Ezekiel as the profanation of the Name of God as protector and forgiver of Israel: he has been compelled, publicly and in the eyes of the world, to act against his nature:

> They have profaned my holy Name among the nations where they have gone, so that people say of them, 'These are the people of the LORD; they have been exiled from his land.' I am acting not for your sake, House of Israel, but for the sake of my holy Name, which you have profaned among the nations where you have gone. (Ezek. 36.20–4)

The basic problem Paul faces in Romans is, then, the irreconcilability of God's wrath with his justice. The burden of the first three chapters is the universal liability of humankind to God's wrath: 'The wrath of God from heaven is being revealed against the ungodliness and injustice of human beings who in their injustice hold back the truth' (1.18). First this is amply illustrated by the sins of the godless gentiles. Then, lest Jews begin to glory, Paul turns on the Jews themselves. The Law will not save them, nor will circumcision. If anything their situation may seem worse: 'You are bringing God into contempt. As scripture says, *It is your fault that the name of God is held in contempt among the nations* (Isa. 52.5)' (Rom. 2.23–4). No one, either Jew or gentile, does in fact keep the Law; all alike are enslaved to sin.

An initial problem is how *dikaiosune* can be predicated of human beings at all. Clearly human beings cannot be 'just' in the sense that God is just, that is, by being true to himself and his forgiveness. It is in fact Paul's constant concern to distance the idea of human 'justness' as far as possible from any relationship to Law. For himself, he claims that he was 'blameless' with regard to the Law, but not that he was just (Phil. 3.6). 'If the Law had been capable of giving life, then certainly *dikaiosune* would have come from the Law. As it is...' (Gal. 3.21). Normally human 'justness' comes from human action related to law; in this case it comes only from divine action on human beings, completely unrelated to law. In any normal sense of 'justice' it is impossible for the unjust to be 'constituted' just: it is the paradigm of injustice that the unjust should be considered just. But in Paul's terminology, 'by one man's action are many to be made just' (Rom. 5.19). Similarly in Romans 6.13–20 the message is that the Christian must be conformed to/given over to/free to the justice of God; *dikaiosune* is not a human quality at all, but a divine attitude or quality to which human beings are made subject, or in which they are enfolded.

The question therefore becomes how human beings may come to participate in this 'justness' of God. Here enters the work of Christ, which Paul describes in Romans principally in two ways, first in a Jewish ritual way, by means of the 'sacrifice for reconciliation' (3.21–6), and then through the concept of the Second Adam, related to all humanity (5.12–21). Each ends with explicit attention to Jesus (3.26; 5.21). Between these two comes the meditation or *midrash* on the faith of Abraham (3.27–4.25), the guarantee of Abraham's own salvation and of the salvation of Jews and gentiles alike; the meditation circles round the statement of Abraham's faith in Genesis 15.6. This opens up reconciliation to all peoples, not only the physical descendants of Abraham, nor those who observe the boundary-markers of Judaism. The sole boundary-marker now is faith. Paul here opens up the quotation from Habakkuk 2.4 with which he began in Romans 1.17, 'Anyone who is upright through faith will live'. Contemporary interpretation in the Dead Sea Scrolls confined its meaning to the observers of the Law in Israel: 'The interpretation of this concerns the observers of the Law in the House of Judah, whom God will deliver from the House of Judgment' (1 QpHab 8.1–2). Paul withdraws the limitation to the House of Judah.

In a way, the whole letter is a celebration of faith. Faith is not any adherence to a particular set of truths, but a world-view, a 'conviction about the difference that God and the lordship of Christ have made for human history' (Joseph A. Fitzmyer, *Romans* [1993], p. 137). It is a trust in God, 'the only possible and sufficient basis to maintain a relationship with God' (Dunn, *Romans*, p. 43). It is correlative to God's own trustworthiness, his fidelity to his promises expressed to Abraham. This correlation is emphasised by the use of the same word, *pistis*, to express both divine trustworthiness/fidelity and human faith/trust. Hence Paul can write of the saving justice of God as a justice, 'from faith to faith' or 'based on trustworthiness and addressed to faith' (Rom. 1.17). It is a view of the structure of the world based on human inadequacy and helplessness and on divine saving power.

5. Christ as the Sacrifice for Reconciliation

The clue here is the rich and strange term *hilasterion*. It is normally translated 'sacrifice for reconciliation': 'God appointed him as a sacrifice for reconciliation through faith by the shedding of his blood'. The concept can be understood only with reference to its Old Testament background. The term is used principally in the Old Testament of the lid of the ark, or the 'mercy-seat'. This is the precise place where God appeared to Moses; it remains the permanent meeting-place between God and man: 'this is where I shall come to meet you, from above the mercy-seat, between the two winged creatures which are on the ark of the Testimony' (Exod. 25.22). Most especially, on the Day of Atonement or Reconciliation the high priest sprinkled the blood of the victims (note 'by the shedding of his blood') on the mercy-seat for the expiation of sins (Lev. 16.14–15). Christ is therefore the place where the reconciliation occurs, as well as the victim by whose blood it is effected.

It is important to stress that there is no shadow of the notion, which sometimes appears in medieval theology, of appeasing the wrath of God. Such was the purpose of pagan sacrifice, wholly foreign to the Hebrew mind. The verb *hilaskesthai* (to reconcile or propitiate) in the Old Testament never has God as its object, as though God were being propitiated. The idea is not 'life for life', as though God's desire for vengeance was being satisfied, or the life of one person being shed in substitution for that of others. The object of the action is always human beings, so that it is a purification of human beings rather than an appeasement of God.

This in fact is also always the function of blood in the Old Testament ritual: its function is to cleanse. 'There is no purification except by blood' is a rabbinic axiom, following Leviticus 17.11, 'blood is what expiates for a life'. Blood is sacred because it belongs to God and contains God's power of life. A victim and its blood are always surrounded with respect and cleanliness (Lev. 6.20; 10.17; Ezek. 42.13). On the Day of Atonement the blood of the victims is sprinkled as a purifying and life-giving factor.

Nor is the sacrifice for reconciliation to be confused with the rite of the scapegoat which also occurs on the Day of Reconciliation (Lev. 16.20–22). This comes from the survival of a primitive and superstitious rite by which the sins of the people were loaded onto a goat, which was then driven off into the wilderness, haunt of evil. Christ is not the scapegoat.

The first way in which the work of Christ is explained is, therefore, in terms of the sacrifice of the Day of Reconciliation. Exactly how Paul understands the effectiveness of this action becomes clear from his view of Christ as the Second Adam.

6. Christ as the Second Adam

Paul uses the name 'Adam' only four times, twice in 1 Corinthians 15 (vv. 22 and 45) and twice in Romans 5.14. The importance of Adam in his thought is out of all proportion to this meagre usage. Principally it occurs in Philippians (see p. 287), and 1 Corinthians (see p. 233) as well as Romans. The contrast between the two Adams is the basis of Paul's teaching in 1 Corinthians 15 on the risen Christ as the first-fruits of resurrection, the forerunner of all the redeemed and risen humanity: 'as in Adam all died, so in Christ will all be made alive' (1 Cor. 15.22). This describes the end-product, the function of the Second Adam in the final transformation, but does not concentrate on the act of reconciliation itself.

In Romans 5.12–20 Paul concentrates on the earlier part of the story, he contrasts the first and second Adam, the Adam of the Genesis-story being the progenitor of the fallen human race, the second Adam being the progenitor of the new humanity. The loving obedience of Christ to his Father undoes the disobedience of Adam; the passage is built on the contrast of disobedience/obedience, condemnation/acquittal, offence/free gift, death/life.

> If death came to many through the offence of one man, how much greater an effect the grace of God has had, coming to so many and so plentifully as a free gift through the one man Jesus Christ! One single offence brought condemnation, but now, after many offences, have come the free gift and so acquittal... Just as by one man's disobedience many were made sinners, so by one man's obedience are many to be made upright (5.15–18).

In this passage the reality behind the sacrificial language of the 'mercy-seat' imagery becomes clear. Christ is the *hilasterion* because his obedience undoes the disobedience of Adam. The two passages may be combined as a statement that the climax of this obedience is the sacrifice 'by the shedding of his blood' (3.25) on the Cross.

Further, against this background it becomes obvious that the thought of the two Adams is more far-reaching. The state of sin in the first section of Romans has in fact been described in terms of fallen Adam. If 'Adam' is substituted for 'they' or 'those people' in 1.20–25 the passage reads almost like a paraphrase of the story of the Fall. All the elements are here in this return to the creation-story, the initial knowledge of God, the refusal to honour or give thanks to God, the attempt to seek knowledge which in fact plunges into deeper ignorance, the loss of glory. The catalogue of sin which follows is again reminiscent of Genesis. First is detailed idolatry (1.24–25), which Wisdom 14.27 says is the beginning, cause and end of every evil (and the allusion to the serpent in v.23). Then comes sexual perversion (1.26–27), which may be an allusion to the intercourse of the angels with the daughters of men in Genesis 6.1–4, or possibly to the rabbinic teaching that lust was the serpent's original temptation. Finally the catalogue of various sins 1.28–32 reflects the general spread of evil which provoked the Flood.

Similarly, when Paul comes to celebrate the freedom from the tyranny of sin which is won by baptism into Christ, he does so in terms of the history of Israel (6.12–7.20), but in terms which recall both the temptation in the Garden of Eden and the sinning of Israel once the Law had been given on Sinai. He speaks in personal terms, making the history of Israel his own history ('*I* used to be alive', '*I* died', '*I* do not do what *I* want to do'). At the same time, this history is the history of every Christian: James Dunn comments on the life-long tension, 'The cry of frustration in Rom 7:24 is the life-long cry of the Christian' (*Jesus and the Spirit*, 1975, p. 338). Thus, in 7.7–11 Sin is represented as present but dormant until the Law comes. The commandment brings Sin to life, 'because sin, finding its opportunity by means of the commandment, beguiled me, and by means of it killed me' (7.11). 'Beguiled' is the word used of the serpent's temptation of Eve, so that Sin is here representing the serpent. 'The commandment' represents the commandment not to eat from the tree of life, and the sinning against the Law, the constant infidelity of Israel, once the Law has been given, is seen in terms of the sin of Eden. The result is the same in each case: Death. Paul conceives Sin, therefore, as well as redemption, in terms of the original sin of Adam in the Garden of Eden. This is approaching the modern view of the story of the Fall, in which it is seen not as the account of an historical event but as an analysis of the ever-repeated temptation and sin of Man ('Adam' means 'Man' in Hebrew) throughout history. Even more far-reaching will be the development of the same theme in Romans 8, where the new creation in Christ is also described in terms of the new Adam.

7. Humanity in Christ

How, then, is the Christian transferred from the sinful regime of the first, fallen Adam to the restored regime of the second Adam? The clue for Paul is faith, expressed in baptism. By baptism *into* (not merely *in*) Christ's death people are incorporated into Christ's being (6.3–4). The symbolism of baptism by immersion in water is a clear image of burial, immersion in the tomb. The understanding of the rite as expressing a sharing with Christ must come from Paul's own experience and that of the Christian communities. It is, of course, expressed in the Acts of the Apostles in the awareness that Christ is in his followers, shown in the account of Paul's vision on the road to Damascus: 'Saul, Saul, why are you persecuting me? … I am Jesus, whom you are persecuting' (Acts 9.4–5). Paul's awareness that he is living with Christ's life is one of his deepest convictions:

> Now, as always, Christ will be glorified in my body, whether by my life or by my death. (Phil. 1.20)
> I have been crucified with Christ, and yet I am alive; yet it is no longer I, but Christ living in me. (Gal. 2.20)

The union of the Christian with Christ was aptly expressed by John A. T. Robinson: 'the new tissues take on the rhythms and metabolism of the body into which they have been grafted' (*The Body* [1966], p. 65). To express this union with Christ, Paul coins a whole series of barbarous neologisms, which occur seldom if ever elsewhere. They are all formed with the Greek prefix *syn-* (compare 'synchronize', 'synthetic', etc):

> *symmorphoi* (Rom. 8.29; Phil. 3.21) 'sharing the form, shape or mould'.
> *symphytoi* (Rom. 6.5) 'con-grown with' – the word is used of a wound healing or a broken bone fusing together again.
> *syntaphentes* (Rom. 6.4; Col. 2.12) 'con-buried with'.
> *synestauromai* (Gal. 2.19) could well be translated 'I *have been and am now* fixed to the Cross with Christ'. This compares with the process signalled as taking place in 2 Corinthians 3.18, 'we *are being* transformed into the

image that we reflect in brighter and brighter glory'. By contrast Romans
6.6 puts in the simple past, 'our former self (the old man/Adam) was
crucified with him'.

synkleronomoi (Rom. 8.17), 'co-heirs' with Christ, claims a shared
inheritance. It is this spirit of adoption as sons, which enables the
Christian to cry out 'Abba, Father'. The Aramaic word *abba* is retained
as a sort of talisman, harking back to Jesus' own use of the term, and
denoting an awareness of sharing in the intimacy of this sonship of
Jesus, though in itself the fact of being an heir is still looking to an
inheritance in the future.

syndoxasthentes (Rom. 8.17) 'con-glorified' again refers to the future,
and is dependent on sharing Christ's sufferings (yet another of these
formations: *sympaschomen*, 'con-suffer').

All this is what Paul sees as sharing the identity of Christ through putting
all trust in him by being baptized into him. He then celebrates the freedom
from slavery to sin by describing the struggles of Israel under the Law in
terms of his own history, his own struggle against sin, but reflecting also
the temptation and sin of Adam in the Garden of Eden (7.7–23). After
this he continues to reflect on the new situation of the Christian under the
influence of the Spirit.

This rises to a climax in 8.14–39. Romans 8 is the chapter of the Spirit;
the word occurs five times in Romans 1–7, but 29 times in Romans 8. In 1
Corinthians 12–14 Paul dwells on the works of the Spirit in the Christian
community. Here he dwells more on the inner transformation of Christians
as sons and heirs to the promises made to Abraham, so able to cry out in
prayer with Christ 'Abba, Father'. Moreover, he sees the transformation as a
transformation of the whole of creation (8.19–22) as a new creation in the
glory of God, rising to a final hymn to the love of God and the glory of God
to which all are called (8.31–9).

Romans 9.5 may be read, 'From them is Christ according to the flesh, who
is above all, God for ever blessed'. This would be the clearest affirmation in
Paul of the divinity of Christ, though he expresses Christ's divinity elsewhere
by means of clear imagery. But the original Greek text has no punctuation,
and may also be read, 'From them is Christ according to the flesh. He who is
above all, God, be for ever blessed.' The latter is slightly awkwardly phrased,
which makes the former reading more likely, though not entirely certain.

8. The Mystery of Israel

From the passionate hymn to the love of God from which nothing can separate us, Paul turns to the mystery of Israel. This cannot, as some have suggested, be a separate sermon subjoined for good measure; it is the climax of the letter. The letter began with the situation of Jew and gentile apart from Christ; we now return to the problem which agonizes Paul, his brothers who have not accepted Christ. This would have been of particular concern to the mixed gentile and Jewish communities of Roman Christians. Paul presents a *midrash*, ranging over the texts throughout scripture which emphasize God's inalienable choice of Israel, an impassioned argument in his prime dialectical (see p. 207) style. He cannot accept that Israel has been rejected, finally resorting to the image of the pruned, dead branches which are to be grafted back into the olive-tree, to join the gentile branches of wild olive already grafted in. Seeing that this horticultural image does not work, he calls on his favourite concepts of election, mercy and obedience (11.28–32) before finally leaving it a mystery and appealing to the eschatological mercy of God and God's unfathomable Wisdom, 'To him be glory for ever!' (11.33–6).

We do not here discuss the Guidelines for a Renewed People, Chapters 12–15. They are much the same as those offered 1 Corinthians. One notable feature is the instruction on good citizenship (13.1–6). This may reflect on the riot for which Jewish Christians were expelled from Rome for a time (Rom. 1). It also expresses a totally different outlook from the Book of Revelation, where Rome and its authority are seen as the great threat to the Christian community, attempting to exterminate it. It is important to realize that such different points of view can exist within the one New Testament.

---

9. Greetings (16.1–27)

One important early papyrus copy of the letter omits Chapter 16, which has led to the suggestion that this typically Pauline chapter was not originally part of the letter; but the ending of 15.33 would be oddly abrupt as a conclusion. The chapter is important for two reasons. First, it shows something of the composition of the Roman communities: it was not a single community, but a group of house-Churches, seemingly – as the Jewish communities of Rome – without any central organisation. Paul, who had never yet been to Rome, seems to be greeting as many people as he can in order to increase the welcome for the letter and perhaps for himself. Secondly, the female name 'Junia' (v. 7) as 'outstanding among the apostles' shows that women, too, played an important part in the early apostolate, despite the reservations (however they are evaluated) of 1 Corinthians 14.34.

Further Reading

Barrett, C. K., *A Commentary on the Epistle to the Romans* (Peabody, MA: Hendrickson, 1991): a classic commentary

Oakes, Peter, *Reading Romans in Pompeii* (London: SPCK, 2009): uses archaeology as background of non-elite Roman Christians

Ziesler, John, *Paul's Letter to the Romans* (London: SCM, 1989): a shorter commentary

16

Paul's Corinthian Correspondence

Corinth in the first century

It is more than usually important to understand the circumstances of the Corinthians to whom this letter is addressed. The ancient city of Corinth had been destroyed in 146BC, in an unusually aggressive and impatient period of Roman history, following a considerable amount of unrest. The geographical situation of Corinth was such that Mediterranean commerce could not get on without it, and the city was re-founded a hundred years later by Julius Caesar. In Paul's time, therefore, the new city was only two centuries old. It had three chief characteristics:

1 It was a port-town, controlling the Isthmus of Corinth, over which passed the major portion of shipping between East and West of the Mediterranean. So feared was the dangerous Cape Malea, the southern tip of the Peloponnese, that merchants normally preferred to transfer their goods or even their entire ships from one side to the other of the isthmus. There was a dragging-track, almost a rail-track, from one side of the isthmus to the other. This made for a very large population of dockers and harbour-folk, with all the attendant difficulties of such people. It also meant a wide diversity of rich and poor. Sosthenes, who partners Paul in writing 1 Corinthians, may have been the same Sosthenes who was president of the synagogue of Corinth in Acts 18.17; this suggests considerable status and possibly wealth. Crispus, whom Paul baptized (1.14), has the same position. Erastus, the city treasurer of Corinth in Romans 16.23, may have risen to be the aedile (one of the chief magistrates) named on an inscription

found at Corinth. The city had developed fast in the previous century. The grand civic buildings betoken considerable wealth. This has a direct connection with some of the problems of the letter, for instance Paul's criticism of eucharistic parties, at which the poor had to sit outside and eat miserable food, while the rich gorged themselves from generous hampers. We have no idea how large this or any other Christian community was, but in fact no room in any house has yet been found in the widely-excavated town which would hold more than 40 people. Houses were built in *insulae*, 'blocks' with rooms facing inwards, round interior courtyards. According to the design of town-houses at the time, one must think of the rich assembled in the dining-room (*triclinium*), while the poor skulk in an obviously under-privileged and neglected position, in the peristyle courtyard outside (11.21–2).

2 It was a university town, renowned for its wisdom. This is related directly to Paul's discussion of Greek wisdom and may well account for the self-confidence, not to say arrogance, of the judgment of some of the Christians, who were so sure of themselves that they held to their opinions in blissful neglect of the feelings of others. In 1 Corinthians Paul seems to throw back at them some of their formulae or slogans which they must have paraded themselves: 'For me everything is lawful' (6.12; 10.23), 'We all have knowledge' (8.1). In 2 Corinthians he is in competition with other teachers who regard themselves as 'super-apostles' (11.5). This chimes in with Paul's representation of Christ as the true wisdom of God and his rejection of Greek wisdom as the worthless wisdom of this world.

3 It was the home of the Isthmian Games, held every alternate year. These were in fact more popular than the quadriennial Olympic Games, because they had more side-shows, more fringe-benefits than the Olympic Games. This would bring in business and money at all levels. Also, at least in the old days, Corinth was known as the fun-city of Greece. Strabo tells us that there were 1,000 licensed prostitutes in Corinth. In the rebuilt city this reputation was perhaps undeserved; there were only two, unimportant, temples to Aphrodite. Certainly by this time the slogan *Non cuivis homini contingit adire Corinthum*, originally said with a leer ('Not every man has the good luck to get to Corinth' – wink, wink), has come to mean something like 'Not everyone gets selected for the Olympic Games'. It has this meaning in Horace (Eph. 1.17.36). In more

general terms it may mean that such a bustling and competitive city was not everyone's cup of tea. It may be that its liveliness as well as its central position were characteristics which made it attractive to Paul. No doubt there would have been plenty of work for him as a tent-maker, lodging, according to Acts 18.3, with Prisca and Aquila. Like Ephesus in Asia Minor, the trade and bustle of Corinth made it a focal point which could have great importance in the spread of Christianity.

4 There was a large Jewish population, as would be expected at such a mercantile centre. Not many Jewish inscriptions have been found, but a certain corporate strength is implied by their courage in unsuccessfully attempting to arraign Paul before the Roman pro-consul (Acts 18.12–17). This may also have some bearing on the problem of meat-eating.

At such a geographical crossroads the situation was not made easier by visits from different preachers with their different approaches and emphases. Apollos from Alexandria had visited Corinth and acquired a following; we may perhaps guess that those who favoured Greek philosophy were among these, since the Jewish community of Alexandria specialized in interpreting the Jewish faith in Greek terms, and Apollos himself was an accomplished orator (Acts 18.24). Possibly Peter, too, who is mentioned (as 'Cephas', the Hebrew form of the name) with unusual frequency in 1 Corinthians, had passed through; he may have been responsible for some of the scruples about breaking away from Jewish customs. But it was to Paul, as the founder of the community, that they turned for answers to their questions.

Further Reading

Blenkinsopp, Joseph, *The Corinthian Mirror* (London: Sheed & Ward, 1964): a clear commentary on various aspects, still enlightening

Meeks, Wayne A., *The First Urban Christians* (London: Yale University Press, ²1983): a classic sociological commentary

Still, Todd G. and Horrell, David R. (eds), *After the First Urban Christians* (London: Bloomsbury, 2010): collection of essays, discussions of Meeks after 25 years

The First Letter to the Corinthians

1. Leading up to the Letter

This complicated community at Corinth kept Paul busy. By the time of the writing of 1 Corinthians a whole series of interchanges had occurred:

1 Paul's first visit to Corinth in which he founded the community. According to Acts 18.11 he spent eighteen months in Corinth. He claims to have 'laid the foundations like a master-builder' (3.10), and 'even though you have 10,000 slaves to look after you in Christ, you still have no more than one father, and it was I who fathered you in Christ Jesus by the gospel' (4.15). In spite of this he protests that he himself baptized only Crispus and Gaius and the family of Stephanas (whom he describes as 'the firstfruits of Achaia', 16.15). Apollos had also been at work in the community, 'doing the watering' (3.6) of the seed Paul planted. Cephas/Peter may well have played some part too,

since he was regarded by some as the patron of their party, though this might conceivably mean only that they appealed to him, perhaps as the authority for some mild kind of Judaising (mild enough not to merit Paul's fury). As Paul says in those two precious passages of literal tradition, he must, in his first visit of catechesis or kerygma, have given them some elementary passages to learn by heart: 'the tradition I received from the Lord and also handed on to you…' (11.23; 15.3).

2   A previous letter (5.9–11) in which he wrote to them that they should have nothing to do with people who live immoral lives. He now focuses those instructions to explain that he meant they must keep away not from all immoral persons but specifically from Christians who indulge in extreme vices.

3   The letter which constitutes the present 1 Corinthians is provoked by two sets of information, one oral and one written. In 1.11 Paul mentions that 'Chloe's people' have told him of the factions which are dividing the community. He may have received more information from Stephanas, Fortunatus and Achaicus, about whose arrival he says he is delighted (16.17). They had also brought a letter containing not information but questions. The way Paul deals with these two sets of information or in-put is entirely different.

a. The sections where he has received oral information about what is going on at Corinth concern:

1   Their boasting and quarrelling, their party divisions (1.11–17; 3.3–4.21), their false idea of wisdom (1.17–3.2, 18–23; 4.1–21).
2   A case of incest (5.1–8).
3   Litigation before gentile courts (6.1–11).
4   Disorder in liturgical assemblies (11.17–24).

In all these sections Paul is writing about the past.

- He is direct and censorious, even angry and sarcastic.
- He speaks with his own authority, not attempting to cajole or persuade, but simply laying down the law.
- His treatment is black-and-white, without any appeal to compassion. He seems to make little attempt to understand the Corinthians' position.

b. The sections where Paul is responding to questions put to him by a letter from Corinth. These are easily discernible because he begins each new topic with the words 'But about…'

1 Marriage (7.1)
2 Celibacy (7.25)
3 Meat sacrificed to idols (8.1)
4 Women's headdresses in the Christian assembly (11.2) – but without 'But about'
5 Gifts of the Spirit (12.1)
6 The Collection (16.1)
7 Apollos' visit (16.12)

Paul uses this formula 'But about' elsewhere only in 1 Thessalonians 4.9 and 5.1, both times about topics on which he says there is no need to write to them – a conventional rhetorical ploy called by Quintilian *praeteritio* ('passing over'). Another literary feature is the quotation of the Corinthians' slogans, which Paul then immediately qualifies or corrects:

6.12 'For me everything is lawful' (repeated 10.23)
6.13 'Foods are for the stomach and the stomach is for foods'
7.1 'It is a good thing for a man not to touch a woman'
8.1 'We all have knowledge'
8.4 'None of the false gods exists in reality'

A vexed question is whether the two verses (14.33b–35) which demand the total silence of women in church are in fact also such a slogan, which Paul then contradicts. They are often cited as evidence that Paul is anti-feminist. The importance of this is that these are the only two verses before the pseudepigraphic Pastoral Letters which warrant such an accusation. However, the next words could be read as expostulation at these ideas expressed by Corinthians, 'Do you really think that you are the source of the word of God, or that you are the only people to whom it has come?' Since they can be excised without trace it has also been suggested that they are a later interpolation.

These two suggestions are not desperate moves to avoid Paul seeming politically incorrect; they are attempts to secure consistency. Elsewhere in Paul there is no trace of this attitude. In his lists of greetings, women feature as 'fellow-workers in Christ Jesus', Prisca, Tryphaena and Tryphosa, in the Romans 16 list alone. The most important name is that of a person whom Paul greets as 'well-known among the apostles', *Junian* (Rom. 16.7, in the accusative case). The nominative of this could be the masculine name, *Junias*,

> though there is no known example of the masculine name Junias.
> On the other hand the female name 'Junia' is common enough.
> There is also strong MS evidence (𝔓46) for 'Julia', which would leave
> no doubt at all that the position of 'well-known among the apostles'
> was being given by Paul to a woman.

In all these sections Paul is writing about the present and the future:

- Often envisaging hypothetical cases. The sentences are full of 'if…'.
- He is systematic and calm, not critical or censorious.
- He seeks to persuade and appeals to authorities.
- He is aware of weaknesses and the need to accommodate them.

Paul's difference in attitude in the two situations is striking, censorious about the news which has filtered to him and sympathetic in the cases about which they have consulted him. He responds sympathetically when he is consulted, but deals vigorously with abuses about which he has been told by others.

2. Plan of the Letter

Hence the letter may conveniently be read as follows:

1. INTRODUCTION and GREETING	1.1–9
2. DIVISIONS IN THE COMMUNITY	1.10–4.21
A. Rival groups in the community	1.10–17
B. God has different standards	1.18–31
C. The power of Paul's preaching	2.1–5
D. True wisdom and the language of love	2.6–3.4
E. The right attitude towards pastors	3.5–4.5
F. Application to the Corinthians	4.6–13
G. Timothy's visit	4.14–21
3. THE IMPORTANCE OF THE BODY	5.1–6.20
A. A case of incest	5.1–8
B. Clearing up a misunderstanding	5.9–13
C. Lawsuits among Christians	6.1–11
D. Prostitution	6.12–20
4. RESPONSES TO CORINTHIAN QUESTIONS	7.1–14.40
A. Problems of social status	7.1–40

3. The Trouble at Corinth

It is tantalizing to try to build up a picture of what the basic trouble at Corinth, underlying all the others, can have been. Paul's first concern is about the unity of the community. So, after a brief thanksgiving for the graces they have received, he denounces with vehemence and biting irony the divisions and factions within the community (1.10–16). What the different beliefs of these factions are is not entirely clear: 'I am for Paul, I am for Apollos, I am for Cephas' tells us only the personal adherence of each. The fourth, 'I am for Christ', must be the ultimate in irony, a *reductio ad absurdum*, insinuating that only one quarter of this bitterly divided Christian community claim Christ as their leader. Possibly the Cephas-faction were in favour of Jewish observances, and presumably the 'Pauline' faction were for freedom from Jewish observances. In fact, however, it was the dividedness of the opinions rather than the actual opinions which disturbs Paul.

Perhaps this was the result of an overflowing confidence in their liberty, for they were no longer subject to the Jewish Law, or indeed any other; hence the repeated 'for me everything is permissible'. This is combined with a certain arrogance ('all of us have knowledge'; 'none of the false gods exists in reality'). The result is a certainty that they can transcend the temptations of the flesh ('It is a good thing for a man not to touch a woman'), and that sexual relations can be treated with the utmost liberty. Some of them have the confidence to disregard food-taboos, while others lack that confidence (8.1–13).

Paul here provides a fascinating little piece of discussion, where he is at his most genuine, frank and human. The issue was whether meat sacrificed to idols was so tainted that Christians could not eat it. Such meat was attractive because it was sold off cheap in the market. There was also the social problem, which might have worried the higher-class members: what do you do at dinner-parties if such meat is offered? (I once found myself lunching with the Queen Mother on Ash Wednesday.) Paul sensibly says that, since the gods to whom it has been offered do not exist, the meat cannot be tainted. More importantly, he then warns 'the strong' who can accept this argument not to upset the consciences of 'the weak' who cannot. Every individual conscience is sacred.

It may also extend to the unfeeling contempt for the poor criticized in Paul's complaints about the Eucharistic assembly (11.20–2). Paul is probably mocking this over-confidence when he contrasts them with himself in 4.8–10. He sets about puncturing their self-satisfaction with really sharp sarcasm: they are honoured, wise, wealthy, kings, while he is the opposite of all these. These are all terms used by Philo (the Jewish philosopher of Alexandria, and Apollos came from Alexandria) to describe the heavenly man, the model of all human beings. This fierce irony must have been uncomfortably galling when the letter was read out in full community, though he can also be affectionate:

> How many of you were wise in the ordinary sense of the word? How many were influential? How many came from noble families? No, it was to shame the wise… I treated you as sensual men, still infants in Christ. I fed you with milk, not solid food, for you were not ready for it, and indeed you are still not ready for it. Isn't that obvious? (1.10–2.16)
>
> I am saying all this not just to make you ashamed but to bring you, my dearest children, to your senses. You might have a thousand guardians in Christ, but not more than one father, and it was I who begot you. (4.14–15)

Paul is also distinctly ironical about speaking in tongues. He says that he himself has the gift but does not use it (14.18). He compares it to thrumming on a lyre or a flute in which the notes are indistinguishable, and to a badly played bugle (13.7–8). He complains that it lacks decorum, fails to edify and fails to communicate – unlike prophecy. Possibly also he refers to speaking in tongues when he speaks of the childish babbling which he has now put aside (13.11). Paul's criterion for valuable gifts of the Spirit is that they build up the community, and accordingly his hesitation about the gift of speaking in tongues rests on its failure to give any message to the community or edify the community unless there is also someone present with the gift to interpret what is being said.

What, then, does Paul think of the phenomenon of the gifts of the Spirit in the modern Church? In the modern Church the word refers principally to speaking in tongues and such ecstatic states as 'slaying in the Spirit' and expulsion of evil spirits. Of these only the first appears in Paul. The same criterion must surely still apply, whether these gifts truly build up the Church and are ordered to this purpose. Individual judgments must be made in each case.

4. The Body of Christ

On the positive side Paul bases all his teaching about the community on the concept of the body of Christ. The incorporation of the Christian into the body of Christ is basic to his whole thinking. He uses the term 'body' indistinguishably in several different ways, just as in Romans he uses each of the terms 'law' and 'spirit' in different ways.

1 The first occurrence is in his condemnation of sexual union with a prostitute. Such is the realism with which he views the body of Christ, that sexual union with a prostitute is forbidden because the body of the Christian is Christ's body: 'Do you think one can take parts of Christ's body and join them to the body of a prostitute? Out of the question!' (1 Cor. 6.15). The bodily union of the Christian with Christ is as real as the full sexual union, which, according to Genesis, makes the two partners a single living being.

2 On the level of eating, too, the Christian is given a share in Christ by sharing in the eucharistic meal. Paul is here using the term 'body' indistinguishably, on two levels at once: 'The blessing-cup which we bless, is it not a sharing in the blood of Christ? And the loaf of bread which we break, is it not a sharing in the body of Christ?' (10.16) Here the parallel with 'blood' shows that he means the real and physical flesh and personality of Christ. But then he goes on to conclude: 'And as there is one loaf, so we, although there are many of us, are one single body, for we all share in the one loaf' (10.17). Here Paul is using 'body' in the sense of a body of people. The eucharistic body of Christ means for Paul equally the loaf and the community which shares it.

Paul touches the subject of the Eucharist twice in this letter, at 10.15–16 and again 11.17–34. Both are precious passages, the former passage because of its teaching on the union with Christ and with the community in the body of Christ. Again in the latter passage it is unclear whether the failure to recognize the body (11.29) is failure to recognize the presence of Christ in the loaf or in the community; Paul does not distinguish. The latter passage is precious also for its exact tradition of the institution of the Eucharist. Paul uses the formulae of rabbinic traditioning, 'received…and passed on' (11.23); he is clearly quoting the tradition, learnt by heart. He uses these formulae again about the death and resurrection of Christ and the witnesses to the Risen Christ. These are two precious nuggets of the most ancient tradition of the Church. They contain minor variations from Paul's own style and vocabulary. In the nugget on the Eucharist there are minor variations between the tradition as presented in Mark-Matthew and that of Paul-Luke. The former seems to be that of the Aramaic-speaking Church, the latter that of the Greek, gentile tradition.

3 Only after this does Paul apply the concept of the body of Christ to the community. The idea of the parts of a political body as interdependent and interacting was a commonplace of political thought in the ancient world. Paul develops this idea in his discussion of the various functions of the body in the different gifts and capacities of the members. One is like an ear, one like a hand, one like a head, each with its own particular function contributing to the whole (12.12–30). But his thinking is at the same time wholly different from any previous use of this figure. Only in Paul is this body some*one*, namely Christ. When he uses the figurative language of the different members, he is building on the reality of the Christian's belonging to Christ, which he has already used independently of the metaphor. Now he brings it to its climax, insisting that the multiple and varied gifts of the Spirit which the members of the community enjoy are not for their own satisfaction and self-congratulation, but for the building up of the body of Christ, living with Christ's life. Their only true function is as manifestations of that true love which he describes so delicately and sensitively (12.31–13.12), the life-functions of the body of Christ. The gift of tongues is pointless unless there is someone who can interpret what is said for the benefit and building of the community (14.9–12). At one stage Paul attempts to rank the gifts, 'In the Church, God has given the first place to apostles, the second to prophets, the third to teachers, after them miracles and after them the gift of healing,

helpers, good leaders, those with many languages' (12.28); but he soon abandons it and returns to the assertion of the equality of the gifts, all given by the same Spirit (12.10–11). All the gifts are equally important for building up the body of Christ. Their variety provides a valuable snapshot of the various functions, various manifestations of the Spirit, exercised within that heterogeneous and enthusiastic community.

5. Paul's Gospel: The Resurrection

It is not immediately clear why Paul moves from his teaching about the activity of the Spirit in the community to the subject of the Resurrection. It has been suggested that the experience of the Spirit in the life of the community was so vivid that they neglected any dimension of future resurrection. In any case, 1 Corinthians 15 is, of all the Pauline writings, the passage where we come nearer than anywhere else to seeing the nature of the risen life, transformed by Christ's resurrection. Since Christ is the first-fruits of resurrection, the risen life of Christ is the exemplar and cause of all risen life. Just as Adam was the exemplar and progenitor of all human life, so Christ is the exemplar and progenitor of the risen life: 'Just as all die in Adam, so all will be brought to life in Christ' (v. 22). What is said of the risen Christ is true of the risen Christian too. Paul can, of course, only use images. He proceeds step by step (vv. 35–49):

1. Firstly he wishes to establish continuity between the present life and the risen life. He uses the comparison of the seed. The continuity is the same as that of the seed to the plant germinated. This is shown by the fact that certain seeds produce certain plants. Grain produces wheat and acorns produce oak-trees.

2. Secondly Paul establishes the principle of analogy. The risen body, that is, the risen personality, is physical, but this is not an end of the matter. Paul tries to explain the principle of analogy: 'not all flesh is the same flesh; there is human flesh, animals have another kind of flesh, birds another and fish yet another' – just as there are different kinds of brightness. So the risen personality is a physical personality, but not physical in the sense to which we are accustomed. Paul is saying that 'flesh' and 'brightness' are alike analogical terms.

3. The change from one form of 'flesh' to another is summed up in four contrasts, the first three issuing in the fourth. Each of these changes indicates a transference into the divine sphere:

1   From perishable to imperishable (the divine immutability),
2   From contemptible to glorious ('glory' is *par excellence* a divine concept),
3   From weak to powerful (and power is above all a divine property).
4   These three are summed up in the life principle: the life-principle is no longer the *psyche* but the *pneuma*; that is, the Christian transformed in the final resurrection is informed and enlivened no longer by the ordinary human life-principle, but by the Spirit, the life-principle of God.

6. Christology: Christ, the Wisdom of the Father

One of the basic difficulties which Paul sets out to combat is the Corinthians' search for Greek wisdom: 'While the Jews demand miracles and the Greeks look for wisdom, here are we, preaching a crucified Christ' (1.22–3). This search for wisdom could conceivably be at the root of one of the rival factions, for Apollos, according to Acts 18.24, was 'an eloquent man' from Alexandria, one of the centres of Greek wisdom at this time. On the contrary, God 'will destroy the wisdom of the wise' (1.19, quoting Isa. 29.14), and 'Christ is the power and the wisdom of God' (1.24). This seemingly chance remark has an important depth, for Paul is describing Christ's position as the Wisdom of God in an utterly new way.

In the Wisdom Literature of the Old Testament, divine Wisdom is the means by which God creates the world, and is not only the agent but also the template or design of creation. God's Wisdom is not exactly God, but is described as existing beside God before creation, and active in creation itself.

> The LORD created me, first-fruits of his fashioning
> before the oldest of his works
> From everlasting I was firmly set,
> from the beginning, before the earth came into being.
> The deep was not when I was born…
> I was beside the master-craftsman
> delighting him day after day. (Prov. 8.22–31)

Finally in Wisdom 7.22–8.1 comes a series of images attempting to express equality with God, a Wisdom somehow separate from God yet wholly dependent on him, a reflection of God with all the divine qualities:

> She is the breath of the power of God,
> pure emanation of the glory of the Almighty…

she is a reflection of the eternal light,
untarnished mirror of God's active power,
and image of his goodness.

Later in the letter Paul uses this concept with astonish boldness. The basic Credo of Judaism was (and is) the so-called *Shema*, the passage in Deuteronomy 6.5 beginning, 'Listen, O Israel! The LORD our God is the one, only LORD. You shall love the LORD your God with your whole heart…'. This passage is the most familiar and beloved of the whole Bible, recited daily, worn in the *tefillin* for prayer, affixed in the *mezuzoth* to every observant doorpost. Paul takes this passage and adapts it to include Christ in the *Shema* as divine Wisdom, as the agent and template of creation:

'For us there is one, only God, the Father,
from whom all things come and for whom we exist'

This is the basic creed of Judaism, but Paul goes on:

'and one Lord, Jesus Christ,
through whom all things come and through whom we exist.' (8.6)

The concept of the godhead has been expanded. There are not two gods, but by the use of the word *kyrios*, which is the standard Greek translation of the divine name otherwise rendered 'the LORD', the title 'Lord God' has been split so that Jesus Christ is included in it. There are now two persons confessed in this central statement of monotheism. The one God and one LORD has become the one God the Father and the one Lord Jesus Christ. The reverence and worship accorded to the LORD God is to be accorded to Christ as the divine Wisdom through whom all things exist.

Further Reading

Blenkinsopp, Joseph, *The Corinthian Mirror* (1964)
Collins, Raymond, *First Corinthians* (1999)
Murphy O' Connor, Jerome, *Paul, A Critical Life* (1996)
Talbert, Charles *Reading Corinthians* (1987)

18

The Second Letter to the Corinthians

1. The Interval between the Letters

After 1 Corinthians, the further communication between Paul and Corinth was stormy. It seems that 1 Corinthians did nothing to allay the troubles. On the contrary Paul's opponents were so riled by the vigour of Paul's sarcasm and criticism (especially of their wisdom, for people who vaunt their wisdom are seldom open to criticism) that it had wholly a negative effect. Between 1 and 2 Corinthians various events occurred which are referred to in the second letter. There seems to have been a series of further communication between Paul and the Corinthians:

1. A brief and painful visit (2 Cor. 1.23–2.1).

2. The visit of a representative of Paul to sort out the problems. In fact this visit only made matters worse, for his authority was flouted (2 Cor. 2.5–10; 7.12).

3. A severe letter from Paul, 'written in agony of mind' (2 Cor. 2.3–9). Despite his severe criticism, Paul still retained a warm affection for those Christians he had 'fathered' at Corinth.

4. News to Paul via Titus that this letter had been effective in bringing them to their senses (2 Cor. 7.8–13).

2. Division of Second Corinthians

It seems most likely that 2 Corinthians is not in fact a single letter, but at least two letters, perhaps a collection of several letters. These would have been put together when Paul's letters were being sent in to whoever made the collection of the letters, and lumped together as a single letter. The components in question are:

2 Corinthians 1–9. Basically Paul is here celebrating his reconciliation with the Corinthians after all the foregoing troubles. He is obviously still rather tentative and lacking in confidence, careful not to alienate them by criticism, and still anxious to win them to his side. Within this unit it has been suggested that there are two passages which once constituted separate letters.

6.14–7.1. This little passage has a quite different tone, and can, moreover, be cut out of the text without spoiling or interrupting any argument: it stands up on its own, and the sequence of thought from 6.13 to 7.2 runs smoothly. It is a strong warning to Paul's correspondents to separate themselves from some evil partners. The Corinthians should not associate with 'unbelievers'. It has been argued that this xenophobia is so contrary to Paul's normal missionary openness (e.g. over food offered to idols, 1 Cor. 8.1–6) that it cannot have been written by him. Paul does not forbid Christians to associate with non-Christians, and indeed encourages a Christian spouse to remain with a non-Christian spouse, in order to convert the non-believing partner (1 Cor. 7.12–16). There is also a series of words used rarely or never elsewhere by Paul. The exclusiveness and the series of oppositions listed is, it is argued, reminiscent of the dualism familiar from the Qumran texts, belief and unbelief, uprightness and lawbreaking, light and darkness, Christ and Beliar. On the other hand, the thought that the Christian is the Temple of the Spirit (v. 16) comes also in 1 Corinthians 3.16.

9.1–15 has no specific reference to Corinth, but mentions Achaia, the province of which Corinth is the capital. Chapter 8 concerns the collection for the Church at Jerusalem, which bulked so large in Paul's thoughts at this time (see p. 206, 246). Chapter 9 starts afresh, as though no mention of the collection had been made, 'About the help to God's holy people there is really no need for me to write to you'. This is, of course, the familiar rhetorical figure of *praeteritio* or 'passing over' ('I don't need to tell you about…'), but it rings strangely immediately after a whole chapter on the matter! Could it be an independent letter, written to all the Churches of of Achaia, which has simply been inserted here after the other passage about the collection which formed part of the appeal addressed specifically to Corinth?

A final decision on either of these matters is not crucial to an understanding of the letter as a whole. Much more important is the status of Chapters 10–13. Here the tone is utterly different from anything which precedes. Instead of being conciliatory or even wheedling, reaching out for the friendship and sympathy of his correspondents, Paul is again explosively ironical and sarcastic. At the very least, his mood has changed drastically between the writing of these two sections. However, the more convincing explanation is that Chapters 10–13 were written separately, some time after the earlier part of the letter, and that some events intervened which left Paul no alternative to justifying himself and re-asserting his authority in this aggressive manner. Accordingly, we shall treat the two passages as separate letters:

Letter A = 2 Cor 1–9
Letter B = 2 Cor 10–13.

It is possible that the editor who collected the letters which we know as 1 and 2 Corinthians put the three letters together in decreasing order of length. Either before or after this collection was made, the two short pieces, discussed above, were inserted.

3. The Purpose and Strategy of Letter A

As all Paul's letters, this letter begins with a normal greeting, followed by a thanksgiving which sets the tone of the letter. In this case the emphasis is on Paul's worries, and on the consolation he eventually received from the Father and passed on to the Corinthians (1.3–11).

This letter indeed, far more than others, is a personal letter, built on and building up the relationship between Paul and the Corinthians, as a result of the stormy situation which had preceded the letter. Despite his repeated protests that he is not commending himself (3.1–2; 5.11–12; 6.11–7.4), Paul is all the time concerned to win over the loyalty of the Corinthians. He constantly stresses his affection for them, calling them 'my dear friends' (2 Cor. 7.1), stressing that he wishes to work for their joy (1.24), not to cause them pain, that they are a letter 'written on our hearts' (3.2, as opposed to the Ten Commandments, written on stone tablets; 7.3). What criticism there is remains tactful and gentle. Nevertheless, after the reconciliation and acceptance of Paul's rebuke which was reported by Titus (7.6–16), he still had some fences to mend. Principally and first, he has to explain why he changed his plan to come to Corinth (1.12–2.17). This leads him on to a reflection on the glory of the apostolic ministry (3.1–4.6), a most valuable and personal meditation by Paul on Christ's ministry of reconciliation, and his own ministry as a ministry of light and glory. To complement this he breaks off to describe his own personal trials and hopes (4.7–5.10), following this up with a return to the idea of the consistency of God's promises, fulfilled in the reconciliation of the world to himself (5.11–6.10). Finally he appeals to them for their loving support (6.11–7.4, though perhaps 6.14–7.1 is inserted in here). After this varied reflection on his ministry, Paul returns to the story of his apostolic travels and his meeting with Titus (7.5–16).

Plan of Letter A

1.12–2.17	Paul's behaviour is consistent, not random
3.1–4.6	The glory of the apostolic ministry
4.7–5.10	Trials of the apostolate
5.11–6.10	Reconciliation and new creation in Christ
6.11–7.4	An appeal for support
7.5–16	Paul's apostolic travels

---

4. Paul's Consistency

First, he sets out to explain why he changed his plans to come to Corinth.

Paul's opponents at Corinth had obviously accused him of inconsistency and unreliability in not coming as he had promised:

> I had been meaning to come to you first... both on my way to Macedonia and then to return to you from Macedonia... Since that was my purpose, do you think I lightly changed my mind? (2 Cor. 1.15–17)

To this accusation he replies on two levels, first historically, explaining that his change had been out of consideration for them, and secondly that he had behaved not unreliably but with the reliability of Christ. This first argument shows just how deep the cleft between Paul and the Corinthians had been. If he had fulfilled his intentions of coming, it would have been 'a painful visit', and consequently he refrained from coming in order to spare them (1.23–2.4). He felt that a visit would be counter-productive until they were in a better frame of mind. In all the letter he is conciliatory and sympathetic. Now he commends their obedience, approves of the forgiveness of the offender (2.5–11), and stresses that they are his letter of commendation, written on his heart (3.1–3)

The second, more theological, explanation Paul gives is also rich in showing his conception of Christ. It is the first instance of the frame of mind which recurs so repeatedly throughout the letter and is the background of all Paul's thought: his assimilation to Christ in his apostolate. Paul claims that he has behaved as Christ did, for Christ is the reliability of God, the fulfilment of the promises of God, the living proof of God's own trustworthiness. Christ is the 'Yes' of God (1.20), in whom we answer 'Amen' to give praise to God. Christ shows the fidelity of God to his promises, and so his reliability. This had been the theme of much of Romans, but there Paul did not seem to have thought of this useful little pun on the word 'Amen'.

In Hebrew the root of 'Amen' means 'true, firm, sure'. So 'Amen' expresses acceptance for myself of the words of others, 'that goes for me, too'. At the great thanksgiving, when Ezra promulgated the Law, at the end Ezra praised the LORD, the great God, and all the people raised their hands and answered, 'Amen, Amen' (Nehemiah 8.6). Saying 'Amen' to a prayer therefore means acceptance of that prayer as one's own. Hence there is a Jewish proverb, 'Only a fool says "Amen" to his own prayer'.

Paul also now gives the clue to all his thought on the matter, making another pun, this time not requiring a knowledge of Hebrew, but only of Greek! The verse 1.21 reads literally: 'God fixed us firmly with you in Christ and christed (*chrisas*) us, who also sealed us and gave us the pledge of the Spirit in our hearts.' The word I have rendered 'christed' is etymologically as well as phonetically related to 'Christ', for 'Christ' means 'anointed', whence the conventional translation, 'God...anointed us'. Paul hints, however, that this anointing made us into Christ, assimilated us to Christ. The pun expresses the intensity with which Paul feels his integration into, or identification with, Christ. Similarly the gift of the 'pledge' of the Spirit of Christ bespeaks the same integration, for the word used for 'pledge' is used of a first down-payment or deposit, a payment which makes sense only if further payment is to follow. It is as though to say, 'We have received the first down-payment of the Spirit, as an earnest of further payments.' Writing to the Spirit-people at Corinth, Paul consistently stressed that we are all transformed by the Spirit, or rather that we have begun to be transformed by the pledge of the Spirit (1.22, and again 5.5). He will stress that his ministry is a ministry of the Spirit (3.6, 8, 17, 18).

The other expression which Paul uses here to express his relationship with Christ is also rich and somewhat involved. In 2.14 Paul writes of God 'always leading us in the triumphal procession in Christ'. Already in 1 Thessalonians Paul had used the image of Christ's triumphal procession, meeting Christ in the clouds (see p. 295). Here the imagery is rather darker. Immediately afterwards Paul twice uses the imagery of 'fragrance of Christ'. For a Jew such imagery conjures up 'the sweet smell of sacrifice' which arises to God in the Temple. Paul is being led in Christ's triumphal procession precisely as a sacrifice, for the conclusion of a Roman triumphal procession was the slaughter of captives in the Temple. He differentiates between the smell of death that leads to death and the sweet smell of life that leads to life.

5. The Glory of the Apostolic Ministry

Much more important than this imagery, however, is the contrast between the ministry of Moses and the ministry of the Spirit, or rather between the glory of each ministry. This may well be designed to appeal especially to the Jews in the Christian community of Corinth, for Paul is drawing on one of the supreme moments of the Old Testament, the moment of the covenant on Sinai, when Moses saw all that could be seen of the glory of God. When

Moses begged the LORD to allow him to see the divine glory, God put Moses in a cleft in the rock while he passed by, shielding Moses with his hand, allowing Moses to see only the back of himself, 'for my face is not to be seen' (Exod. 33.23). It was then that God made the Covenant which was the basis of Israel's life. Ever afterwards the face of Moses was so marked – conventionally translated 'horned', but better translated 'calloused' – by the brightness of the glare of the splendour of God's glory that he veiled his face.

> If the administering of death was accompanied by such a brightness that the Israelites could not bear looking at the face of Moses, how much greater will be the brightness that surrounds the administering of the Spirit! If what was so temporary had any splendour, there must be much more in what is going to last for ever.' (3.7–10)

Then Paul, somewhat unfairly, changes the image and puts the veil on the face of the Israelites who failed to recognize Christ. 'Yes, even today whenever Moses is read, the veil is over their minds, and it will not be removed until they turn to the Lord' (3.16). However he ends on the supremely optimistic note of the Spirit, which would, of course, appeal especially to the Corinthians who so valued the works of the Spirit: 'And we, with our unveiled faces reflecting like mirrors the brightness of the Lord, all grow brighter and brighter as we are turned into the image that we reflect; this is the work of the Lord who is Spirit' (3.18), 'to radiate the light of the knowledge of God's glory, the glory on the face of Christ' (4.6).

6. The Trials of the Apostolate

Throughout this letter Paul continually reminds his listeners of the trials associated with the work of the apostle. These are part of his living with Christ's life and imitating Christ's life, a source of strength. He had already said in the initial greeting, 'Just as the sufferings of Christ overflow into our lives, so too does the encouragement we receive through Christ. So if we have hardship to undergo, this will contribute to your encouragement and your salvation'. (1.5)

So now, as so often, using images from the games, he gives more detail:

> We hold this treasure in pots of earthenware, so that the immensity of the power is God's and not our own. We are subjected to every kind of hardship but never distressed, we see no way out but we never despair, we are pursued

but never cut off, knocked down but still have some life in us. We carry with us in our body the death of Jesus so that the life of Jesus too may be visible in our body. Indeed, while we are still alive, we are constantly being handed over to death. (4.7–11)

The imagery is drawn from wrestling, and provoked by the image of an earthenware pot. Wrestlers oiled themselves before a bout. After the number of falls onto a clay floor suggested by Paul ('knocked down') they would themselves look like clay pots. The other antitheses also fit wrestling-bouts well. The same sort of recitation of his trials and sufferings occurs also in a later passage, again with the repeated antithesis of refusing to be quelled by the hardships:

But in everything we prove ourselves authentic servants of God; by resolute perseverance in times of hardships, difficulties and distress, when we are flogged or sent to prison or mobbed, labouring sleepless, starving, in times of honour or disgrace, blame or praise, taken for impostors and yet we are genuine, unknown and yet we are acknowledged, dying, and here we are alive, scourged but not executed, in pain yet always full of joy, poor and yet making many people rich, having nothing and yet owning everything. (6.4–10)

He will return to the same theme in Letter B, and there contend that the lack of such sufferings in his opponents shows that they are not authentic apostles (11.23). By relating his own sufferings to those of Christ he shows what a central part in his own spirituality is played by the cross of Christ: 'we carry in our body the death of Christ … so that in our mortal flesh the life of Jesus, too, may be openly shown' (4.10–11). In consequence, Paul longs to be perfectly united with Christ and to bear the weight of eternal glory (5.17).

The puzzling passage 5.1–5, in which Paul writes of the tent of this present life being replaced by an everlasting home in the heavens, and of another garment being put on to cover his nakedness, has been read in a Platonic sense as though Paul was expecting a new and heavenly body to replace or even to cover over his earthly body. However, the apocalyptic writings of the time (*1 Enoch* 39.3–4 and Jn 14.2) speak freely of the dwelling places in heaven, and of being clothed with heavenly garments as opposed to being stripped naked to reveal sinfulness. This is an imaged way of speaking not about a new body but of a whole new mode of existence in the eschaton.

7. Reconciliation and New Creation in Christ

In this final section of Paul's teaching in this part of the letter he combines the two themes of reconciliation in Christ and his own apostolic ministry as an ambassador of Christ, passing on this reconciliation. This is one of the most important passages in Paul on the work of salvation. In fulfilment of his covenant with Israel, God has in Christ finally completed the purpose of the covenant through the reconciliation in Christ. In Greek and pagan religion and sacrifice, reconciliation is something done by human beings on God, turning away God's wrath by providing a conciliatory sacrifice. There are remnants of this in the primitive rites of the scapegoat. This is, however, utterly different from the Hebrew conception of reconciliation. In the Hebrew Bible God is not reconciled, but it is always God who does the reconciling (e.g. Deut. 21.8; Jer. 18.23); God is the grammatical subject of the verb 'to reconcile', not the object (5.18–20). So in Romans 3.25 God puts forward Christ Jesus 'as a sacrifice of reconciliation through faith in his blood in order to show his justice', and as here in 5.21, the 'justice of God' is his fidelity to his promises (cf. discussion in Romans). This is also the message of Isaiah 49.5–15, which Paul quotes in his summing up in 6.2., God is the author of reconciliation, and it is the apostle's task to hand on this reconciliation.

What of God 'made the sinless one into sin' (5.11)? Paul cannot here mean that God actually made Christ sinful. He must mean that for our sake Christ underwent death, the consequence of sin. He may also be playing on the Hebrew word *hatta't*, which means both 'sin' and 'sacrifice for sin', suggesting that Christ was the perfect sin-offering, as in Romans 8.3, 'sending his own Son…to be a sacrifice for sin'. See L. Sabourin, *Sin, Redemption and Sacrifice* (Rome, 1970, Chapters 3 and 4), who shows that the idea that Christ was 'made into sin' in the sense of a penal substitution originates only at the Protestant Reformation. As R. Haight insists (*Jesus, Symbol of God*, 1999, p. 241), the idea that Christ sustained God's wrath and suffered the punishment for the sins of others is a paradigm of injustice. See also this volume on Galatians 3.13.

Thus at the end of his exposition Paul sums up the teaching of the letter by returning to the idea of Christ as the 'Amen' of the Father, completing the Father's promises made in the covenant. This completion is the new creation (5.17). It remains only to appeal once more to the Corinthians for their support, and once again to explain the necessity of the abrasive letter he had sent.

8. The Collection

A feature of several letters of Paul is the collection for the Church of Jerusalem. Writing to the Romans, Paul mentions a present of money which he plans to take to the Church in Jerusalem (15.24–33). Macedonia and Achaia had already decided to send a generous contribution, which Paul regards as repaying a debt in gratitude for the spiritual contribution received from the mother-Church there. The same collection is mentioned also in 1 Corinthians 16.1–4. It may also have been intended to restore or smooth over relationships between Paul of his gentile communities and the Jerusalem Church, for Galatians 2.2–14 shows that there had been massive disagreements between them about the observance of the Jewish Law by Christians. Whether it succeeded or not remains doubtful, for we hear nothing in Acts of any rapturous welcome when Paul made his final visit to Jerusalem. Had it occurred, this is just the sort of event which Luke would have painted in glowing colours, for he is always eager to stress the unity and brotherhood of the Christian community. On the contrary, after the elders have briefly acknowledged Paul's work, they immediately reproach him for drawing Jewish converts away from observance of the Law, and demand that he show his good faith by being purified in the Temple and paying the expenses of four others (Acts 21.21–4). It is almost as though he is being asked to launder the money first. After Paul made his speech in the Temple and had to be rescued from a riot, we do not know what happened to the money.

In these chapters, 2 Corinthians 8–9, Paul presses with all his persuasiveness, while at the same time underlining that the gift must be entirely free. He points out that they initiated the idea in the first place, and should finish it off (8.10). He puts forward the example of Christ's generosity (8.9), and that of the Macedonian Church, despite their own acute poverty (8.2–3). He spurs on the Corinthians by the example of the Macedonians (8.1–4) and the Macedonians by the example of the Achaeans (9.2)! It has been suggested that Paul's expression of hope that there will be no accusations of maladministration on his part (8.20) precisely implies that there had been such accusations; this is hardly justified.

9. Letter B

If these chapters originally formed a separate letter, the immediate question is chronological: where do they fit into the correspondence? Paul says that he is all prepared to go to Corinth for the third time (12.14), but this still leaves the question open. The first visit was the initial evangelisation, the second the 'painful visit' mentioned in 2 Corinthians 1.23–2.1, but this third visit could have been at any later time, even before 2 Corinthians 1–9, especially if an editor put the three letters together simply in order of length: 1 Corinthians, 2 Corinthians 1–9, 2 Corinthians 10–13 without regard for the chronological order. (This would assume that Chapter 8 belongs with Chapters 1–7, and Chapter 9 was added to that because of the similarity of the subject, the Collection).

This question, however, need not affect a reading of the letter. We will consider these chapters as a separate letter, independent of all others. The most striking features are that it is entirely different in mood from the earlier part of 2 Corinthians, and that it is more autobiographical than any of the other Pauline letters. Especially if one is reserved towards the biographical information on Paul given in Acts, it is valuable as almost our chief biographical source for Paul's ministry. The most striking feature of all is the extended and bitter sarcasm, the same sort of sarcasm as we have met in the early chapters of 1 Corinthians. This sort of parody was a well-known form of literature, and was assiduously practised and rehearsed in the rhetorical schools. Now, however, it is directed not primarily against the Corinthians, though they do also merit the sharp edge of Paul's tongue ('I know how happy you are to put up with fools, being so wise yourselves', 11.20), but against a group of people who were attempting to withdraw Paul's community there from their loyalty to him and from his view of Christianity.

Plan of Letter B

10.1–11	Paul's task and his authority at Corinth
10.12–18	Contrast with his rivals
11.1–11	Paul's devotion to the Corinthians

11.12–33	Contrast with his rivals
12.1–13	The revelation to Paul
12.14–13.10	Paul's impending visit to Corinth
13.11–13	Final Blessings

Who were these rivals?

- They begin with personal abuse, suggesting that Paul is insufficiently forceful in person, so that Paul replies sarcastically, 'I, the one who is so humble when he is facing you but full of boldness at a distance... Someone said, "His letters are weighty enough and full of strength, but when you see him in person he makes no impression and his powers of speaking are negligible"' (10.1, 10). Presumably there is some truth in their claim that he was not a polished orator – 'but as for knowledge, that is a different matter' (11.6).

- They claim to be more Jewish than Paul, pure representatives of Israel, so that Paul replies, 'Are they Hebrews? So am I. Are they Israelites? So am I. Are they descendants of Abraham? So am I. Are they servants of Christ? I speak in utter folly – I am too, and more than they are' (11.21–2). This claim was presumably based on Paul's teaching that it is unnecessary for Christians to obey the Jewish Law. They claim to be true Christians, but Paul replies that he is more faithful to the meaning of descendance from Abraham. So we are back to the old controversy about Jewish observance, which had rumbled on ever since the beginning of the inclusion of gentiles in the Christian community. Paul feels that he is on solid ground after the decision he records in Galatians 2.7: 'They [the leaders at Jerusalem] recognised that I had been commissioned to preach the Good News to the uncircumcised just as Peter had been commissioned to preach it to the circumcised.' But there were still difficulties about table-fellowship in view of the laws about clean food. The eating habits of gentile Christians could well upset Jewish Christians. Had the letter of Acts 15.28–9 already been widely promulgated or is Luke there pre-dating a later decision?

- They claim equal authority to Paul's (10.12), or even more, if Paul's ironical description of them as 'super-apostles' is their own language (12.11). After the manner of imposters, even in the ancient world, they write their own letters of reference.

- Paul's repeated claim that he was no burden to the Corinthians, and his determination not to accept money from them (11.7–10), may suggest that his rivals, the 'counterfeit apostles, dishonest workmen disguised as apostles of Christ', did just that.

- The heart of their claim against Paul is perhaps never stated in clear terms, but lies behind the 'fool's boast' of the visionary experience. We know from the traditional formula in 1 Corinthians 15.3–5 (see p. 233) that the Risen Christ 'appeared to more than five hundred of the brothers at the same time'. It may be that the arch-apostles claimed that Paul, not having experienced the Risen Christ in this way, fell behind them in authority. Paul's account of his own visionary experience – whether this is the same as the experience on the road to Damascus or not – may be set in deliberate opposition to this claim of superior authority.

What was this experience, described in such strange terms in 12.2–4? Is it to be equated with the vision of the Risen Christ on the road to Damascus described in Acts 9.3–6 and elsewhere? There have been many reconstructions of the chronology of Paul's ministry, but the chief common factor is their flimsiness of evidence. One striking factor here is that on the only two occasions when Paul himself mentions his remote past, each time it is 14 years ago (here and Galatians 2.1). Is this a conventional figure (2 x 7)? Is Paul now describing in terms of his own experience the same incident as Acts described from an external point of view? The language is that of Jewish apocalyptic (see p. 362), in which journeys to and from another world are common enough. In some schemes there are seven heavens, but the preposition used by Paul (*eos*=right into, all the way to) suggests a journey to the extreme, to total intimacy with the divine. The uncertainty about in or out of the body is not a lapse into Platonic language about incorporeal existence, but rather stresses Paul's total incomprehension of how it happened. The (literally) 'unspeakable words which a human being cannot say' is a characteristic expression of a mystical experience. It may also be Paul's way of stressing that this experience and any similar experiences claimed by Paul's rivals are irrelevant to their message. More likely, it is a way of showing that Paul's special intimacy with God goes beyond words.

All this is controversy, and well within the conventions and spirit of the times. Paul was thoroughly at home in Hellenistic rhetoric. It is possible that the whole of Galatians is built on the plan of a rhetorical speech for the defence. Now he uses the well-known convention of Comparison. Meleager's comparison of pease-porridge to lentil soup was a famous exercise of the schools. Plutarch develops a great series of *Parallel Lives*, comparing Greek and Roman statesmen. So now Paul mounts his attack on his critics by comparing himself to them. To a modern ear Paul's method at this stage may seem distastefully boastful. It is important to realize that the modern conventions of modesty and self-deprecation were not yet valued. Self-praise was an accepted convention, though there were firm conventions also about its limits. Thus two contemporaries, Lucian, in *A Professor of Public Speaking* (13.21) claims to drive out his rivals 'as trumpets drown flutes or cicadas bees'. Plutarch, on the other hand, lays down rules *On Praising Oneself Inoffensively*. So Paul is constrained to compare himself to his rivals, but when he comes to describing his heavenly experiences slips into anonymity by referring to 'a man in Christ... whether in the body or out of the body, I do not know' (12.2–5).

The brunt of Paul's positive *apologia* is two-fold. One plea is that he loves the Corinthians and serves them by preaching the gospel to them (11.7–8). This is expressed especially in Old Testament terms, drawn from Jeremiah 1.10, 'The Lord gave me authority for building you up and not for pulling you down' (10.8), or by means of the frequent biblical metaphor of the spouse: 'I arranged for you to marry Christ, so that I might give you away as a chaste virgin to this one husband' (11.2).

More important still in his *apologia* is his claim to imitate Christ in his sufferings. As Christ was the Servant of the LORD in his Passion, so Paul is the servant of Christ. He has already described himself as such in 1 Corinthians 3.5, as servant of the new covenant in 2 Corinthians 3.6. Now he develops this:

> Servants of Christ? I must be mad to say this, but so am I, and more than they; more, because I have been in prison more. I have been flogged more severely, many times exposed to death. Five times I have been given the thirty-nine lashes by the Jews; three times I have been beaten with rods; once I was stoned; three times I have been shipwrecked and once I was in the open sea for a night and a day; continuously travelling, I have been in danger from rivers, in danger from brigands, in danger from my own people and from the gentiles, etc. (11.23–9)

The same claim will be made in Colossians 1.23, 'the Good News, of which I, Paul, have become the servant'.

Further Reading

Lambrecht, Jan, *Second Corinthians* (1999)
Stegman, T. D., *Second Corinthians* (2009)
Murphy O'Connor, Jerome, *The Theology of the Second Letter to the Corinthians* (1991)

19

The Letter to the Galatians

---

1. Background: Christians and the Law of Moses

The Gospels and Acts leave little doubt that Jesus did not make clear any position with regard to observance of the Law by his followers. The Gospels show Jesus in dispute with Pharisees about *how* the Law should be observed, and ways in which Jesus' interpretation differs from that of mainstream Pharisees. However, the disputes of Jesus with the Pharisees may even suggest that Jesus was an unorthodox Pharisee, but still working within the Pharisaic framework, though the Son of Man has authority over the Law, and may introduce adjustments, for example on divorce (Mk 10.3–12). Mark (writing for gentile Christians) is much more dismissive of observance than is Matthew (writing for Christians sprung from Judaism). Thus Mark reads Jesus' comments on cleanliness ('Nothing that goes into someone from outside can make that person unclean; it is the things that come out of someone that make that person unclean' Mk 7.15) as sweeping away all culinary restrictions: 'Thus he pronounced all foods clean', Mark explains (7.19). Matthew, however, deliberately omits this telling explanation, which suggests that in his community the restrictions still held. He teaches, with examples, that the Law-observance of Christians must exceed that of the scribes and Pharisees, not that Christians need not observe the Law (5.17–48). He also suggests that the Sabbath continued to have some importance (e.g. 24.20).

It was by no means obvious that non-Jews should be admitted to Christianity at all. Jesus had made contact with them only exceptionally. The Syro-Phoenician (gentile) woman had to win the cure of her daughter by the ready wit coupled to her faith in Jesus (Mk 7.24–30). The Gerasene demoniac, whose legion of unclean tormentors drowned themselves in the Lake, may or may not have been a gentile; all we know is that he lived in the gentile area of the Decapolis (5.1–20). It is, of course, significant that the first human being to recognize that Jesus was Son of God was the gentile Roman centurion after his death.

The Acts of the Apostles reflects the uncertainty about the matter in the earliest Christian community. One of its main purposes is to show that the extension of Christianity to the gentiles was divinely inspired. So Peter is sent to the first gentiles to be received by means of that strongest of Lukan divine persuasions, an interlocking vision (Cornelius is told by a vision to send for Peter [10.32] and correspondingly Peter is told by a vision to go to him [10.22]). When Peter arrives, the reception of Cornelius and his family is pre-empted by the Spirit coming down, before Peter has finished his introductory speech (10.44). Further stress is laid on this story by its repetition twice, in Chapters 11 and 15 before the Christian assembly. Similarly the vocation by the risen Christ of Paul, the apostle to the gentiles, is thrice repeated. Again thrice, in each area of the expanding mission (Asia Minor, Greece, Rome), Paul begins his mission to the Jews, but is forced to turn to the gentiles. This he does with a biblical gesture, hinting that this was the divine will. The heavy stress on the divine guidance of this move to include the gentiles suggests that it needed justifying.

But the inclusion of gentiles did not settle the questions of observance by Christians of the Law of Moses or the relationship between Jews and non-Jews within Christianity. There had already been one upset between the Hebrew and the Hellenistic followers of the Way, even in the ideal early Jerusalem community (Acts 6.1–4). Before Galatians was written we know of one, possibly two, stabs at solving the problems:

1 *The 'Letter from Jerusalem'* (Acts 15.23–9), addressed to 'the brothers of gentile birth in Antioch, Syria and Cilicia'. This letter does not even hint that converts must obey the Law in such important matters as

Sabbath and circumcision. It lays down basically three restrictions, banning food sacrificed to idols, blood in meat, and illicit marriages (presumably marriage within the family degrees forbidden by Jewish Law, but permissible in Roman law). These conditions would avoid situations which would make association with gentile Christians highly distasteful for Jewish Christians. But the relationship of this letter to Paul remains obscure: certainly, when writing to the Corinthians, he does not forbid the use of food sacrificed to idols. Was the letter a merely local ruling? When was it made, before or after the writing of Galatians and First Corinthians? We have suggested that the account of the 'Council of Jerusalem' in Acts 15 is an amalgam of different events at different dates (see pp. 169, 176).

2 *The Row between Peter and Paul at Antioch*, described in Galatians 2.11–14. Two factors in this ugly scene particularly deserve note:

a It concerns association of Jews with gentiles, not gentile observance of Jewish Law. Of course if gentile Christians had observed Jewish Law, there would have been little or no problem. But it is not suggested that the only reasonable solution would be to prescribe such observance. Another reasonable solution (one which might have been preferred) would be to have two separate eucharistic communities within Christianity.

b The dispute remained unresolved. Paul tells us that he publicly rebuked Peter/Cephas, but he never tells us Peter's reaction. Did Peter admit that he was in the wrong? Did he even think he was? If Peter had conceded the point, Paul would surely have trumpeted the fact, since it would have been an impressively strong argument on his side. The fact that Paul says nothing, leaves his question in the air (Galatians 2.14), constitutes a strong argument *e silentio* that Peter never conceded. This would also account for Paul's seeming isolation after this event. It could be at this point that Paul split off from his erstwhile colleague and leader, Barnabas. Luke attributes the split to a 'sharp disagreement' over the suitability of John Mark (Acts 15.37–39). This may be less than the whole story. Paul admits ruefully that at the Antioch incident 'even Barnabas was carried away by their insincerity' (Gal. 2.13). There is no sign later in the Acts that Paul is working in conjunction with any of the other Jewish apostles, and his reception when he brought the fruit of his collection to Jerusalem was distinctly frosty (Acts 21.17–25).

2. Paul's Argument in Galatians

a. Disclaimer, what Paul's argument is not

Traditionally, and especially as a consequence of controversy in the sixteenth century, Paul's argument has been seen as a squabble between faith and works. According to the traditional understanding of Jewish piety, helped by Christian anti-semitism, pious Jews believed that salvation was earned by the works of the Law, circumcision, observance of the Sabbath and especially the alimentary precepts. Life consisted in building up a positive balance by successive acts of observance of the Law. This led to the widespread hypocrisy, criticised by Matthew, the most Jewish of the gospels, which castigates the Pharisees for parading their good deeds 'to win human admiration' (e.g. Mt 6.1–18; 23.13–32). Such a view of Judaism was further confirmed by the Reformation controversies, in which Catholics were caricatured in the same way as the Jews, attempting to earn salvation by indulgences, multiplication of Masses, pilgrimages and other external exercises. The focus of Martin Luther's polemic against certain practices of the Catholic Church was the misuse of indulgences, and the apparent implication that salvation could be won by actions such as monetary donations without any repentance for sin. This rapidly escalated into controversy about the relative saving value of faith and works.

However, this view has finally been recognized as a caricature. E. P. Sanders in *Paul and Palestinian Judaism* (1977), carried further by James Dunn in the essays published in *Jesus, Paul and the Law* (1990) and in his short commentary on Galatians (Cambridge University Press, 1993), have shown that it is a fundamental misunderstanding. For the basic Jewish understanding of the Law at the time, Sanders has coined the phrase 'covenantal nomism'. The Law (*nomos* in Greek) was the gift of God and the revelation of his love for his covenant people, the children of Abraham. Salvation was offered in the covenant, and only within the covenant. Obedience to the Law was a response to this love and a sign of being within the covenant people. Belonging to the covenant people was certified primarily by circumcision, but also by the appropriate behaviour. Salvation was not earned, for it was a free gift. The purpose of circumcision and the other observances (especially food laws and Sabbath-observance) was to show that a person belonged to the covenant people; the observances were 'boundary-markers'. God gave the Law to show how people should live within his covenant, so that obedience to the Law was a sign of belonging. These were the customs by which Jews in the ancient world were recognized as such, both by themselves and by outsiders. Dunn calls them 'badges of covenant membership' (*Jesus, Paul and the Law*, p. 192).

b. The Letter

The most striking feature of the letter is its lack of thanksgiving at the beginning. Standard in Paul's letter-writing is a thanksgiving immediately after the initial greeting (p. 196), including often fulsome praise for the recipients of the letter. No such thing in Galatians! There is neither praise nor thanksgiving. Instead Paul launches immediately into reproaches, 'I am astonished that you are so promptly turning away from the one who called you' (1.6). Such hostile and wounding remarks are repeated at intervals throughout the letter: 'You stupid people in Galatia' (3.1) or 'I am beginning to fear that I may, after all, have wasted my efforts on you' (4.11), or 'I am quite at a loss with you' (4.20). It is almost more upsetting that at the end of the letter, when Paul has had his say, he still cannot find it in his heart to send the personal greetings with which he usually concludes. He does manage the final 'grace', but before that almost pushes them away with, 'After this, let no one trouble me' (6.17) and a final reaffirmation of the authority he earns by sharing in Christ's sufferings (compare p. 241). So there is real poignancy in the agonised 'My children, I am going through the pain of giving birth to you all over again' (4.19).

Further light is thrown on the nature of the letter, if Hans Dieter Betz is correct that the letter is composed according to the formal rules of rhetoric. It can be classified according to the well-known genre of an 'apologetic letter'. This means not that Paul is apologising, but that he is arguing and explaining a situation, justifying his stance (as John Henry Newman in his *Apologia pro Vita Sua*). The more formal it is, the more chillingly impersonal, contrasting with Paul's warm, vibrant letters to other communities.

The formal, rhetorical structure, corresponding to the rules laid down for a speech by the defence in Cicero's works, is in fact easily traced:

1.1–5 *Praescriptio* (address)
1.6–11 *Exordium* (introduction) – statement of the issue, the Galatians' rejection of Paul's gospel.

1.12–2.14 *Narratio* (narration of events) – the story, intended to establish Paul's authority.

2.15–21 *Propositio* (argument to be proved) – Salvation comes to all not by the Law but by faith in God's fidelity to his promises in Christ.

3.1–4.31 *Probatio* (proof)

3.1–5	The evidence of experience: the Spirit
3.6–14	The evidence of scripture
3.15–18	The analogy of a will
3.19–29	Digression on the purpose of the Law
4.1–11	Children of God entering upon the inheritance
4.12–20	A personal appeal
4.21–31	The allegory of Hagar and Sarah

5.1–6.10 *Exhortatio* – this is not quite a normal feature. The *exhortatio* normally consists in an appeal for sympathy to the listening jury, and invocation of the gods. Paul, however, here exhorts his correspondents to give full rein to the freedom of the Spirit.

6.11–18 *Conclusio*

Praescriptio

Each of the four main central sections deserves some special comment. But before that we should note that the letter begins, not with his usual warm greeting, followed by a thanksgiving, but with a strong or even strident assertion of Paul's own authority: 'Paul, an apostle appointed not by human beings nor through any human being but by Jesus Christ and God the Father'. Paul leaves no doubt of his right to teach and lay down the law. This is followed, not by a thanksgiving for their faith, but by the forthright statement, 'I am astonished that you are so promptly turning away…to a different gospel' (1.6).

It is, however, a feature of all Paul's opening paragraphs that he alludes to the principal subject-matter. Here he mentions both the risen status of Christ ('God the Father who raised him from the dead') and Jesus Christ's own sacrifice for our sins ('who gave himself for our sins'). These two qualities will play their part throughout the letter, in which Christ's own story is basic. It is the Cross and the vindication of Christ by the Father which are added to the promises to Abraham to give a new quality to the story of Israel. This is a radical newness, a 'rescue from this evil world', freedom from the elemental principles of this world, a new creation.

Narratio (1.12–2.14)

This section provides us with the fullest piece of consecutive autobiography of Paul that we possess. He is concerned to establish both that his authority is of divine origin and that it is not opposed to the teaching of the human authorities in the Christian community at Jerusalem.

First he gives them the account of his own call. The version of the story in the Acts of the Apostles is familiar enough; it is modelled on the biblical conversion-experience of Heliodorus in 2 Maccabees 3. Here Paul gives his own version, not so much of a conversion-experience as of a call, for he likens it to the call of the prophet Jeremiah 'called from his mother's womb' (1.15; Jer. 1.5). It is a call to announce God's will. But astonishing also is the change from his 'limitless zeal' for the Law (1.14), for the word 'zeal' has a long and fierce history, referring to relentless defence of the Israel's Law and traditions even to the point of bloodshed and killing, particularly by Phinehas (Num. 25.6–13), Elijah on Mount Carmel (1 Kgs 18.40) and Mattathias (1 Macc. 2.15–28). He is called to leave behind this zeal and carry Israel's traditions and promises to the gentiles.

However, Paul's sense of divine vocation did not exclude his learning from human tradition. In First Corinthians he gives two excerpts of credal statements (on the eucharist and on the resurrection) which must have been learnt by heart, first by Paul and then by the converts to whom he passed them on (see p. 232). Paul speaks of a visit of 15 days to Jerusalem (Gal. 1.18). If Paul was educated at the feet of Gamaliel (the greatest of this generation of rabbis), he would certainly have been trained in learning by heart. Rabbi Resh Laqish learnt the whole of the *Torat ha-Qohanim* (the Torah of the Priests) by heart in three days (b. Yeb. 72b).

The situation is, however, not quite so simple. In the last analysis, Paul does not succeed in sheltering behind the human authorities of the Christian community. Although he had previously twice 'checked out' his message with the authorities in Jerusalem, it is precisely against these authorities, James and Cephas, that he takes up his stand in the Antioch incident. On the human level he can claim only that in Jerusalem they recognized 'that the gospel for the uncircumcised had been entrusted to me' (2.7). When it came to the point, this did not stop the 'trouble-makers' taking a different point of view on the relationship of circumcised and uncircumcised Christians.

Propositio (2.15–21)

This is, of course, the nub of the whole argument of the letter. The whole burden of the letter is that some outsiders had attempted to divert the Christians of Galatia from the gospel preached by Paul, persuading them to return to the practice of the Law. Paul does not bother to tell us exactly who they were, nor exactly what they taught. But their stress on the Law was enough to induce Paul to formulate and express the attitude of the Christian to the Law.

a. There are clear hints in the letter which suggest that those who pressed the claims of the Law were distinguished from the Galatian Christians themselves, that they were outsiders:

1 He always refers to the trouble-makers in the third person, while he addresses the Galatians in the second person (1.7–8; 3.1).
2 To Paul it seems as though they want to cut the Galatians off from him, so that they can hold the loyalty of the Galatians (4.17).
3 They want to avoid being persecuted for the Cross of Christ (6.12).
4 They are circumcised (6.13).

b. It is also difficult to see what they taught, because Paul does not see any need to give a fair and balanced picture of their teaching. Rather he caricatures it:

1 It can be presented as a 'gospel'. Paul denies that it is a gospel (1.6), but this denial suggests that the proponents put it forward as such.
2 It is concerned with the flesh rather than the Spirit (3.2). This, however, says little, for to Paul 'the flesh' opposed to 'the Spirit' is merely unredeemed humanity (see p. 264). This contrast is more a value-judgment than an explanation.
3 They depend on the works of the Law (3.10).
4 It concerns 'those powerless and bankrupt elements whose slaves you now want to be all over again' (4.9). This again is difficult to evaluate. Are the 'elements' the principles behind the Law, or some sort of powers which might be thought to rule the world? In the previous verse Paul refers to being 'kept in slavery to things that are not really gods at all'. Paul may mean merely false principles of conduct, or some powers which stand behind them.
5 It involves keeping special days and months, and seasons and years, presumably the festivals prescribed by the Law of Moses (4.10).

6 It implies being fastened again to the yoke of slavery from which Christ has set us free (5.1); this could be no more than an image of return to the Law, as in 4.1–7.

7 It requires acceptance of circumcision (5.2).

c. The main thrust of Paul's reply, and the principal advance of the whole letter, is that faith in Christ and baptism into Christ effect such a change that legal observance now becomes irrelevant. To return to such observance is therefore to fail to recognize faith and baptism for what they are. At beginning and end of the *Propositio* Paul expresses this negatively and positively.

> First and negatively, saving justice does not come through the Law (vv. 16 and 21): 'No human being can be found upright by keeping the Law' and 'if saving justice comes through the Law, Christ died needlessly'.

> Secondly and positively, the heart of the teaching is in the two paradoxes, 'through the Law I am dead to the Law' (v. 19) and 'I have been crucified with Christ and yet I am alive' (v. 20).

Probatio (3.1–4.31): This proceeds in several stages

3.1–5 The evidence of experience: the Spirit.

Paul's argument is that fulfilment has arrived, and to prove this the first argument is the fulfilment of the promises of the outpouring of the Spirit, and the obvious phenomena of the Spirit. It is an appeal to their own religious experience. To anyone versed in Judaism the outpouring of the Spirit is evidence of the fulfilment of the last days, as Peter proclaimed at Pentecost, quoting Joel 3.1. He could have added innumerable passages from Isaiah, such as 11.2–9, or 32.15–16, or 42.1–4. Here Paul appeals briefly to the power to work miracles (v. 5), but principally in Galatians he appeals to the quieter manifestations of the Spirit, the awareness and experience of being sons which they could feel in their hearts: 'God has sent into our hearts the Spirit of his Son, crying "Abba, Father"' (4.6). Just as striking is the guidance by the Spirit, which they are assumed to experience in their own consciences (5.16), leading to the fruits of the Spirit, 'love, joy, peace, patience, kindness, goodness, trustfulness, gentleness and self-control' (5.22).

3.6–14 The evidence of scripture.

Here Paul turns to the promises to Abraham to re-define the people of God. Already in the promise to Abraham the key is faith, and 'all nations' are included (Gen. 12.3; 15.6). As a good rabbinical scholar he adds to the quotation of the Law a quotation also from the prophets, Habakkuk 2.4. On the other hand, the Law brings only a curse, not by itself but by our inability to fulfil the Law.

> In what sense can Christ be described as 'cursed for our sake' (3.13)? Paul cannot resist a neat rabbinical use of *gezerah shawah*, one of the principles of exegesis codified at about this time by Rabbi Hillel: if the same words appear in different verses, they can be used to interpret each other. So *'cursed be everyone who* is hanged on a tree' (the expression used for crucifixion) can be related to *'cursed be everyone who* does not persevere…' It is an argument for showing that Christ too put himself under the obligation of fulfilling the Law, rather than an argument that Christ was accursed. The curse which Christ took on was the Law, which could not be fulfilled.

3.15–18 The analogy of a will

What then was the purpose of the Law? Paul first explains negatively: it cannot have altered the promise, for, like a will, the dispositions once made cannot be changed. So it could not add to or alter the promise made to Abraham. Above all, the promise was made to Abraham and his seed, Christ. Paul argues from the use of the noun 'seed' in the singular that there can be only one descendant, not two. We are baptized into Christ and there cannot be two Christs, a Jewish and a gentile Christ: 'you are all clothed in Christ and there is no more Jew and Greek, slave and free, male and female; you are all one in Christ Jesus' (v. 28).

3.19–29 The Law as a *paidagogos*

Then what was the positive function of the Law? It was added because of transgressions/sins, as a *paidagogos*, the slave who looked after a young child, kept him in check, led him to school – a sort of nanny or childminder, a figure regarded (like school teachers) with a mixture of affection, awe and patronizing mockery, but above all a temporary figure.

4.1–11 Entering upon the inheritance

The conclusion of the argument is full of allusion to the Exodus from Egypt, when God called his son out of slavery in Egypt to give him the promised inheritance of Canaan. Through the gift of the Spirit we can call God 'Father'. Paul is thinking principally of Hosea 11.1–4:

> When Israel was a child I loved him, and I called my son out of Egypt...
> I led them with reins of kindness, with leading-strings of love,
> I was like someone who lifts an infant close against his cheek,
> Stooping down to him I gave him his food.

An important point is obscured by the English term 'adoption as sons', implying some sort of secondary rank or substitution as sons. The Greek term holds no such implication, merely 'placement as sons', with full title as heirs. This new liberation into the inheritance is not, however, merely a matter of personal status, but of a whole new world-condition. Formerly the world was subject to 'elemental principles' (4.3), 'the present wicked world' (1.4), from which it is now liberated. Now it is a new creation (6.15) in which the old categories of Jew and gentile, male and female, slave and free, have lost their validity.

4.21–31 The Allegory of Hagar and Sarah

After Paul's personal appeal (4.12–20), he completes his picture rather wickedly with this allegory. Just as he had turned upside-down the view of the Law, seeing it as a curse, not a blessing, so he turns upside-down the conventional relationship of Hagar and Sarah. The full sting, not to say offensiveness, of this figure comes from its reversal of the natural and expected meaning of the contrast, which indeed the trouble-makers may well have used. Paul's Judaising opponents would no doubt have used the contrast between Sarah and Hagar to reinforce their own view: the Jews were the promised inheritors, descended from Abraham through Sarah, while the gentiles, excluded from the promise, were linked to Ishmael, son of the slave-girl. Outrageously, Paul uses his contrast of slavery and freedom to reverse this, and relegate the Jews to descendance from Ishmael.

To deepen the insult yet further, Paul applies the same figure to the city of Jerusalem. When Moses is commanded in Exodus 25 to make the sanctuary and its furnishings, God promises to show him a design for them. Ezekiel also sees a vision of a heavenly Jerusalem and describes its design in minute detail (Ezek. 40–48). In the first century apocalyptic writings this heavenly Jerusalem was considered to be about to appear. Paul appropriates this 'Jerusalem above, that is our mother' (4.26) for his law of freedom, relegating to the Jews the currently enslaved Jerusalem, a city captive to the Romans.

Exhortatio (5.1–6.10)

The final exhortation gives two important conclusions of Paul's argument. First (5.1–12), he focuses the conclusion of the whole thrust of his argument about Jewish observance on circumcision as the symbol of, and the opening to, such observance: there is no point in perversely binding yourself to the slavery of the Law. Secondly (5.13–6.10), the obvious corollary to answer the obvious question: if Christians no longer have the Law as a guide in morality, what guide can there be? The quick answer is the same as that given in 1 Corinthians 13, the single commandment, 'Love your neighbour as yourself' (5.14). The longer answer is that Christians need no external restriction, since they have the Spirit of Christ as an inspiring motivation.

This leads on to the two lists, the works of the flesh and the works of the Spirit. These two are opposed to each other (5.17), but the works of the flesh should not be understood as necessarily bodily, since they include not only physical and sexual sins such as drunkenness, but also bad temper, feuds, jealousy and envy. The bodily element is present, for circumcision enables people to 'put a good face on it' in the flesh (6.12, cf. Phil. 3.3–4). In Paul, 'flesh' signifies more the weakness and sinfulness of humanity as opposed to the strength of the Spirit: Romans 6.19, 'I speak in human terms because of the weakness of your flesh… as you presented yourselves as slaves to uncleanness and lawlessness'. However, the 'flesh' is not always bad, for Onesimus is to be a member of Philemon's household 'in the flesh' as well as 'in the Spirit' (Phlm. 16). It can mean 'by worldly standards' (1 Cor. 1.26), not necessarily evil, and 'From now on we know no one according to the flesh. Even if we had known Christ according to the flesh, we do not so know him now' (2 Cor. 5.16). Perhaps the best understanding of 'the flesh' is of human nature and its drives, not yet transformed by the Spirit. The works of the Spirit issue from the person transformed by the Spirit of Christ.

Conclusion

The letter ends as it began, with an impassioned personal note, a contrast between Cross and circumcision: 'They want you to be circumcised only so that they can boast of your outward appearance. But as for me, it is out of the question that I should boast at all except of the Cross of our Lord Jesus Christ' (6.14). It ends as it began, also, by the overarching statement of the radical difference Christ has made, stretching back to the initial statement: at the end, in the last analysis it is not circumcision or lack of it that matters, but the new creation in Christ (6.15); at the beginning, Christ has rescued us from the present evil world (1.4).

Further Reading

Dunn, James, *The Theology of Paul's Letter to the Galatians* (1994)
Witherington, Ben, *Grace in Galatia* (1998)

20

The Letter to the Ephesians

The so-called Letter to the Ephesians is different from all the other Pauline. Why 'so-called'? Because 'at Ephesus' in the first verse is missing in the early manuscripts (e.g. the authoritative P46 from about 200AD, the Codex Sinaiticus from the fourth century) and in quotations by early second-century writers. It is difficult to believe that Paul, having spent some three years at Ephesus, should have written with such detachment as to include no personal greetings and to say merely 'having *heard about* your faith in the Lord Jesus' (1.15). It may have been a letter intended for several communities, possibly with a gap left for the insertion of the name of the community. Apart from the swift mention of the trustworthy Tychicus (6.21) there are no details of persons, questions, problems, struggles which would link this writing to any particular community or circumstances. It has only a shadow of the conventional elements of greeting at beginning and end of a letter. On the other hand, the conventional Pauline element of a thanksgiving for the faith of the recipients is hugely expanded in the early chapters. We regard Ephesians as the first great meditation and commentary on Paul's view of the world and of salvation in Christ. It makes use of the contemporary convention of pseudepigraphy, by which a writing could be attributed to a great figure of the past, presenting what that figure *would have* written about the matter in hand (see p. 283).

> **Plan of Ephesians**
> 1.3–14 The Blessing
> 1.15–23 The Prayer
> 2.1–3.13 Salvation in Christ
> 3.14–21 The Praise
> 4.1–6.9   Christian Behaviour
>   4.1–16 United in Christ
>   4.17–5.20 New Life in Christ
>   5.21–6.9 Family Relations
> 6.10–24 Concluding Encouragement

1. The Authorship of Ephesians

Heinrich Schlier characterized the author of Ephesians as a 'Paul after Paul'. 'The apostles' are mentioned in a hagiographical way as foundations in the past, and 'holy' (2.20; 3.5). Paul is no longer just a prisoner, but is 'the prisoner in the Lord' (3.1; 4.1). The style is even more expansive and liturgical than that of Colossians, with the long sentences, the repetitions and insistent addition of descriptive clauses by a genitive ('according to the working of the power of his strength', 1.19). There is particularly a remarkable overlap with Colossians in both words and topics, perhaps between a third and a half of all the verses. In the passage recommending Tychicus (Eph. 6.21) 23 consecutive words are the same as Colossians 4.7. The section 4.17–24 takes up words and phrases used in Colossians 3.5–11, but in a different order and with a different sense; for example, 'in the name of our Lord Jesus Christ' now refers not to all the activity of the Christian, as in Colossians, but specifically to thanksgiving. Recently it has been suggested (by John Muddiman, 2010) that Ephesians is an expansion, by an author thoroughly conversant with Paul, of the lost letter to the Laodiceans, in much the same way that the gospel of Matthew is an expansion of that of Mark.

2. The Genre of Writing

The whole of Ephesians is framed in broad and expansive, almost liturgical language, meditating on the Christian mystery, particularly from Pauline angles but with notable developments. One significant and typical change is that, in the earlier Pauline letters, 'Church' always refers to a particular community in a particular place, whereas in Ephesians all nine references are to the Church as a worldwide community, expressive of the triumphant ecclesiology of Ephesians. A further important development concerns 'mystery'. The word has occurred rarely in Paul, but in important contexts, to express the final revelation at the end of time (e.g. Rom. 11.25; 16.25; 1 Cor. 2.1, 7). In the Dead Sea Scrolls it is a 'buzz-word' for the eagerly awaited final revelation. In Ephesians it occurs six times to designate the final revelation, and nowhere more significantly than at the centre of the great opening blessing (1.9).

3. The Prayer of Ephesians

If Ephesians is regarded as a meditation and reflection, looking back on Paul's message, the first three chapters should be seen as a prayer. They begin with the lyrical blessing of 1.3–14, leading directly into the prayer (1.15–23) for an understanding of the 'mind-blowing Christology' (James D. G. Dunn) of its final verses. There follows a meditative break on the renewal of humanity (2.1–3.13) before the final burst of praise in 3.14–21.

a. The Blessing (1.3–14)

The paradox of Ephesians is fully expressed in the paradox of this capacious blessing. It grows out of the whole richness of the Old Testament traditions of the choice of Israel, and yet opens out to stretch this choice beyond the bounds of Israel. In time it extends from 'before the world was made' to 'when the times had run their course'. In space it extends from heaven to earth. In form it adopts the biblical formula of a blessing to God, frequently used in the psalms. It is full of the key concepts of Israel's choice, many of which have been familiar in Paul's thought, adoption as sons, inheritance, God's love leading to forgiveness, the Beloved Son (in the Old Testament this is Israel, but here the concept is transferred to Christ). There are also the concepts which became central in Romans, freedom through Christ's blood and the plan of God's purpose finally revealed.

In shape this blessing is a parabola. It starts with the Father, descends to gather up all humanity, as 'he would bring everything together under Christ as head' (v.10), finally returning to the Father with 'the praise of his glory'. From the human point of view the richness of this blessing is that it expresses in so many ways the Christian experience of forgiveness and acceptance in Christ. It has been divided into seven distinct blessings showered upon humanity:

v. 4 God's call	v. 13b Seal of the Spirit
v. 5 Adoptive sonship	v. 13a Call of the gentiles
v. 7 Forgiveness	v. 11 Inheritance
v. 9 Revelation of the mystery	

All are centred on Christ, and all could be considered different ways in which the experience of forgiveness and acceptance in Christ has been experienced. The focus of the whole hymn lies in the great word *anakephalaiosasthai*, (1.10), a compound of *kephale* (= 'head'), so 'to head up all things in Christ'. Christ is the head and completion of the whole universe, the purpose and goal of creation.

b. The Prayer (1.15–23)

The prayer continues the elevated vein of the blessing. It is a prayer for a deep understanding, in the Spirit of wisdom, of the mystery revealed. It is a prayer not for mere knowledge, but for perception: 'may he enlighten the eyes of your mind' (1.18). The object of this understanding is the position of Christ. Perhaps more striking is the supremacy of Christ to all the powers which might seem to determine the course of world events, 'every principality, ruling force, power or sovereignty, or any other name that could be named'. Most notable of all is the immense power by which God has placed the exalted Christ in this position. Conflict with, and comparison to, these powers has already occurred in Colossians 1.16 and 2.15. The author does not deny their existence, but uses Psalm 110 (109) to show the exalted Christ's superiority to them. Christ's exaltation was effected by 'the overriding greatness of his power... according to the energy of the power of his strength' (1.19).

The climax of the assertions about Christ's position in the world comes by use of the term *pleroma* (1.23). In its basic and normal sense this term means 'the filling-up', the cargo of a ship, the population of a town, the contents or completion. In Colossians, Christ is filled with the fullness of divinity: 'because God wanted all fullness to be found in him' (1.19). In Ephesians 1.23 this fullness is active, perhaps – by a typically Pauline play on words – both active and passive, both filled with God and filling all things with the divine presence. Later it seems that the fullness transfers to God's holy people by the fact of Christ indwelling them and filling them: 'so that Christ may live in your hearts … and that you may be filled with the utter fullness of God' (3.17–19), or 'until we all form the perfect Man, fully mature with the fullness of Christ himself' (4.13).

c. Meditation on the changed condition of humanity (2.1–3.13)

The themes of this middle section are all familiar from earlier letters. First the writer outlines the condition of humanity without Christ and lost in sin (2.1–10). But, whereas in Paul salvation was always in the future, now it has already been won: 'it is through grace you have been saved, and raised up with him and given a place with him in heaven, in Christ Jesus' (2.5–6). In Romans the union of Jew and gentile Christian was described in terms of being grafted into the olive-tree; it is only in the eschatological future that this grafting will be complete. In Ephesians the image used is a wall destroyed: Christ is the peace between Jew and gentile, and has already destroyed the hostility between them, fashioning 'a single New Man out of the two of them' (2.15).

The climax picks up again the image of a building, the building being the new Temple. The living Temple of the Church has taken the place of the Temple of Jerusalem as the place of God's presence. Jesus Christ is the corner-stone, and the foundation stones are apostles and prophets (2.20). The image is used in such a way as to suggest again the organic unity of the Body of Christ in Paul: it is 'knit together in him' and still 'growing into a holy temple … being built into a dwelling-place of God' (3.21–2). It will be further developed by the comparison of the unfailing love of Christ for his spouse, the Church, to the unbreakable bond between husband and wife (5.23).

Finally (3.1–13), the author describes Paul's part in the work of salvation. This was a feature of the earlier letters of Paul; it now occurs in quite a new fashion. In the earlier letters the emphasis was on Paul sharing the sufferings of Christ (e.g. 2 Cor. 11.22–9; Phil. 1.13–26); now, after a mere mention of imprisonment, it is a triumphant summing up of Paul's ministry.

d. The Praise (3.14–21)

Prayer and wonder have never been far below the surface. Now the writer breaks out again explicitly into a noble trinitarian prayer. As in the initial blessing, the Father is the source of all 'fatherhood' or even 'family'; the prayer looks ahead to the counsels on the family which will be given in 5.21–6.9. This astonishingly positive and forward-looking prayer sums up the objectives of the initial blessing of the letter.

4. Exhortation – the Basics of Christian Life

The moral advice on living the Christian life is marked by several notable features.

1 The heading is a call to support one another in love, preserving the unity of the Spirit (4.2–6). God's love and generosity are to be the pattern (5.1). All relationships are to be 'in the Lord' (15 times in Chapters 5 and 6).

2 The conventional submission of wife to husband is softened and balanced by a comparison of the love of husband for wife with the generosity and self-sacrifice of Christ.

3 The conventionally absolute authority of parents over children is mitigated by the counsel to parents 'never drive your children to resentment, but bring them up with correction and advice inspired by the Lord' (6.4).

4 Similarly the institution of slavery is not itself questioned, but the obedience of slaves to their masters is seen as a Christian obedience, 'as to Christ' (6.6–7). The direct address to slaves dignifies them as full members of the congregation (6.1, 5), who render their obedience willingly and with their own responsibility.

5 Finally the biblical image of God as a warrior is brilliantly applied to the struggle against the powers of evil (6.11–17), supported by the prayer of the whole community. Having previously presented the members of the Church as seated with Christ in triumph (2.6) and walking worthily of their vocation (4.1, 17, etc), this conclusion of the letter tells them now to stand their ground in battle (6.14).

Further Reading

Lincoln, Andrew, *Ephesians* (1990)

Muddiman, John, *The Epistle to the Ephesians* (London: Continuum, 2010): an
   acclaimed commentary

The Letter to the Philippians

1. The City of Philippi

According to Acts 16.11 Philippi was the first town in Europe at which Paul spent any length of time when he crossed from Troas. It was an ancient town, built on a fertile agricultural plain. Originally called Krenides, it took the name 'Philippi' in 356BC, when it made a protective alliance with Philip of Macedon. However, after the battle of Actium, Octavian (later to receive the title 'Augustus') planted there a *colonia*, a colony of demobilized veterans, giving them generous grants of land in lieu of pension. There was, therefore, a mixed combination of Greeks and Romans. It is striking that Acts does not mention any synagogue, despite the presence of Lydia, who welcomed Paul; her customary place of prayer was by a river outside the city, which suggests that there was none. The names which Paul mentions (also Euodia, Syntyche and Clement) are gentile rather than Jewish names. Furthermore, Paul makes liberal allusion to the games and athletic events which were so important in Greco-Roman culture: 'I had not run in the race and exhausted myself for nothing' (2.16); 'I have not won yet, but I am still running, trying to capture the prize for which Christ Jesus captured me …

I am racing for the finish' (3.12, 14). Writing to such a city it is especially forceful that Paul insists that Christian citizenship is different from the citizenship of other inhabitants of the city. To a city where the Emperor was regarded and worshipped as a saviour god, he proclaims that the Christians' saviour and the Christians' Lord is not the Emperor but Christ: 'For for us our citizenship is in heaven, from where we are expecting a Saviour, the Lord Jesus Christ' (3.30). On the other hand, it is notable that Paul's letter, by contrast to many of his letters, contains almost no clear allusions to scripture (possibly only two or three). This suggests that a strong proportion of the Christians had little Jewish or biblical background. The lively polemic against Judaism (3.2–7) should therefore perhaps be considered more as part of Paul's personal statement than as polemic against Judaism and Jewish opponents at Philippi.

It is only in his greeting to the Philippians that Paul mentions *episkopoi*. The word, 'overseers', has a wide meaning. It later becomes 'bishop', and by the time of the Pastoral Letters has taken on ecclesiastical meaning (cf. p. 309). The *diakonoi* are also greeted, but again we do not know their function. According to Acts 14.23, Paul and Barnabas appointed elders in the new Christian communities of southern Asia Minor. This would conform to the normal pattern of the Jewish communities of the Diaspora, ruled by a council of elders, presided by an *archisynagoga*. The leadership of the non-Jewish community at Philippi could have been entirely different; as they are in the plural, these officials provide no evidence of what will in the next century become the 'monarchical episcopate' attested by Ignatius of Antioch. Phoebe, who carried the letter to Rome, is described in Romans 16.1 as *diakonos* of the Church at Cenchreae.

The letter is perhaps the warmest and most affectionate of all Paul's letters. He says it is only from this community that he has accepted gifts of money, which betokens a special relationship (4.14–16), and the expressions of affection are so frequent that there is no point in listing them. He obviously has a comfortable and easy relationship with them, and writes full of joy, partnership and happiness, despite his imprisonment.

2. The Components of the Letter

As for Second Corinthians, a case has been made for dividing Philippians into several separate letters. For two reasons it is odd that Paul launches a few verses from the end of the letter into a thanksgiving for the gift of money which he has received from the Philippians. First, a thanksgiving is normally at the beginning of the letter, and, secondly, Paul always wades immediately at the opening of the letter into his primary concern (witness the abrupt condemnation at the beginning of Galatians, and the opening diatribe in First Corinthians against the divisions within the community). Why should he save up till this late stage his thanks for the gift of money which they have sent him? The preceding paragraph, with its personal messages (4.2–3) and its advice in valedictory style as though concluding (4.4–9a) and final blessing of peace (4.9b), seems to be an interrupted conclusion. These difficulties are solved if 4.10–20 is regarded as a separate letter, Letter A. Its tone is somewhat defensive, as though Paul needs to justify himself against the accusation of accepting money unnecessarily. Such a tone appears again when the Collection for Jerusalem is at issue (2 Cor. 8.18–20).

A conclusion of a letter appears to occur also at 2.19–3.1a, again with personal news about Timothy and Epaphroditus, and Paul's own plans, and a final blessing, 'Finally, brothers, I wish you joy in the Lord'. It may be that this first part of Philippians (1.1–3.1a) is also a separate letter, Letter B. From this fragment we learn that Paul is in prison, no doubt awaiting investigation, and envisaging the possibility of being put to death (1.19–26; 2.16–18). The backwards-and-forwards of Epaphroditus and the proposed mission of Timothy (2.19–30) suggest that Paul is not too far from Colossae, which may indicate that his imprisonment is at Ephesus. This is only a guess, for we do not know that Paul was ever imprisoned in Ephesus; but Acts does not give us enough information about his stay there to fill adequately the eighteen months he spent there (Acts 18.8–20.1). Imprisonment at Ephesus would fit the mention of the Praetorium (1.13), for the governor of Asia at Ephesus was a Praetor.

This leaves 3.1b-4.1 as a third, separate letter, Letter C. This section of Philippians is perhaps the bitterest and most caustic personal attack in all Paul's letters, on those who practise and urge circumcision. To begin with, in a single verse Paul calls them 'dogs', 'evil workmen' and 'mutilators'. The injurious name used by Jews for gentiles is now turned back on Jews who hold this point of view, suggesting that they put themselves outside the true people of God. The prime good work of Judaism is characterised as an evil work. Further, the sacred operation of circumcision is degraded (by a neat play on words, *katatome*, rather than *apotome*), into a mere mutilation. Later on (v. 8), he spurns as 'filth' – 'shit' would not be an unjustified translation – all the noble titles in which Jews took their pride. Finally (v. 19), he mocks the regulations about food as making a god out of the stomach. Worse still, by 'they glory in what they should think shameful', he actually goes over to the side of the gentiles, whose contempt and disgust for circumcision made it impossible for Jews to take part in athletic contests unless they somehow disguised their circumcision. Paul would not go to these lengths of coarse abuse on an intimate and delicate matter unless he felt that strong pressure was being put upon the Philippians to embrace the practice of the Law.

These three letters – if indeed they are separate letters – which we have labelled in possible order of writing (B, C, A), are given in descending order of length, i.e. B, C, A. This parallels the ordering of the possible components of 2 Corinthians, also in descending order of length.

3. The Hymn to Christ

Paul illustrates his first exhortation to the Philippians about their relationship to one another with a hymn which contains one of the richest statements of Christ's divinity. It seems likely that this hymn is culled from elsewhere. In the early communities Christians were encouraged to compose hymns and bring them to the liturgical assembly, and it is not impossible that this is such a piece, for the balanced and rhythmical structure is not characteristic of Paul himself. In 1 Corinthians 14.26 Paul says, 'When you come together each of you brings a psalm or some instruction or a revelation'. Two passages in Ephesians, 5.19 and 3.16, closely parallel to each other, urge Christians to 'sing psalms and hymns and inspired songs among yourselves'. Early in the next century Pliny describes the Christians as coming together to sing hymns 'to Christ as to a god' (*Epistles* 10.96). In any case the original hymn may have proceeded in six couplets, using Hebrew parallelism, by which the second line of the couplet completes the first:

> Being in the form of God
> he did not count equality with God something to be exploited
> but he emptied himself
> taking the form of a servant

becoming as men are
and being in all respects as a man
he humbled himself
becoming obedient unto death, *death on a Cross.*

Therefore God raised him high
and gave him the name above every other name
so that at the name of Jesus every knee should bow
in the heavens, on earth and in the underworld
and every tongue acknowledge Jesus Christ as Lord
to the glory of God the Father.

Quite apart from the obvious Semitic parallelism and the elevated style, this gives fine balances within couplets (God – God; man – man; every – every), antithesis (form of God – form of a servant; humbled himself – raised him high; servant – Lord) as well as assonances audible only in the Greek text. If the original hymn was not composed by Paul, he would himself have been responsible at least for adding to the fourth couplet his characteristic stress on the Cross, 'death on a Cross', and to the final couplet the overloading and thoroughly Greek 'in the heavens, on earth and in the underworld' and the last line.

The hymn receives its full sense from the allusion to Isaiah 45.22–3 in the third quatrain. This part of Isaiah was written during the exile in Babylon, when first the exiles found themselves face-to-face with the plethora of Babylonian gods. Their reaction was an unhesitating and unbending assertion of the uniqueness of YHWH, the God of the whole earth, of which this verse is a primary example: 'I am God unrivalled. By my own self I swear it. What comes from my mouth is truth, a word irrevocable. Before me every knee shall bend, by me every tongue shall swear, saying, "From the Lord alone come victory and strength"'. The Pauline hymn takes this strong assertion of monotheism and applies it to Christ. Every knee shall bend, not to YHWH but to Jesus. Every tongue shall swear not by YHWH but by Jesus. Most of all, the unrivalled divine personal name YHWH, which is above all other names, so holy that it may not be pronounced but only rendered into Greek as 'Lord', is given to Jesus. This seeming blasphemy is not blasphemous, but on the contrary is 'to the glory of God the Father'. A further rich allusion to Jesus as the Servant of the LORD is given by 'raised him high' which harks back to the beginning of the hymn of the Suffering Servant of the LORD, 'See, my servant shall be lifted up, exalted, rise to great heights' (Isa. 52.13).

In addition it is strongly held by some that there is an underlying comparison and contrast of Jesus to Adam, that this might be the origin of Paul's theology of Christ as the Second Adam, which occurs in Romans 5.14 and 1 Corinthians 15.22 and 45. The contrast is:

> Adam grasped at equality with God – Christ did not
> Adam exalted himself – Christ emptied himself
> Adam was disobedient – Christ was obedient to death
> Adam was humbled by God – Christ was raised high by God

In using this figure Paul turns upside-down current theories on the first and second Adam. In Jewish thought at this time it was held that there were two Adams, a heavenly and an earthly Adam, corresponding to the two Adams of the two creation-stories in Genesis. The heavenly Adam came first, perfect in every way, a model and an ideal for the second. The second Adam is the earthly (or even earthy) Adam who fell. Paul turns this over: the first Adam was earthly and became the model for fallen humanity, while the second Adam is the sinless one, the true model for humanity. Whether this figure is intended in Philippians turns on whether the initial 'being in the form of God' can be translated 'being in the image of God', a reference to the creation of Adam 'in the image of God'. The difficulty is that Paul here uses a different word, *morphe*, instead of the *eikon* of Genesis.

4. Faith in Christ

Following on from this abasement and raising up, Paul sees his own trajectory as one of loss and gain. He compares himself to those who seek their salvation through belonging to the People of God by means of 'relying on physical evidence'. This leads on to a recital of his Jewish credentials:

> Take any man who thinks he can rely on what is physical: I am even better qualified. I was born of the race of Israel and of the tribe of Benjamin, a Hebrew born of Hebrew parents, and I was circumcised when I was eight days old. As for the Law, I was a Pharisee; as for working for religion I was a persecutor of the Church; as far as the Law can make you perfect, I was faultless. (3.4–6)

But all this is rejected in favour of belonging to Christ personally. This is expressed with passionate personal warmth: 'All I want is to know Christ and the power of his resurrection and to share his sufferings by reproducing the pattern of his death' (3.10). For the Jew what was important – and what had been important to Paul – was belonging to the People of God; of this the sign was circumcision. The rest, observance of the Law and its justice, was merely the outworking of belonging to the People. Paul has rejected this manner of belonging to the People of God, and declares his passionate adherence to Christ. Now his boast is in Christ, and not in circumcision (3.3). He wants the perfection which comes through faith in Christ, so that he 'may be found in Christ'. Writing to the Corinthians he speaks of his longing to be 'exiled from the body and make our home with the Lord' (2 Cor. 5.8), but writing as a prisoner to his friends the Philippians he is even more explicit: 'My one hope and trust is that … I shall have the courage for Christ to be glorified in my body, whether by my life or by my death. Life to me, of course, is Christ, but the death would bring me something more … I want to be gone and to be with Christ' (1.20–3; cf. 3.21). Then God will 'fulfil all needs according to his richness in glory in Christ Jesus' (4.19).

Further Reading

Oakes, Peter, *Philippians, from People to Letter* (Cambridge: Cambridge University Press, 2007): commentary based on archaeology and sociology of the city
Verhoef, Edward, *Philippi: How Christianity began in Europe* (London: Bloomsbury, 2013): development of Christianity in Philippi

22

The Letter to the Colossians

One of the clearest data in Acts about Paul's missionary activity is that he had centres for each part of his activity, first Antioch in Syria, then Ephesus on the west coast of what is now Turkey, then Corinth on the isthmus which joins the Greek Peloponnese to northern Greece. It seems likely that Paul was imprisoned at Ephesus, and this may be the imprisonment mentioned in 4.10. Paul sends a message also to Archippus (4.17), whom we meet also in the letter to Philemon (v. 23). He has written also to Laodicea (4.16). The impression is given that there is fairly easy communication between the place of imprisonment and these cities some 150km to the East, up the valley of the Lycus. We know from classical sources that there was a large Jewish population of this area, some of whom must have become Christians.

1. Authorship

Two letters of the Pauline corpus need to be considered together, namely the letters to the Colossians and to the Ephesians. The same question is asked about both of them, whether and in what sense they are indeed by Paul, though the same answer need not be given for both. The phenomenon of pseudepigraphy was widespread in Jewish and Christian circles, that is, documents were attributed to respected figures of the past in order to give them authority. Thus in Jewish circles the biblical Greek Book of

Wisdom, written at Alexandria in the first century BC. claims to be written by Solomon, the *First Book of Enoch* and the *Psalms of Solomon*, of approximately the same date, were not written by Henoch and Solomon respectively. The list may be lengthened indefinitely: the *Letter of Barnabas, Gospels of Peter, Philip, Judas* and others. It is far from certain that the Gospels of Matthew and John were written by Matthew and John the apostles, though it must be added that they make no claim to this authorship. Within the New Testament it is highly unlikely that 2 Peter was written by the apostle (see p. 339). So it is both historically possible and theologically acceptable that writings of the New Testament were not written by authors whose name they bear.

An objection made to pseudepigraphy in the Bible, and particularly in the New Testament, is that it involves deceit, by not merely claiming the authorship of a distinguished figure of the past but also by putting in personal details to make it seem more plausible, like the personal greetings and news at the end of Colossians (4.10–18) or Titus 3.12–15. This is, however, part of the convention: in the Old Testament Qoheleth (Ecclesiastes) 2.4 gives details of the revelry of Solomon, the supposed author. Within the convention it is no more deceitful than the 'Dear' and 'Yours' at the beginning and end of a courteously hostile modern letter.

Colossians has several features which differentiate it from the genuine Pauline letters:

1 Sentence-structure. The cut-and-thrust of diatribe (see p. 207) has given way to an ample, rhetorical or even liturgical style. Thus in Colossians 1.3–8 and 9–20 may each be construed as a single sentence, phrase piled upon phrase. There are none of those darting Pauline questions-and-answers, none of that vivacity and energy. As one commentator said, a sparkling stream has given way to a massive slow-moving avalanche.

2 Grammatical construction. Far less logical connectives ('accordingly', 'therefore', 'indeed'), but instead more relative clauses, doubled synonyms ('grovel to angels // and worship them'; 'joints // and sinews'; 'where Christ is // sitting at God's right hand'), participial constructions and loosely added genitives, 'the wealth *of the* glory *of this* mystery' (1.27).

3 Difference of approach. There is none of the fierce controversy against Jewish practices: instead of polemic against circumcision (Rom. 2.25–29; Philippians 3.3), circumcision is used as an image of Christian

self-denial (2.11). There is no need to inveigh against legal observance, for the Law has been nailed to the cross (2.14). Observance of Jewish festivals is not a sign of desertion of Christ (Gal. 4.10); it does not deserve criticism, for such festivals are merely the shadow of a reality (2.16–17). So allusive is any attack on false ideas that it is difficult to see exactly whether the author envisaged Pythagoreanism, Essenism, Gnosticism, or the various syncretistic mystery cults close to Judaism.

So far it would be attractive to hold that the letter was written well after the 'genuine' letters, when the heat of controversy against Judaism had subsided. The chief target of controversy is the 'thrones, ruling forces, sovereignties, powers' (1.16) over which Christ has triumphed, or the 'sovereignties and ruling forces' which Christ has paraded in public, behind him in his triumphal procession (2.15 – reverting to the image of a Roman triumphal procession, already used in 1 Thessalonians 5.16–17). Attention to angels and celestial powers was a feature of Jewish religion at this time, and may have been carried to excess. Since they are targeted also in the letter to the Ephesians (1.21), there may have been a special cult of angels in the Lycus valley, which the author describes by 'anyone who chooses to grovel to angels and worship them' (2.18).

A curious feature is that Colossians shares several verbal characteristics with the letters to the Philippians and to Philemon, which may also have been written during this imprisonment. Does this show that Colossians is genuinely by Paul, or that the pseudepigraphical author has carefully worked in these similarities to add verisimilitude? Both Philippians and Colossians have an important hymn to Christ, stressing his divinity. Both pray for an increase in the community's knowledge (Phil. 1.9; Col. 1.9), both describe the community as 'unblemished' (Phil. 2.15; Col. 1.22), both use circumcision as an image of the community (Phil. 3.3; Col. 2.11), both point out that their citizenship is in heaven (Phil. 3.19-9–20; Col. 3.1-1–5), both mention Epaphroditus/Epaphras as a link between Paul and the community (Phil. 4.18; Col. 4.12). Similarly with Philemon: in the greeting, Paul has heard of his/their love and faith (Phlm. 5; Col. 1.4); Paul thanks God for him/them in his prayers (Phlm. 4; Col. 1.3). A number of Paul's co-workers are mentioned in the final greetings of both letters (Phlm. 23-3–24; Col. 4.10–13).

At least this shows close contact between the three letters. Although Mark Kiley who points out these similarities takes them as signs of careful pseudepigraphy, they could be taken also as signs of genuine authorship of all three letters. At the very least it shows such contact between the authors that whether the letters are penned by the same hand becomes less important: unless the author of Colossians was carefully working to make a modern-style pastiche, he was thoroughly imbued with the thoughts of Paul. He was writing at a different time, about different problems, with a more expansive approach and less febrile energy than Paul, but nevertheless a close disciple of Paul, with the same theology. It might even have been Paul himself!

Plan of Colossians

1.3–14	Thanksgiving and Prayer
1.15–20	Hymn to Christ
1.21–2.5	Paul's Labours for the Colossians
2.6–3.4	Warning against Errors
3.5–17	Christian Behaviour
3.5–17	New Life in Christ
3.18–4.1	Family Relations
4.2–6	Prayer
4.7–18	Concluding News and Greetings

---

2. The Hymn to Christ

As the hymn to Christ is the jewel of the letter to the Philippians, so the hymn to Christ is the masterpiece of Colossians. It provides an ideal focus for the Christological thought of the letter. It may be an earlier hymn in two strophes. Despite the characteristically Pauline mention of the Cross, it has an unusually high proportion of non-Pauline words and words which do not occur elsewhere in these letters (see E. Lohse, *Colossians and Philemon*, 1971). The first strophe is a meditation on the Logos which penetrates the universe, which could well stem from Hellenistic-Jewish circles. The second strophe is a meditation which applies this to Christ. The whole has been adapted by the letter-writer to his own purposes. The two strophes correspond to each other:

[15]**Who is** the image of the unseen God **the firstborn** of all creation,	**Who is** the beginning, **the firstborn** from the dead so that he be supreme in every way

¹⁶**for in him all** things were created
in heaven and on earth,
visible and invisible,
whether thrones or ruling forces
or sovereignties or powers
all things were created
through him and for him.

¹⁹**for in him** it pleased **all** fullness to
dwell,

²⁰to reconcile **all things**
through him and for him (making
peace
through blood of his Cross
whether **on earth or in heaven**.

¹⁷He exists before all things
and in him all things hold together
¹⁸and he is the head of the body
(the Church).

Notes:

1. The insertion in v. 20 is characteristic of Paul's emphasis on the Cross, which otherwise plays little part in this letter. Grammatically it is awkward, giving two uses of 'through' in the same sense. It is, however, unmistakably Pauline, for outside the gospels virtually only Paul in the whole of the New Testament refers to the Cross itself (elsewhere once in Heb. 12.2) or crucifixion (elsewhere once in Rev. 11.3). It goes unmentioned in the Pastoral Letters, and the whole of the Catholic Epistles.

2. The application of 'the body' to the Church in v. 18 is again characteristic of the letter, as we shall see later.

The first stanza fits well into the milieu of Hellenistic Jewish speculation about the Logos as it appears in Philo and other writers. There was constant concern to explain Judaism to the Hellenistic public in terms of philosophies familiar to them. The Logos, or reason, was the perfect means of welding philosophy to Jewish Old Testament speculations about Wisdom, which we considered in relation to 1 Corinthians (see p. 234). The first stanza can be understood only in the light of all these. Perhaps the most striking features are 'image' and 'firstborn'. The former corresponds to Wisdom texts where Wisdom is referred to as 'shining brilliance' of God; for the ancients an image is not a mere external look-alike, but is thought to have in some way the same power as the original. The latter clearly refers to Wisdom in Proverbs 8.22–3.

The hymn has similarities to the thought patterns of Paul which we saw with regard to Christ as the Second Adam. In Romans, Christ is seen as the principle of the new creation, the re-founded humanity, contrasting with Adam in whom humanity was first created. Now, however, the thought goes back beyond the Garden of Eden to the Creation itself and before. Christ is the Wisdom of God, existing before all things, in whom the creation of the world itself occurred, the agent of creation (Prov. 3.9; Ps 104.24; Phlm., *Fug.* 109). This is not a departure from Paul's earlier thought, but a development of it, for in 1 Corinthians 8.6 already Christ was seen as the Wisdom of God. Colossians, however, goes further than previous writings, for now Christ is also the goal of creation ('created *for* him'), which formerly had been God alone.

It is suggested that the Colossians were bemused by speculation about cosmic forces, Thrones, Principalities, Powers. What was the relationship of Christ to these powers? 'Do not be cheated of your prize by anyone who chooses to grovel to angels and worship them' (2.18). Were these powers superior, parallel or inferior to him? Just as in the Old Testament, during the Babylonian exile, the contact with the gods of Babylon forced the Jews to think out the relationship of the LORD to the creation and to other forces said to rule creation, so this challenge led the author to greater clarity about the relationship of Christ to the so-called ruling powers of the universe: Christ 'has stripped the sovereignties and ruling forces, and paraded them in public, behind him in his triumphal procession' (2.15). Christopher Tuckett concludes: 'Some real sense of the pre-existence and pre-existent cosmic creative activity of Jesus seems to be asserted here. Jesus is here being put up into the realm of the divine in a way that exceeds much of the rest of the New Testament' (*Christology and the New Testament*, 2001, p. 79).

The second stanza mirrors the first, applying it to Christ by means of two ideas which both fit Pauline thought. As in 1 Corinthians 15, Christ is seen as firstborn from the dead. This echoes also the conception of Christ as the Second Adam, the exemplar and model of the new humanity. Here, however, the conception is wider than in the earlier letters, for it extends to the whole of being. He is 'supreme in every way, for in him it pleased all fullness to dwell" Secondly, the reconciliation takes place through the Cross, as so often in Romans, where Christ is seen as the sacrifice of reconciliation. The same language, 'through him … making peace through the blood of his cross' (1.20), is used as at Romans 5.1, 'we are at peace with God through Jesus Christ'.

The third change, which is especially characteristic of these letters rather than the Pauline writings as a whole, is the restriction of Christ's headship to the Church. By the addition of 'the Church' in v. 18 the universality of the original hymn is focused on human beings. This is further reinforced by the verses following the hymn, which refer it to the recipients of the letter. There is, indeed, a constant wavering in these letters over what is envisaged by 'the Body'. Accordingly, the differing relationship can be discovered only by a consideration of the teaching of the letter on the body of Christ.

In the earlier Pauline letters the author uses the expression 'Body of Christ' in three different ways, without seeming to realize that these are different ways (see p. 231). For him they are all interlocked, and form one idea. In the Deutero-Paulines the image of the body expressing the interdependence of the members is touched only in two related passages, Ephesians 4.14, 'We shall grow completely into Christ who is the head, by whom the whole body is fitted and joined together, each joint adding its own strength, for each individual part to work according to its function' (cf. Col. 2.19). Here the Body is the Christian body or the Church, but the optic has changed. No longer do all the parts go to make up the body of Christ, but Christ stands over against the body as its head. This is in consequence of the new perception of the position of Christ. Furthermore, Christ is now head not of the Body only but of the whole cosmos. In the hymn at the beginning of Ephesians everything in heaven and on earth is to be brought together under Christ as head (1.10); the body is wider than the Church. The basic idea is the same as that already expressed in 1 Corinthians 15.24–8, that all creation is subject to Christ. On the other hand, in Ephesians 1.22–3 'God has put all things under his feet, and has given him, as he is above all things, to the Church as head'. The concept of head has three principal connotations:

1 The head is the classic concept in Hebrew history for a ruler or authority, a king at the head of his people.
2 In ancient medical writers the head is the source of nourishment and co-ordination, ruling the nerves and functioning of the body.
3 The head is also in Philo (*Quaestiones in Exodum*, 2.117), the source of order and logic by means of the Logos or Reason by which God rules the universe, the ruling principle of the cosmos.

So instead of all the members of the Church together making up the Body which is Christ, now, Christ is seen as the Head, giving life, nourishment and meaning to the Body which is not merely the Church but is the whole universe of all creation. It is this vast and noble vision which the author has come to see through the consideration of Christ in comparison to the world-powers who were held in the valley of the Lycus to hold sway over the world.

Further Reading

Lincoln, Andrew and John Wedderburn, *The Theology of the Later Pauline Letters* (1993)

The First Letter to the Thessalonians

1. Background

The modern city of Thessalonica, the second largest city of Greece, is built over the ancient town. As soon as the northern part of Greece began to open out, in the reign of Alexander the Great, this city was built because of its natural geographical advantages. It has an excellent natural harbour, and stands at the end of a natural road-route into the interior. The modern motorway from Belgrade and the Danube dips down to the sea there. In Roman times it was also the point at which the trunk-road Via Egnatia hit the sea-coast. This important road was the land link between Rome and the East, running from the West coast of Greece to Constantinople. Such has remained the importance of this link that, from the motorway now following the same route, the ancient bridges, dating in part back to Roman times, can still be seen. Perhaps more important in an age when transport by sea was immeasurably easier than transport by land, Thessalonica provided the opening onto the Eastern sea for goods both from Rome and from the northern part of the Empire up to the Danube. It was and is a bustling sea-port, at which convoys to and from the interior would be constantly loading and unloading. There would be pack-animals, carts and traders everywhere.

Most of the big trading cities of the Mediterranean had an important Jewish presence. The Jewish community at Thessalonica was large enough to have a synagogue. According to Acts 17, when Paul reached the city, he preached there about Christ on three consecutive Sabbaths. Then the Jews opposed to him 'enlisted the help of a gang from the market-place, stirred up a crowd, and soon had the whole city in uproar'. With this gang they set about persecuting Paul, who in fact escaped from the city. The impression of uproar throughout the city may be something of an exaggeration, for Luke regularly stresses the violence of the rejection of the Christian message by the majority of Jews. He depicts similar scenes at Ephesus and at Corinth. Luke does not actually tell us that Paul spent only three weeks there, and this impression may be a foreshortening of a much longer period. A short stay might account for the gaps in their knowledge of Christianity, but the affection with which he writes to the Thessalonians suggests that they were long-term friends. He calls them 'brothers' 14 times and stresses his impatience to hear how they are faring! There are plenty of expressions of affection: 'like a mother feeding and looking after her children...' (2.7), or 'we treated every one of you as a father treats his children' (2.11), or 'you are our pride and joy' (2.20).

Acts stresses that in each city some of the Jewish community accepted the message, but the opposition of the majority forced him to turn to the gentiles. Paul's letter itself makes it clear that the gentiles formed a significant part of the Christian community, for they 'broke with the worship of false gods' (1.9), which would not have been said of Jews. Paul confirms that this was already the case during his stay at Thessalonica: 'God gave us the courage to speak his gospel to you fearlessly, in spite of great opposition' (2.2). The state of affairs clearly continued. Paul stresses that he had warned them that they were certain to have hardships to bear, 'and that is what has happened now' (3.4).

Plan of 1 Thessalonians

1.2–10	Thanksgiving
2.1–19	Paul's Mission to Thessalonika
3.1–13	Timothy's Mission to Thessalonika
4.1–12	Life in Christ
4.13–5.11	The Second Coming
5.12–28	Final Encouragement and Greetings

2. The Day of the LORD

After all these statements of affection and worry, somewhat assuaged by Timothy's reassuring visit (3.1–10), Paul gives them some general advice about living a holy life (3.11–4.12). Such advice is normally placed at the end of the letters, but in this case Paul immediately afterwards cuts down to the problem of the Christian dead. The problem was no doubt that Paul had taught that Christ had conquered death, and in the meantime Christians had died. The Thessalonians, swiftly instructed as they had been, may well have taken Paul's teaching to mean that Christians would never die. Paul's teaching could be understood in this sense: 'We know that Christ has been raised from the dead and will never die again. Death has no power over him any more. In the same way, you must see yourselves as being dead to sin but alive for God in Christ Jesus' (Rom. 6.8–11). Or again, writing to the Corinthians, 'Death, where is your victory? Death, where is your sting? The sting of death is sin' (1 Cor. 15.55). What he really meant was not that death does not occur any more, but that it has lost its sting and its victory.

Paul answers this worry with a brilliant composition which draws together two different sets of imagery, the Israelite idea of the Day of the LORD, and the Roman conception of a triumphal procession.

a. The Concept of a Day of the LORD

The idea first occurs in Amos 5.18 (see p. 6). A prime element in Amos is his campaign against social injustice. The rich and comfortable of Samaria are secure in their consciousness of election, which has only to be consummated at a Day of the LORD. The prophet rounds on them to say that this Day they are expecting will be one of deserved disaster:

> Disaster for you who long for the Day of The LORD.
> What will the Day of The LORD mean for you?
> It will mean darkness not light,
> as when someone runs away from a bear
> only to meet a lion.

This conception of the Day of the LORD grows in importance and immediacy as prophetic and national awareness of the corruption of Israel increases, and the punishment of Israel and then of Judah by the exile approaches.

With the exile of the Jews in Babylon the application of this Day of the LORD changes sharply. The Day of the LORD becomes a day when the oppressors of the now helpless Israel will be punished: 'The Day of the LORD is near for all the nations. As you have done, so will it be done to you: your deeds will recoil on your own head' (Obad.15). It will become a day of comforting for Israel (Joel 3.4; Zach. 12.1; Mal. 3.2). Increasingly, with the awareness of God's rule over the whole of creation (which was not yet clear in Amos' time), this Day takes on cosmic dimensions (e.g. Isa. 24.21–3):

> When that Day comes, The LORD will punish
> the armies of the sky above
> and on earth the kings of the earth.
> They will be herded together like prisoners in a dungeon
> and shut up in gaol
> and after long years punished.
> The moon will be confused and the sun ashamed
> for The LORD Sabaoth is king.

This is the imagery of the *Dies Irae*, based on Joel 2.10–11:

> As they come on, the earth quakes, the skies tremble,
> sun and moon grow dark, the stars lose their brilliance.
> The LORD's voice rings out at the head of his troops,
> for mighty indeed is his army,
> strong the enforcer of his orders,
> for great is the Day of The LORD
> and very terrible – who can face it?

This imagery is, of course, also reflected in the scene of the crucifixion, not only by the darkness at noon – no mere casual meteorological observation, but an allusion to Amos 8.9 – but also by the earthquake, the splitting of the rocks and the opening of the tombs described in Matthew 27.51–2. Such cosmic imagery, involving heaven and earth in turmoil, becomes a standard feature in the apocalyptic writings of the first century (see p. 362). In this letter of Paul such imagery is represented not only by the name 'the Day of the LORD' (5.2), but also by the trumpet of God, the voice of the archangel, the sons of light, the suddenness of the event and the transition between heaven and earth.

A highly significant difference is the identity of the LORD. In the Old Testament in general and specifically in the expectation of the Day of the LORD, the LORD is always the Lord God, with the use of the sacred name, translated into Greek as *Kyrios*. This word can be used in the vocative, *kyrie!*

to mean simply 'Sir!'. With the definite article *o kyrios*, it seems always to mean 'the LORD', that is, the LORD God. In Mark it is never clearly used of Jesus in this way (doubtful possible uses are Mk 5.19; 11.3). It will be used of Jesus with a divine reference sparingly in Matthew (18.31; 21.3) and more frequently in Luke (7.13, 19; 10.1; 10.39, 41; 11.39; 13.15; 17.5; 19.8; 22.61; 24.3, 34). The really significant factor is not so much the word as the context of the title: the LORD who comes on the Day of the LORD can only be the LORD God. So here, in the earliest writing of the New Testament Jesus is already being given divine honours and divine prerogatives.

b. Paul's Use of the Idea

Paul combines this standard biblical imagery with that of a Roman triumphal procession: 'We who remain alive will be taken up in the clouds to meet the Lord in the air' (4.17). The LORD's triumphal procession will be in the clouds – always a symbol of divinity – rather than in Rome. The word used for 'to meet' is *eis upantesin*, a Hellenistic word for a solemn, usually processional, meeting with the Emperor on a state visit. Elsewhere Paul uses similar technical terminology, that of the triumphal procession (2 Cor. 2.14; cf. Col. 2.15). The imagery is that of joining Christ's own triumphal procession. A Roman triumphal procession, consisting of the victorious general (normally the Emperor), his troops, spoils and captives marching through the streets of Rome, ended with the offering of the spoils of battle to God. In the Roman rite the offering was made to Jupiter on the Capitol hill, including the slaughter of captives. Paul adapts this language, making a bridge between this Roman custom and the apocalyptic scenes familiar to us from Jewish apocalyptic writings of the first century. But again, the significant factor is that to make his point Paul takes a ritual of the imperial cult and transfers it to Jesus, so that Jesus stands in the place of the divine Emperor. In the same way, it is an attractive idea that Paul takes a dig at the Roman proclamation (on coins and inscriptions) that Roman rule brings peace and security when he says (5.3): 'It is when people are saying "Peace and security" that the worst suddenly happens'. On the Day of the LORD, the LORD Christ, rather than the Emperor, will lead the procession and Christians will solemnly come to meet him in his triumphal procession, in which those who have already died will already be participants. This is already a clear statement of the total Lordship of Christ.

Further imagery makes this additionally clear, for:

- In 3.13 Jesus will come *with all his holy ones* – as the Lord God in Zachariah 14.5.
- In 4.16 the *ram's horn* will sound for the coming of the Lord, as in Isaiah 27.13.
- In 4.16–17 the *dead* will come back to life, the *corpses* will rise again, as in Isaiah 26.19 at the coming of the Lord.
- In 5.2–3 the image of sudden *labour-pains* is used of the coming of Christ, as in Isaiah 13.8 of the coming of the Lord.

24

The Second Letter to the Thessalonians

---

1. Authorship

With this second letter we come up against the problem of pseudonymity. There was a convention at the time that a writing could be ascribed to a famous author in order to give it authority. This is less dishonest than it seems to us, for it was considered an act of homage to a revered author. It was not only before any laws on copyright, but seemingly before there were any conventions about ownership of a piece of writing. The attitude towards copying was quite different before printing and photocopying made diffusion of a text a simple matter. In these cases it seems that the later author felt that he was carrying on the tradition of the famous figure of the past, and interpreting his mind for the present, applying it to the new situation. One important factor, especially with regard to the inspiration of scripture, is whether the author was trying to deceive his readers. If, as seems to be the case, pseudonymity was a literary convention of the time, there was no deception involved, for readers would understand that ascription to an authoritative figure of the past was merely a convention of authorship.

Examples from the first century are numerous. The *Testaments of the Twelve Patriarchs*, the *Book of Enoch* and *3 & 4 Esdras* are clearly pseudonymous. Nor is pseudonymity a bar to inclusion in the canon of scripture. In the Book of Proverbs several of the collections of proverbs are attributed to Solomon, no doubt on the grounds that his reputed wisdom (1 Kings 3) was considered the basis of all wisdom in Israel. Similarly the Book of Wisdom is called 'The Wisdom of Solomon', though composed probably in the mid-first century BC. The 'Psalms of Solomon', included in the Greek Septuagint though not in the Latin Vulgate, is similarly a Pharisaic collection from about the same time.

In the New Testament also it has been vigorously argued that the gospels were originally anonymous and were subsequently (in the second century) attributed to their named authors. It is unlikely that Matthew, one of the Twelve, wrote the gospel that bears his name; he would have been too old by the time it appeared at the end of the first century. At the end of the New Testament period there is no doubt that Second Peter is also pseudonymous. Nor is there any particular positive reason why the letters which bear the names of Peter, James and Jude were written by members of the Twelve. Why, then, were they included in the New Testament? Bearing the name of a member of the Twelve was certainly only one factor in such inclusion, not sufficient in itself, for the 'Gospels' of Thomas, Peter, Philip and others (known in the second century) were never included. Mark, Luke and 'the Elder' (responsible for some of the Johannine corpus) make no claim to have been members of the Twelve, but they are considered to have been of the apostolic generation. By contrast, at the end of the second century Bishop Serapion of Antioch forbade the reading in the Church of Rhossus of the 'Gospel of Peter', on the grounds that its Christology was unsatisfactory. Those documents and only those documents which were held to be foundation-documents of the universal Christian Church were included in the New Testament as expressions and guides of the beliefs of the Church.

Is this particular letter genuinely by Paul? It is undeniable that there are many purely Pauline phrases in 2 Thessalonians. The difficulty is that there are too many exactly similar words and phrases, combined with differences of thought. It looks as though an imitator has carefully imitated the phrases, sometimes with variation, sometimes woodenly, in order to suggest Pauline authorship of the letter. Of course another solution would be that the same author has simply repeated himself, saying the same things with slight changes of expression, consciously or unconsciously repeating himself by heart. One major difficulty about this hypothesis is that there is so little difference between the two letters, apart from the eschatological passage in 2 Thessalonians 2.1–12. There is the same structure, for example, the renewed thanksgiving in 1 Thessalonians 2.13 and 2 Thessalonians 2.13. The exhortation to live according to the gospel is much the same in both letters. If the main purpose of the second letter is this eschatological passage, there would have been no need to wrap it up in so much repetition! After all, Paul knew how to correct pretty sharply any misinterpretation of his letters, as in 1 Corinthians 5.9–11. So:

---

1 Thessalonians 1.2: We always thank God for you all … faith … love … perseverance.

2 Thessalonians 1.3: We *should* always thank God for you … faith … love … perseverance.

1 Thessalonians 2.9: We worked with unsparing energy, night and day, so as not to be a burden on any of you (repeated verbatim in 2 Thess. 3.8).

1 Thessalonians 5.12–14 (in the closing section): We urge you, brothers, in the Lord (repeated verbatim in the closing section of 2 Thessalonians 3.12–15).

1 Thessalonians 3.12 (just before the closing section): May God our Father himself and our Lord Jesus Christ … strengthen your hearts.

2 Thessalonians 1.16 (just before the closing section): May *the Lord Jesus Christ* himself and God our Father…*console* your hearts and strengthen you.

Note the reversal of order, putting the Lord Jesus first. Several times 2 Thessalonians gives more prominence to Jesus in these dual formulas. So 2 Thessalonians 1.12 'by the grace of our God and Lord, Jesus Christ' states the divinity of Christ more clearly than almost any other Pauline passage. Similarly *kyrios* ('Lord') is frequently used of Jesus, and frequently replaces 'God' (2 Thessalonians 3.16 for 1 Thessalonians 5.23 in a blessing, 'the God/Lord of peace'; similarly 2 Thessalonians 3.5 for 1 Thessalonians 3.11).

It is often said that the Second Letter is notably less warm and more formal than the First: in the First the Thessalonians are called 'brothers' fourteen times, in the Second only eight times, and then only 'formulaically'; however, it does contain passages of warmth and affection – readers must make their own judgment! It might be claimed that the 'signature' at the end is a proof of authenticity: 'The greeting in my own hand, Paul, is a sign in every letter. That is how I write' (3.17). Paul, does, it is true 'sign' other letters somewhat similarly, but not wholly similarly. In other letters the 'signature' in Paul's own hand is for emphasis (Galatians 6.11) or for warmth of friendship (1 Cor. 16.21; Col. 4.18). He never uses it to stress the authenticity of the letter.

One likely solution, therefore, is that 2 Thessalonians is a letter facing a different situation. It assumes a realized eschatology, such as is expressed in Ephesians and Colossians some years later; such an eschatology must lie behind the suggestion that 'The Day of the Lord has already arrived' (2.2). The developed apocalyptic writing of 2.3–8 has no parallel in earlier Pauline letters. It was deliberately written in a Pauline style, with some involuntary variations and some wooden imitations. It was given the address 'to the Thessalonians' because 1 Thessalonians is the Pauline letter which deals most fully with the problem of eschatology, though in a different situation, with different worries. The unknown author will have attributed the letter to Paul with the intention that it applied the Pauline teaching about the coming of Christ to the different situation of his own day.

Other solutions are possible and cannot be excluded. One attractive possibility is that the letter is basically from Paul, facing a situation some time later, but making use of a different secretary. Paul's flexible creativity in responding differently and aptly to different situations is a feature which will continue to astonish any student of his letters. The somewhat wooden and not wholly exact imitation in 2 Thessalonians of phrases in 1 Thessalonians could be explained by the careful harmonisation of the second letter to the first by a secretary: both letters are from 'Paul, Silvanus and Timothy' (1.1), but perhaps Silvanus and Timothy played a more prominent and different part in the composition of the Second from the First.

Plan of 2 Thessalonians

1.3–12	Thanksgiving
2.1–12	The Delay of the Second Coming

2. The Message

Obviously the purpose and message of the letter will be considered somewhat differently if it is authentically Pauline or not, but the difference is principally only a matter of date. Whether or not it is truly Pauline, the situation must be that of excitement at the imminent coming of Christ, which was such that certain people downed tools and refused to work. The author reacts, perhaps only shortly after the first letter (especially if it is Paul himself), by pointing out that the second coming is not so very imminent. The delay of the second coming is a problem in several of the later letters of the New Testament. Certain apocalyptic events must happen before that second coming, namely the Great Rebellion, and the appearance of the Rebel, the Lost One or the Evil One. This figure will be enthroned in the Temple. The scenario is reminiscent of the Emperor Gaius Caligula's attempt to have an equestrian statue of himself erected in the Temple, an attempt which caused outrage in the early 40s, and was staved off and eventually avoided by Gaius' death in 44AD. Such a date is too early for this letter, even if it is genuinely Pauline; but the upset and outrage caused by the attempt serves as a symbol of exaltation of the evil Anti-God, the Enemy. It also shows that worship of the Roman Emperor could stand as the symbol of all evil opposition to Christianity. However, all the language of the passage is highly biblical and symbolic, dependent on the prophets, Ezekiel 28.3, Daniel 11.36 and Jewish apocalyptic writings. There is no need to search out exact historical equivalents to 'the Lost One' and 'Satan'. This figure may or may not be the same as the AntiChrist of 1 John 2.18–22. It may or may not be the same as the claimants to be the Messiah envisaged in Mark 13.5–6. In any case it is clear from the Book of Revelation 20 that some early Christians saw the final events as occurring in two stages.

25

The Pastoral Letters to Timothy and Titus

The two letters to Timothy and one to Titus are known as the Pastoral Letters, a name coined in 1726 by P. Anton. The name indicates that they are concerned with the Christian community settling in the world, rather than letters from the first missionary efforts of the Church, and that they are largely concerned with pastors and their qualifications. The order in which they are printed indicates nothing about their priority, for the letters attributed to Paul are printed in decreasing order of length, first letters addressed to communities, then those addressed to individuals. In fact few scholars now accept the attribution of these letters to Paul, though some accept that 2 Timothy may stem from Paul. The order in which the letters were written can, then, be determined only from internal evidence. There is little to indicate any succession. Of course, if 2 Timothy is viewed as a farewell testament of Paul would this situate it as the first of the three.

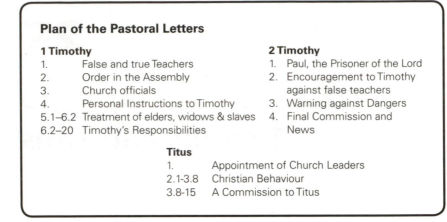

Plan of the Pastoral Letters

1 Timothy		2 Timothy	
1.	False and true Teachers	1.	Paul, the Prisoner of the Lord
2.	Order in the Assembly	2.	Encouragement to Timothy
3.	Church officials		against false teachers
4.	Personal Instructions to Timothy	3.	Warning against Dangers
5.1–6.2	Treatment of elders, widows & slaves	4.	Final Commission and
6.2–20	Timothy's Responsibilities		News

Titus
1.   Appointment of Church Leaders
2.1-3.8   Christian Behaviour
3.8-15   A Commission to Titus

1. Authorship of the Letters

These letters appear to be written by Paul at a late stage of his life. They do not fit into the outline of his life as given by Acts, so that, if the historical details are taken seriously, they show a 'second career' after the time in Rome with which Acts concludes. The differences of the Pastoral and earlier letters are explained in two ways. Scholars who are determined to retain genuine authorship by Paul paint a portrait of an old man, broken by hardship and years, fearful for the future, unable any longer to think through to his magnificent old doctrinal formulations and concerned only to instruct his two beloved disciples in the preservation of doctrine and Church structure after his fast-approaching death. Others accept the convention of pseude-pigraphy (see p. 297–8). There is, however, a distinction between 2 Timothy and the other two letters.

2 Timothy has a character of its own, corresponding to the contemporary convention of a last will and testament, testifying to Paul's own efforts, but also an appeal from the great apostle to continue his work of spreading the gospel, inspired by his heroic example. Again and again Paul's heroism and perseverance in his task are stressed, but without the detail of the autobio-graphical passages of earlier letters, and without the sense of 'filling up the sufferings of Christ' (2 Cor. 1.5; Phil. 3.10).

Paul is no longer in 'free captivity' in Rome, but in close confinement. He has presented his defence once, and expects the Lord to rescue him, 'when he has fought the good fight to the end' only to 'bring him safely to his heavenly kingdom' (2 Tim. 4.7, 16–18). Some scholars (e.g. Raymond

Brown) tentatively hold that this letter, though not written by Paul himself, is pseudepigraphical, but written 'not long after Paul's death as a farewell testament by someone who knew Paul's last days'. It might, then, be the first of the three letters to be written, and would fall into a different category from the other two.

This genre of farewell speech of a great leader was well-known and frequent in ancient literature, both within and outside the Bible, from Genesis 49 onwards, from Plato's *Apology* of Socrates onwards. Particularly obvious examples in contemporary Jewish literature were *The Testaments of the Twelve Patriarchs*. In the New Testament there are two other examples, the final discourse of Jesus after the Last Supper (Jn 14–17) and Paul's parting speech to the elders of Ephesus at Miletus (Acts 20.17–38). Features of such a discourse are regular and appear in 2 Timothy:

	Acts 20	2 Timothy
a résumé of the life-work	v. 19	1.8–12
announcement of approaching death	vv. 22–23	4.6–8
self-justification	v. 26	4.7
disciples are counselled to continue the work	v. 28	2.1–13
to preserve unity	v. 31	2.14
to beware of dangers and opposition to come	v. 30	3.1–9; 4.2–5.

The other two letters show Paul still travelling in the East: 1 Timothy, written to his previous companion and disciple in Ephesus, mentions a journey to Macedonia (1.3), and 2 Timothy (4.13) a journey to Troas, while Titus (1.5) was 'left behind' by Paul in Crete. This gives the outline of a 'second career' of mission in the eastern Mediterranean, presumably intended as later than the journey to Rome with which Acts concludes. A major difficulty about genuine Pauline authorship is that the instructions include elementary advice with which any companion of Paul would have been thoroughly familiar; the implied readership is the community, not Paul's own lieutenants. By contrast, another difficulty is that, even when allowance is made for different subject-matter and the advance of time, it is surprising that there should be no trace of so many distinctively Pauline interests, such as the Cross, the Body of Christ and the Covenant. It is difficult to conceive of Paul, such an innovator and such a lively thinker, settling in old age to write such elaborate and worthy manuals of discipline!

2. The Situation of the Letters

a. False teaching

There is clearly false teaching around, but what this teaching was is more difficult to establish. 2 Timothy tells us little, for 'wrangling about words' and 'pointless philosophical discussions' (2.14) may be applied to any opponent's theories. 1 Timothy 1.4 mentions 'myths and endless geneal-ogies' which tend to raise doubts. This could indicate either pagan myths of the endless amours of the gods and goddesses, or Jewish *haggadoth* founded on the genealogies of the Pentateuch, which certainly seemed to play a part in contemporary Jewish interpretation of the Bible. They could also indicate the succession of demiurges from some creator-figure which became popular in speculations on the fringes of second-century Christianity and are associated with what later became known as Gnosticism. There is some suggestion in 1 Timothy 4.1 of a new revelation, coming from deceitful spirits and demons; the fact that Timothy is told (v. 14) to trust in the spiritual gift which he himself possesses may indicate that he is being urged to press his own right to interpret revelation. Similarly, in Titus 1, the 'nonsense' taught by the undisciplined, 'particularly those of the Circumcision' (v. 10. 14) merely signifies the disapproval of the writer. Almost the only clear false doctrine mentioned is that of Hymenaeus and Philetus (2 Tim. 2.17–18), who teach that the resurrection has already taken place.

b. Positive teaching

However, while we have little information about the errors to be avoided, we do have precious hints in all three letters of what the author considers 'sound doctrine'. All these seem to be concerned with salvation and the way to salvation, several of them being also rhythmical, the sort of material and form which is learnt by heart. The paradigm case is 2 Timothy 2.8–13, which starts off, 'the Gospel that I carry, Jesus Christ risen from the dead' and then develops into:

If we have died with him, then we shall live with him.
If we persevere, then we shall reign with him.
If we disown him, then he will disown us.
If we are faithless, he is faithful still,
    for he cannot disown his own self.

In 1 Timothy it is first given briefly as 'a saying you can rely on': that Jesus Christ came into the world to save sinners (1.15). More elaborately, in 3.16 it is called 'the mystery of our religion' (for 'mystery' see p. 00) and set out, obviously for memorization:

'Who was   Manifested in flesh
            Justified in Spirit
            Perceived by angels
            Proclaimed to nations
            Believed in the world
            Taken up into glory.'

Other instances of a 'trustworthy saying' are in 2.14–3.1, 'She [any woman] will be saved by child-bearing', or the saying given in 4.9, 'We have put our trust in the living God, and he is the Saviour of the whole human race'. Or again, Titus 3.7, 'saved by his kindness we should become heirs according to the hope of eternal life'. All concern the message and the means of salvation.

This stress on 'salvation' is particularly significant as Christianity is beginning to settle into a world where multiple cults of saviour-gods were current, and it was possible to be initiated into a variety of 'mystery'-religions in the search for salvation. Frequently on inscriptions also the Emperor is given the title of 'Saviour'. In the gospels God is called 'Saviour' only once (Lk. 1.47), and Jesus twice (Lk. 2.11; Jn 4.42). Suddenly in these letters the title becomes frequent: 'God our Saviour' (1 Tim. 1.1; 2.3; 4.10; Tit. 1.3; 2.10, 13; 3.4), and 'Jesus Christ our Saviour' (2 Tim. 1.10; Tit. 1.4; 2.13; 3.6). This change in language must be in direct opposition to the mysteries and the imperial cult, proclaiming where salvation is truly to be found.

A similar Christological development takes place with the title 'Lord'. Again the imperial cult uses this title frequently of the Emperor. In the gospels 'Lord' is rarely used of Christ, and normally reserved to God, predominantly as the Greek translation of the sacred Hebrew name, YHWH. In both letters to Timothy (oddly, not at all in Titus) the title 'Lord' is used frequently, and often indiscriminately, of Christ and God. For the first time little distinction is made between Christ and God (1 Tim. 1.2; 6.13). Another technical term deliberately inherited from the imperial cult is 'Epiphany' (five times, elsewhere in the New Testament only 2 Thess. 2.8), indicating the final coming and appearance of Christ. In the imperial cult it is used to designate the ceremonial and quasi-divine coming of the Emperor on the visitation of a city, in which he was greeted as a god. At the end of 1

Timothy (6.15–16) this Epiphany of our Lord Jesus Christ is celebrated in the most splendid of the rhythmical sayings: the Epiphany revealed by

The blessed and only Ruler
The King of kings and Lord of lords,
Alone having immortality
Inhabiting inaccessible light,
Whom no man sees or can see,
To whom be honour and power eternal.

3. Order in the Community

a. General morality

A principal concern of 1 Timothy and Titus is order and discipline in the community, 'so that we may be able to live peaceful and quiet lives with all devotion and propriety' (1 Tim. 2.2); 'set an example of good works … so that any opponent will be at a loss, with no accusation to make against us' (Tit. 2.7). These are the virtues of public and private life stressed by Greek and Roman contemporary writers on morals, centred on moderation and restraint, piety and godliness. This is indeed a Christian morality, founded on mercy and grace and the salvation won by Christ (1 Tim. 1.13–15). The first advice given is on prayer, 'petitions, prayers, intercessions and thanksgiving'; this includes intercession for those in authority, but the only quality mentioned is reverence (1 Tim. 2.1–8).

In general the morality recommended is to conform in its practical applications to the acceptable behaviour of the time. It is significant that the two chief virtues, *sophrosune* ('moderation'; 1 Tim. 2.9, 15; 3.2; Tit. 1.3; 2.2, 5) and *eusebeia* ('piety, godliness'; recommended 11 times in the two letters) do not feature in the less conventionally Hellenistic morality of the earlier Pauline letters. Correspondingly, the conventional leanings are shown by quotation from a non-biblical 'prophet' that all Cretans are liars (Tit. 1.12), and another saying of popular Hellenistic wisdom, that money is the root of all evil (1 Tim. 6.10). 'Healthy' teaching is preferred to excessive questioning and argument about words (1 Tim. 6.4). Institutional morality is re-affirmed, in that a woman should not have authority over a man (5.12). This must, of course, be read against the background of the position of women in the societies of the time.

The mechanical argument for the subordination of women, based on Genesis, hardly bears the weight put on it. It should not, however, be taken as the only position accorded to women in the New Testament or even the Pauline writings. A diametrically opposed evaluation is put forward in 1 Corinthians 11.11–12, each sex being dependent on the other. Is it for the sake of good order that women are forbidden to ask questions in the assembly and told to ask their husbands later (1 Cor. 14.34–5)? In any case there can be no doubt that women had an important role in the Pauline communities, notably Chloe of 1 Corinthians 1.11. The deaconess Phoebe was entrusted with the letter to the Romans (Rom. 16.1). The catechist Prisca is classed as Paul's co-worker (16.3), and other women at Rome 'work hard for the Lord' (16.7, 12). On Junia see p. 219.

Nor is the institution of slavery questioned, but rather the obedience of slaves becomes more valuable if it is given to Christian masters (6.1–2). No more than the earlier Pauline letters are the Pastorals prepared to upset the very fabric of society.

b. Special cases

Special instructions are given for certain classes of persons, which gives us an important insight into the incipient institutionalization of the Church. It is not always clear who or what is intended by these instructions, but a certain order and organization is beginning to develop in the Christian communities.

(i) *Episkopos*. This word literally means 'overseer', but, later, from the beginning of the second century, comes to mean 'bishop', the single leader of a Christian community. It is not clear whether here he is yet a single office-holder. The word is here always in the singular, though it is used in the plural in Acts 20.28 and Philippians 1.1. No clue is given about his duties or function, but the qualities required are those of the head of a household, especially leadership, ability to teach, discretion and good reputation (1 Tim. 3.1–7; Tit. 1.7).

(ii) *Widows*. In the society of the time a widow without a man to support her and without family could be destitute and helpless; it is for such distress that the enrolment as a widow is intended. The author is mistrustful of the behaviour of young widows, and is concerned that widows should be enrolled for alms only if they are truly without support and unlikely to marry again – as well as minding their own business! (5.3–16).

(iii) *Presbyteroi*. The normal constitution of Jewish communities of the Diaspora was a council of elders (*presbyteroi*), presided by an *archisynagoga*. Acts 14.23 tells us that Paul set up *presbyteroi* in each of the Christian communities of his first journey. The word means 'seniors' or 'elders'. Coming immediately after instructions for elderly women, this could be a matter merely of seniority in age, which conveys a certain standing. In these letters some of the *presbyteroi* are envisaged as playing a leading part, preaching and teaching, but this may not imply a special administrative office. They are to receive 'double reward' for significant service, and accusations against them must be upheld by two or three witnesses. This may mean that they especially should not be judged on gossip alone. On the other hand the 'imposition of hands' (5.22) normally (not always: Acts 9.17; 19.6) conveys the imparting of the Spirit for some task in the Church. The instruction to set up *presbyteroi* in every town in Crete suggests some definite position, such as the arrangements made by Paul in Acts (Tit. 1.5).

(iv) *Diakonoi*. In Acts 6 these officials are notionally appointed for the distribution of alms, but in fact they (e.g. Stephen and Philip) have a wider ministry of teaching and baptising, similar to that of the Twelve, but for the Hellenists, whereas the Twelve minister primarily to the Hebrew-speakers. The qualities here required overlap widely with those of *presbyteroi*, but again there is no indication of their duties (1 Tim. 3.8–13). There is no judging whether the 'women' of 1 Timothy 3.11 are female deacons or the wives of deacons. No argument for or against the ordination of women to the diaconate in the early Church can be based on this.

Further Reading

Young, Frances, *The Theology of the Pastoral Letters* (1994)

26

The Letter to Philemon

Paul's letter to Philemon is a fascinating document. It conforms entirely to the conventions of letter-writing at the time, and yet is entirely different. We do not know when it was written, but Paul proclaims himself a prisoner and an old man (v. 9). He mentions Archippus and the community which meets at his house, and both Onesimus and Archippus appear in the letter to the Colossians (4.9, 17). Since Colossae was not too far from Ephesus, we may guess that the imprisonment was at Ephesus, from where at least part of Philippians was written; the letter presupposes fairly easy travel between the writer and the recipients. An additional scrap of information may be that half a century later Ignatius of Antioch mentions an Onesimus as bishop of Ephesus.

Paul writes asking Philemon to receive back his slave Onesimus, who has sought refuge with Paul. On the surface it is a typical Greco-Roman letter, of the class of a request or reference sent for another person. The letter bears multiple similarities especially with an analogous letter from Pliny the Younger, some half-century later, in which Pliny asks his friend, Sabinianus, to take back a slave who has fled to him (Pliny, *Letters* 9.21). That letter, like all Pliny's letters, was written for publication. As always, Pliny is very pleased with himself, confident in his high status, rather arch, and talks down to Sabinianus in a patronizing way.

Paul is not writing for publication, but his letter is a fairly public letter, to be read out in the assembly, for his greeting and his final blessing are addressed to 'you' in the plural, not to Philemon alone (vv. 3 and 25). *So, to his embarrassment or otherwise,* Philemon would know that the whole group of Christians would hear the letter! While superficially insisting that he is leaving Philemon free to accede to or refuse the request (v. 14), Paul brings a great deal of pressure to bear – some might say too much pressure. It is a letter full of art: Paul begins with the conventional ploy of *captatio benevolentiae*, a string of compliments to ensure a welcome for his letter (vv. 1–7). He puts forward his own needy situation (v. 9, 12), that he is a prisoner for Christ's sake, and subtly reminds Philemon of his immeasurable debt to Paul (v. 19). At the same time he appears light-hearted and witty, playing on Onesimus' name, which means 'useful': 'he was useless to you before, but now he will be useful to you, as he has been to me' (v. 11). It is a prime example of the delicate word-play which we find throughout Paul's letters. The Greek words he uses for 'useless' and 'useful' sound like 'unChristed' and 'Christed' respectively – Onesimus' conversion is another and the vital persuasive factor. Another word-play on Onesimus' name is 'I would *have this gain* from you, brother' (v. 20): *onaimen*, the only time this word occurs in the New Testament. Paul uses the same sort of word-play with 'christed' in 2 Corinthians 1.20 (see p. 00).

At the heart of the letter, however, is a deeply affectionate and religious message. It is all about the warmth which Christians show to one another within the Christian family. Both Onesimus and Philemon are 'beloved', beloved son and beloved brother respectively. Three times (vv. 7, 12, 20) Paul speaks of his deepest feelings of love (*splanchna*, literally 'guts', usually used for a mother's instinctive love). Twice (v. 6. 17) he uses that vibrant Christian word *koinonia* or community; the paradigm case of *koinonia* is the perfect unity and sharing, practised in the earliest Christian community at Jerusalem. Philemon should welcome Onesimus as a family member (a special word signifies this welcome, v. 17). By becoming a Christian Onesimus has changed from being a slave into being an equal and beloved family member. Paul has fathered him (v. 10) into a new life.

In order to understand the significance of the change it is essential to understand the condition of slaves and their status – or rather, complete non-status – in the Roman world. The great philosopher, Aristotle, regarded some humans as being naturally slaves, that is, being chattels, not possessed of personal rights. Some slaves worked in the mines, some had important administrative jobs, but in any case a slave was to be discarded (like a soiled paper towel) when finished with. The politician and philosopher Cicero chides himself complacently for being sensitive to the sickness of his slave-secretary. By becoming a Christian brother, Onesimus has really become a new creation.

Although this letter played its part in the eventual abolition of slavery, the absence of any general condemnation of slavery has meant that it was also used for many centuries as a justification for slavery. It may well be asked why Paul did not point out that the whole institution of slavery was incompatible with the Christian message, especially as he says (Galatians 3.28) that in Christ there is neither slave nor free. One answer has been that he thought the end of the world too close for such a social revolution to be practicable or necessary: 'It is good for a man to stay as he is... The world as we know it is passing away' (1 Corinthians 7.26, 31). Another answer is that the required mental upheaval was too great to be possible; it takes time to absorb the full implications of the Christian message.

Opinion is divided about the background to Paul's appeal. Had Onesimus run away from his master Philemon and taken refuge with Paul? This would have been a daring step, followed by a daring appeal, for the penalty for a re-captured fugitive slave was death by torture. Flight to an imprisoned friend of the master is a curiously risky procedure. Had Philemon lent Onesimus' services to Paul for a fixed time, so that Paul is now asking for Onesimus' services for a renewed period? Is v.18 a hint that Onesimus has wronged his master, and has a debt to pay? Is Paul gently suggesting that Onesimus should be set free, to remain with Philemon 'for ever' ('and ever'? v. 15)? In the Bible a freed slave might well remain a member of the household (Exod. 21.2–6), and in the Roman world also. These issues are unimportant to Paul in comparison to the overwhelming novelty that, by baptism into Christ, Onesimus has become a beloved brother to himself and to Philemon.

Questions on Part Three

1 Should Paul rather than Jesus be considered the founder of Christianity?
2 If Paul had fathered a son, would he have had him circumcised?
3 Did Paul think Jesus was God? How does he express his view?
4 Do Paul's letters show him as a successful pastor? Have you any advice to give him?
5 What was the chief problem besetting Christianity in Paul's time?
6 Does Paul's attitude to women destroy his value as a teacher?

Part IV

The Catholic or Universal Epistles

27

The Letter to the Hebrews

1. Authorship, Origin, Destination

The letter gives away hardly any clues about its author, its origin or its destination. Indeed, in some ways it would be better if this writing was not classified as a letter: it has no epistolary introduction, and the only letter-features are the brief details at the end (13.18–25). The full and frequent passages of encouragement and advice might indicate that it would be better classified as an exhortation. Some ancient manuscripts position it after Paul's Letter to the Romans, thereby showing that at one moment someone thought it was written by Paul. This could be a conclusion drawn from mention of 'our brother Timothy' in 13.25, but Timothy was a fairly common name. Another unhelpful clue is the greeting from 'those from Italy' (13.24), which shows only that the author was in contact with some Christians in Italy. An external clue is its quotation in *1 Clement*, written at Rome no later than 110AD, and perhaps a score of years earlier, which shows that it was known at Rome by the writer of that letter. This does not, of course, show that it was written either at or for the Christian community in Rome.

Scholars have argued that the silence of the letter about the Jerusalem Temple, despite its interest in Jewish ritual, argues some say for, some say against, the conclusion that it was written after the destruction of the Temple. H. Attridge comments succinctly and forcefully that the author 'is interested in biblical symbolism not the fate of a cultic rite'. The principal rite to which Christ's sacrifice is compared is, in any case, not the Temple of Jerusalem, but the tabernacle of the desert wanderings. The widespread use of biblical examples, the foundation of so many arguments on scriptural texts and the frequent use of methods of contemporary Jewish exegesis go a long way to justify the title, 'To the Hebrews'. Scriptural argument is the chief means of exposition. For instance, the first two arguments to be developed are contrasts of Jesus to the angels who mediated the Law, and to the revered figure of Moses.

Some of the exegetical moves made seem strange to modern exegesis. For instance the argument of 4.6–11 depends on the interpretation of Psalm 95(94).11 (entering a place of rest) in reliance on Genesis 2.2 (God's place of rest), because of the use of the same word: the rest envisaged for the pilgrim people is the final rest of God after creation. This utilizes the exegetical principle *gezerah shawah*, one of the rules codified by Rabbi Hillel in the first century: it is legitimate to interpret a word obscure in one context by its meaning in another context. Another such rabbinic principle is the *a fortiori* argument in 9.13–14, 'how much more…'.

At the same time, the skilful use of polished Greek rhetorical devices and of the Greek language show that it is at home in Hellenistic culture. Both of these aspects would fit a Jewish community in Rome – but also in many other cities of the Roman Empire.

2. Outlines

The structure of this 'word of encouragement' (13.22) is not always easy to discern. Does it indeed have a single coherent and advancing argument? It might almost be taken as a series of expositions of isolated scriptural texts, building up to the general idea of Christ as high priest, using these texts to show that Christ is their true meaning and that he supersedes the cult and ritual of the sacrifices of the Temple. A theme which is constantly recurring is fidelity and perseverance. The Greek word *pistos* means both 'trustworthy' and 'trusting' in the sense of persevering. It can thus be used both of Moses and Christ, of God and of the enduring heroes of Israel. The corresponding noun, *pistis*, therefore denotes both belief or trust and the perseverance which goes with it.

Plan of the Letter

1.1–4	Introduction
1.5–2.18	Christ, the Son crowned with glory, superior to the angels. This is built upon a catena of scriptural quotations, strung together in the manner of rabbinical exegesis.
3.1–4.14	Christ compared to Moses. Moses was faithful as a servant; Christ is faithful as a Son, a faithful high priest. The argument revolves round the fidelity of these two figures. This is punctuated by a warning, built upon an exegesis of Psalm 95, of the failure of those who were not faithful to their vocation (3.7–4.11), confirmed by a statement of the power of God's word (4.12–13).
4.15–8.5	Christ as a merciful and sympathetic high priest. This is built on two texts: Genesis 14 and Psalm 110. In the former Melchizedek is introduced as superior to Abraham. In the latter it is argued that Christ, exalted to God's right hand, is the true recipient of the promise of an eternal priesthood sworn to Melchizedek. This is enriched by an exhortation on the dangers of human lack of fidelity and a reminder of God's own fidelity (5.11–6.20).
8.6–10.21	Christ as the high priest of the new and eternal covenant. This is built on the promises of a new covenant in Jeremiah 31.31–4, quoted in 8.8–12, and a reminder of the ineffectiveness of the old ritual (Exodus 24.8). It is seen as the fulfilment also of Psalm 40.
10.22–12.17	A eulogy of faithfulness in the history of Israel. This begins with an encouragement to perseverance and a warning about failure (10.22–39). The centre of the argument is the recital of the fidelity of the great figures of history,

and their achievements. Such a list is a standard feature of Jewish historical writing at this time, such as Ben Sira (Ecclesiastes) 44–50 or 1 Maccabees 2.51–60. Here it is expressed with a fine anaphora, each example beginning 'by faith…', in praise both of the faith and of the perseverance of the hero of God's people.

12.18–29   A final comparison of the two covenants.

13.1–24   Conclusion and final greetings.

3. The Revelation of the Wisdom of God

The letter opens with perhaps the most glorious assertion in the whole of the New Testament of Christ's position, as the climax of revelation. It is introduced by a reflexion on two moments of revelation: God's self-revelation to the Fathers was good enough, but now a greater revelation still has occurred. In the Greek the news begins with a little trumpet-fanfare in the form of the alliteration: *Polymeros kai **p**olytropos **p**alai o theos lalesas tois **p**atrasin en tois **p**rophetais,* followed by a title already familiar enough from Paul's message, 'son' and 'heir'. What follows, however, binds the Son even more closely to the Father, 'through whom he also made the ages'. This itself is followed by an explanation in terms which relate to the Wisdom literature of Judaism: in Wisdom 7.26, divine Wisdom is called the radiance of God's glory, the communication of God's glory which somehow is-and-is-not God himself. The struggle is always to explain how God can communicate, transfer himself to the world in creation; of this the second noun, 'imprint of his being', is another attempt: the imprint of a seal has the same shape and power as the seal itself. There follow two further participial clauses, the first expressing the permanence of this creative act ('carrying all things by the word of his power'), and the second more soteriological and eschatological, related to the final triumph, before the main verb, the first of many references in Hebrews to Psalm 110, 'has *taken his seat at the right hand* of the Greatness on high'; this Psalm is used throughout the letter to tell of Christ's exalted position. These first four verses contain almost the whole Christological message of Hebrews.

4. Jesus, the Angels and Moses

After this initial statement in terms of divine Wisdom in creation, the position and the work of Jesus begins to be explained by two comparisons, the first between Jesus and the angels, the second between Jesus and Moses. Both are particularly apt to Judaism, and so apposite to the letter to the Hebrews. The position of the angels bulked large in the Judaism of this time, as we see from the mention of 'thrones, dominions, sovereignties, powers' in Colossians 1.16 and 'the worship of angels' in Colossians 2.18 (cf. Eph. 1.21), where they seem to be put forward as rivals to Christ. Galatians 3.19 and many passages in the contemporary *Book of Jubilees* show the importance of angels in the mediation of the Law. The catena of verses from the Psalms paints the true picture, underlined by the explanation in 2.1–5 that the angels are no more than messengers and ministers. At the same time we are given the first hints of how the author sees the 'great salvation' (2.3), the work of Jesus, who had to become man and submit to death in order to be exalted and bring with him, as a faithful and trustworthy high priest, his brothers who share his human nature. Here for the first time (2.10), but again and again throughout the letter, the task of Christ, or his 'perfecting' and the salvation which he brings, is expressed as bringing his brothers into God's presence to share the divine glory.

The second contrast, between Jesus and Moses, is less sharp, in fact almost a partnership. Both are 'trustworthy', an epithet which is most important in Hebrews, in Greek *pistos*. The noun *pistis* means 'faith', and is the basis of the eulogies of the ancestors for their faith in Hebrews 11. The adjective can be used both actively and passively, that is, for someone who is trustworthy, that is, earns faith (as Moses here and in Num. 12.7), and for someone who trusts, is full of faith. The contrast between them is in the quality of their faith: Moses is trustworthy because his promises will be fulfilled, Jesus because he is already in possession. This is expressed by the contrast familiar from Galatians 4, between slave and free.

5. Jesus the High Priest

Jesus as high priest is the message at the heart of Hebrews. Nowhere else in the New Testament is this title given to Jesus, though there have been elements which might well have led to this. In the messianic expectation of the Dead

Sea Scrolls at Qumran, the sectaries awaited not only a warlike Messiah but also an anointed priest, so a Messiah of Aaron and of Israel (1 QS 9.11), though it is not clear whether this is one or two different figures. The final, prophesied Day of Peace will be inaugurated by an anointed one, and will be a Year of Peace for Melchizedek (11 Q Melch.), always a priestly figure. In the contemporary *Testaments of the Twelve Patriarchs* there is frequent expectation of a priestly figure (*Testament of Levi* 18.8). In the gospels there is no explicit mention of Christ as a priest, unless perhaps the seamless robe of Jesus in John 19.23 is a symbol of the high priest's garment. However, the discourse after the Last Supper is full of hints in this direction. Jesus fulfils the priestly function of interceding for his followers (Jn 14.16; Rom. 8.34; 1 Jn 2.1), and speaks of sanctifying himself so that they too may be sanctified in truth (Jn 17.19). Paul, of course, speaks of Christ 'giving himself for me' (Gal. 2.20), and on one occasion uses the terminology of sacrifice in calling Christ the *hilasterion* or 'sacrifice of reconciliation' (see p. 212). The same cultic language is used rarely elsewhere, 'Jesus Christ, the sacrifice to expiate our sins' (1 Jn 2.2).

However, in Hebrews such language is brought explicitly into the focus of the High Priest. The author is seeking to wean his readers from their yearnings for the old order of sacrifice and cult. The stress of this focus has several dimensions:

- 4.14–16 A high priest who is 'not incapable of feeling our weakness' so that 'we may have no fear in approaching the throne of grace to receive mercy' The word for 'mercy' is the normal equivalent of the Hebrew *hesed*, the quality of family love and understanding which brings repeated and unfailing forgiveness. This aspect of shared sympathy through shared suffering in the humanity of Jesus is stressed also in 5.7, 'During his life on earth he offered up prayer and entreaty with loud cries and with tears'.

When was this incident in the life of Jesus? He offered up prayer with loud cries and tears, and his prayer was heard. Could this be the Agony in the Garden? In what sense was his prayer ('Take this cup away from me, but not what I want but what you want', Mk 14.36) heard there? The tradition varies widely between the synoptic gospels and John, for in John there is no prayer in the garden; in John 12.27–8 Jesus prays almost the same prayer, but on an earlier occasion. Was Mark's scene built up by the evangelist on the basis of this saying, using the typical Markan triple repetition? It is possible that there were several traditions on Jesus' prayer before the Passion, of which the synoptic gospels have one, John another and Hebrews a third.

- 5.8 'Winning a hearing by his reverence, he learnt obedience through his sufferings; when he had been perfected he became for all who obey him the source of eternal salvation'. Here the stress is on obedience, the obedience which was the heart of Jesus' self-offering and won salvation. This is underlined again by the quotation of the psalm in the summary at 10.7, 'I am coming to do your will'. It is also the message of Romans 5.12–21: the loving obedience of Christ throughout his suffering reversed the disobedience of Adam, that is, of the human race.

- 7.1–28 The abrogation of the old order of levitical priesthood and the attachment of Christ's priesthood to 'the order of Melchizedek' is argued from the two texts of Genesis 14.17–20 and Psalm 110.4. From these texts the author argues the superiority and the eternity of Christ's priesthood (7.3): Abraham gave tithes to Melchizedek and Melchizedek blessed Abraham. Both of these are taken to show that Abraham recognized the superiority of Melchizedek's priesthood to the priesthood of his own line. The oath sworn in Psalm 110 to David 'for ever' establishes the perfection and permanence of the covenant of which Jesus is the guarantee (7.22). Here the multiple meaning of the Greek *diatheke* is exploited; it means 'covenant' or 'testament' or simply 'disposition' or 'arrangement'. So there is no need to claim a New Covenant, superseding the covenant made on Sinai, but only a 'new arrangement', a new means by which it is activated. This is then explained (8.8–10.10) on the basis of the text of Jeremiah 31.31–34.

- 9.11–14 It is an important principle that there is no purification without blood. Christ's blood, offered once and for all (also 7.27 and 10.10) is superior to the annual purification sacrifices of the Day of Atonement because it is the blood of the Son, who has passed through the 'greater, more perfect tent', probably a metaphor for the heavens through which Christ passed in his journey of exaltation. Here there is perhaps a reflection of popular Platonic philosophy: Christ's sacrifice is the perfect, heavenly and permanent sacrifice, of which the earthly sacrifice of the Temple was only a shadow or passing reflection (9.24).

6. Pilgrimage to the Place of Rest

The little homily built upon Psalm 95 is valuable both as an excellent example of the contemporary scriptural exegesis of the author and as a meditation on the whole thrust of the letter. The purpose of the letter is to inspire the readers, disgruntled at the loss of the cult, with the hope that its objectives will be better fulfilled through the promises realized in Christ. It is the primary exemplar of a typology used several times in the New Testament, that the followers of Christ, the new People of God, are engaged on the same journey through the desert as the followers of Moses, with the same dangers and temptations (1 Cor. 10.1–22; Jude 5), and ending in the perfect Sabbath-day rest of God after creation. This theme is neatly stressed by allusion to the name 'Joshua'. The leader of the People of God into the hoped, but incomplete, place of rest was the successor to Moses, Joshua. In Hebrew this name is the same as 'Jesus', so that the Old Testament Joshua can be seen as the type for Jesus, and the High Priest Jesus seen as the successful leader into a place a rest which was never reached on the earlier journey (4.8–9, 14).

Indeed, the rest for which the People of God must hope is only a copy of the heavenly reality of God's rest in which it reaches its perfection. This motif of hope for the fulfilment of the promise, and its actualization 'today' recurs constantly: 6.12, 17 on the unalterability of God's promise; 7.6; 8.6 on the promise transferred to Melchizedek; 9.15 on the fulfilment of the promise in Christ; and especially on the fidelity of the ancestors to the hope of the promise 11.9, 13, 17, 33, 39, the message of the triumphant historical recital.

Further Reading

Lindars, Barnabas, *The Theology of the Letter to the Hebrews* (1991)

The Letter of James

1. Authority and Provenance of the Letter

a. Authority

The letter was received into the Canon of scripture only slowly. The name of 'James' was not, of course, sufficient to win it acceptance, for in the second century there were many writings which claimed apostolic authorship which were not accepted into the Canon of scripture. The first mention of this letter is by Origen, c. 200AD; he calls it scripture, and uses it as such. A century later Eusebius places it among 'disputed books', but by the time of Athanasius' authoritative Festal Letter in 367 it is included in the full list of books of scripture.

b. Which James?

There is a certain amount of confusion over the common name Jakob/ James, which was borne both by one of the Twelve and by another figure, 'James, the brother of the Lord'. However, 'James, the brother of John', so one of the paired sons of Zebedee, one of the Twelve, was beheaded by Herod Antipas (Acts 12.2) early in the history of the Jerusalem community, leaving James 'the brother of the Lord' (whatever blood-relationship this implies), in an authoritative position in the community (Acts 15.13–21; Gal. 1.19). It is presumably to this figure that the letter is attributed.

c. Is the letter pseudepigraphical?

Several weak arguments speak against authorship by James, brother of the Lord. The letter shows none of the interest in Jewish legal observance which characterizes the James, head of the Jerusalem community. The depth of culture shown in the letter, both Jewish and Hellenistic, would be unlikely, but not impossible in a Galilean fisherman; in any case he could have used secretaries, or simply taken responsibility for a document elaborated by a more literary figure. Would a brother of the Lord not have written a letter more focused on Jesus? Some reputable scholars (e.g. R. Bauckham) still maintain that it is genuinely a letter from James, the leader of the mother-community, to the communities of the Diaspora. To others this seems simply the result of a dislike of pseudepigraphy. In any case the literary authorship makes little difference to the reading or appreciation of the letter.

2. The Literary Genre of the Letter

The first verse of this writing proclaims that it is a letter from James to the Twelve Tribes of the Diaspora. This is the only indication that it is a letter, for the rest of the standard features of a letter (address, greeting, thanks-giving, see p. 196) are absent. It stands therefore in a different tradition, represented also by the biblical Letter of Jeremiah (Jer. 29) and 2 Maccabees 1–2, which are presented as letters from communities at Jerusalem, offering moral advice to the Jews of the Diaspora, and other contemporary works not included in the Bible, e.g. the 'Epistle of Enoch' in the *Book of Enoch* or the *Apocalypse of Baruch* 78–86.

The nature of the advice offered is typical of the wisdom of the time. There is no straining for originality, and the author is quite content to teach in his own way the wisdom of the ancients. The same may be seen in other first-century writings, both Jewish (such as the *Pirke Avoth*) and Christian (the *Didache*). The ordering of the letter is typical of the Wisdom Literature of the Old Testament, especially Proverbs and Ben Sira (Ecclesiastes), a series of wise sayings, grouped only loosely. In James, however, these sayings are seen to be embedded in a certain amount of commentary. The commentary is conducted in the manner of Hellenistic works, with two dominant features:

a A wealth of lively illustrations drawn from life (e.g. looking in the mirror, 1.23; ushering to a place in the synagogue, 2.2; the helmsman, 3.4); and

b The rhetorical technique of diatribe (dialogue with an imaginary opponent, 2.18–20; 3.10–12, cf. p. 00).

The letter is unmistakably Christian. Not only is the Lord Jesus Christ explicitly mentioned (1.1; 2.1), but the 'coming of the Lord' in 5.7–15 is most simply understood as the second coming of Christ. The lack of clarity of whether 'the Lord' applies to God or the Christ suggests that the author believes in the divinity of Christ. Many of the themes of the letter may be found also in the tradition of the sayings of Jesus, particularly in the Q-material. Almost every one of Matthew's Beatitudes has an equivalent saying in James.

	James	Matthew
Joy in suffering persecution	1.2	5.11
Be perfect and complete	1.4	5.48
Not only hear the word but do it	1.22	7.24
The poor will inherit the kingdom	2.5	5.3
Mercy will earn mercy	2.13	5.7
Can a fig-tree bear olives or a vine figs?	3.12	7.16
Peacemakers	3.18	5.9
Do not swear but for 'yes' say 'yes'	5.12	5.34–7.

The order of these themes, however, is different and (in this letter) random. There are no grounds to suggest direct dependence in either direction; rather, both series depend on the oral tradition of the teaching of Jesus and the ethical instruction of the times.

3. The Listening Disciple

The first chapter is built round two related series of aphorisms. The first is centred on perseverance under testing, the second on listening to the word of Wisdom. Thus the eight central sayings could be classified as:

1.2 When trials come, treat them as a happy privilege.

1.5 If any of you lacks wisdom, he should ask God who gives to all in simplicity.

1.12 Blessed the man who stands firm under testing.

1.14 Everyone is tested by his own desires.

1.17 Every good gift and every perfect donation is from above.

1.19 Be quick to listen but slow to speak.

1.23 To listen to the word and not obey is like looking at your own features in a mirror and then going off and forgetting what you looked like.

1.26 If anyone seems religious without reining in his tongue but deceiving his heart, his religion is empty.

These are commented with a lively wit: the waves of the sea represent wavering (vv. 7–8), the Old Testament image of grass scorched by the sun represents reversal (vv. 10–11), failure to listen is illustrated by neglect of an image seen in a mirror (vv. 23–4). The second theme is summed up in the saying of v. 17a (which is in the form of a classical Greek hexameter), whereas the sayings of v. 12 and 19 are taken from the Old Testament. At the same time, the aim of the whole is said to be 'completeness' or 'perfection', a quality much lauded in ancient literature, a word frequent in James (1.4, 17, 25; 2.8, 22; 3.2) and a quality insistently demanded in the Community Rule of Qumran (1 QS). This is a perfect example of the combination of biblical and classical learning in Hellenistic Judaism.

4. Rich and Poor

The contrast and the reversal between rich and poor is a theme which appears frequently, already in 1.10–11 and again in 4.13–5.6, showing that the community to which the letter is addressed is settling into the Hellenistic world. The same preoccupation occurs in Luke, who is writing for a situation where there are wealthy people, warning of the dangers of wealth (cf. p. 107). The pictures of the rich man being ushered respectfully into the best seats and the poor being casually brushed off with unrealistic good advice (2.15–16) are brilliantly drawn. Society was built on patronage; the rich might expect such fawning respect in return for their protection and advancement. All the more important was the commandment of real, genuine love, which Jesus puts equal to the first commandment: 'love your neighbour as yourself' (2.8). Such an attitude is translated as *eleos*, mercy (2.13), which in turn is the translation of the Hebrew *hesed*, generous, unfailing family love. In Jesus' command this love is extended beyond the family to apply to all people.

The passage broadens out into the application which led Luther to dismiss the letter as 'a right strawy epistle' (2.18–26). Against the background of a mistaken impression that Jews thought salvation could be won by observance of the Law, Luther sees this passage as expressing an opposition between faith and good works. In Galatians and Romans, Paul is concerned to teach that faith rather than observance of the Jewish Law is the way to salvation. In fact there is no allusion in 2.18–26 to that controversy; this passage teaches merely that faith is expressed in action, of which Abraham and Rahab are cited as startling examples. Their actions are applauded as good not in themselves, but rather as expressions of faith. The only possible reminiscence of Paul here is the splendid title of love as the 'law of freedom' (2.12), for those who express their faith in love are the free heirs of the Kingdom (cf. Gal. 5.6). If this passage were intended as a riposte to Paul's teaching, it would surely have been more direct and forceful.

5. The Wicked or Winning Tongue

This chapter consists of a collection of lively aphorisms about speaking and the power of the tongue for good or ill, many of which have parallels in Jewish and other wisdom literature.

v. 1	Teachers, beware!
v. 2	Two stock images: the horse's bit and the rudder have an effect beyond their size.
v. 5b	The tongue is like a bush-fire wreaking uncontrollable disaster. (This series is particularly full of neat alliteration in the Greek).
v. 9	Double-effect: blessing and curse. (three images: clean and dirty springs – figs and vines – sweet and salt water).
v. 13	Cleverness both heals and harms.
v. 17	Seven (the perfect number) qualities of wisdom from above.

6. Misdirected Efforts

There follows a whole series of rebukes before a final return in 5.7–11 to the original counsels of patient endurance until the Lord's coming. In all these, the author builds on the received wisdom of the times, based in the Wisdom tradition of the Old Testament.

4. 2   Grasping and quarrelling for unattainable aims.
4. 3   Prayer for wrong ends.
4. 4   Friendship for the world implies enmity to God.
4. 7   Seven imperatives to submit to God's purposes.
4. 11   Prohibition of slander and judgment of brothers.
4. 13   The futility of preoccupation with worldly advancement.

7. Anointing the Sick

This passage is the only warrant in the New Testament for the prayerful anointing of the sick with oil, though the healing of the sick by the apostles with prayer in the name of Jesus is frequent enough in the stories of the early community in Acts 3.6, 16; 4.10; 9.34. The disciples sent out by Jesus also 'anointed many sick people with oil and cured them' (Mark 6.12). In the ancient world oil was of major importance in soothing wounds, and is still an ingredient in many such modern remedies. The word used in both these passages (*aleipho*) is quite different from the anointing of priests, prophets and the Messiah in the Old Testament, which bestowed the power of the Spirit for Wisdom, government or prophecy. Since the anointing is 'in the name of the Lord' it is clearly conceived as continuing the healing mission of Jesus himself. It is an action of the whole Church, carried out by the elders, representing the people as a whole. This is the only reference in the New Testament to what subsequently became a regular Christian healing practice.

Whether these 'presbyters' were appointed officials or simply senior members of the community is not clear. Jewish communities of the Diaspora were normally governed by a council of elders, presided by an elected chairman (chairwomen are not unknown). Acts 14.23 shows Paul appointing 'presbyters' in the communities of his first mission; they also existed at Philippi (Phil. 1.1). The Pastoral Epistles lay down a process for selection and appointment of 'presbyters' (1 Tim. 5; Tit. 1.5, see p. 310).

In the next generation the bishop was assisted by a council of presbyters. Different communities may have developed in different ways, and the stage of development pre-supposed by James is unclear.

The anointing with prayer brings also forgiveness of sin, and the informality of the process – without any specially appointed minister – is suggested by the instruction which follows, 'confess your sins to one another' (v. 16), a practice which continued in the Church for many centuries, e.g. before battle.

Further Reading

Martin, Ralph, P., *James* [Word Biblical Commentary] (1988)

The First Letter of Peter

This writing presents itself as a circular letter written by Peter the apostle. It has enough of the regular features of a letter (introductory greeting, initial blessing, some final personal items) to make this claim plausible, though authorship by Peter has been strongly disputed. Many consider it pseudepigraphical. It is not easy to discern a pattern in the letter, or to see how it fits together. The Christians to whom it is addressed seem to be new Christians, 'new born, and like babies, hungry for nothing but milk, the spiritual honesty which will help you to grow up to salvation' (2.2). Because of the stress on new birth and becoming a new people, and on Noah's flood as a type of baptism (3.20–1), it has been thought that the letter is based on a baptismal liturgy, or at least on a paschal homily.

The five places named in the first verse as destinations are to be found on a circular route in the north of Asia Minor, the modern Turkey. The Dispersion, or 'Diaspora', named in v. 1 is often used for the Jewish communities scattered around the shores of the Mediterranean. It may suggest that many of the recipients were Christians sprung from Judaism, though the author stresses that formerly they were not a people at all, and that they have been called out of darkness (2.9–10). The thinking is based on forceful use of biblical texts, though quotations are not nearly as frequent as in Paul's letters to communities where Judaism predominated.

Plan of 1 Peter

1.3–2.10	New-born Christians
2.11–4.11	Moral Guidance
4.12–5.14	Conclusion

---

1. New-born Christians

The first section is suffused with the joy of becoming Christians (1.6, 8), a new people of God (2.9). This is expressed by means of exodus-symbolism, dwelling on the themes of the exodus from Egypt. By the very act of becoming Christian the recipients have become aliens from the world around them (1.1). But, after a testing of their faith by all kinds of trials, an inheritance awaits them (1.4, 6–7). They are commanded to be holy as God is holy, which is one of the principles of the Law given to Israel in the desert. Israel is constantly told in the Book of Leviticus to be holy as God is holy (1.16, quoting Leviticus). There are several references to the ransom paid in the blood of the lamb (1.19; 2.5), so understanding the sacrifice of Christ in terms of the blood of the paschal lamb, or in terms of the sacrifice of the covenant on Sinai, or both. The final part of the first section stresses that formerly they were not a people at all, and have become a chosen race, a royal priesthood, a consecrated nation, a people set apart. Three biblical texts are central to this, one about the original covenant (Exod. 19.5–6), and two (Isa. 43.20–21 and Hosea 1.9, quoted in 2.9–10) about the renewed covenant. The new Christians have passed through the exodus experience of Israel, but are still in movement, still 'exiles and pilgrims' (Psa. 39.12, quoted in 2.11) wandering through the desert. The image of Christ, the precious cornerstone (2.6–8) brings to mind the symbolism used by Paul in 1 Corinthians 10.4: Christ as the rock which followed them in the desert, a symbolism used also by Philo.

2. Moral Guidance

This pilgrimage mentality is developed in guidance on how to behave as 'visitors and pilgrims' in this world. Christians are strangers to this world, but a major concern is to fit into society and to earn a good reputation. Some points are raised which do not come in other household codes, such as Ephesians 5.21–6.9; Titus 2.1–3.3. Perhaps women come off slightly better here than in other such household codes. They are told to be submissive to their husbands, and their finery is limited, but husbands are also told to treat their wives with consideration. Contrary to existing custom, which would assume that wives would accommodate to the religion of their husbands, it is even envisaged that the Christian wife may convert her husband (3.1).

There is no criticism of society, even though the recipients of the letters are envisaged as living in a hostile world, to which they are only provisionally attached as strangers – a nation set apart. There are frequent exhortations to bear angry words, accusations and insults patiently. This may be a sign of unpopularity of the Christians. Their refusal to take part in the unbridled festivities of pagan celebrations (4.3–4) must have seemed to Hellenistic society strangely divisive, even prudish. Many routine activities such as games and theatrical presentations, so important in the Roman world, would probably have been barred to Christians by the pagan sacrifices which accompanied them. The new converts would no doubt have forfeited previous friendships and even become isolated. Nevertheless, they are to respect the established order, obey the Emperor and remain good citizens (2.14). Slaves are not only to obey their masters but also to accept unjust punishment after the model of Christ; there is no corresponding counsel to masters to treat their slaves well, as in Colossians 4.1; are the Christians addressed so depressed that they do not even have slaves?

3. Conclusion

The final section, introduced, as was 2.11, by the affectionate address 'beloved', gives renewed assurance of the reward for perseverance under persecution. Two features especially deserve comment. Here occurs one of the three instances in the New Testament of the term 'Christian'. It was first given to the followers of Jesus the Christ at Antioch (Acts 11.26), and the form of the word suggests that it was originally a mocking nickname. This would fit also the other New Testament usage, in the mouth of the sarcastic King Agrippa (Acts 26.28). In addition, the author here describes himself as an 'elder' (5.1): is this a claim to a position or merely to seniority in age? Does the claim to be a witness to the sufferings of Christ constitute a claim to have been a companion of Jesus to the last, or merely to have shared in the sufferings of Christ as the recipients of the letter were doing?

Discussion of the identity of the author is tedious and inconclusive: there are weak indications in either direction. The greeting from 'your sister in Babylon' (5.13) uses a cryptic name for Rome employed by Jews towards the end of the first century. It could fit with the tradition that Peter was martyred in Rome; it could also have created that tradition. It is unlikely that the Galilaean fisherman would learn to write such polished Greek; but Peter could certainly have left the composition to a secretary. Whether the letter is authentically by Peter or is pseudepigraphical, the conditions it presupposes and the inspiring message it gives fit the situation of many places, including northern Asia Minor in the late first century. The validity of the message springs from the inclusion of the letter in the Canon of Scripture rather than from authorship by any particular person.

4. A Christ triumphant through suffering

Against this background the triumph of Christ as a cause for hope and confidence becomes all the more important. Whenever Christ is mentioned it is in connexion with his sacrificial death and its triumphant outcome. Right from the beginning the emphasis is on the Passion, for Christians are 'sprinkled with the blood of Jesus' (1.2). In the initial formal blessing (1.3–5) the keynote struck is hope in the resurrection as assurance of inheritance and of new birth as sons. In a quasi-liturgical summary at the centre of the reflection on the exodus, again Christians were set free and brought to glory by the blood of Christ as the spotless Passover lamb (1.18–21). At the conclusion of this development (2.4–10) the union of Christ and his followers is depicted by the image of the precious cornerstone, supporting, and knit into, the building of living stones – again with the sacrificial image, represented by 'a royal priesthood'. The same sacrificial imagery recurs in the little meditation (2.21–4) on the poem of the Suffering Servant, the most explicit treatment in the New Testament of this Chapter 53 of Isaiah. The most triumphant passage of all comes in the final verses about Christ raised from the dead and going 'to proclaim to the spirits in prison' before entering heaven, where he 'is at God's right hand, now that he has made the angels and Dominations and Powers his subjects' (3.19, 22).

> This verse 3.19 is the basis of the statement, 'he descended into hell', introduced into the Creed of the Council of Sirmium in 359AD. The apocalyptic imagination has developed this into the rich imagery of the Harrowing of Hell, the Risen Christ trampling the devil underfoot and drawing Adam and the saints of old from their tombs. This is a development of the text, which says only 'he proclaimed to the spirits under guard' as a herald. There is no further biblical warrant for this picture.

Again in the conclusion of the letter (4.13; 5.10) the same themes are stressed: 'Be glad, for you will enjoy a much greater gladness when his glory is revealed' (4.13) and 'the God of all grace who called you to eternal glory in Christ after a little suffering will see that all is right again' (5.10). The constant presentation of Christ is, then, of a sacrificial victim, who has triumphed and brought his people with him to triumphant joy. The suffering Christ is the model for Christians in suffering (2.21–5).

Further Reading

1 Peter, David Horrell, T&T Clark 2008 – introduction to the letter
Martin, Ralph P., *The Theology of The Letters of James, Peter and Jude* (1994)

The Second Letter of Peter

1. First Peter – Jude – Second Peter

The Second Letter of Peter has been the subject of considerable controversy:

First, it is quite doubtful whether it is in fact a *second* letter of Peter, a letter of *Peter*, or indeed a *letter* at all. To take these in reverse order:

1. This writing conforms partially to the format of New Testament letters, e.g. the letters of Paul. They normally begin with greetings, a blessing and thanksgiving for the Christian qualities of the recipients, and end with items of personal news and a final blessing. This script does begin with a greeting and a short blessing, but has little or none of the usual personal material at the end. If it is a letter at all, it is a circular letter, addressed to 'all who treasure the same faith as ourselves' (v. 1), so lacking anything personal or accommodated to a particular situation. It has been characterized as a 'homily fitted into a minimal letter format'.

2. It explicitly claims to be 'from Symeon Peter, servant and apostle of Jesus Christ'. The form of the name is slightly strange: this

double name 'Symeon Peter' occurs nowhere else, and the leader of the apostles is called 'Symeon' (with this spelling) only in Acts 15.14. As with several others of the letters of the New Testament, there is a strong question whether the attribution to an apostolic author is in fact pseudepigraphical, an attempt to grant authority to the writing, conventional in Judaism at this time. One oddity would be, if it was truly written by Peter, the impersonal way in which he refers to 'the words of the Lord and Saviour spoken beforehand by the prophets and your apostles' (3.2); why would he not be more personal about his own part as an apostle and his own experience?

3 The letter claims to be 'my second letter to you' (3.1), although the addressees are not mentioned in 2 Peter. There is a strange assemblage of similarities with and differences from 1 Peter. The opening greeting is as though copied from 1 Peter, and the use of the Transfiguration in 2 Peter 1.17–18 naturally refers back to the claim of 1 Peter 5.1 to be a witness to Christ. On the other hand:

- 60 per cent of the words used in 2 Peter do not occur in 1 Peter. Although a cookery recipe would have a different vocabulary from a love letter, for two letters from the same person on roughly the same subject this is a wide divergence.
- The style of 2 Peter is very different from that of 1 Peter. 2 Peter has none of the joy of 1 Peter, and is bombastic and condemnatory (e.g. 2.10–12, 17–18). This is a style called 'Asian rhetoric' full of repetition, exaggeration and elaborate figures (e.g. 1.5–7).
- The chief event awaited by both writings is the coming of Christ. In 1 Peter this is called a 'revelation' (*apocalypsis*, 1.7, 13; 4.13), in 2 Peter it is a 'presence' (*parousia*, 1.16; 3.4, 12). Why the different words for the same key event?

A salient characteristic of 2 Peter is its relationship to the Letter of Jude. They both inveigh vigorously but a little vaguely against false teachers. Both make use of the same examples of well-earned disaster (the angels, Noah's Flood, Sodom and Gomorrah: 2 Peter 2.4–7; Jude 6–7), and the deviation of Balaam (2 Pet. 2.15; Jude 11). A significant difference is that 2 Peter sticks to canonical Old Testament examples (e.g. Prov. 26.11), whereas Jude uses non-canonical works such as *1 Enoch* and *The Assumption of Moses*, which

2 Peter avoids. On the other hand, 2 Peter uses the Greek classical word 'Tartarus' (2.4), while Jude 6 uses 'in chains in the darkness' to express the punishment of the fallen angels. It is possible that both the letters are independently using well-known horror-examples, but it is more likely that 2 Peter is directly reliant on Jude.

None of this, however, explains the literary genre of the writing. The clue to this is given by the insistence in 1.12–15 that the author is about to depart: 'the time for taking off this tent is coming soon, as our Lord Jesus Christ has foretold to me'. It belongs to the well-known genre of a last will and testament, in which an authoritative figure gives instructions to his disciples for their conduct after his death, and warns them of difficulties and trials to come. In the New Testament the familiar examples of this are the Last Supper discourse in John 14–17 (and to a lesser extent Lk. 22.21–38), Paul's final speech to the elders of Ephesus at Miletus (Acts 20.18–35) and 2 Timothy (see p. 305).

It is a fascinating speculation to ask to what extent the atmosphere of impending departure in 2 Peter, combined with the cryptic indication of Rome in the 'Babylon' of 1 Peter 5.13, have contributed to the development of the legends surrounding Peter's martyrdom at Rome.

2. Date

It is much easier to give a comparative date for 2 Peter than an absolute date. The only useful absolute date is that the letter was known to Origen of Alexandria in about 200AD; he discusses whether it is part of scripture. It is also preserved on a fragment of papyrus ($\mathfrak{P}$72) of the third century. One of the difficulties pointed out already by early Christian scholars (e.g. St Jerome) is the difference of style from 1 Peter; they judged it unlikely that the two writings were from the same author, but 2 Peter was eventually accepted into the Canon of Scripture.

- The atmosphere and background, the concern about unauthorized teachers and the lack of any firm machinery for dealing with the matter is similar to that of Jude. From a literary point of view it seems likely that 2 Peter is later than Jude and depends on it.
- The letter assumes that a collection of the letters of Paul has already been made and was considered authoritative (3.15).
- Some sort of teaching or interpretative body is also presupposed by the comment, 'We must be most careful to remember that the

interpretation of scriptural prophecy is never a matter for the individual' (1.20), which implies that there is some authoritative body to do the interpretation. In the early modern period this assertion was heavily criticised as a sign of 'Early Catholicism' creeping in, on the assumption that the plain meaning of the words of scripture was obvious and sufficient. Against this view it must be remarked that Luther himself was content to accept 2 Peter as belonging to the Canon of Scripture.

3. The Eschatological Message

This letter is often regarded as having little value. Its principal contribution to the Christian life is, however, its eschatological message. From this the bulk of Chapter 2, on false teachers (on which the author gets rather carried away by his own rhetoric), is a distraction between Chapters 1 and 3. The earliest Church seems to have had difficulty over the eschaton. Paul is waiting for the Lord Jesus to come imminently in a triumphal procession and a blare of angelic trumpets. This is so imminent that it is doubtful whether it is reasonable to carry on with the normal processes of life: 'those who have to deal with the world should not become engrossed in it. I say this because the world as we know it is passing away' (1 Cor. 7.31). In Jesus' own proclamation of the Kingship of God there is a tension: has the Kingship already arrived? In what sense is the moment of the Crucifixion and Resurrection the long-awaited Day of the Lord? The message of the different gospels is not quite the same on this matter. In Mark the Kingship of God has come near (cf. p. 82). In Matthew it is more distant, so that there is time for good works before the Final Judgment (Mt. 25.31–46). The Book of Revelation seemed to teach that a thousand-year earthly reign of Christ would precede the end of all things (Rev. 20). So many thinkers understood this literally that one could almost say that, in the second century, millenia-rism was the majority opinion (see p. 376).

It is clear from 2 Peter that the failure of the eschaton to arrive was a worry and a puzzle. People were getting tired of waiting; they needed to be reminded that divine time is not like human time: 'You must never forget, my friends, that with the Lord "a day" can mean a thousand years, and a thousand years is like a day' (3.8). Much of Chapter 1 (1.16–21) is taken up with the argument that the prophecies and the apostolic witness are reliable. The vehemence of the denunciations of Chapter 2 can distract from the message that God again and again gives time for repentance, that Noah and Lot were able to be saved from the general condemnation. In the same way, Christians can 'escape corruption in a world that is sunk in vice' (1.4; 2.20). Then come the heavy warnings: things do not just go on as they have since the Fathers died (3.4); God does punish (3.5–7). In the end, 'the Day of the Lord will come like a thief, and then with a roar the sky will vanish, the elements will catch fire and fall apart, the earth and all it contains will be burnt up' (3.10). Despite delays, the eschaton is still a force to be reckoned with. The habitual violence and colourful language of biblical apocalyptic imagery is such a well-defined genre that the discerning reader needs to 'cash' these symbols, but not to wipe them away.

The First Letter of John

1. A Letter?

The first Letter of John is a puzzling document. It is rich in teaching, especially about love and loyalty, but its form, author, recipients, relationship to the gospel of John and exact purpose are all difficult to elucidate. There were firm conventions about letter-writing in the ancient world, to which 1 John does not adhere. A letter began, as do all Paul's letters, with a greeting to the named recipient, normally good wishes or a blessing, and the name of the sender. Normally also, except in the most formal of letters, there would be some personal chit-chat at the end. 1 John has none of these. Recipients are addressed as 'my dear friends', often passionately (2.12–14), but there is constant denunciation of others as liars and children of the devil (2.4; 3.10); this makes it too personal to be a mere proclamation or exhortation. It is more akin to an internal memorandum addressed to one group within the community, warning them against another group who have seceded. There is heavy opposition to this group, who are characterized (with a vehemence which is not extreme for the period) as liars (2.4, 22; 4.20, cf. 2.9. 11, 15, 18–19, 26).

An attractive suggestion is that 2 John is intended as a covering note to 1 John, sent to a number of Churches, since 1 John lacks the usual features of letters. The only trouble about this is that 2 John contains only the slightest possible reference to another letter, 'And now I am asking you, not as though I were writing you a new commandment, that we should love one another' (2 Jn 5).

2. From John?

Our investigations into the gospel of John are based on the hypothesis that there were at least three progressive editions of that gospel, of increasing clarity and reflection. Although these may each have been penned by different authors, there is a coherence of approach and style, vocabulary and argumentation throughout the gospel, which argues for a single school of authorship. Rather than identify a single person as *author* it is more profitable to speak of an *authority* which stands behind the writing. An impressive list can be assembled of similarities between the two writings, chief among which are antithesis (truth/falsehood, light/darkness, child of God/child of the devil) and generalisation ('anyone who...', 'no one who...'). There are, however, also significant differences, which might suggest that the two writings come from different authors, though perhaps within the same school, for example, in the gospel, Jesus is the light of the world (Jn 8.12), whereas in 1 John 1.5 God is the light. 'The beginning' in John 1.1 refers to the beginning of time, but in 1 John 1.1 to the beginning of Jesus' mission. The Greek language and grammar of the letter are possibly the worst in the New Testament, and certainly less good than those of the gospel of John .

Von Wahlde, who has elaborated the three editions of the gospel most carefully (see p. 120), places 1 John before the third and final edition of the gospel. He maintains that it represents a crisis in the community, to which the high Christology of the third edition responds by stressing the dignity and pre-existence of the Word. At the turn of the first/second century, however, where it is appropriate to locate 1–3 John, problems are expressed more in terms of splits and divisions than in terms of 'heresies'. True, there was already the great controversy about the propriety of eating food offered to idols (1 Cor. 8–10; Rev. 2.14), and the shadowy group called 'Nicolaitans' (Rev. 2.15) about whom we know nothing. But the great problem was lack of unity rather than choice of doctrines. It is significant that Clement of Rome (?90AD) mentions 'schism' five times, 'squabble' nine times, but 'heresy' never. Similarly Ignatius of Antioch, 15 years later, mentions 'heresy' twice, but 'division' six times, and constantly stresses the need for unity with the bishop. The concept of 'orthodoxy' had not yet arisen. The problem in 2–3 John certainly seems to be division of leadership, for 'the Deceivers' are mentioned (2 Jn 7) and the hostile Diotrephes (3 Jn 9), who is circulating personal slander, without any attention to the errors of their teaching. The stress on the need to love one another within the community is already present in the Last Supper Discourse of the gospel: 'This is my commandment, love one another as I have loved you' (Jn 15.12), and especially in the great prayer for unity (Jn 17.21). This may well be a reaction to the sort of division presupposed by 1 John, against which the author writes so fervently in the second half of the letter.

In addition, it is always difficult to reconstruct a coherent and positive account of a teaching from its refutation. In a controversial tract the positive points tend to be neglected and the points criticised tend to be presented without a context which might make them more palatable. This is, however, the only course open to us if we wish to reconstruct the points of view which the author of 1 John criticises. All attempts to link those he criticises to later known deviations and 'heresies' have failed (for most of these deviations remain very shadowy and obscure). Von Wahlde reckons that the opponents of 1 John held a radical pneumatology, that 'the true purpose of Jesus' ministry was the announcement of and preparation for the eschatological outpouring of the Spirit' (*The Johannine Commandments*, p. 115). The reason why 1 John so stresses the earthly work of Jesus would be that his opponents held Jesus' human role to be irrelevant. Presumably they thought that the only point of Jesus' earthly life was his death (at which point he handed over the Spirit) and his gift of the Spirit after the Resurrection. This goes beyond the evidence, though it is significant that the first positive teaching of 1 John stresses the experience of Jesus as a real man, heard, seen, watched and touched (whereas the prologue to the gospel starts with his heavenly pre-existence). It may be significant that 2 John 7 mentions that many deceivers refuse to admit that Jesus Christ has come in the flesh, especially if 2 John was written to the same community as 1 John; this is, however, quite uncertain, and the community addressed by John 1 could well not have had this deviation. The stress on the physical side of Jesus is reiterated in writing on the Passion, in 1.7, 'the blood of Jesus purifies us from all sin' and 2.2, 'his is the sacrifice that takes our sins away'. This emphasis might suggest that the physical side of the Passion had not been given due place, though the only clear designation of the teaching of the opponents concerns Jesus as the Christ or Messiah: 'One who denies that Jesus is the Christ is the liar, the Antichrist, and denies the Father as well as the Son' (2.22), and the commandment that we should 'believe in the name [that is, the power] of his Son Jesus Christ' (3.23).

The way in which Jesus' act of redemption functions here receives a description which comes nowhere else in the New Testament (though see p. 212), and which has led to a whole theological emphasis. Jesus is twice described as the *hilasmos* (reconciliation? propitiation?) for our sins (2.2; 4.10). What does this mean? It has often been taken to mean that Jesus was a substitutionary victim who by his bitter death paid the price due for my sins.

This depends on the pagan idea of sacrifice to appease an angry god, which is quite foreign to the Bible. In the Bible it is God who reconciles us, not we who reconcile God. God is always the subject of the verb *hilaskesthai*, 'to reconcile', and God bring us back to himself. The verb translates the Hebrew word which basically means 'to cover over'. (In the Bible animal sacrifice is a recognition that God is the Lord and Master of all life. The blood of the sacrifice belongs to God because it is the sign of life; it is sometimes wiped or sprinkled on the offerer as a sign of new life.)

The death of Jesus is the *hilasmos* because his perfect obedience to the Father unites humanity to God again after the estrangement caused by Adam's disobedience, as Paul explains in Romans 5.12–21.

There is also an obscure passage about the three witnesses to Jesus, 'who came by water and blood, not with water only but with water and blood, with the Spirit as another witness' (5.6). If this is understood in any connection with the gospel of John, it must refer to the crucifixion, where Jesus breathes out his Spirit, and water and blood flow from his wounded side (Jn 19.30–4), which again puts the emphasis on the physical Jesus. Since all the accent in the Passion narrative of the gospel of John is on the triumph of Jesus, it could be that the author of 1 John sees that the physical side of the Passion needs to be accentuated.

Another difference between the two writings is that in 1 John 2.1 Jesus *is* himself the Paraclete, 'our advocate with the Father', whereas in the gospel Jesus *sends* the Paraclete, 'another Paraclete' to continue and complete his work on earth. This may be connected with a significant difference in the eschatology. In the gospel, the believer already has eternal life and has passed from death to life (Jn 5.24), whereas 1 John uses language of future apocalyptic events: the AntiChrist is yet to come (2.18), and God's children are still to be transformed when the full revelation happens at some future time (3.2).

3. The Message of the Letter

The message of the letter falls into two halves, which cannot be clearly separated, the first concerning faith and the second love. After a meditation on each of these and their consequences, the two are joined together in a reflection on the eternal life which this brings (4.7–5.13).

a. Faith (1.5–2.29)

Faith, trust, belief have been the watchword of Israel's stance since the beginning. Starting with Abraham this has coloured everything. The call of Abraham in Genesis 12 is a call to trust in this unknown protector and champion. It is hideously tested in the story of the Sacrifice of Isaac, where Abraham's love for his only son is so dramatically illustrated, only to be overcome (and rewarded) by his trust in the LORD. We are reminded of the centrality of trust occasionally throughout the Bible, as in Isaiah's challenge to Ahaz to trust in the LORD in the face of the threatened invasion by the alliance of northern kings (Isa. 7.1–9), or in Habakkuk's vision telling him to record the undying trustworthiness of the LORD (Habakkuk 2.4 – the passage quoted by Paul in Romans 1.17 as the clue to the whole of that great letter).

In giving faith such prominence the author is continuing the message of the gospel, for faith in Christ is there repeatedly central. In the conclusion the author tells us that the message is recorded, 'so that you may believe that Jesus is the Christ, the Son of God, and that believing you may have life through his name' (Jn 20.31). In the central verse of the Prologue 'to those who believe in his name he gave power to become children of God'. The same is seen in so many stories of the gospel, at Cana (2.11), in the story of the woman of Samaria (4.41–42), the reaction to the Bread of Life discourse, 'You have the message of eternal life and we believe' (6.68–9), the climax of the Man Born Blind (9.17).

In 1 John belief is presented under the image of light. The author proclaims that the Word who is life 'is our subject', and the message we are announcing is that 'God is light; there is no darkness in him at all' (1.1, 5). It is an exhortation to live in the light. For this it is necessary to be aware that the blood of Jesus has purified us from all sin, and that we have Jesus as our advocate or Paraclete with the Father. It is necessary also to live the commandment of love, and not to love this passing world which is coming to an end.

b. Love (3.1–4.6)

Throughout the Bible love is a central concept. This is a real affectionate love, both whole-hearted and emotional. God's love for Israel is presented in different ways according to the many modalities of family love, as spouse loves spouse or as parent loves child (Hosea 2.21; 11.1–4), with an everlasting and forgiving love (Isa. 54.8). It is also the model for a demanding and generous human love, such as the indissoluble family love which supports members of the family through thick and thin, no matter what the cost. Perhaps its most delicate analysis is St Paul's in 1 Corinthians 13. In the Old Testament the basic structure of life is to love the LORD God with all your heart, all your soul and all your strength, to have the love of God before your eyes and on your hands at every moment. The faithful member of the people of Israel declares this daily (Deut. 6.5). Nor is it a new commandment to love your neighbour as yourself (Lev. 19.18). What is new is that Jesus equates these two commandments, putting them on the same level (Mk 12.29–31). Who is my neighbour? Jesus extends the concept of the neighbour beyond Israel to include all people. This is the new commandment of love (1 Jn 2.7–8), which is the central requirement of the letter (3.10–24; 4.7–5.4). The demand is put with daunting force: 'anyone who fails to love can never have known God' (4.8). Lack of love means lack of understanding of the nature of God; without love, the search for God is vain. Knowing God, in both gospel and epistle, is a matter not of intellectual knowledge but of direct experience, as in knowing a person rather than a fact. This lies at the heart both of Jesus' teaching in the Last Supper discourse (Jn 13–17) and in this Letter.

Further Reading

Brown, Raymond E., *The Community of the Beloved Disciple* (London: Geoffrey Chapman 1979): detective work on the community

—*The Gospel and Epistles of John* (Collegeville: Liturgical Press, 1988): a concise commentary

Van der Watt, J., *Introduction to the Johannine Gospel and Letters* (London: T&T Clark, 2007): a model scholarly short textbook

32

The Second and Third Letters of John

These are short notes, in form typical of the many short papyrus letters of the period discovered in the lands around the Mediterranean. Standard features are the named greetings, followed by the opening words of praise and encouragement. The second and third were not necessarily written in that order, but are so called simply because they are arranged according to length; the third is 26 words shorter than the second. It is possible that either of them may have formed a covering letter to First John, which lacks the standard features of a letter – more likely 2 John, for 3 John is addressed throughout to a single person, Gaius (the 'you' is here consistently in the singular), which gives it a more private and personal tone.

These two letters attest both the harmonious love and the serious divisions within the early communities. Particularly, the denial of hospitality (2 Jn 10; 3 Jn 10) was a drastic statement of hostility in the mobile world of those days, all the more striking in that 3 John is a letter of reference for brothers on their travels (v. 5).

We do not know who any of the persons mentioned are. The mention of the Antichrist (2 Jn 7) provides a link to 1 John 2.18, and the emphasis on love and truth is an inspiration in all the Johannine writings. 'The Elder' occurs nowhere else in the New Testament, though the Jewish communities around the Mediterranean were normally governed by a council of elders, a practice taken over by Paul for his communities (Acts 14.23). Scholars differ about whether early stories in the Christian tradition about John the Elder at Ephesus are derived from, or independent of, these letters. The 'Chosen Lady' (2 Jn 1, 13) is a designation of the community itself.

33

The Letter of Jude

The Letter of Jude witnesses to the age after that of the Apostles. There is no sign of any hierarchical structure of the Church, such as may be seen in the sub-apostolic letters of Clement to the Corinthians and Ignatius of Antioch (bishop, presbyters and deacons), or even of the structure of presbyters and deacons, such as may be seen in the Pauline Pastoral Letters (see p. 310). On the other hand there are itinerant teachers, possibly prophets, who both instruct and confuse the members of the community, and must be guarded against as well as appreciated. A further sign of date is the use made of sacred Jewish writings, current in the first century, but not finally incorporated into the Canon of Scripture in either Judaism or Christianity, which began to take shape in the early second century. The situation of the letter therefore makes abundant sense in the Christian communities towards the end of the first century. It presents a fascinating glimpse of the workings and difficulties of the sub-apostolic community.

1. Authorship

In verse 1, the letter claims the authorship of 'Jude (or Judas), brother of the Lord'. Such a person is mentioned as a close member of Jesus' family in Mark 6.3. He is presumably different from Jude, a member of the Twelve (Lk. 6.16), or he would have claimed this authoritative title. 'Judas' is, however, an obviously common name, and there may have been several in Jesus' company who bore that name. Scholars remain divided whether this attribution is authentic or pseudepigraphical, but the answer makes little difference to the authority and interest of the letter, which comes primarily from the fact that it is included in the final Christian Canon of Scripture.

2. Style

The Greek style of the letter makes it a pleasure to read, far removed from the rough Greek of the gospels, and an indication of the extent to which a community so immersed in Judaism and its writings could also feel at home in the Hellenistic sphere. The general outline accords with the rhetorical conventions of the time (see p. 197), proceeding by the three steps *narratio* (recounting the situation which gives rise to the writing, v. 4), *probatio* (proof or substantiation of the case, vv. 5–16) and *peroratio* (conclusion, vv. 17–23); this is common and obvious enough. Pleasing also are the illustrations, not only the succinct historical allusions but the lively images of instability, storm-tossed clouds, uprooted barren trees, white-capped waves and shooting stars (vv. 12–13). On the verbal level, the balanced row of participles in the warnings of vv. 18–23 gives a lilting flow to the presentation. The author sharpens his argument by the repeated apodeictic accusation, as though pointing the finger, 'these are the ones who' or 'these people' (vv. 8, 10, 12, 16, 19), and the neat Greek opposition of *men* and *de* (clumsily rendered 'on the one hand … on the other') in vv. 8, 10, 22. This is a writer who knows how to use language.

3. Structure of the Letter

1–2   Greeting and blessing
3–19   False teachers in the community
        Three examples of disaster from taking a false path:

4. Comments

Three features deserve note and comment.

a. No Guidance

Any current authoritative guidance is lacking, suggesting that there was no authoritative guiding body in the community. The writer is concerned to rebut false teachers, who have infiltrated the community and whom he likens to wind-swept clouds, uprooted trees, shifting waves and shooting stars, all images of instability. No significant details are given of their teaching, for the accusations made are merely generalities; the letter does not really explain what is wrong with their teaching. One factor about these false teachers agrees with the warnings of the *Didache* 11–13 against wandering teachers who come merely for food (cf. v. 12):

'Every apostle who comes to you should be received as the Lord, but shall not stay more than one day, or if necessary a second. If he stays three days he is a false prophet. When he leaves he should receive nothing except food; if he asks for money he is a false prophet.'

The author appeals to his readers to adhere to the apostolic teaching (v. 22), citing a saying which occurs nowhere else in the New Testament, but there is no mention of any active personal guide or authority in the community.

Apart from the final doxology, the most prominent doctrinal teaching stressed is the lively expectation of the coming of Christ for judgment (vv. 18, 21). This letter does not make it clear whether the false teachers had denied a future second coming in judgment. It may be that this coming is mentioned only as a threat against any false teaching and misbehaviour. However, it may be legitimate to interpret the emphasis on the coming in judgment by reference to the closely related 2 Peter, which combats (2 Pet. 3.1–10) impatience at the delay of this event.

b. Old Testament Reference

Plenty of reference is made to the Old Testament, but hardly any detailed reference to the New Testament. On the other hand, there are important uses of Jewish sacred writings which were not finally accepted into the Canon of Scripture. Most likely the first three examples of disaster are given in chronological order. In this case the fall of the angels who left their appointed spheres and are now 'kept down in the dark, in spiritual chains, to be judged on the great day' (v. 6) refers to the popular interpretation of Genesis 6.2, that the fall of the angels consisted in the marriages between the 'sons of God' and 'the daughters of men', the last straw of wickedness which preceded Noah's flood. Similarly, the struggle between the archangel Michael and the Devil over the body of Moses (v. 9) is nowhere mentioned in the Old Testament, but occurs in the apocryphal *Assumption of Moses*. Most of all, in the course of the letter there are several reminiscences of *1 Enoch*, perhaps the most widespread of all non-biblical Jewish writings of that era. This is a collection of writings pseudepigraphically attributed to the mysterious patriarch Enoch, who 'walked with God and God took him' (Gen. 5.24); in Judaism he was considered the prime revealer of divine secrets. This work is actually quoted as an authority in v. 14. All this shows that such writings were an important part of the formation, imagining and thinking of some of the early Christian communities at this era. It is striking that narrative material about the ministry and sayings of Jesus seems to have contributed little to the formation of the parts of the New Testament other than the gospels.

c. The Doxology (24–5)

The final blessing or doxology is one of the noblest in the New Testament, centred on the glory of God. The word '*doxa*/glory' in secular Greek means 'reputation, good name, fame', but in biblical Greek it has a far more profound sense. The glory of God is an awesome, attractive and daunting concept. No human being can see God and live. When Moses begs to see God, he is allowed to glimpse God's glory, but only from behind and sheltered (Exod. 33.18–19). In the Temple the prophet Isaiah (Isa. 6.1–4) sees God's glory and is overcome by the sense of his own uncleanness and inadequacy. The prophet Ezekiel similarly glimpses God's glory in the vision of the chariot-throne (Ezek. 1.26–8). The Prologue of the gospel of John sums up the experience of the disciples by saying, 'We saw his glory' (Jn 1.14), a glory which Jesus shares with the Father (Jn 17.1–5). In this doxology the prayer is to be placed in joy in the presence of this glory. The divine glory is joined to divine greatness, power and limitless authority, and yet God is 'our Saviour'. All this is 'through Jesus Christ our Lord'. The title 'Lord' translates the ineffable and unpronounced Name of God, which in this letter is used interchangeably of God (vv. 5, 9) and Christ, the Lord who will come again in judgment (vv. 4, 14), a judgment in mercy which will give eternal life (v. 21). As in the final vision of the Book of Revelation, the divine properties are already shared by Christ. There is a single throne, and a single worship is offered to God and to our Lord Jesus Christ (cf. Rev. 22.3–5).

At the same time, there are other properties attributed to God: he is our Saviour through Jesus Christ. In the New Testament God is called 'Saviour' outside the Pastoral Letters only here and in Mary's canticle of the Magnificat (Lk. 1.47). It probably has connotations of opposition to the saviour-gods of the Hellenistic world, for the Emperor was frequently hailed as a divine saviour, and there was a plethora of saviour-cults into which many were initiated. This therefore constitutes an energetic affirmation that the true Saviour is God alone, and that this salvation is imparted uniquely through Jesus Christ. It will be remembered that in the preface to the letter (v. 3), before the crisis of the itinerant preachers occurred, the author had been intending to write about 'the salvation that we all share'; he does so in the final blessing. Linked to the salvation through Jesus Christ is the love or loving mercy of Jesus Christ unto eternal life which the recipients of the letter are told to await (v. 21); this is that steadfast and unbreakable love within the family, the *hesed* of the Hebrew tradition and in Greek *eleos*. Matthew, the most Jewish of the gospels, three times pronounces this the key to the observance of the Law: 'What I want is loving mercy (*eleos*) not sacrifice (9.13; 12.7; 23.23).

Questions on Part Four

1 Do the Catholic Epistles add anything important to the Christian revelation?
2 Does pseudonymity destroy the value of these letters? Why/why not?
3 Is love the only thing that matters?
4 What is the teaching of the New Testament about priesthood?
5 As the Church is guided by the Spirit, is there really any need for human authority?
6 Has the Hellenistic influence enriched or distorted Christianity?

Part V

The Book of Revelation

34

The Book of Revelation

---

1. Authorship and Background

a. Title and Author

The Greek title of this last book of the New Testament is simply *Apokalypsis*, which means 'revelation'. In modern languages the term 'apocalypse' was coined in 1822 by the German scholar K. I. Nitsche. The book is often called also 'Revelations' or 'the Apocalypse of John'. The book claims to be by John (1.1; 22.8), but, as we shall see, it is a feature of this kind of literature that it is attributed conventionally to a great religious figure of the past. In the mid-second century Justin Martyr thought the author was the Apostle John. However, already in the third century Dionysius, bishop of Alexandria, used linguistic analysis to prove that it was not written by the author of the gospel or epistles which bear that name. The language used is barbarous and full of solecisms which show that the author thinks in Hebrew or Aramaic, while writing in Greek. There is also complete lack of many key concepts of those writings (life, light/darkness, love, Spirit, truth). The use of the Bible is entirely different, for there is no single literal quotation of the Bible, but constant use of biblical allusion and imagery which draws its sense from the Bible. The angle of the Christology is very different, for in the gospel the emphasis is on the Son doing on earth the works of the Father, whereas in Revelation the victorious Lamb shares the worship given to Almighty God. Above all, the eschatology is entirely different: the gospel concentrates on the presence of the Spirit in the Church now, whereas Revelation concentrates on looking forward to a future world beyond history.

Doubts about the authorship of the book contributed to the delay of its acceptance into the Canon of scripture, especially in the Eastern Church. One straightforward argument against its authorship by the Apostle John is that the vision of the twelve gates of the New Jerusalem has gates inscribed with the names of the twelve apostles (Rev. 21.14). It is wise to accept that we do not know who wrote the work.

b. The Genre of Apocalyptic

This biblical Book of Revelation stands not alone but in a specific type of literature which proliferated in the Jewish and Christian spheres both within and outside the Bible during the last centuries before Christ, and continued until about 200AD. In the Bible the clearest parallels are the Book of Daniel, and some chapters of Isaiah (24–7) and Zachariah (9–12). However the characteristic use of vivid imagery and some of the actual images can already be seen in Ezekiel at the time of the Babylonian Exile (e.g. Ezek. 1; 37.1–14; 47.1–12), and the vision of the heavenly throne-room has its roots in earlier prophecy (1 Kgs. 22.19–23; Isa. 6). Literature of this type became widespread around the turn of the eras, especially in such extra-biblical books as the *First Book of Enoch* and the scrolls of Qumran (e.g. 4QAmram). There are traces of it also in the New Testament, for instance Paul's description of his celestial experience in 2 Corinthians 12.1–3, and in some gospel passages, notably the Baptism, the Testing in the Desert, the Transfiguration and the Synoptic Apocalypse.

Apocalyptic writing is characteristic of oppressed societies which find themselves in humanly hopeless situations, promising them deliverance and salvation by some sort of supernatural transformation. In the biblical sphere it occurs principally at three moments, the Babylonian Exile (586–548BC), the persecution by the Syrian King Antiochus Epiphanes (167–160BC) and the time leading up to the two Jewish revolts of 66 and 132AD. Such writings continue to appear till the end of the second century, both in what was later recognized as orthodox Christianity (*The Shepherd of Hermas, the Apocalypse of Peter*) and in circles later condemned as Gnostic (*The Apocryphon of John, the Apocalypse of Paul*). Characteristics are:

1 Pseudonymity, attribution to a great figure of the past who is in fact not the author.
2 Reports of mysterious visions seen, but explained by otherworldly figures.
3 Bizarre imagery, normally dependent on biblical imagery.
4 Otherworldly journeys, easy transition between earth and heaven.

Thus the early example of the Apocalypse of Isaiah (Isa. 24–27) uses cosmic imagery of the earth lurching and jolting, the moon confused and the sun ashamed, promising that the oppressor will be destroyed and the oppressed lifted up. In 27.2–11 it reverses the Song of the Vineyard in Isaiah 5.1–7. Ezekiel 8 uses the technique of the heavenly vision and the otherworldly interpreter. Zachariah 14.6–14 re-uses much imagery from earlier prophets, much of which will be used again in Revelation 21.

Full apocalyptic begins to be seen in the Book of Daniel 7–12. The pseudonymous name 'Daniel' is derived from that of the ancient sage Danel (Ezek. 14.14). The burden of the Book is to promise deliverance from the persecution of Antiochus Epiphanes, the Syrian king attempting to stamp out Judaism in 168–164 BC. The paradigm example is the Vision of the Four Beasts and the Son of Man (Daniel 7), a dream-vision whose bizarre imagery is explained by a supernatural interpreter as a promise of the eventual triumph of Judaism.

A further non-biblical example is the *First Book of Enoch*, a composite work spread over two centuries, purporting to stem from the mysterious figure of Enoch who 'walked with God and God took him' (Genesis 5.24). The Son of Man, moving between heaven and earth, brings coded messages of deliverance in the future, expressed with the aid of biblical imagery. The Letter of Jude 14–15 quotes this book as prophecy, but Jerome and Augustine are definite that it is not part of scripture. The book disappears from view in about 800AD, until a copy in Coptic was re-discovered in Abyssinia nearly a thousand years later. Since then, other Greek copies have confirmed the text.

c. The Purpose of the Book

After the introduction, the first section of the Book comprises letters to the seven Churches of Asia Minor. This is itself prefaced by an epistolary greeting in the style of contemporary letters (1.1–8), reassuring the readers of the letters that they are a line of kings and that Christ is the triumphant Lord of the universe. This is confirmed by the majestic vision of Christ which launches the book as well as the letters to the Churches (1.9–20).

The book is to be an account of the lethal struggle between good and evil, good represented by God, Christ and his forces, angelic and human (the Church or the Elect enumerated in various ways), and the forces of evil, represented by such images as the Beast, the Dragon and Babylon, the Great Prostitute. Under these figures is represented the Roman Empire, and in particular its claim on the worship due to the divine Emperor from all its inhabitants. Before, however, the struggle is depicted in its apocalyptic symbolism, the prophecy is to be firmly rooted in historical circumstances by the seven letters to the seven Churches of Asia to whom primarily the book is addressed. These letters are therefore no mere accidental preface to the major part of the book, but are integral to its purpose, for the seven Churches of Asia are the scene envisaged by the author in which the drama is played out. This local attachment constitutes the particular scene in which the struggle between Christian good and imperial evil is at work. The regular mention in these letters of suffering 'for the sake of my name', and of endurance or lack of it (2.3, 10, 13, 19; 3.5, 10, 21), are integral to the message of the book as a whole, and form a preparation for the apocalyptic struggle which is to follow.

The book is therefore not only an apocalypse, but also a prophecy. This does not mean that the book is primarily about what is going to happen in the future, as would be suggested by some modern uses of the term. This is a frequent misconception of the nature of prophecy. On the contrary, the primary function of biblical prophecy is to explain the divine view of the present, to see the present through the eyes of God, rather than to predict the future. The 'pro' of 'prophet' means that the prophet 'speaks on behalf of' God rather than necessarily 'beforehand'. Accordingly, the purpose of Revelation is not so much to reveal what will happen at the end-time as to reveal to the hearers/readers the true nature of the forces at work in the struggle in which they are currently engaged, to help them to understand the crisis and the suffering which is dominating their lives. Revelation is in fact six times called a prophecy (e.g. 1.3; 19.10; 22.7, 10, 18, 19), and the warnings and admonitions of the Seven Letters are typical of prophecy. It is therefore, of course, a fundamental error to interpret the Book – as some literal fundamentalists do – as a sort of encrypted prediction of actual events and personalities which are to appear and herald the end of the world.

This means that it is a fundamental mistake to identify – as has frequently been done, and is still done in some fundamentalist sects – the forces of evil portrayed in Revelation as particular historical personages or movements, as though the book was a coded prediction of events still to come. The narrow purpose is to interpret to its contemporaries the contemporary struggle between good, exemplified in Christian values, and evil, exemplified in the values of the Roman Empire, and to proclaim the outcome of that struggle. The broader purpose is to interpret to all believers all struggles between Christian values and evil however manifested, and to proclaim the final outcome of those struggles.

The book must therefore be understood against the background of the Roman imperial power. In the countries bordering the eastern Mediterranean there was a long tradition of regarding monarchs as in some way divine. From the time of Alexander the Great they are represented on coins as wearing the horns which symbolise divinity. When the Romans increasingly took over the rule of these lands, beginning with the Province of Asia in 133BC, they picked up on this imagery. For the most part they left the existing constitutions in place, allowing the local rulers to exercise rule but superimposing a religious cult. This increased in importance after the Battle of Actium in 31BC. Among a plethora of differing nations, city-states and provinces, loyalty to the emperor was secured and expressed in the religious cult of Rome and Augustus, and the status of cities of the East could be judged by whether they were allowed to have an altar, a Temple or an even more splendid Games in honour of Rome and Augustus. It was this cult that bound them together with one another and with Rome. In the early second century, Pliny the Younger, governor of Bithynia, made his criterion for whether suspects were Christians or not whether they would anathematize Jesus and proclaim, in front of an image of the Emperor, *Kyrios Kaisar*, 'Caesar is Lord', thus giving to the Emperor the title used in the Old Testament of God (Pliny, *Letters* 10.96). The same testing may be reflected in 1 Corinthians 12.2–3: 'No one can be speaking under the influence of the Holy Spirit and say, "Jesus is accursed", and on the other hand, no one can say, "Jesus is Lord" unless he is under the influence of the Holy Spirit.'

While Christianity remained under the aegis of Judaism it was protected as a *religio licita*, allowing a certain tolerance, but when it became separate from Judaism the pressure to conform would have been all the greater.

Already, when Nero in 64AD declared that the Great Fire of Rome had been caused by Christians, they were considered, according to Tacitus, 'a destructive superstition', 'hated for their crimes' (*Annals* 15.44). No doubt it will be this unpopularity which induced Nero to fasten the blame upon them. Persecution will have waxed and waned; it was acute during the reigns of Nero (54–68AD) and Domitian (81–96AD).

The Date of the Book of Revelation

The earliest external witness, Irenaeus, at the end of the second century, dates the book from the end of the reign of Domitian, which may be the best solution. In the past, various minor duplications and inconsistencies have convinced many scholars that there must have been two separate editions, conveniently dated to the reigns of Nero and Domitian respectively. Recently this idea has become less popular. Was this sort of inconsistency important enough to indicate two editions? Look at the differences between the two Creation narratives stuck side-by-side! Or the two accounts of the Ascension!

As internal evidence, Revelation 17.10–11 has seemed to provide an answer, 'The seven heads are also seven emperors. Five of them have already gone, one is here now, and one is yet to come. The beast, who once was and now is not, is at the same time the eighth and one of the seven'. If Julius Caesar is to be considered the first emperor, this would put Nero on the throne; if Augustus is considered the first, the calculation falls to the ground. The final sentence might suggest Nero, who was widely expected to return to life and come back in power after his death. Such could also be the meaning of the fatal wound that seemed to have been healed in one of the seven heads of the Beast emerging from the sea (13.3). Another engaging but tricky argument is that the Hebrew letters of 'Nero Caesar', when used as numbers, add up to 666, the number of the Beast (13.8). This could attach the historical reference to that emperor. However, the number could also mean radical insufficiency, triply short of 777, the perfect number!

All this assumes that the passage is a carefully encrypted historical riddle. It is just as likely that the author is playing with numbers based on 7, the number of completion. In Revelation there are seven 7s (letters, seals, trumpets, signs, cups of wrath, heavenly voices, visions of the end). The author may be indicating near-completion and using obscurity to slightly hedge his bets.

2. Structure and Plan

No overall plan of Revelation has won general acceptance. It may be convenient to outline three possibilities:

1 Four major sections, each marked by beginning 'in spirit' (not 'in *the* Spirit', which occurs ten times, more randomly). Certainly each of these begins a major section of the Book.

1.10 'It was the Lord's day and I was in spirit': the Letters to the Churches.
4.2 'I was in spirit and behold a throne': the inaugural vision of heaven, which will lead onto the combat between good and evil forces portrayed in sequences of judgment (6.1–16.21).
17.3 'He took me in spirit' to see the punishment of Babylon, the evil city.
21.10 'In spirit he took me' to see the reward of the New Jerusalem, the holy city.

2 The revelatory experience in two halves (Raymond Brown), preceded by the Seven Letters. Certainly there is a significant change of scene between these two.

4.1–11.19 God's judgment of the world.
12.1–22.5 The Church and God's control of the demonic.

3 The visions are organized in series of seven.

Seven letters (2.1–3.22)
    The heavenly throne-room (4–5)
Seven seals (6.1–8.1) – the destruction of world empires
Seven trumpets (8.2–11.19) – heralds of the holy war
Seven thunderclaps (10.3–4) – signal of the end
    The Woman and the Dragon (12–13)
    Mount Zion and the angelic heralds of Judgment (14)
Seven plagues (15–16) – praise or retribution
    The Punishment of Babylon, the evil city (17.1–19.10)
    The Eschatological Battles (19.11–20.15)
    The Vision of Jerusalem, the holy city (21.1–22.5)

This plan is not entirely tidy, but there is a good deal of interlocking and balance. The One sitting on the Throne in 4 is balanced by the Lamb on the Throne in 5. The scroll unrolled (a symbol of the unrolling of history) in 5.1 is balanced by the scroll unrolled in 10.2. The immense numbers round the

Throne in 5.11 return in the 144 thousand on Mount Zion in 14.1. The Beast of 11.7 prepares for the Beast of 13.1–10. The fall of the evil city, the whore of Babylon, in 17 is balanced by the triumph of the Bride, the holy city of Jerusalem, in 21. The two eschatological battles and the two resurrections balance each other in 19.11–20.15.

Throughout Revelation numbers are importantly symbolic. Most prominent is 7, the number of completion, to which are linked both 3½ and 6 as numbers of radical incompletion. 1,260 days or 42 months are, of course, 3½ years. Twelve is the number of the tribes of Israel, so that 144 is the number of all the saved, especially when multiplied by 1,000, the biblical equivalent of almost-infinity.

3. Theology

a. Symbolic Figures

Much of the meaning of Revelation is enshrined in the symbolic figures which give definition to the narrative. All are rich in varied biblical imagery. George Caird's comment on this is invaluable and applies to the whole use of imagery in the Book: 'to compile a catalogue is to unweave the rainbow. John uses his allusions not as a code in which each symbol requires separate and exact translation, but rather for their evocative and emotive power' (*The Revelation of John the Divine* [1966], p. 25).

b. One like a Son of Man (1.12–16)

This figure is not to be confused with the gospel title for Jesus, '*the* son of man', for here it is '*a* son of man', so an Aramaic expression for a human being. The principal reference is to the one like a son of man in Daniel 7.13, who receives all power on earth from the One seated on the throne. But at the same time the figure is more like the One seated on the throne himself, for his hair is white as white wool and his eye blazing flames. The sound like the sound of the ocean also suggests God himself, as Ezekiel 43.2. The figure also includes the divine messenger of Daniel 10.5–6, and the seer's reaction is as to a heavenly messenger. But the words 'it is I, the First and the Last, the Living One' leave no doubt that the figure is divine. The allusion to the Resurrection ('I was dead and now I am alive') brings in firmly the concept of the human Risen Christ, and the seven stars, representing the seven Churches, in his right hand present him as the lord of human history, reinforced by the teaching authority of the double-edged sword. This gives assurance to the whole message of Revelation.

c. One seated on the Throne and the Lamb standing as though Slain (4–5)

There have been scenes of the heavenly throne-room several times in the Bible, each one growing from its predecessors, beginning with 1 Kings 22.19–23, next the vision of Isaiah 6 in the Temple, then the mobile throne of God in Ezekiel 1, going on to Daniel 7, and finally in the Inter-Testamental period *1 Enoch* 14. It is not a series of transient scenes of events, but a repeated statement of the permanent relationship of creation to its Lord. The scene in Revelation draws elements from each of these, but is the most lively and dramatically developed of all.

'Look' (4.2) and 'Come up' are personal invitations, drawing the reader in. There is the unending noisy chorus, extending to the whole of creation, the constant movement of the prostrations of the 24 elders, the dramatic silence after the angel's unanswered question. The most striking element, however, is the approach of the Lamb, who has won his place by his blood and receives (5.7) the same sevenfold doxology as the One seated on the Throne, a doxology from all creation. The Lamb has seven horns and seven eyes, symbols of total strength and total oversight. Again the figure of the Lamb is human as well as divine, for by his blood he has himself won the victory and the right to open the scroll as the Lord of history. Future history is the outworking and consequence of that victory, for 'you bought men for God, to serve our God and to rule the world'. The stress on the hard-won victory is central to the whole message of Revelation, for throughout the message for this persecuted community the triumph is won not by the sort of domination exercised by the evil powers but by the acceptance of martyrdom.

The final scene of Revelation makes the equal honour of the Lord God and the Lamb even more explicit, for – as we shall see – together they form a single object of homage and worship.

d. The Woman robed with the Sun (12.1–6)

The first of the three female figures to be presented is the Woman robed with the Sun. She and the New Jerusalem are on the side of the good, as Babylon is the very embodiment of evil. The Woman robed with the Sun can be understood on several levels. At the most basic is the widespread myth of combat between the Woman, the mother representing fertility and life, and the Dragon, the pitiless, inhuman, infertile forces of evil, destructive of life. One form of this is the conflict in the Garden of Eden between Eve and the Serpent ('serpent' and 'dragon' are the same word in many ancient languages). Another important form, particularly close to Revelation 12 in its use of the wind and the sea, is the Greek legend of Delphi, the seat of the oracle: when Leto was pregnant with the god Apollo. The dragon Python (who originally controlled and provided the oracular responses at Delphi), forewarned that Apollo would replace him, sought to kill the child. Things turned out otherwise: when Apollo was born he killed the dragon and took over his position. Leto was carried off to Delos, just as the Woman is carried off to the desert. This is particularly apposite because it gives a strongly anti-Roman and anti-imperialist slant to the scene; for Augustus and Nero, whose worship is presented as a major evil force, both identified themselves strongly with Apollo.

This legend may be at the basis of the Woman and the Dragon in Revelation. But who is the Woman? The story can be understood at many levels, for it is in the nature of such a story that it should be polyvalent. There are overtones of the Genesis story, in which the seed of the Woman will crush the head of the Serpent, denoting that evil will not triumph for ever. There are also overtones of the Messiah, in that the boy is to 'rule all the nations with an iron sceptre' (Ps. 2). In this case the statement 'the child was taken straight up to heaven' (Rev. 12.5) may be a proleptic description of the Ascension. Or is the primary allusion to Isaiah 26.17–27.1, in which case it might be understood of the re-birth and re-establishment of God's people in triumph? This allusion would present the Woman primarily as Israel, the Mother of the Messiah.

Christian tradition has, however, always seen the Woman as a representation of Mary, but at what level should this be understood? The most appropriate context is that of Mary as Mother of the Church, for at some level the people of God is certainly indicated. Whoever the Woman represents, this picture is trenchantly subversive of current Roman imperial myths. Revelation adopts the imagery, but claims that the true son is Christ.

e. The Great Prostitute (17–18)

a. The Figure of the Prostitute.

This third of the major visions is again introduced by 'He took me *in spirit*'. The vision is unlike all the others which we have hitherto come across in

Revelation. First, it is a 'still', rather than a moving picture. There is no angel rising where the sun rises or blowing trumpets or emptying bowls, simply the woman mounted on the scarlet beast. Secondly, for the first time in Revelation, the vision is an enigma which needs an explanation, a sort of key to be given by an *angelus interpres,* that stock figure of apocalyptic, the interpreting angel. At the end the visionary says that he is completely baffled and the angel offers to interpret. Such an interchange is a stock feature of biblical visions, especially Ezekiel 3 and Daniel 7.15–16; 8.15–16, but has not yet been utilized in Revelation.

The details of this vision are perhaps based on a coin of Vespasian depicting Rome seated in this pose, for the description is a satire. The resemblances are striking:

Revelation 17	Coin of Vespasian
She is seated by many waters (17.1)	Roma's foot touches the River Tiber
seated on the beast (17.3)	The wolf of Romulus and Remus is below her
she is a prostitute (17.4)	*lupa* (=she-wolf) is slang for 'prostitute'
on seven hills (17.9)	Roma is seated on seven hills
holding a winecup (17.4)	Roma holds aloft a cup
drunk with blood of martyrs (17.6)	Roma holds a short sword or dagger.

The description of the woman as a prostitute characterizes her not so much as a sexual temptation but as the figure of seduction to any infidelity, a caricature of any kind of depravity, with a particular focus on the depravities of Rome and its empire. Just as virginity is the symbol of faithfulness to the Lord, so harlotry is the symbol of infidelity. Babylon, the icon of seduction and iniquity at the time of the Babylonian Exile, is described in Jeremiah 51.7 as a golden cup in God's hand, 'she made the whole world drunk, the nations drank her wine, and then went mad'. The extent of this harlot's domination is suggested by the waters, which are interpreted in 17.15 as 'all the peoples, the populations, the nations and the languages'. The glittering jewels are reminiscent of the description of another icon of iniquity, the King of Tyre, in Ezekiel 28 – and Tyre was also a symbol of seduction, for it was the homeland of Queen Jezebel, who led Israel into infidelity. The woman enthroned on the beast is also a satirical antitype of God enthroned in Revelation 4–5. This is made clearer by the blasphemous titles (17.3) and by the repeated caricature of the divine title, 'who is, who was and who is to come' in 17.8, 'the beast who was once alive and is alive no longer and is still to come', and in 17.10: 'five have already gone, one is here now and one is yet to come', both of which stress the ineffectiveness of the apparition.

At the same time there are features which indicate a special focus on the temptation to the infidelity of worship in the Roman imperial cult: she is drunk with the blood of martyrs (17.6). She is seated on seven hills, always a conventional indication of Rome, given further focus here by being described also as the seven emperors (17.9). This receives still further focus by the reference to the legend of *Nero redivivus*, in 'the beast who was once alive and is alive no longer and is still to come' (17.8). This is flagged up as code by the indication that it 'calls for shrewdness'. It is soon interpreted as 'the beast who is at the same time the eighth and one of the seven' (17.11). To add yet more clarity we are told in so many words that 'the woman is the great city which has authority over all the rulers on earth' (17.18). Other features of the vision are already familiar from earlier visions. Some are purely conventional, such as the ten horns, symbolizing totality of strength, and already familiar from Daniel 7.24 as the symbols of the kings hostile to the people of God but doomed to destruction. A more significant detail is the location of this crowned woman in the desert, making her an antitype and caricature not only of God enthroned but of the Woman who appeared in heaven, robed with the Sun, carried off into safety in the desert (12.6).

As soon as this figure has been fully described, attention is turned to its destruction by the Lamb, the 'Lord of lords and King of kings'. Again, overlapping images are used for this humiliating experience: clothes torn off and the prostitute stripped naked – the conventional punishment for a prostitute (Nahum 3.5, and Ezekiel 23.25–9 of the prostitute symbolizing unfaithful Judah), beasts eating her flesh, as was prophesied of the seductress Jezebel (2 Kgs 9.37). The victory of the Lamb, 'standing as though slain', is no military victory, won by force of arms. Triumph through aggression has been replaced by triumph through endurance. The victory of the Lamb is won by his endurance of suffering and martyrdom. Similarly the followers of the Lamb triumph by their endurance of suffering. In each of the letters at the beginning of Revelation a promise is made to those who conquer (2.7, 11, 17, 26; 3.5, 12, 21). But this victory is won not by aggression but by perseverance (1.9; 2.2, 3, 19; 3.10; 13.10; 14.12).

b. The Laments

After the description of the fall of Babylon/Rome under the image of the enthroned woman, an ironic lament or taunt-song predicts its fall. This figure is familiar from the biblical prophetic books, predicting the fall of Babylon and other oppressors of Israel, such as Tyre and Moab (Isa. 14; Jer. 50–1; Ezek. 26–8). Rome is the culmination of the evil empires of history, and the luxury goods she provides are the gifts of a courtesan. It is a promise that the corrupt dominance of Rome will not last, but also a warning that Christians should distance themselves from this corruption. Babylon's complacent pride is part of the reason of her downfall, combined with the extortion by which her wealth was acquired and the shedding of the blood of martyrs. Kings, merchants and seafarers join in the lament, and the list of cargoes (vv. 12–13) highlights the centralisation of the empire on Rome and the exploitation by Rome.

The seafarers' lament finishes with the two explicitly Christian allusions of the chapter, calling on the martyrs to join in the celebration of Babylon's downfall (v. 20). The chapter will end with the reason for her downfall, responsibility for the blood of martyrs (v. 24). These surround a repeat of Jeremiah's prophecy of the fall of Babylon, hurled into the sea as a sign of finality (Jer. 51.63–64). After this succeeds an eerie silence (18.22–3), when all the cheerful and productive sounds of the city have disappeared, the music of celebration, the hammering of craftsmen, the incessant grinding for cookery, the promise of a future in the loving voices of the young married couple.

f. The New Jerusalem, the Bride (21)

Answering the city of Babylon, doomed to destruction, we are shown the new city of Jerusalem ('Come and I will show you the punishment of the great prostitute', 17.1 and 'Come and I will show you the bride of the Lamb', 21.9). Every element has biblical significance, some drawn from the description of the New Jerusalem in Ezekiel (the high mountain, the 12 gates with the names now of the Apostles rather than the 12 tribes: Ezek. 40.2; 48 31), the precious stones of the High Priest's breastplate (Exod. 28.17), the river of life from Ezekiel 47. The city is cubed as the Debir of the Temple (1 Kgs 6.20), but of enormous size, 2,400 kilometres, an image of its limitless capacity and the totality of salvation. The bridal imagery recalls the imagery of the stormy relationship of Israel to the Lord (Hosea 2.16), coming to a perfect consummation in the bridal adornment of Isaiah 61.10 and Jesus' own imagery of the Wedding Feast (Jn 2.1–12; Mk 2.19; Mt. 22.1–10). The climax comes in the presence of God, no longer in the Temple but face to face (22.4).

Perhaps the most striking element of all is the parity and unity of God and the Lamb. The Lord God almighty and the Lamb *is* (not 'are') the Temple. The glory of God enlightens it, and the Lamb is its torch. The throne of the Lord God and of the Lamb will be (singular) in it, and *his* servants will worship *him* and see *him* face to face (not 'their' or 'them'). There is one Temple, one light, one throne, one worship, for the Lord God and the Lamb constitute one divinity (21.22–3; 22.1, 3).

4. Letters to the Seven Churches of Asia

Before the revelatory experience begins, the book is firmly anchored in geography and history by these Letters to the Churches. These Churches are no doubt the sphere in which will be played out the struggle between good and evil dramatically and symbolically presented in the body of Revelation. Each of the Letters has a fourfold set formula: an address, a balance-sheet of the Church's activities, an admonition and a promise of reward; this corresponds to the fourfold form of imperial edicts sent to city-states. The criticisms are unsparing and abrasive, and must have had a devastating effect when read out in public, though we have no idea how large the communities were. Each is carefully accommodated to its recipients. Geographically the cities form a continuous circle, which could reflect a route taken by the messenger carrying the Letters.

a. Ephesus

This great city (the ancient theatre accommodates 25,000 people) was the capital of the Province. It had served as Paul's base in Asia Minor and was also an important centre for the worship of Augustus and Rome. They are complimented for their hard work, but also threatened with ceasing to be a Church (losing their lamp-stand) if they do not repent of their laxity. The mention of the tree of life may be an allusion to the great shrine of Artemis, the deity of the city, which was centred on a tree-shrine.

b. Smyrna

A few miles south of Ephesus, this Church at the modern Izmir is spared any criticism. Perhaps the pressing threat of persecution fanned their zeal.

The great martyr-bishop Polycarp was martyred there at an advanced age in 160AD. Was he already a member of the community when the letter arrived? The mention of the 'crown of life' may play on the victor's laurel-wreath in athletics, for there were important Games at Smyrna.

c. Pergamum

Attalus, king of this great hill-fortress, was the first to invite the Romans into Asia, and the city was a major centre for the cult of Rome and Augustus which features so notably in Revelation. This may be the meaning of Satan being enthroned in Pergamum. Our author's disapproval of eating food which had been sacrificed to idols is a valuable indication that there could be differing solutions in the Church to moral problems, for Paul had no problems with eating such food, despite protecting the consciences of the weak (1 Cor. 10.23–33).

d. Thyatira

Archaeologists comment that Thyatira seems to have been a city of artisans and craftsmen. This may account for the mention of a burning flame, burnished bronze and earthenware pots, though these must have been present in every city. The image of adultery for infidelity which will be so important in Revelation already appears here, but the dominant impression is of fidelity in the face of temptation.

e. Sardis

Sardis was a great city, the erstwhile capital of the fabulously wealthy Croesus of Lydia. It is the furthest east of the cities on this circular route, some 50 miles inland from Ephesus. The counsel to be alert may allude to the fact that it was twice captured by surprise-attack. This is the only one of the messages which contains reference to two of Jesus' sayings in the gospel, Matthew 10.32 and Mark 13.33.

f. Philadelphia

The promises of this message are uniquely encouraging, unqualified by any reproaches and fully positive about their endurance of persecution. They must have been used to hardship. After a great earthquake in 17AD this fertile valley was recognized as a disaster area, and Tiberius remitted taxes for five years. Sixty years later Pliny says that it was the greatest earthquake in human history, twelve cities being flattened in a single night. The after-shocks were such that many people preferred to live outside the city. This may explain the use of several building images, the promise to make them pillars in the sanctuary and to have a share in the New Jerusalem. David Aune argues, perhaps correctly, that the mention of a New Jerusalem shows that the letters were written and added after the description of the New Jerusalem in Revelation 21 had been composed.

g. Laodicea

The city was an important and prosperous Jewish centre in the Lycus valley, the focus for the collection of the annual half-shekel Temple tax; the amount of this (10 kilos of gold) indicates a population of several thousand adult Jews. After an earthquake in 60AD the city was rebuilt from its own resources without need for any remission of taxes. The author of the Letter ironically mocks the pretentions of this proud city in several ways (3.15–18):

a   The neighbouring city of Colossae was famed for its crystal cold waters, yet Laodicea had a mediocre, emetic, lukewarm water supply, neither hot nor cold, and suitable only to be spat out.
b   The city produced a well-known eye-salve, yet they are blind and need to purchase eye-ointment.
c   The local wool was praised for its raven-black colour, yet they need to buy white robes to hide their nakedness.

They even seem to have lost the Letter sent to them by Paul (Col. 4.16), or at least it never became part of the New Testament! The quality here applied to Christ, the 'Amen', the faithful witness (3.14), is thoroughly Pauline. Paul describes Christ as the 'Amen' of the Father, using the Hebrew root of that word, which signifies firmness, confirmation, stability: Christ confirms and fulfils the promises of the Father.

5. The Problem of Milleniarism

Many important thinkers in the second century expected that Christ and his saints would reign on earth, free from all evil, for some variable time before the final consummation of world history. Such a view of history is frequently presented in the apocalyptic literature. The *Apocalypse of Weeks*, which forms part of *1 Enoch,* represents human history in terms of ten weeks. The eighth week is a period of righteousness, the ninth of destruction and the tenth leads into eternity (*1 Enoch* 9.12–17). Several fragments of this early second-century BC writing have been found at Qumran, which shows that it was popular there in the first century AD. In the late first century AD (so more or less contemporary with Revelation) *4 Ezra* 7.28 envisages a rule of 400 years on earth for the Messiah with the righteous, followed by the resurrection of the dead and the final judgment (cf. *2 Baruch* 29–30). The apocryphal *Ascension of Isaiah* 4.14–17 depicts a rule of Beliar as Anti-Christ, after 1,332 days of which the Lord comes with his saints before the heavenly conclusion. Is this the same as the 'Great Revolt' of 2 Thessalonians 2.3–4, in which 'the wicked one, the lost one, the Enemy' is to appear? Or the 'final hour' of 1 John 2.18, when 'the Antichrist is coming'?

In the New Testament an extremely influential passage can be read in the same way:

> Just as all die in Adam, so in Christ will all be brought to life, but all of them in their proper order: Christ the first-fruits, and next, at his coming, those who belong to him. After that will come the end, when he will hand over the Kingdom to God the Father, having abolished every principality, every ruling force and power, for he is to be king *until he has made his enemies his footstool* [Ps. 110.1], and the last of the enemies to be done away with is death. (1 Cor. 15.22–24)

It is possible to read in this sense also the central petition of the Lord's Prayer, 'Thy will be done on earth as it is in heaven', seeing the prayer for the realisation of God's sovereignty on earth as a prayer for the coming of this temporal kingdom. This view also makes a balanced picture: just as at the beginning of history there was a period of harmony and goodness in the Garden of Eden, so at the end of history there will be a similar period in the earthly reign of Christ. Mythically this position is attractive, emphasizing as it does that peace and harmony is normal and that evil is a temporary abnormality which arose for a time and will again give way to goodness and the sovereignty of God.

This was the world picture of the principal theologians of the second century all over the Christian world, such as Papias, bishop of Hierapolis, Justin Martyr in Palestine, Irenaeus of Lyons, Melito, bishop of Sardis,

Hippolytus of Rome and Tertullian in North Africa. It was not until Origen, Eusebius and Augustine that the picture changed, and this reign of Christ came to be understood as the time of the Church. Through the *glossa ordinaria* based on Bede, that prince of medieval exegesis (he quotes Augustine at length, often through Primasius [d. 558]), the interpretation of the thousand years as the time of the Church became standard: 'He shows what is to happen in these thousand years in which the devil is bound, for the Church, which in Christ will sit upon 12 thrones to pass judgment, is already sitting in judgment.' (*PL* 93, col. 191).

The particular mythical picture put forward by Revelation in 19.11–20.15 is in two, or perhaps three, panels. In the first panel (19.11–20.3) the enemies are dealt with: the beast and his false prophet are thrown alive into the fiery lake of burning sulphur, but the primeval Serpent, the Devil, is confined merely for a thousand years. There follows the first Resurrection, in which the faithful witnesses come to life and reign with Christ for a thousand years (20.4–6). In the final panel Satan is briefly released before being hustled to join the Beast and his false prophet in the lake of fire and sulphur. The stage is emptied of earth, sky, Death and Hades, and there is a general judgment, those whose names are not written in the book of life being thrown into the burning lake (20.7–15). We hear nothing of those whose names are written in the book of life. Presumably they reappear as part of the New Jerusalem.

The period when Satan is active after the thousand years of Christ's reign (20.7–10) may correspond to the spasms of agony threatened for the last times in the synoptic apocalypse (Mk 13.19, 24; Mt. 24.21), the Great Revolt of 2 Thessalonians 2.3–4 and the AntiChrist of 1–2 John. Whether anything more definite is envisaged by these symbolic descriptions than the final throes of the on-going and bitter struggle between good and evil, culminating in the triumph of Christ and his faithful, is quite unclear.

Further Reading

Bauckham, Richard, *The Climax of Prophecy* (London: T&T Clark, 1993): literary insights and theological essays

Boxall, Ian, *Revelation: Vision and Insight* (London: SPCK, 2002): simple, comprehensive commentary

Questions on Part Five

1 Is conflict between the Church and the Beast inevitable?
2 Is it vain to strive for a New Jerusalem on earth?
3 Is the presentation of the Lamb the summit of New Testament Christology?

Glossary

Alexander the Great 356–323BC, King of Macedon from 336. He created the largest empire of the ancient world, stretching as far as modern Pakistan. This marks the beginning of the Hellenistic period, when the same Greek-based culture spread over all this area.

Allegory An extended metaphor in which every detail has its own significance. It is debated whether any of Jesus' own parables were allegories or whether they each held only one central comparison. Mark 4.14–20 gives an allegorical key to the parable of the Sower. Pages 12, 105, 263

Amen Hebrew word from the root meaning 'firm'. It is used to signify agreement, e.g. Nehemiah 9.6. Pages 192, 241

Antiochus Epiphanes King of Syria 175–14BC, he claimed to be a manifest god. His attempt to stamp out Judaism caused the Maccabean revolt in 167BC.

Antitype An event or person foreshadowed by another, its type. The sacrifice of Jesus is held to be an antitype of the sacrifice of Isaac.

Apocalyptic Literally, 'revelatory'. A genre of writing which reveals the future by symbols, often predicting the liberation of the oppressed by a divine intervention, often expressed by means of cosmic symbols, e.g. Daniel 1–7; Mark 13. Pages 56, 362

Archelaus Son of King Herod the Great, ruler of Judea after Herod's death, but in 6AD deposed by the Romans for incompetence.

Augustus Divine title given to Octavian, great-nephew and heir of Julius Caesar in 27BC.

Babylonian exile Period spent in exile in Babylon by the Jews after the Sack of Jerusalem in 587BC. They were allowed to return to Judea in 438. It was a painful but important period of theological advance.

Babylon The capital of the Babylonian Empire, situated between the rivers Tigris and Euphrates. It was at the height of its power from 625–538BC.

Baptism John the Baptist baptized people in the River Jordan to prepare a community for the Messiah. Jesus was baptized by him to begin his public mission. It became the symbol of entry into the group of followers of Jesus.

Beatitudes A formula frequent in Jewish literature, expressing the blessing of God on particular people. Page 55

Bede Monk of Wearmouth and Jarrow, important scripture scholar. He died in 735AD.

Beloved Disciple The authority behind John's gospel (John 21.24). He is not named in scripture, but many believe him to be John, son of Zebedee. Page 118

Bishop English version of Greek *episcopos*=overseer. Title later given to the leader of Christian groups, successor of an apostle.

Blood Blood is the sign of life and as such belongs to God. Hence its role in sacrifice, in reconciliation ('There is no reconciliation without blood') and in sealing a covenant. God reconciles the human race by the blood of his Son, the blood of the New Covenant. Page 213

Body of Christ Given in the Eucharist, Mark 14.22; 1 Corinthians 10.16; 11.24. Page 231

Canon of scripture The inspired and normative writings of the Old and New Testaments. The Jewish canon of scripture was completed early in the second century. The date usually given for the completion of the Christian canon is 367AD. Page 9

Canonical criticism Method of biblical research which investigates a word or concept not just in one passage but throughout the Bible. A concept may develop in the course of the Bible, e.g. life after death. Page 14

Chiasmus A literary device in which words of clauses are repeated in reverse order, e.g. abcdc'b'a'. It usually has two climaxes, one at the beginning, one at the end, e.g. the judgment for Jesus before Pilate in John 18.28–19.15. Pages 103, 127–8

'Christian' Name first given at Antioch to followers of Jesus as Messiah, Acts 11.26.

Christology Teaching or discussion about the nature of Christ.

Codex A book, whose leaves contain writing on both sides, as opposed to a scroll. This form was not invented by Christians, but first became common among Christians at the end of the first century.

Collection Paul was much preoccupied with a collection of money to give to the poor in the Church of Jerusalem as a thank-offering from gentile Churches, e.g. Romans 15.25; 2 Corinthians 8–9.

Council of Jerusalem The first general meeting of Christians to make decisions, described in Acts 15, perhaps in 49AD. Discrepancies from Paul's account in Galatians 2 cause some to hold that the account in Acts is composite, joining together three or more different events.

Covenant An alliance or pact, principally used of the covenant made by God with Abraham and again with Moses and his People on Sinai, and the renewal of the alliance foretold by Jeremiah 31.31, sealed in Christ's blood. Page 210

Cosmic forces Thunder, lightning, earthquake, stars falling from heaven, convulsions of the earth, phenomena associated with apocalyptic writing.

Or supernatural, world-ruling forces as Thrones, Dominations, etc, see Colossians 1.16. Page 288

Cynics A school of philosophers, headed by Diogenes, who despised the world and its bourgeois standards. They delighted in public obscenities.

Day of the Lord A day predicted by the prophets from Amos 5.18; 8.9 onwards, when the Lord would right all wrongs, reward the just and the wicked. Pages 6, 293

Dead Sea Scrolls Scrolls found from 1945 onwards hidden in caves on the Western shore of the Dead Sea. They describe a messianic sect, possibly Essenes. Many of their ideas are highly significant as background to the New Testament.

Demiurge An intermediary creative force, emanating from the deity, important in second-century philosophy and myth.

Deutero-Pauline The letters of the Pauline corpus which some consider were written by a 'Paul after Paul': Ephesians, Colossians, 2 Thessalonians, Pastorals.

Diaspora The Jewish settlements scattered chiefly round the shores of the eastern Mediterranean from the Sack of Jerusalem in 586BC onwards. Page 333

Diatribe A Hellenistic rhetorical device, much used by Paul for arriving at the truth, consisting in lively dialogue with an imaginary opponent. Page 207

Ecclesia Greek for 'assembly', used for the Christian assembly and eventually corrupted to 'Church'. Page 63

Ecclesiology Teaching about the Church.

Emperor-worship Honour paid to the Roman emperor as divine. This practice, originating in the East, was encouraged as a vital factor in holding the empire together. It was strongly opposed by Christians, e.g. in the Book of Revelation. Pages 276, 295, 301, 307, 36

Enoch or Henoch, see Genesis 5.24, revealer of heavenly secrets, reputed author of the *Book of Enoch*. The first *Book of Enoch* is especially important as a background to New Testament ideas (e.g. Son of Man). It was written in several sections in the last two centuries BC.

Epiphany Greek for 'appearance', a term used in emperor-worship for the formal processional arrival of the emperor, and later applied to Christ's final coming.

Erasmus Renaissance scholar (1466–1536) who edited the first printed New Testament.

Eschatology From the Greek '*eschaton*'=end. Teaching about the last four things, conventionally death, judgment, heaven, hell.

Essenes A messianic sect of the Jews, known from Pliny and especially from Josephus (*Antiquities of the Jews*, 18.1.13–18), thought to be authors of many of the Dead Sea Scrolls. Page 31

Eucharist Literally 'thanksgiving', referring especially to the Christian memorial of Jesus' Last Supper.

Exegesis Methods of interpreting, especially the Bible. Pages 7, 192, 318

Farewell speeches Speeches of a leader about to leave his followers, usually warning of dangers and divisions to come, a conventional literary genre in biblical and other literature, e.g. Genesis 49; John 14–17; Acts 20.17–35; 2 Peter. Pages 13, 305

Flesh Often opposed to 'spirit' to designate human nature as frail and perishable, e.g. Galatians 5.16. Page 233

Folk-history Popular, usually pre-literary, account of past events, handed down by word of mouth. Its conventions are less rigid than those of modern historians.

Fulfilment of scripture It is constantly stressed that events in the life of Jesus fulfilled the Old Testament.

Games Athletic fixtures held an important place in popular culture. Paul often uses metaphors drawn from the games. King Herod made huge contributions to the Olympic Games.

Gentiles Non-Jews, often despised by the Jews. Luke especially stresses that they too are heirs of the promises to Abraham.

Glory The awesome otherness of God. Page 320

Glossa ordinaria The standard medieval commentary on scripture, often written in the wide margins round the scriptural text itself.

Gnostics Various schools of thought, especially in the second century after Christ, which considered salvation to be gained by knowledge rather than love.

Gospel Current version of Old English 'god spel', translating Greek *euaggelion* or 'Good News', often including other writings than the four gospels of the Christian canon. Pages 39–40

Goulder, M British scholar (1927–2010), student of Austin Farrer, who championed the theory of dispensing with Q.

Grace The favour of God. See page 197

Griesbach, J German scholar (1745–1812) who produced the first three-columned synopsis of the gospels in Greek. He championed the theory that Matthew was the first gospel and Mark a combination of Matthew and Luke – a theory revived by William Farmer in 1965.

Haggadah see *Midrash*.

Hagiography Biography presenting its subject as a saint, a term often used in a derogatory sense, suggesting uncritical gullibility.

Hellenistic Judaism Judaism affected, for better or worse, by Hellenistic modes of thought.

Hellenistic rhetoric Patterns of rhetoric typical of Hellenistic thought, but often current in Judaism and the New Testament. Pages 13, 172, 192. See 'diatribe'

Herod Antipas Son of King Herod, tetrarch (ruler) of Galilee and Peraea 4BC-39AD.

Herod the Great 74–4BC. King of Judea from 40BC, responsible for re-building the Temple of Jerusalem.

High Priest Ruler of the Jerusalem Temple and often of the city and Judaea itself, combining sacred and secular rule, an office held by Joseph Caiaphas 18–37AD.

hilasterion This Greek word has two related meanings: (1) sacrifice of reconciliation, (2) 'mercy-seat' above the Ark, the dwelling-place of God among his people. See Romans 3.25. Pages 212, 322

Hillel, R A Jerusalem rabbi at the beginning of the first century AD, often paired with R. Shammai, as representing liberal and strict interpretations of the Law respectively

Historico-Critical important method of biblical interpretation, demanding a critical attitude to historical writing. See page 12

Honi, R Charismatic Galilean rabbi, credited with wonder-working in the generation before Jesus. Page 32

Infancy Narratives Matthew 1–2 and Luke 1–2. Pages 58, 94, 111

Inspiration Guidance and preservation of scripture by the Holy Spirit. Page 9

Irenaeus Presbyter, possibly bishop, of Lyons in the late second century.

Irony Use of words to convey a deeper or different meaning from the obvious. Pages 59, 84, 94, 116, 167

James I King James VI of Scotland, James I of England (1566–1625) sponsored the English translation of the Bible, often called 'the Authorized Version' published in 1611.

Jebusite Canaanite tribe whose capital was Jerusalem till David conquered it.

Jewish rhetoric Rhetorical figures such as balance, parallelism and chiasmus common in Jewish literature. Page 13

Journeys On Paul's journeys. Pages 195–6, 243

Judgment Day of Judgment. See Day of the Lord.

Justice of God Page 208

Kingdom of God Page 6, 82

koinonia Fellowship or communion, highly valued by the earliest Christians Pages 174, 312

Lachmann, K Karl Lachmann, German classical scholar (1793–1851) who established that Mark was the first written gospel.

logos Greek for 'word'. A keyword in Christology. Page 118

Lord's Prayer Jesus' prayer in Matthew 6.9–13 and Luke 11.2–4. See page 100

Love Page 357

Luther, Martin Augustinian friar, leader of the sixteenth century Reformers (1483–1546).

Marcion Wealthy second-century ship-owner from Pontus who tried to persuade the Roman Church to expunge parts of the Bible which he found too Jewish.

Messiah The long-awaited Lord's anointed. Pages 39, 178

Messianic secret Theory, stemming from William Wrede in 1902, that Jesus' messiahship was to be kept secret. Pages 86, 144

mezuzah Cigar-shaped case containing parchment copy of Deuteronomy 6.4–9, affixed to the door-frames of orthodox Jewish homes.

midrash Jewish techniques of scriptural reflection and meditation, usually classified into *midrash haggadah* (story-telling) and *midrash halakhah* (moral teaching). Pages 144, 212, 218

Milleniarism Theory that at the end of time Christ would reign for 1,000 years on earth. Page 376

Morality Page 199

Mystery In the Pauline sense, the revelation of God's purpose at the end of time, Romans 16.25; 1 Corinthians 15.51m. Pages 218, 269

Myth Presentation in narrative form of a deeply-held religious truth; this designation in itself makes no claim for or against historical truth.

Newman John Henry Newman (1801–90), a leader of the Oxford Movement, perhaps the most important religious thinker of the nineteenth century. Page 11

Number symbolism Pages 12, 52, 366

Oral tradition Passing on traditions by word of mouth, at some eras held to be more secure than written tradition. Pages 39, 97

Origen Christian scholar and exegete (184–253) born at Alexandria, later resident in Caesarea.

Papias Bishop of Hierapolis in early second century, witness to traditions of earliest Christian writings. The value of his testimony is disputed. Pages 39, 70, 377

Papyrus Durable writing material made from the papyrus reed.

Parable Greek term for Hebrew *mashal*, an imaged and often riddling saying or story. Page 133

Paraclete Greek legal term for 'advocate', used in the Johannine writings, often to designate the Holy Spirit. Page 129

Parallels Balancing pattern much used in Hebrew literature and in Luke. Pages 94, 166

Passion Narrative Pages 153–61

Pentateuch The first five books of the Bible, constituting the Law of Moses.

Pericope Literally 'cut around', technical term for unit of gospel tradition. Page 41

pesher Jewish method of scriptural interpretation, understanding current events in the light of biblical texts, much used in the Dead Sea Scrolls and the New Testament. Page 8

Pharisees The most influential of the three religious groups of the Jews in first-century Palestine, according to Josephus, *Antiquities of the Jews*, 18.1.12–15. Page 29

Philo Jewish neo-Platonist philosopher of Alexandria (20BC–50AD).

pleroma Greek term, literally 'fullness' used by Paul and Deutero-Paulines, e.g. Ephesians 1.10; Colossians 1.19. Page 270

Pneumatology Teaching about the Holy Spirit (*pneuma* in Greek).

Pompey the Great In the course of his campaign to settle the Eastern Roman empire Pompey established Judea as a client state in 63BC, confirming Hyrcanus II as high priest but no longer king.

Prefect Official title of the Roman governors of Judea 6–41AD. Pontius Pilate was prefect 26–36AD. After the brief reign of Agrippa I, the Roman official was, from 41AD, entitled 'procurator'.

Prophet One who speaks on behalf of God, seeing things with God's eyes and announcing God's judgment. In Luke, Jesus is often described as a prophet. Page 98

Presbyters Literally 'elders', leaders of Jewish and Christian communities. The word is later corrupted in English to 'priests'. Page 310

Pseudepigraphy The convention, common in the first century, of attributing a writing to a great figure of the past to lend it authority. Page 283

Q The nickname of a lost collection of 'Sayings of the Lord' mentioned by Papias, and postulated by some scholars as the source of material shared by Matthew and Luke but not derived from Mark. Page 43

Rabbinic arguments Rabbi Hillel is said to have codified a set of seven rules for interpreting the scriptures; these are called the *middoth* of Rabbi Hillel. They are frequently used also in the New Testament. Page 192

Redaction Criticism A method of scriptural interpretation focused on the theological message of individual authors or editors ('redactors') of biblical Books. Page 13

Rhetorical analysis A method of interpretation focussed on the conventions of Jewish or Hellenistic rhetoric. Page 13

Rome Capital of Empire.

Sacrifice of Christ Page 212

Sadducees One of the three factions in Palestinian Judaism, described by Josephus, *Antiquities of the Jews*, 18.1.16–17. Page 29

Sandwich technique Markan technique of 'sandwiching' one incident between two halves of another incident related to it. See page 73

Sanhedrin Literally 'sitting together', a Jewish gathering, informal or formal (e.g. Mk. 13.9). After the Fall of Jerusalem in 70AD, the 'Great Sanhedrin' became the theoretical ruling body of Judaism.

Saviour Title of Christ, especially in Luke, Deutero-Paulines and 2 Peter. Used also for the emperor and Hellenistic saviour-gods. Pages 101, 180, 276

Scribes Literally 'writers', a title of literate persons, learned in Jewish Law. Page 30

Second Adam Title of Christ. Page 214

Second Coming Eschatological return of Christ in triumph. Pages 88, 295, 376

Second Moses Title of Christ. Pages 59, 319, 321

Sepphoris Capital city of Herod Antipas in Galilee.

Septuagint Greek translation of the Bible (abbreviated 'LXX'), according to legend (*Letter of Aristaeus*), the work of 70 scholars, begun in Egypt about 250BC.

Shammai See Hillel

Shema '*Hear*, O Israel', the basic Jewish statement of faith, Deuteronomy 6.4–9. Page 235

Slavery Greco-Roman society was built on the institution of slavery, an institution which is not questioned in the New Testament. Pages 272, 309, 312

Son of David Title of Jesus. Pages 6, 58

Son of God Title of Jesus. Pages 83–4, 158

Son of man Aramaic expression meaning 'human being', also a self-description of Jesus. Pages 32, 66, 88, 91, 101, 224

Speaking in tongues Page 230

Synoptic problem Problem of the interrelationship of the synoptic gospels. Page 40

Tefillin Small boxes containing the *Shema*, worn by observant Jews during prayer. Also called phylacteries.

Temple of Jerusalem Pages 149, 171, 301

Theophany An appearance of the divine. Page 79

Triumph A Roman triumph, a procession of victors and captives to the Capitol Hill in Rome, celebrating a victorious general.

Tyndale William Tyndale (1494–1536), first translator of the Bible into modern English, garrotted as a heretic.

Typology Study of symbolic figures in the Old Testament, seen as prefiguring New Testament persons or events, e.g. Jonah, emerging from the whale after three days, is a type of Christ's resurrection. Pages 8, 12, 324

Vulgate Common translation of the Bible into Latin. The Old Testament and the gospels were translated by Jerome (383–420).

Wisdom Christ is the power and the Wisdom of God. Pages 8, 68, 118, 234, 287

Wycliffe John Wycliffe (1320–84), Master of Balliol College, Oxford, sponsored a translation of the Bible into English, but it was banned in 1410.

Yelammadenu Sermon Literally, 'he will teach us', a first-century type of Jewish sermon of which John 6.31–58 is an example. Page 389

Yohanan b. Zakkai An important Jerusalem Rabbi at the time of the Sack of the city in 70AD. He later presided over the reconstitution of Judaism at Jamnia.

Zeal Zeal for the Law was greatly treasured, even to the shedding of blood. The two archetypal examples of zeal were Phinehas in Numbers 25 and Simeon and Levi in Genesis. This no doubt influenced Saul/Paul in his persecution of Christians.

Zealots Also known as *sicarii* or 'dagger-men', leaders of the revolt against Rome in 66AD. According to Josephus (*Jewish War*, 7.8.389–406) they made their last stand at Masada and in 73AD committed suicide rather than fall into the hands of the Romans. Page 31

Bibliography

Attridge, Harold T., 'Hebrews' in the *Oxford Bible Commentary* (2001)

Barrett, C. K., *A Commentary on the Epistle to the Romans* (1991)

—*Paul, an introduction to his thought* (1994)

Bauckham, Richard, 'James' in *Eerdmans Commentary on the Bible* (2003)

Blenkinsopp, Joseph *The Corinthian Mirror* (1964)

Boxall, Ian *Revelation: Vision and Insight* (2002)

—*Discovering Matthew* (2014)

Brown, Raymond, E., *The Community of the Beloved Disciple* (1979)

—*The Gospel and Epistles of John – A Concise Commentary* (1988)

Clark Kee, Howard, *Good News to the Ends of the Earth* (1990)

Duff, Jeremy, in *The Oxford Bible Commentary* (2001)

Dunn, James D. G., *The Theology of Paul's Letter to the Galatians* (1993)

Edwards, Ruth, *Discovering John* (2014)

Ehrmann, Bart D., *Misquoting Jesus* (2007)

Farkasfalvy, Denis, *Inspiration and Interpretation* (2010)

Finegan, Jack, *Encountering New Testament Manuscripts* (1974)

Fitzmyer, Joseph A., *Paul and his Theology, a brief sketch* (1988)

—*Luke the Theologian, aspects of his teaching* (1989)

—*The Interpretation of Scripture* (2008)

France, R. T., *Matthew, Evangelist and Teacher* (1989)

Goodacre, Mark, *The Synoptic Problem* (2001)

Goodman, Martin, *Rome and Jerusalem* (2007)

Green, Joel B., *The Theology of the Gospel of Luke* (1995)

Harrington, Daniel, *The Gospel of Matthew* (1991)

Harrington, Wilfred, *John, Spiritual Theologian*

—*The Jesus of John* (1999)

Hooker, Morna, *The Message of Mark* (1983)

—*Paul, a Short Introduction* (2003)

Johnson, Luke Timothy, *Acts* [Sacra Pagina] (1992)

Lambrecht, Jan, *Second Corinthians* [Sacra Pagina], 1999.

Lincoln, Andrew T., *The Theology of the later Pauline Letters: Ephesians* (1993)

Lindars, Barnabas *The Theology of the Letter to the Hebrews* (1991)

Martin, Ralph P., *James* [Word Biblical Commentary] (1988)

—*The Theology of the Letters of James, Peter and Jude* (1994)

Matera, Frank, J. *Galatians* [Sacra Pagina] (1992)

McGrath, Alistair, *In the Beginning* (2001)

McKnight, Scot, *Eerdmans Commentary on the Bible* (2003)

Meeks, W. A. *The First Urban Christians* (1983)

Moloney, Francis, *Mark, Storyteller, Interpreter, Evangelist* (2004)

Muddiman, John, *The Epistle to the Ephesians* (2010)

Murphy O'Connor, Jerome, *The Theology of the Second Letter to the Corinthians* [New Testament Theology] (1991)

—*Paul, a Critical Life* (1996)

Oakes, Peter, *Philippians, from People to Letter* (2001)

—*Reading Romans in Pompeii* (2009)

Paul for Everyone by N. T. Wright (c. 2001)

Rowland, Christopher, *Christian Origins* (2002)

Sanders, E. P., *The Historical Figure of Jesus* (1993)

Senior, Donald P. *The Passion of Jesus in the Gospel of Matthew* (1985), *of Mark* (1984), *of Luke* (1985), *of John* (1991)

—*Jesus: a gospel portrait* (1992)

Stanton, Graham, *Gospel Truth?* (1995)

—*The Gospels and Jesus* (2002)

—in *Eerdmans Commentary on the Bible* (2003)

Vermes, Geza, *Christian Beginnings from Nazareth to Nicaea* (2012)

Wansbrough, Henry, *The Story of the Bible* (2006)

Wedderburn, A. J. M., *The Theology of the Later Pauline Letters, Colossians* (1993)

Young, Frances, *The Theology of the Pastoral Letters* (1994)

Ziesler, John, *Paul's Letter to the Romans* (1989)

General Further Reading

Specific suggestions for further reading are given at the end of chapters throughout the book, where appropriate. The following list provides general pointers towards series and individual titles that will strengthen the reader's understanding of the New Testament and its world

Background

Barton, J., *The Biblical World* (London and New York: Rutledge, 2004): an excellent survey, covering many aspects of that world

McKenzie, John L., *Dictionary of the Bible* (Denver, CO: Touchstone, 1995 repr): despite its age still the best for quick reference on any puzzle

One-Volume Commentaries

The Oxford Bible Commentary, ed. John Barton and John Muddiman (Oxford: Oxford University Press, 2001)

Eerdmans Commentary on the Bible, ed. James D. G. Dunn and John W. Rogerson (Cambridge: Eerdmans, 2003)

both of these are excellent, many authors writing for both volumes – some articles better in one volume, some in the other – Eerdmans has more general articles, Oxford more space on individual books.

Murphy, E., (London: Geoffrey Chapman, 1989) – Roman Catholic, with useful general articles, including ecclesiastical guidance.

The New Jerome Biblical Commentary, ed. Raymond E. Brown, Joseph A. Fitzmyer, Roland

Introductions to the New Testament

Brown, Raymond E., *An Introduction to the New Testament* (London: Doubleday, 1997): complete and clearly written – fuller than this volume (898 pages)

Burridge, Richard A., *Four Gospels, One Jesus?* (London: SPCK, 1994): useful popular introduction to each gospel

Drane, John, *Introducing the New Testament* (Tring: Lion Publishing, 1986): still popular, illustrated

Johnson, Luke T., *The Writings of the New Testament* (London: SCM, 1999): a full and readable introduction (694 pages)

Perkins, Pheme, *An Introduction to the Synoptic Gospels* (Grand Rapids: Eerdmans, 2009): a thorough introduction to many aspects of the synoptic gospels

Shillington, V. George, *The New Testament in Context* (London, Bloomsbury,
2009): a serious study, treating each Book of the New Testament in its context

Theissen, Gerd, *The New Testament* (London: T&T Clark, 2003): short (206
pages) but comprehensive

Series of Commentaries

Many of these are excellent, though they vary from book to book. They are
not mentioned again here under individual books.

Matthew [etc] *for Everyone,* Tom Wright (London: SPCK, c. 2000): short,
popular commentaries on each book by N.T. Wright.

New Testament Theology, ed. James D. G. Dunn (Cambridge: Cambridge
University Press, 1990s): general treatment of theology of each book (some
200 pages each)

Sacra Pagina, ed. Daniel J. Harrington (Collegeville: Michael Glazier, 1990s):
continuous commentaries on each book, easy to read and clear

Sheffield New Testament Guides (London: Sheffield Academic Press, c. 2000):
simple, clear guides to each book

Word Biblical Commentaries, ed. Ralph P. Martin (Dallas: Word Publishing
(1980s–1990s): detailed and scholarly commentaries

General Introductory Books

Chancey, Mark A., *Greco-Roman Culture and the Galilee of Jesus* (Cambridge:
Cambridge University Press, 2005): recent archaeological data and
conclusions

Ehrmann, Bart D., *Misquoting Jesus* (New York: HarperSanFrancisco, 2005):
introduction to textual criticism, with explained examples

Farkasfalvy, Denis, *Inspiration and Interpretation* (Washington: Catholic
University, 2010): theological essays on exegesis, inspiration and canonicity

Finegan, Jack, *Encountering New Testament Manuscripts* (London: SPCK,
1974): illustrated introduction to the chief manuscripts of the New
Testament

Fitzmyer, Joseph A., *The Interpretation of Scripture* (New York: Paulist Press,
2008): a collection of articles explaining methods of scriptural study,
especially the historico-critical method.

Goodman, Martin, *Rome and Jerusalem* (London: Allen Lane, 2007): the clash
between them, leading to the Jewish War in 66AD

McGrath, Alister, *In the Beginning* (New York: Doubleday, 2001): the story of
the making of the King James Bible

Saldarini, Anthony J., *Pharisees, Scribes and Sadducees* (Wilmington: Michael
Glazier, 1988): the evidence and discussion

Wansbrough, Henry, *The Story of the Bible* (London: Darton, Longman &
Todd, 2006): the evolution of the biblical text from the beginning till today

Index